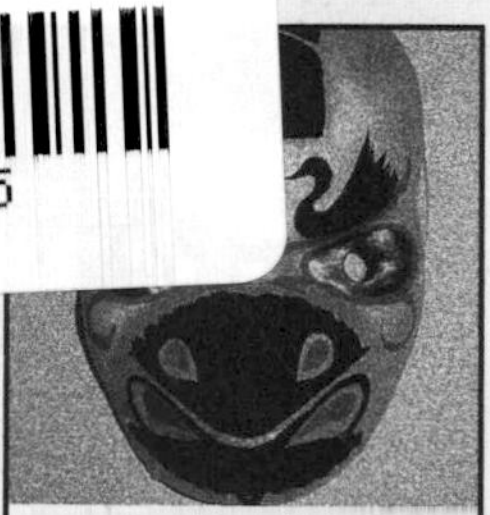

武井宏之

The Japanese kanji for "busy" is composed of separate parts that, when read together, literally mean "losing your heart." It makes sense, because even if you try not to say you're busy, if you can't spare time for the things in life that truly matter, you have already begun to lose your heart. Pretty smart design, I think.

—*Hiroyuki Takei*

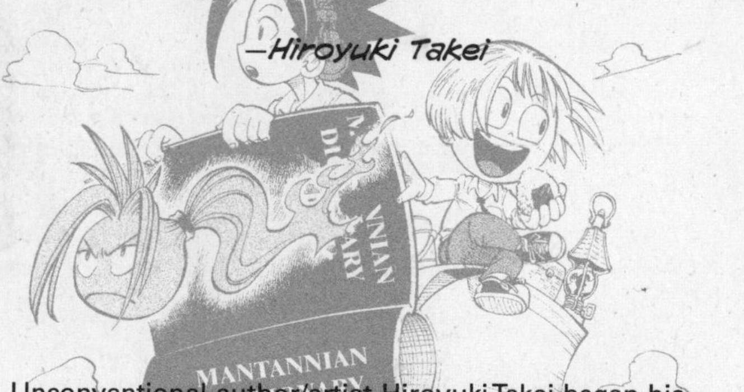
MANTANNIAN

Unconventional author/artist Hiroyuki Takei began his career by winning the coveted Hop Step Award (for new manga artists) and the Osamu Tezuka Award (named after the famous artist of the same name). After working as an assistant to famed artist Nobuhiro Watsuki, Takei debuted in **Weekly Shonen Jump** in 1997 with **Butsu Zone**, an action series based on Buddhist mythology. His multi-cultural adventure manga **Shaman King**, which debuted in 1998, became a hit and was adapted into an anime TV series. Takei lists Osamu Tezuka, American comics and robot anime among his many influences.

SHAMAN KING VOL. 23
The SHONEN JUMP Manga Edition

STORY AND ART BY
HIROYUKI TAKEI

English Adaptation/Lance Caselman
Translation/Lillian Olsen
Touch-up Art & Lettering/John Hunt
Design/Nozomi Akashi
Editor/Carol Fox

Editor in Chief, Books/Alvin Lu
Editor in Chief, Magazines/Marc Weidenbaum
VP, Publishing Licensing/Rika Inouye
VP, Sales & Product Marketing/Gonzalo Ferreyra
VP, Creative/Linda Espinosa
Publisher/Hyoe Narita

Printed in the U.S.A.

Published by VIZ Media, LLC
P.O. Box 77010
San Francisco, CA 94107

SHONEN JUMP Manga Edition
10 9 8 7 6 5 4 3 2 1
First printing, July 2009

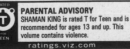

SHONEN JUMP MANGA

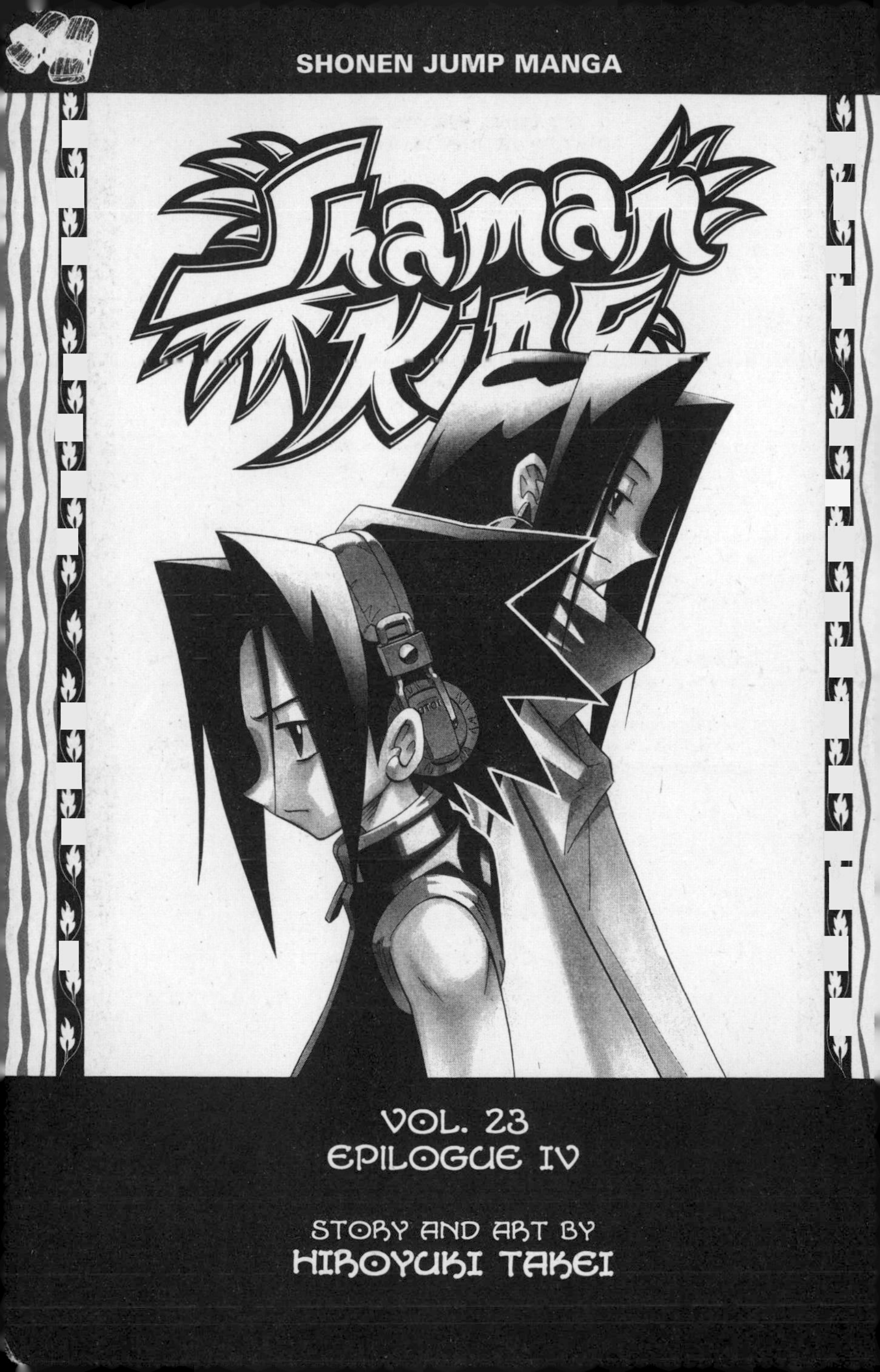
Shaman King

VOL. 23

EPILOGUE IV

STORY AND ART BY

HIROYUKI TAKEI

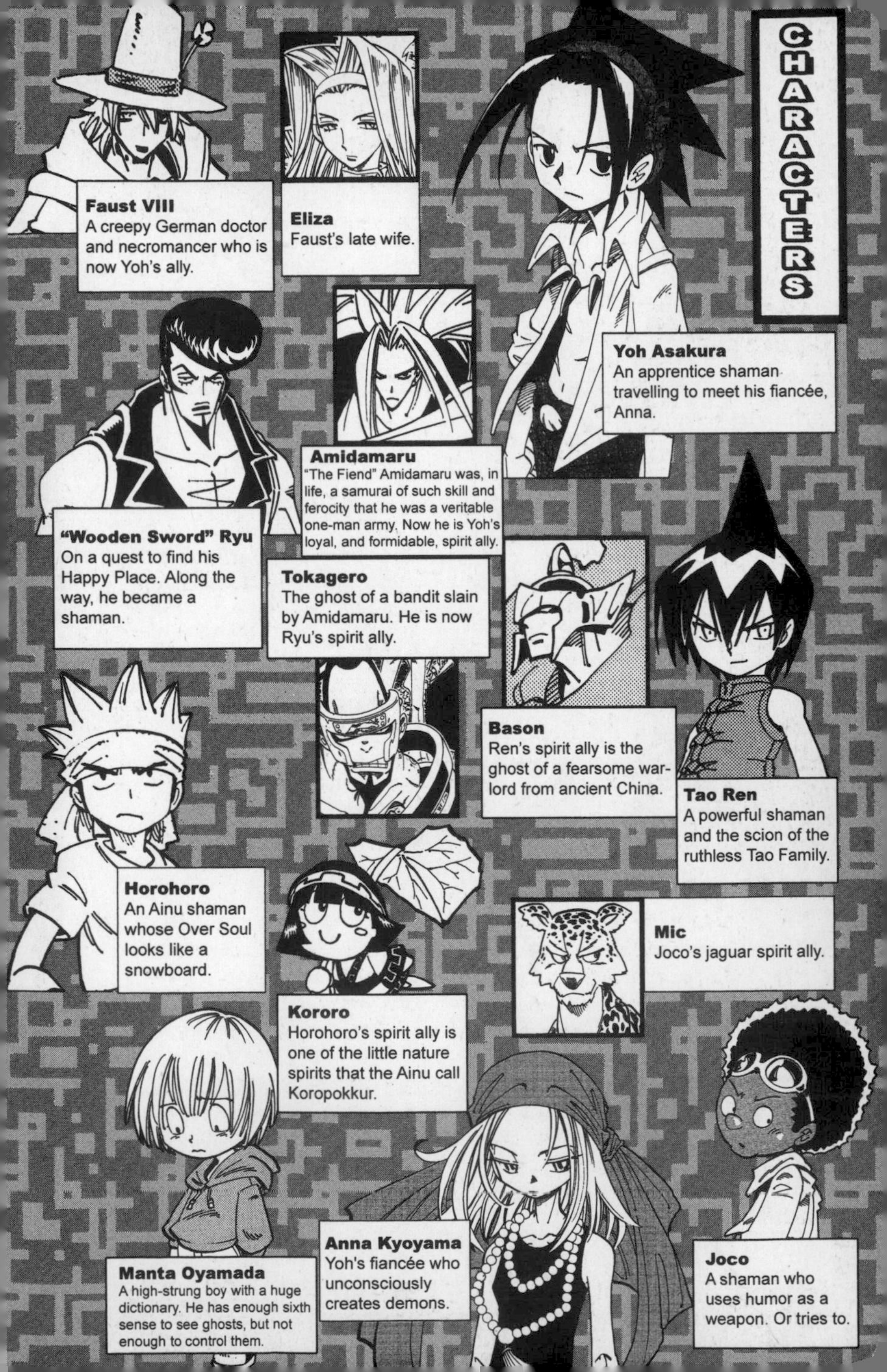
CHARACTERS
Yoh Asakura
An apprentice shaman travelling to meet his fiancée, Anna.
Eliza
Faust's late wife.
Faust VIII
A creepy German doctor and necromancer who is now Yoh's ally.
Amidamaru
"The Fiend" Amidamaru was, in life, a samurai of such skill and ferocity that he was a veritable one-man army. Now he is Yoh's loyal, and formidable, spirit ally.
"Wooden Sword" Ryu
On a quest to find his Happy Place. Along the way, he became a shaman.
Tokagero
The ghost of a bandit slain by Amidamaru. He is now Ryu's spirit ally.
Tao Ren
A powerful shaman and the scion of the ruthless Tao Family.
Bason
Ren's spirit ally is the ghost of a fearsome warlord from ancient China.
Horohoro
An Ainu shaman whose Over Soul looks like a snowboard.
Mic
Joco's jaguar spirit ally.
Kororo
Horohoro's spirit ally is one of the little nature spirits that the Ainu call Koropokkur.
Joco
A shaman who uses humor as a weapon. Or tries to.
Anna Kyoyama
Yoh's fiancée who unconsciously creates demons.
Manta Oyamada
A high-strung boy with a huge dictionary. He has enough sixth sense to see ghosts, but not enough to control them.

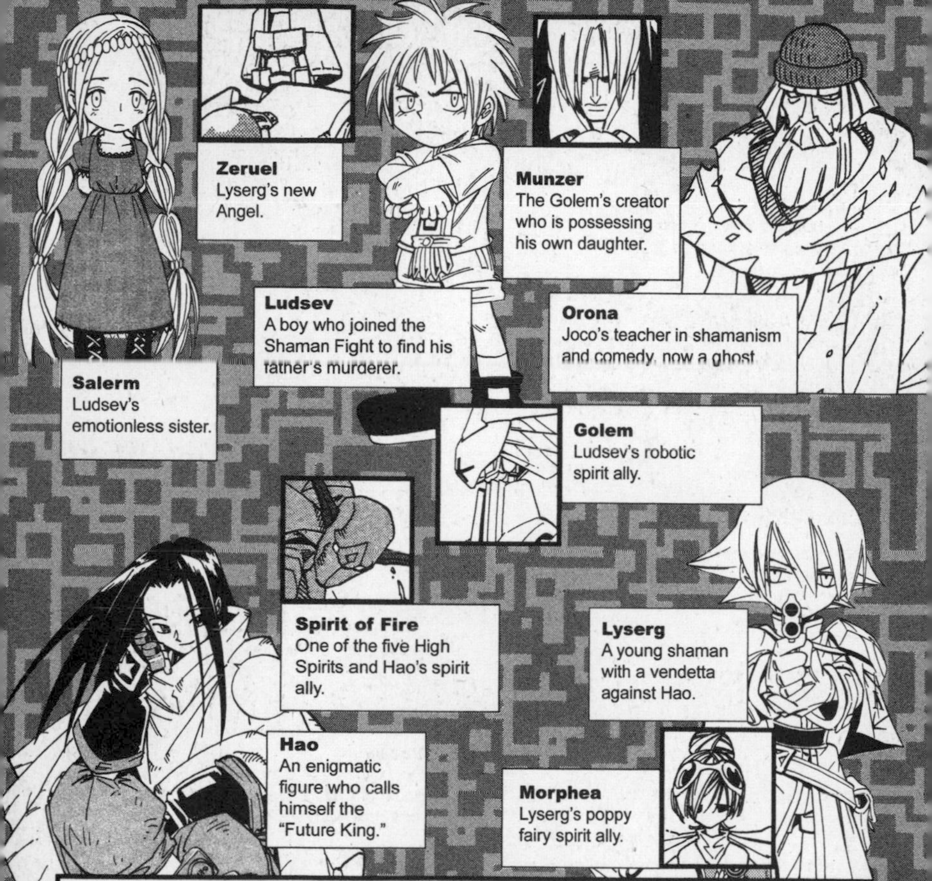
Munzer
The Golem's creator who is possessing his own daughter.
Zeruel
Lyserg's new Angel.
Orona
Joco's teacher in shamanism and comedy, now a ghost
Ludsev
A boy who joined the Shaman Fight to find his father's murderer.
Salerm
Ludsev's emotionless sister.
Golem
Ludsev's robotic spirit ally.
Spirit of Fire
One of the five High Spirits and Hao's spirit ally.
Lyserg
A young shaman with a vendetta against Hao.
Hao
An enigmatic figure who calls himself the "Future King."
Morphea
Lyserg's poppy fairy spirit ally.

THE STORY THUS FAR

Yoh Asakura not only sees dead people, he talks and fights with them, too. That's because Yoh is a shaman, a traditional holy man able to interact with the spirit world. Yoh is now a competitor in the Shaman Fight, a tournament held every 500 years to decide who will become the Shaman King and shape humanity's future.

Having dropped out of the Shaman Fight in order to save Ren's life, Yoh still finds himself in a swirl of lethal conflict. Before he can prevent it, Ludsev and Salerm exact their revenge on Joco for the murder of their father. And soon Yoh finds himself facing not only the fearsome Golem but Hao's entire team!

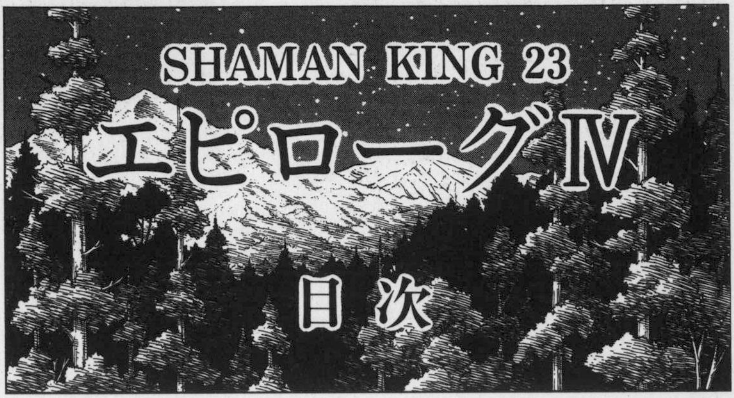
SHAMAN KING 23
エピローグⅣ
目次

VOL. 23
EPILOGUE IV

CONTENTS

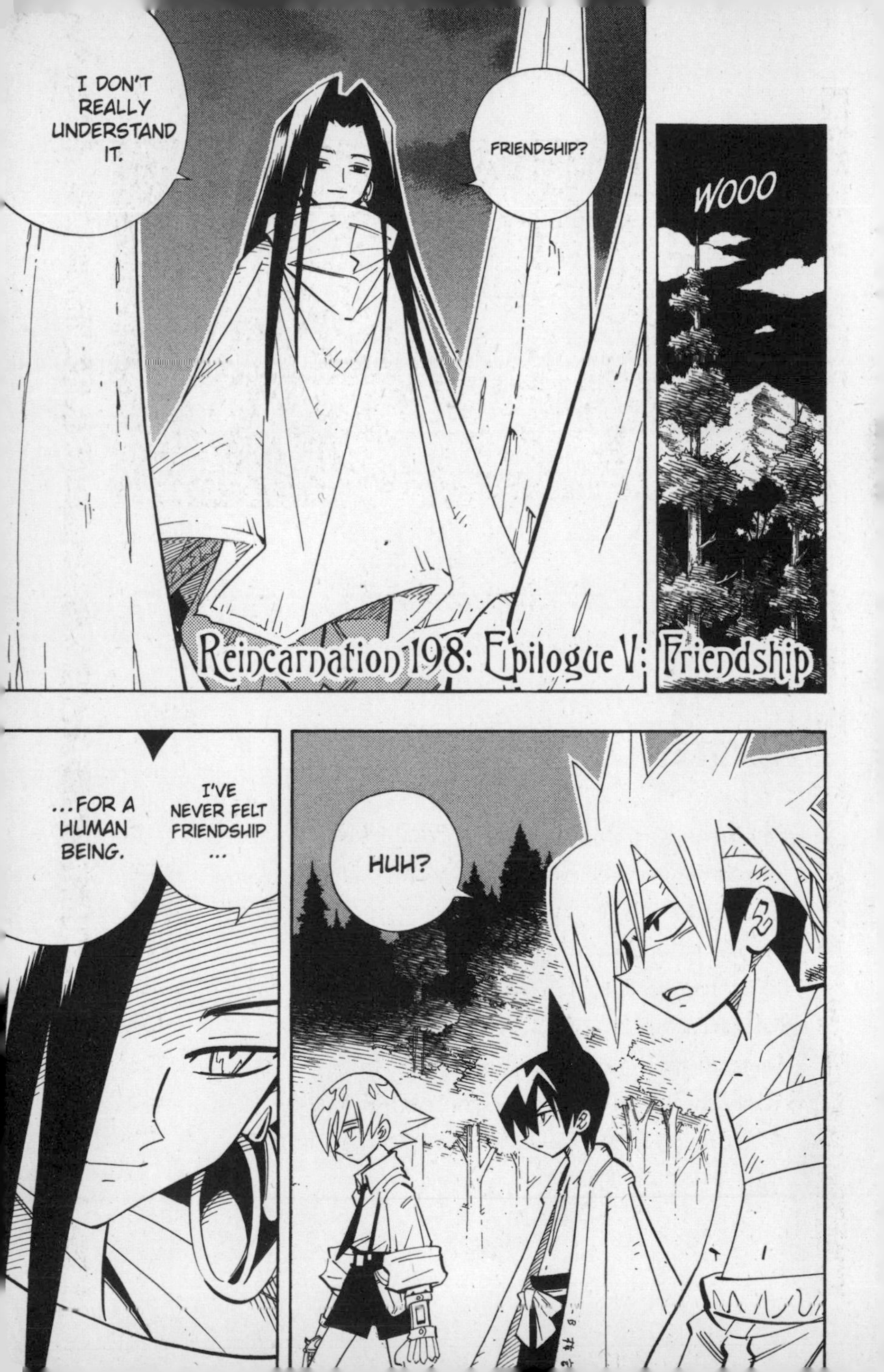
WOOO
Reincarnation 198: Epilogue V: Friendship
FRIENDSHIP?
I DON'T REALLY UNDERSTAND IT.
HUH?
I'VE NEVER FELT FRIENDSHIP...
...FOR A HUMAN BEING.

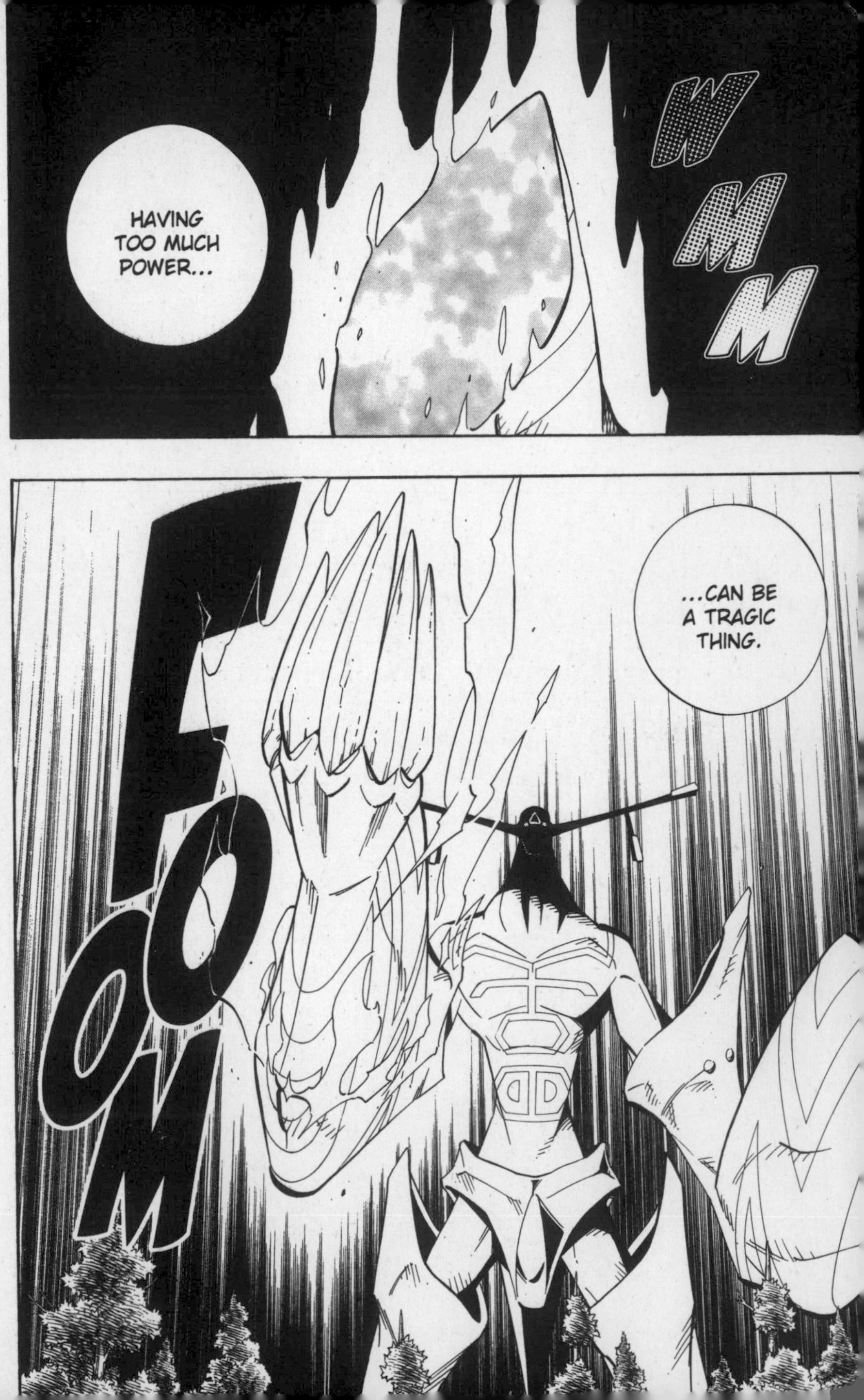
WMM
HAVING TOO MUCH POWER...
...CAN BE A TRAGIC THING.
FOOM

Reincarnation-198:
Epilogue V:
Friendship

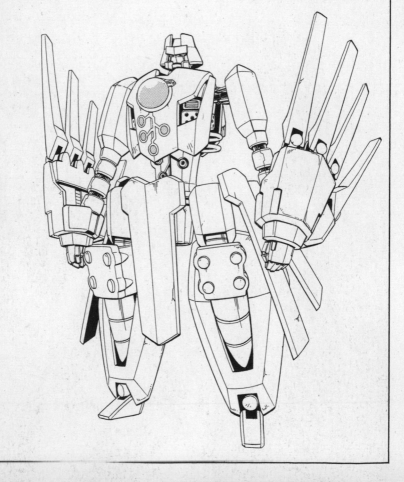

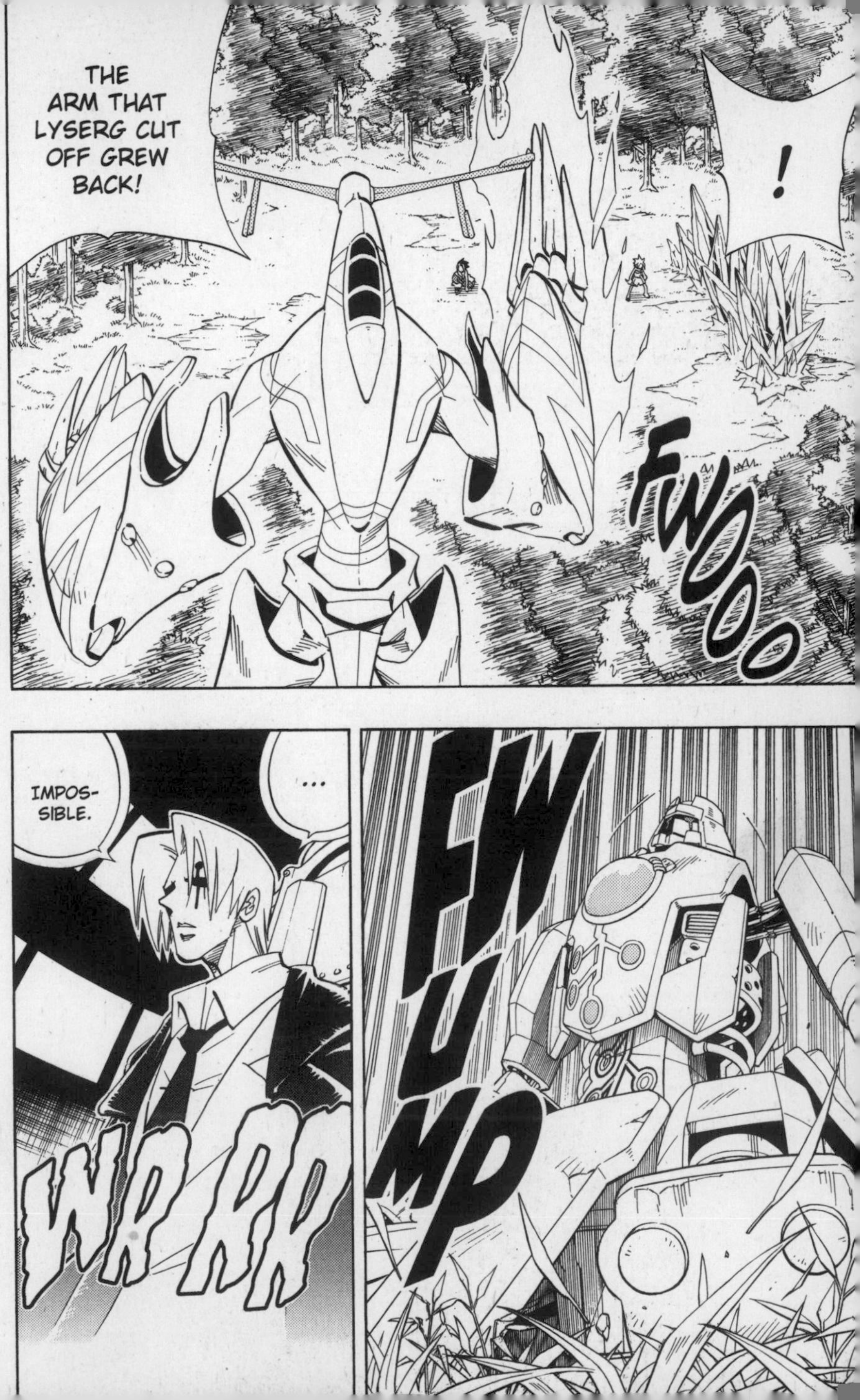
!
THE ARM THAT LYSERG CUT OFF GREW BACK!
FWOOOO
FWUMP
...
IMPOS-SIBLE.
WRRR

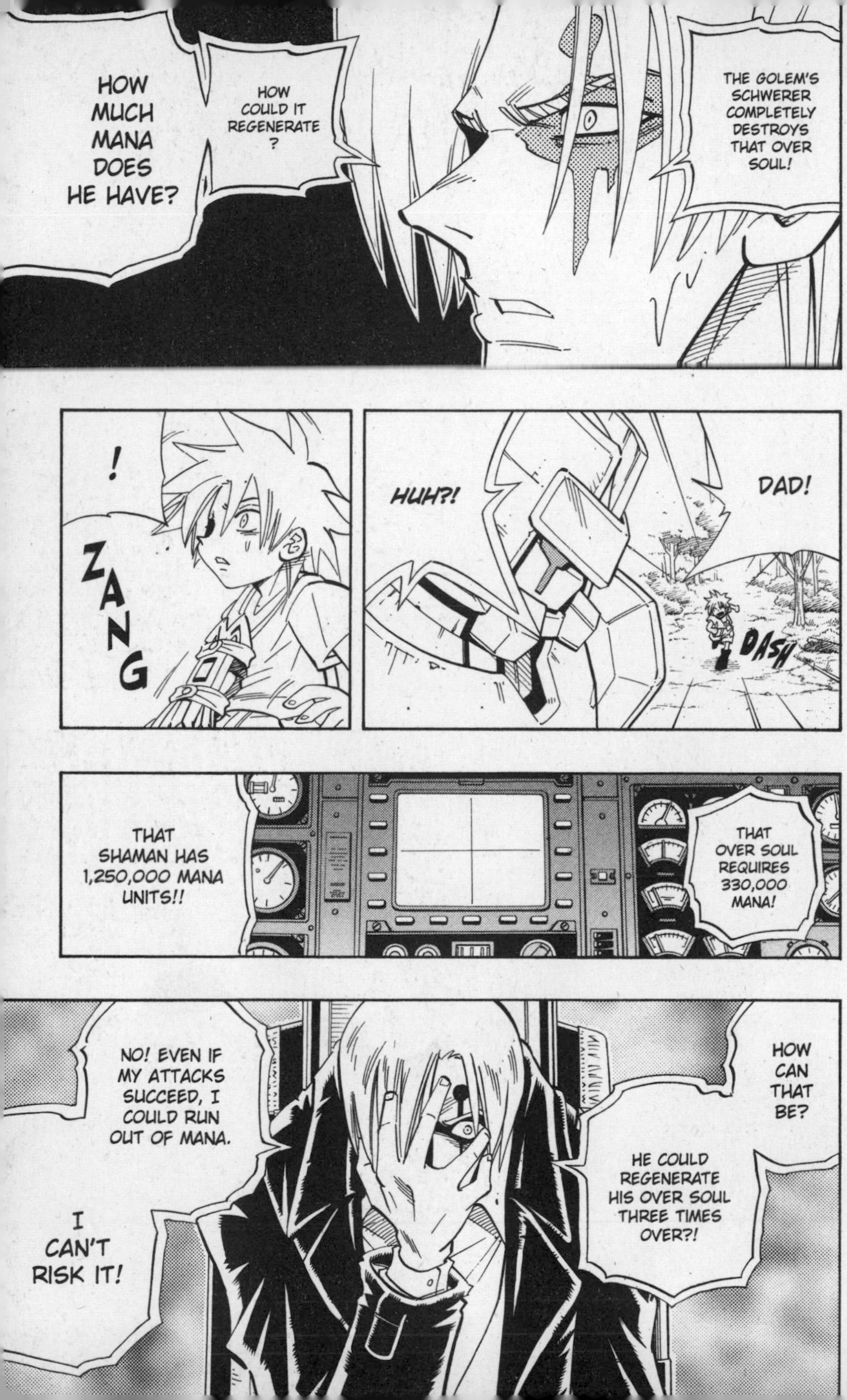
THE GOLEM'S SCHWERER COMPLETELY DESTROYS THAT OVER SOUL!
HOW COULD IT REGENERATE ?
HOW MUCH MANA DOES HE HAVE?
DAD!
DASH
HUH?!
!
ZANG
THAT OVER SOUL REQUIRES 330,000 MANA!
THAT SHAMAN HAS 1,250,000 MANA UNITS!!
HOW CAN THAT BE?
HE COULD REGENERATE HIS OVER SOUL THREE TIMES OVER?!
NO! EVEN IF MY ATTACKS SUCCEED, I COULD RUN OUT OF MANA.
I CAN'T RISK IT!

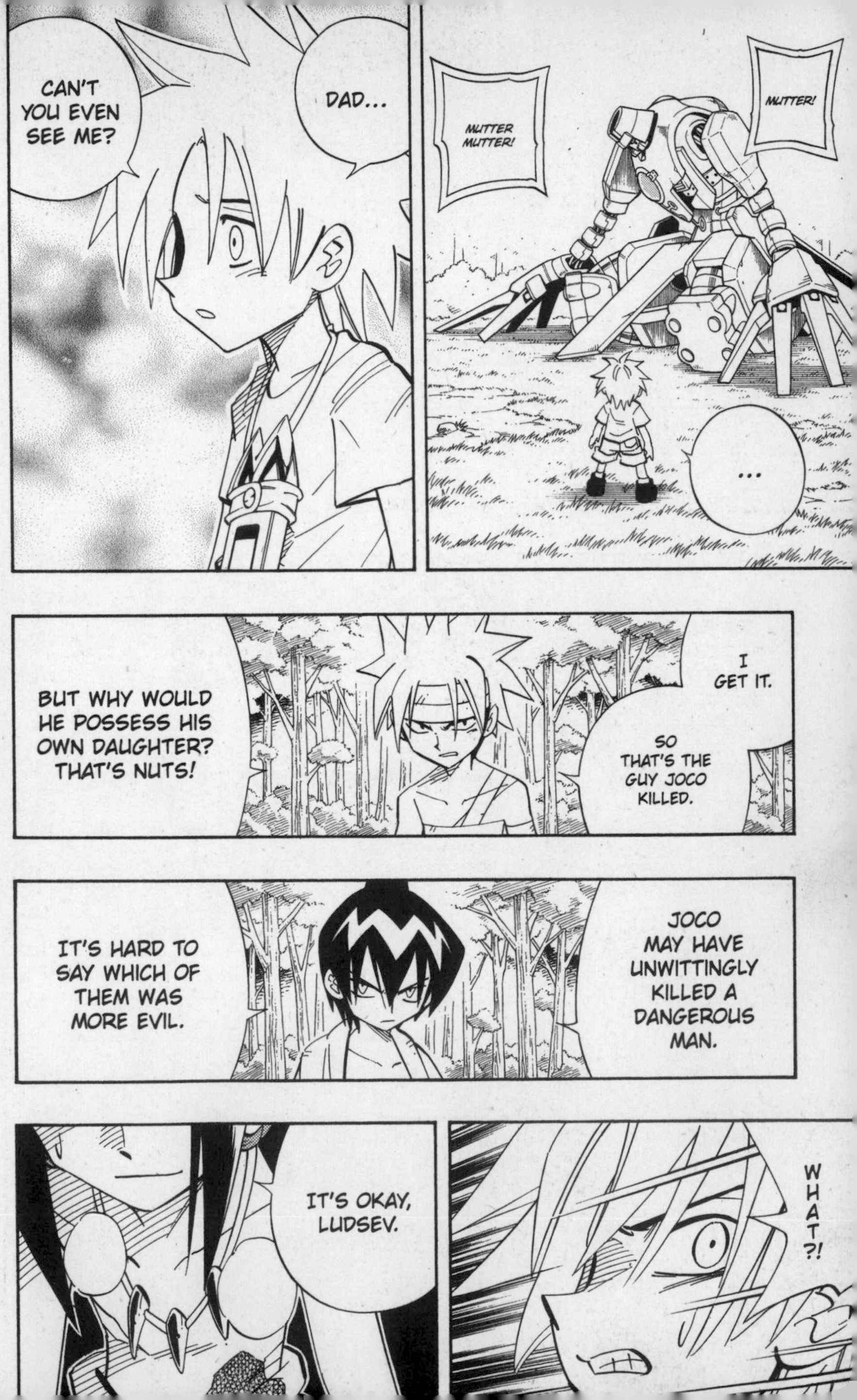
MUTTER!
MUTTER MUTTER!
...
DAD...
CAN'T YOU EVEN SEE ME?
I GET IT.
SO THAT'S THE GUY JOCO KILLED.
BUT WHY WOULD HE POSSESS HIS OWN DAUGHTER? THAT'S NUTS!
JOCO MAY HAVE UNWITTINGLY KILLED A DANGEROUS MAN.
IT'S HARD TO SAY WHICH OF THEM WAS MORE EVIL.
WHAT?!
IT'S OKAY, LUDSEV.

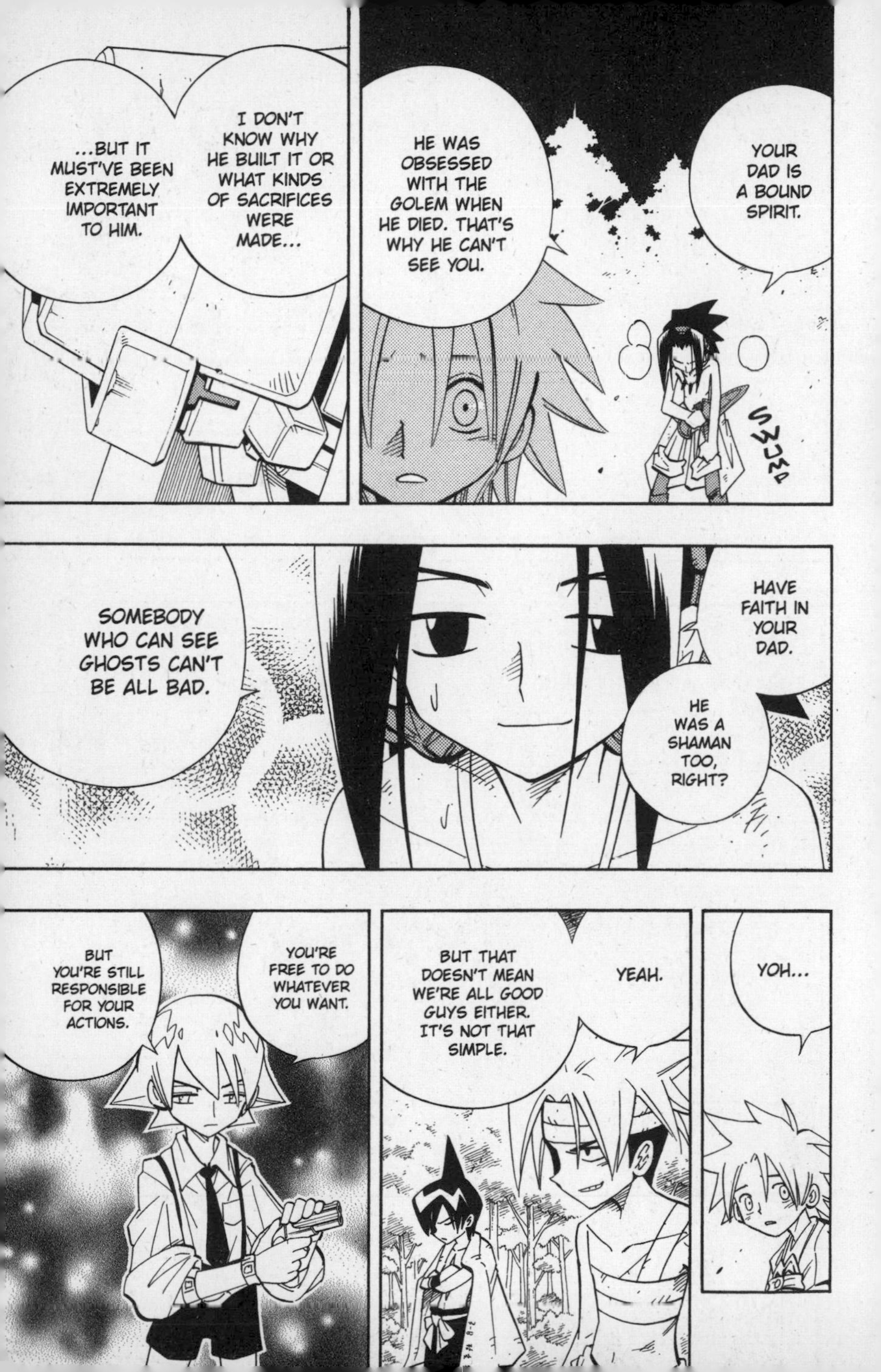
YOUR DAD IS A BOUND SPIRIT.
HE WAS OBSESSED WITH THE GOLEM WHEN HE DIED. THAT'S WHY HE CAN'T SEE YOU.
SWUMP
I DON'T KNOW WHY HE BUILT IT OR WHAT KINDS OF SACRIFICES WERE MADE...
...BUT IT MUST'VE BEEN EXTREMELY IMPORTANT TO HIM.
HAVE FAITH IN YOUR DAD.
HE WAS A SHAMAN TOO, RIGHT?
SOMEBODY WHO CAN SEE GHOSTS CAN'T BE ALL BAD.
YOH...
YEAH.
BUT THAT DOESN'T MEAN WE'RE ALL GOOD GUYS EITHER. IT'S NOT THAT SIMPLE.
YOU'RE FREE TO DO WHATEVER YOU WANT.
BUT YOU'RE STILL RESPONSIBLE FOR YOUR ACTIONS.

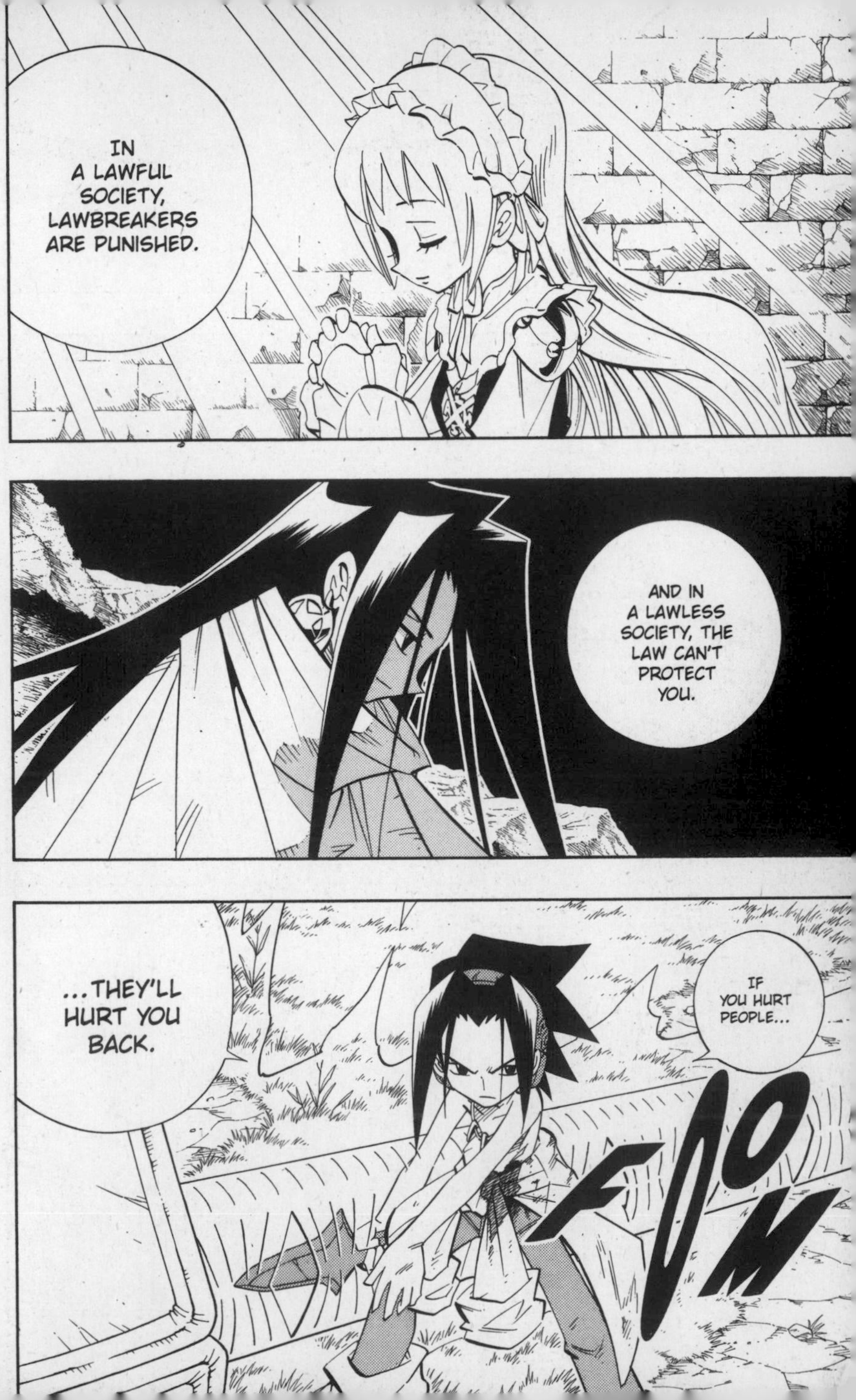
IN A LAWFUL SOCIETY, LAWBREAKERS ARE PUNISHED.
AND IN A LAWLESS SOCIETY, THE LAW CAN'T PROTECT YOU.
IF YOU HURT PEOPLE...
...THEY'LL HURT YOU BACK.

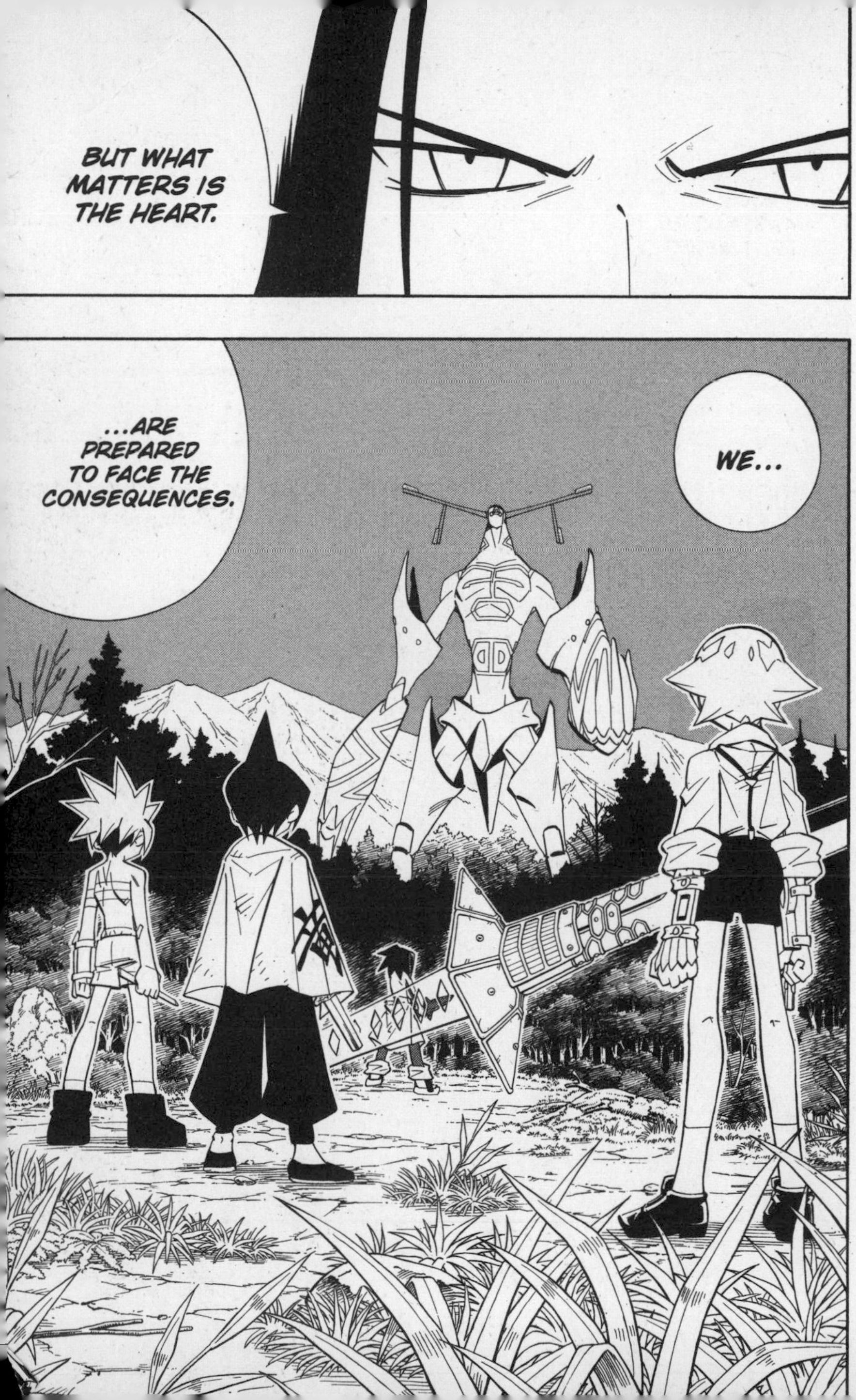
BUT WHAT MATTERS IS THE HEART.
WE...
...ARE PREPARED TO FACE THE CONSEQUENCES.

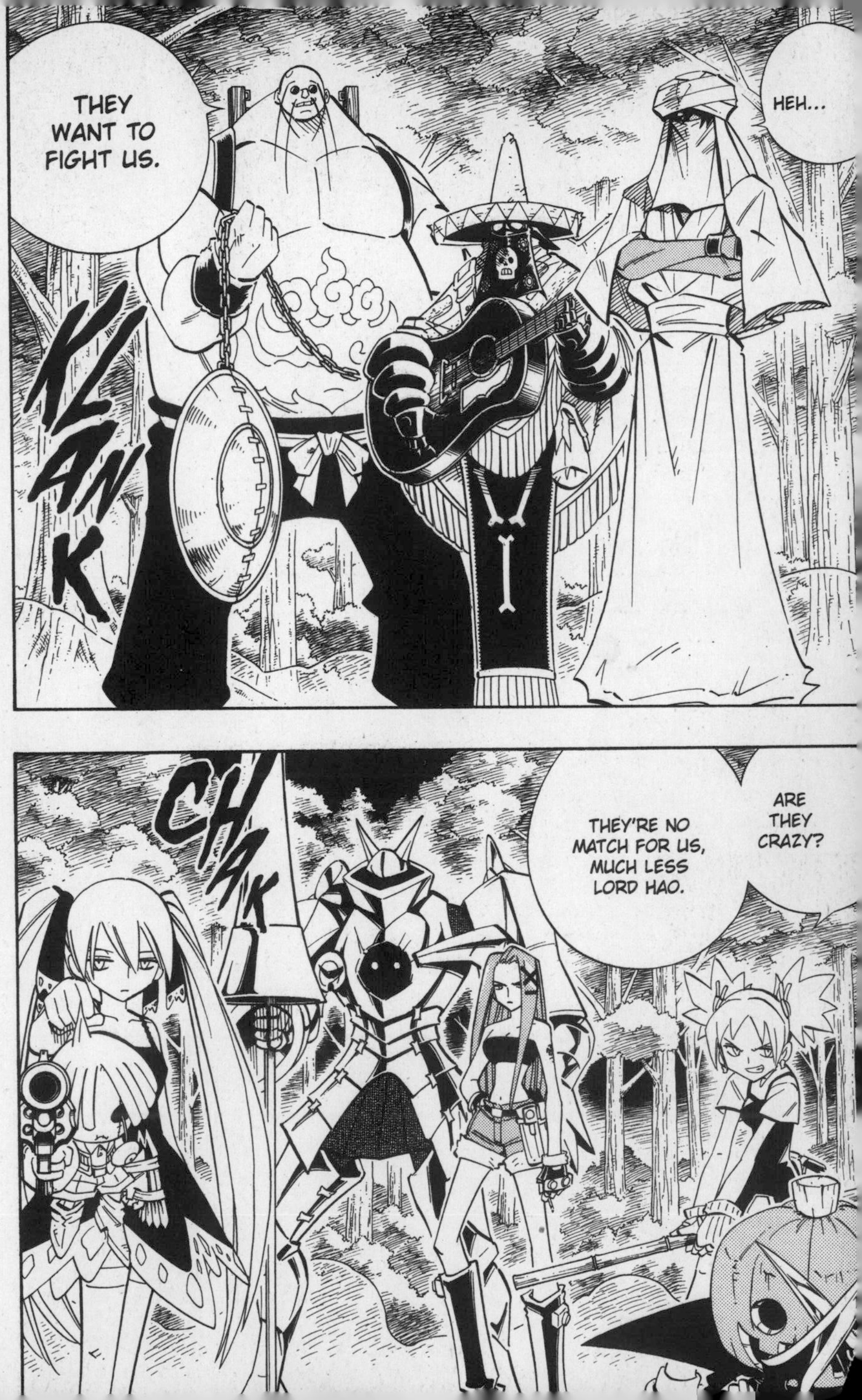
HEH...
THEY WANT TO FIGHT US.
KLANK
ARE THEY CRAZY?
THEY'RE NO MATCH FOR US, MUCH LESS LORD HAO.
CHANK

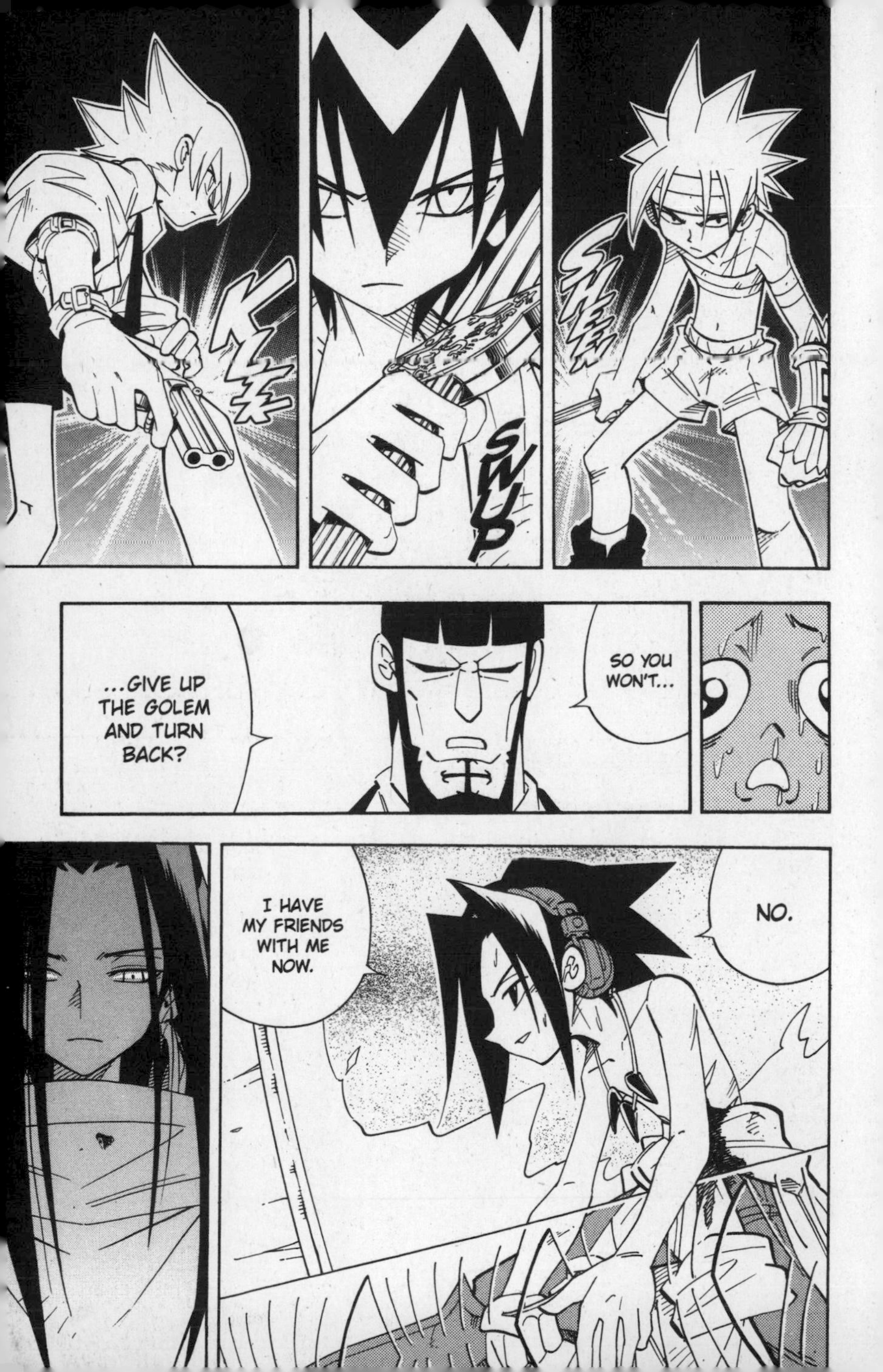
SWUP
SO YOU WON'T...
...GIVE UP THE GOLEM AND TURN BACK?
NO.
I HAVE MY FRIENDS WITH ME NOW.

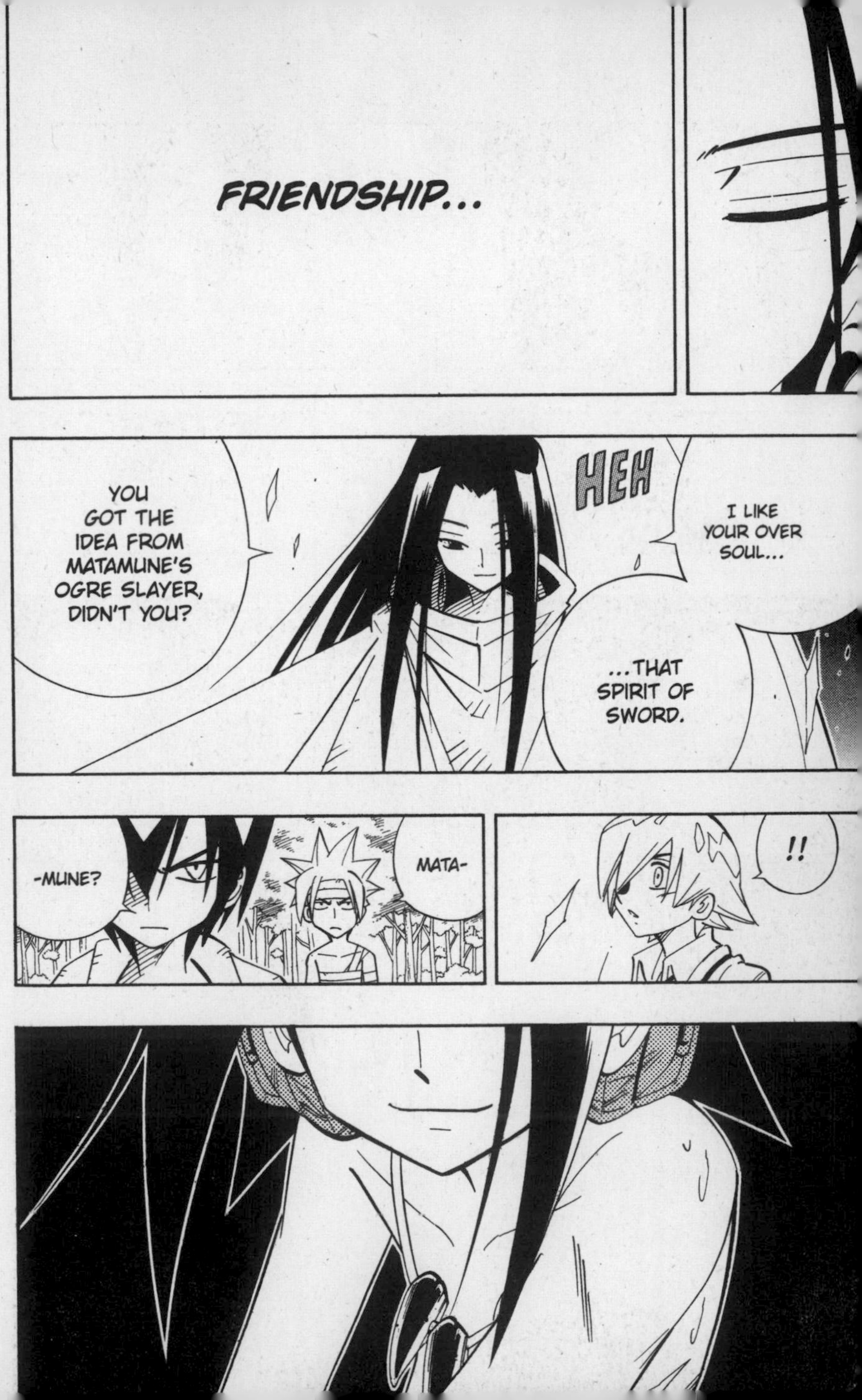
FRIENDSHIP...
HEH
I LIKE YOUR OVER SOUL...
...THAT SPIRIT OF SWORD.
YOU GOT THE IDEA FROM MATAMUNE'S OGRE SLAYER, DIDN'T YOU?
!!
MATA-
-MUNE?

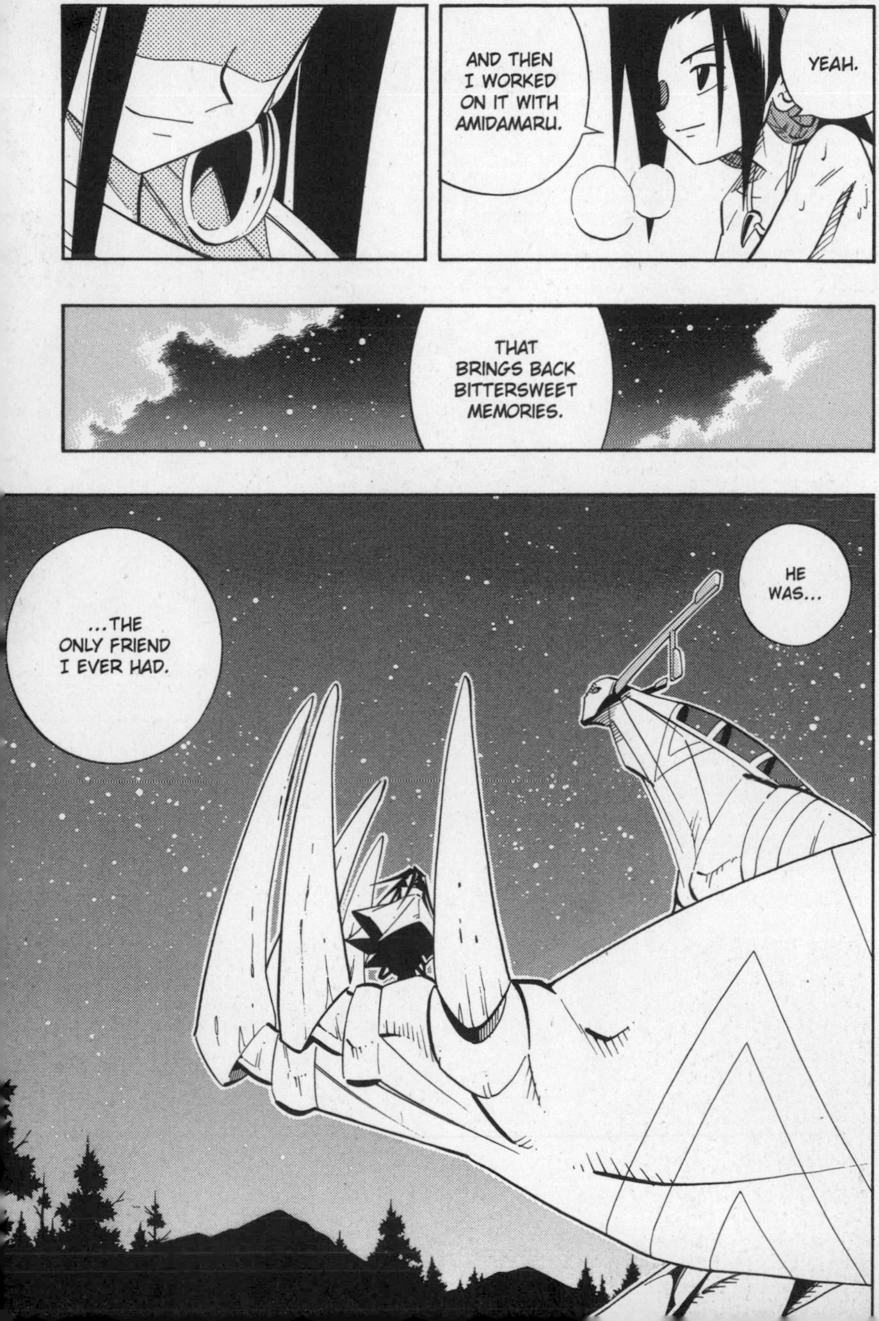
YEAH.
AND THEN I WORKED ON IT WITH AMIDAMARU.
THAT BRINGS BACK BITTERSWEET MEMORIES.
HE WAS...
...THE ONLY FRIEND I EVER HAD.

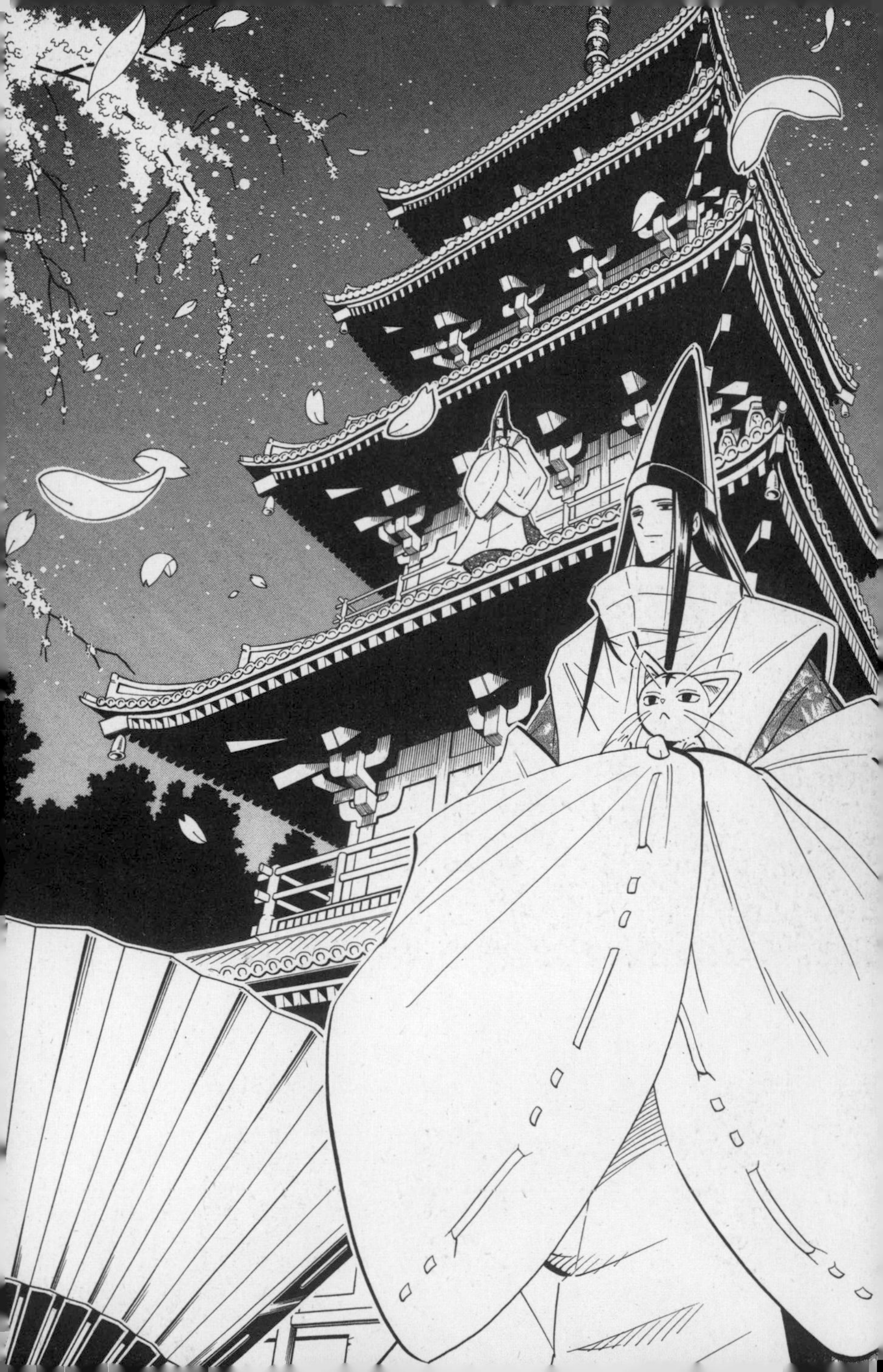

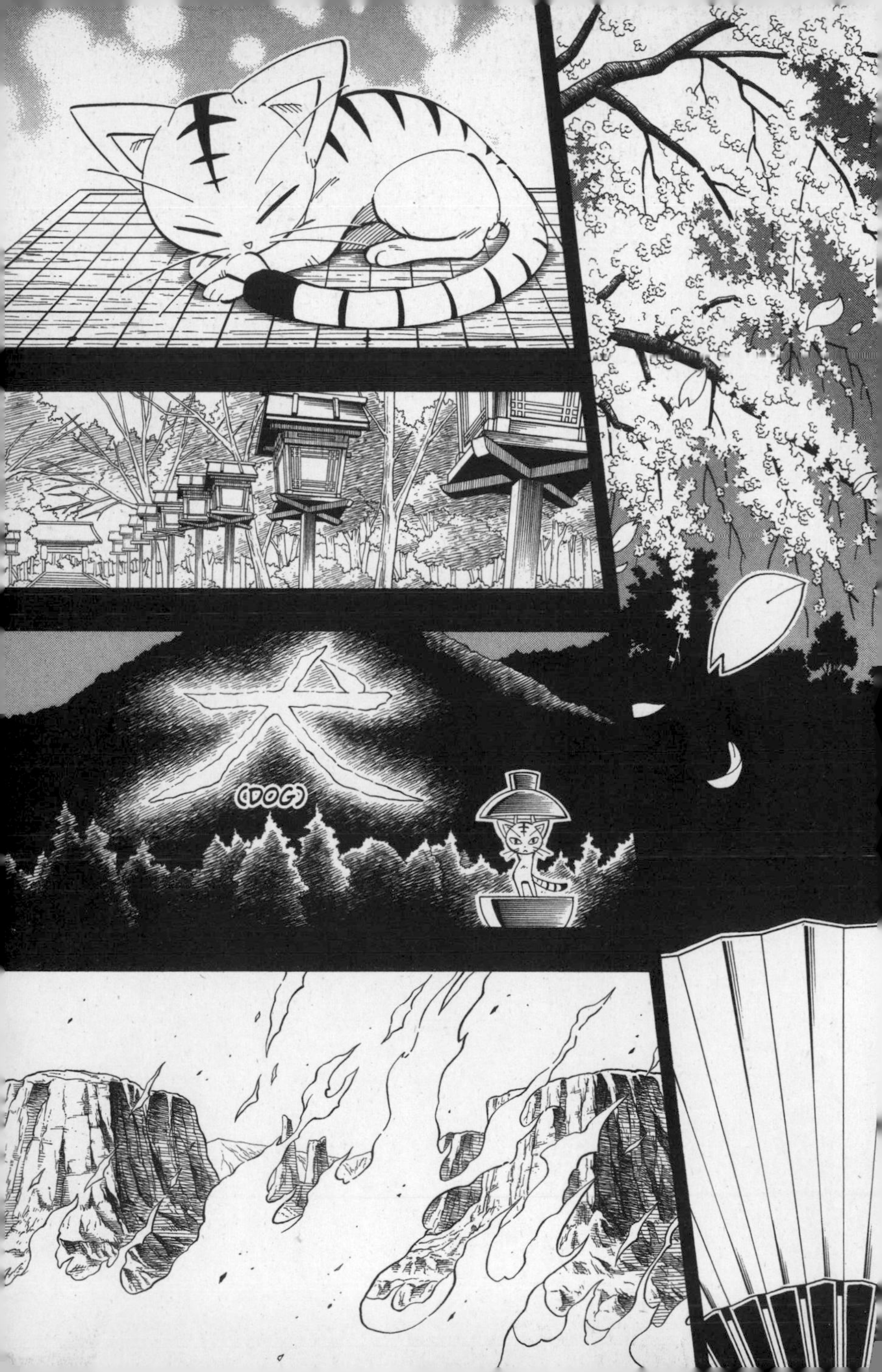
(DOG)

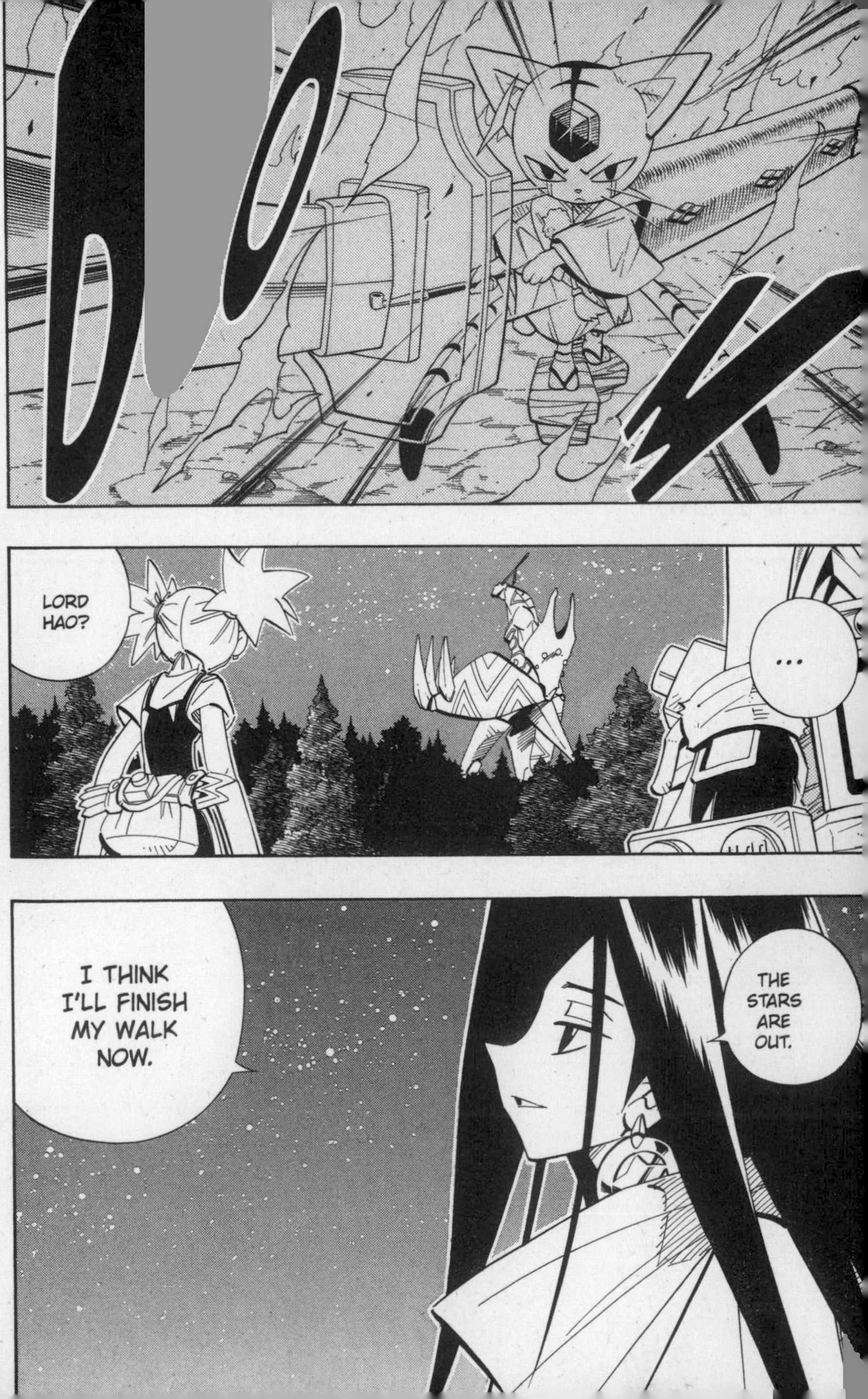
...
LORD HAO?
THE STARS ARE OUT.
I THINK I'LL FINISH MY WALK NOW.

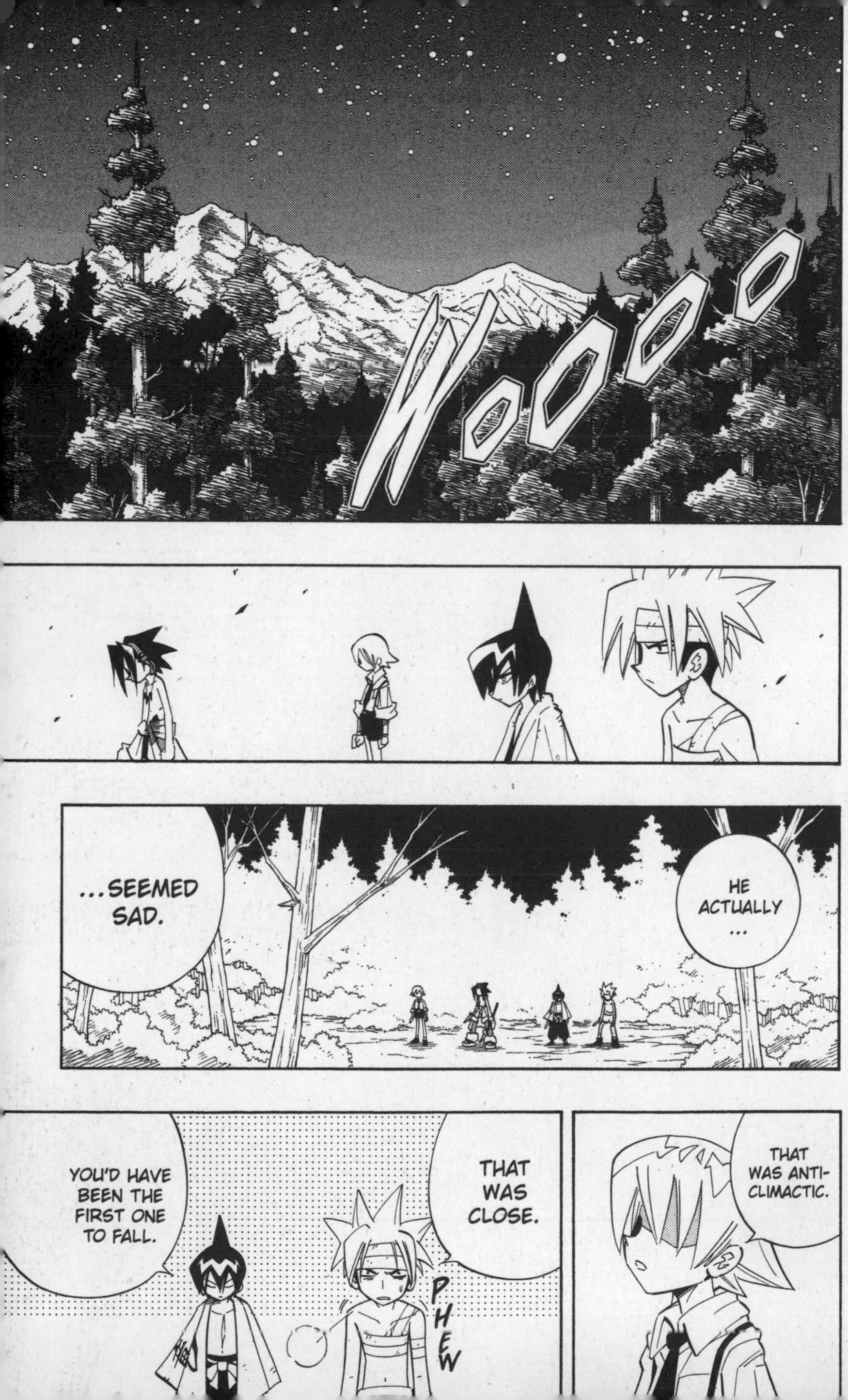
WOOOOO
HE ACTUALLY ...
...SEEMED SAD.
THAT WAS ANTI-CLIMACTIC.
THAT WAS CLOSE.
PHEW
YOU'D HAVE BEEN THE FIRST ONE TO FALL.

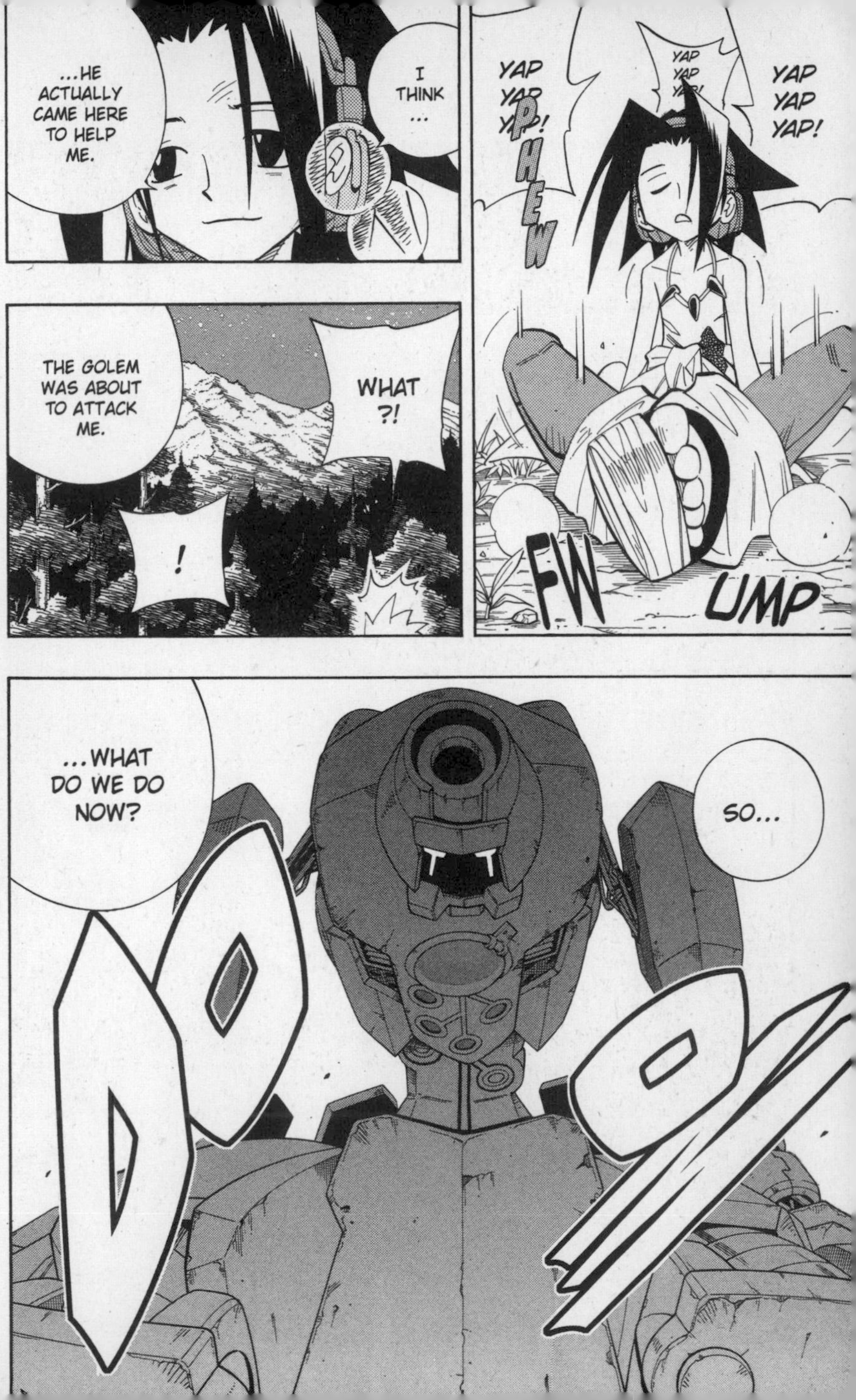
YAP YAP YAP!
YAP YAP YAP!
YAP YAP YAP!
PHEW
FWUMP
I THINK...
...HE ACTUALLY CAME HERE TO HELP ME.
WHAT?!
THE GOLEM WAS ABOUT TO ATTACK ME.
!
SO...
...WHAT DO WE DO NOW?

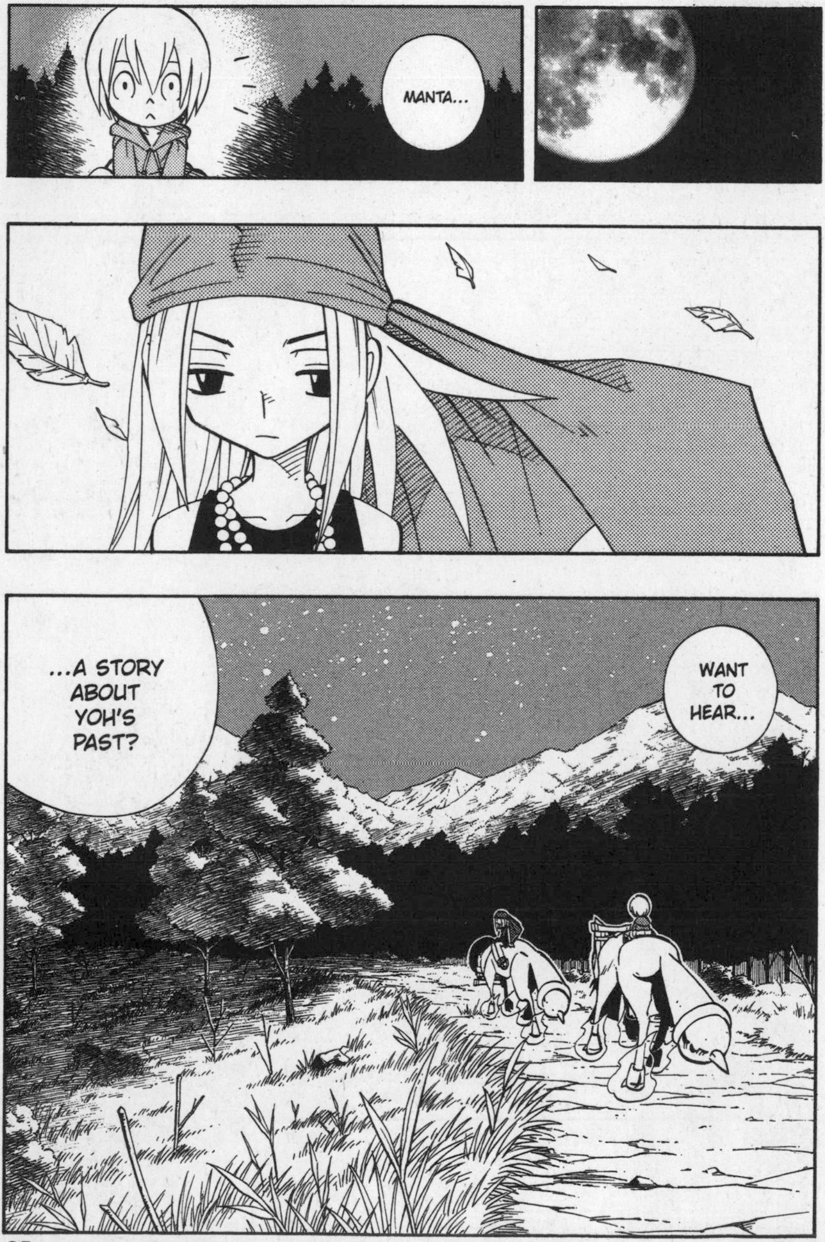
MANTA...
WANT TO HEAR...
...A STORY ABOUT YOH'S PAST?

SHAMAN KING CHARACTER FILE No.122

2001
(JAN)

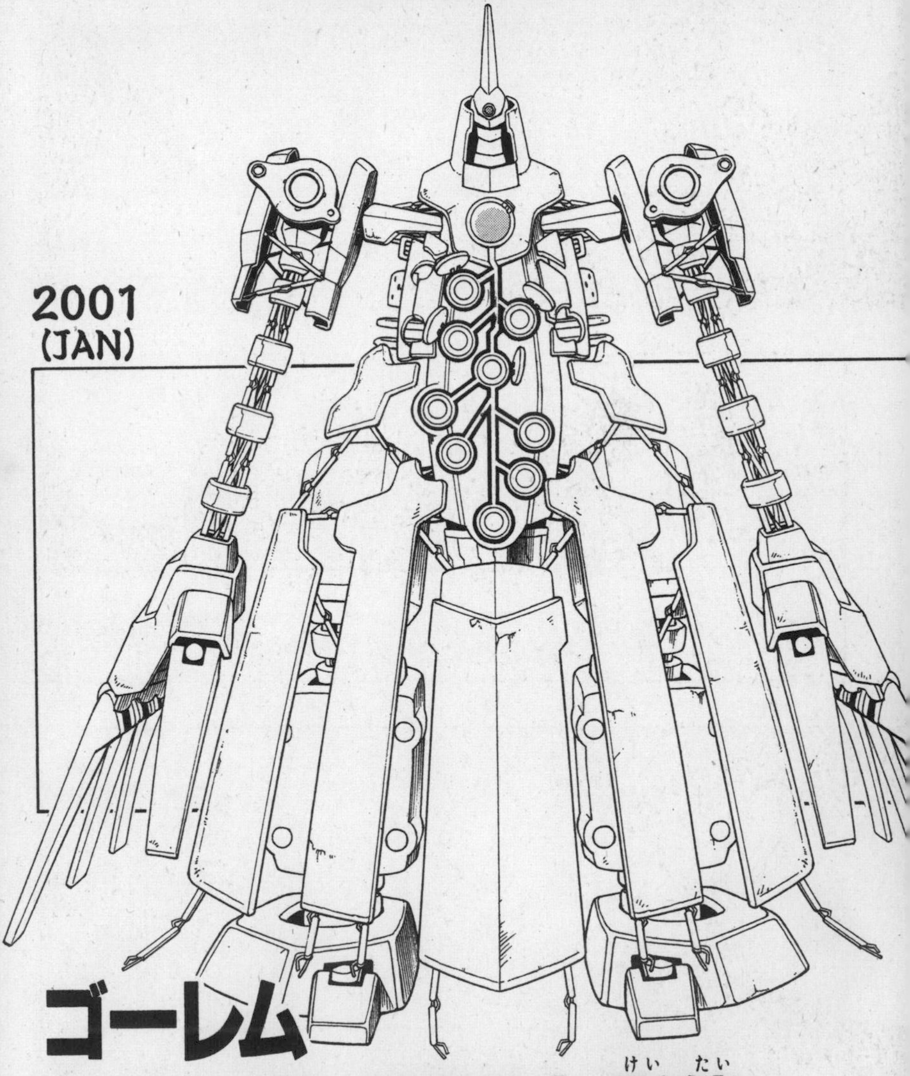

ゴーレム
セフィロトブラスト形態(けいたい)

GOLEM SEPHIROT: BLAST MODE

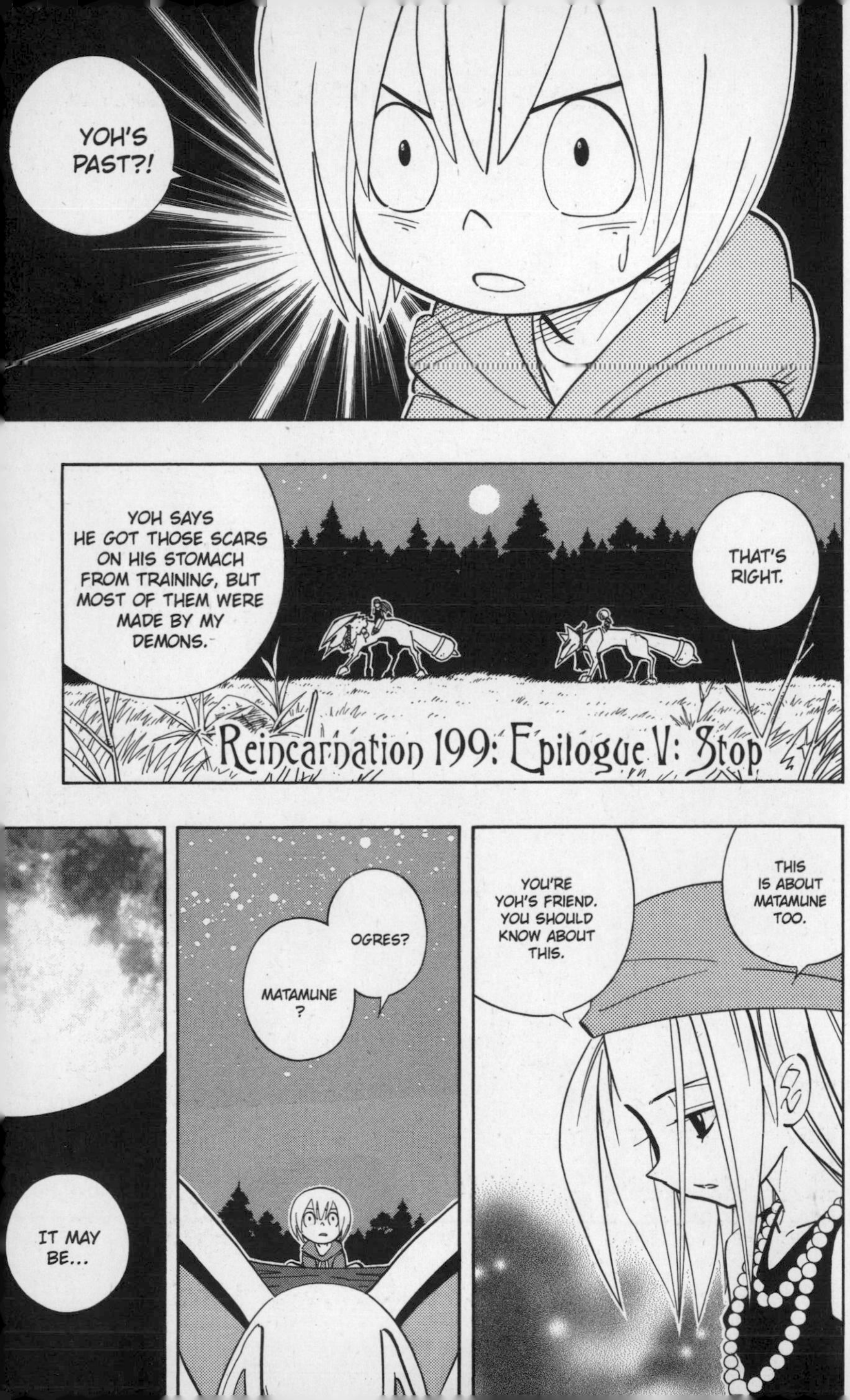
YOH'S PAST?!
THAT'S RIGHT.
YOH SAYS HE GOT THOSE SCARS ON HIS STOMACH FROM TRAINING, BUT MOST OF THEM WERE MADE BY MY DEMONS.
Reincarnation 199: Epilogue V: Stop
THIS IS ABOUT MATAMUNE TOO.
YOU'RE YOH'S FRIEND. YOU SHOULD KNOW ABOUT THIS.
OGRES?
MATAMUNE?
IT MAY BE...

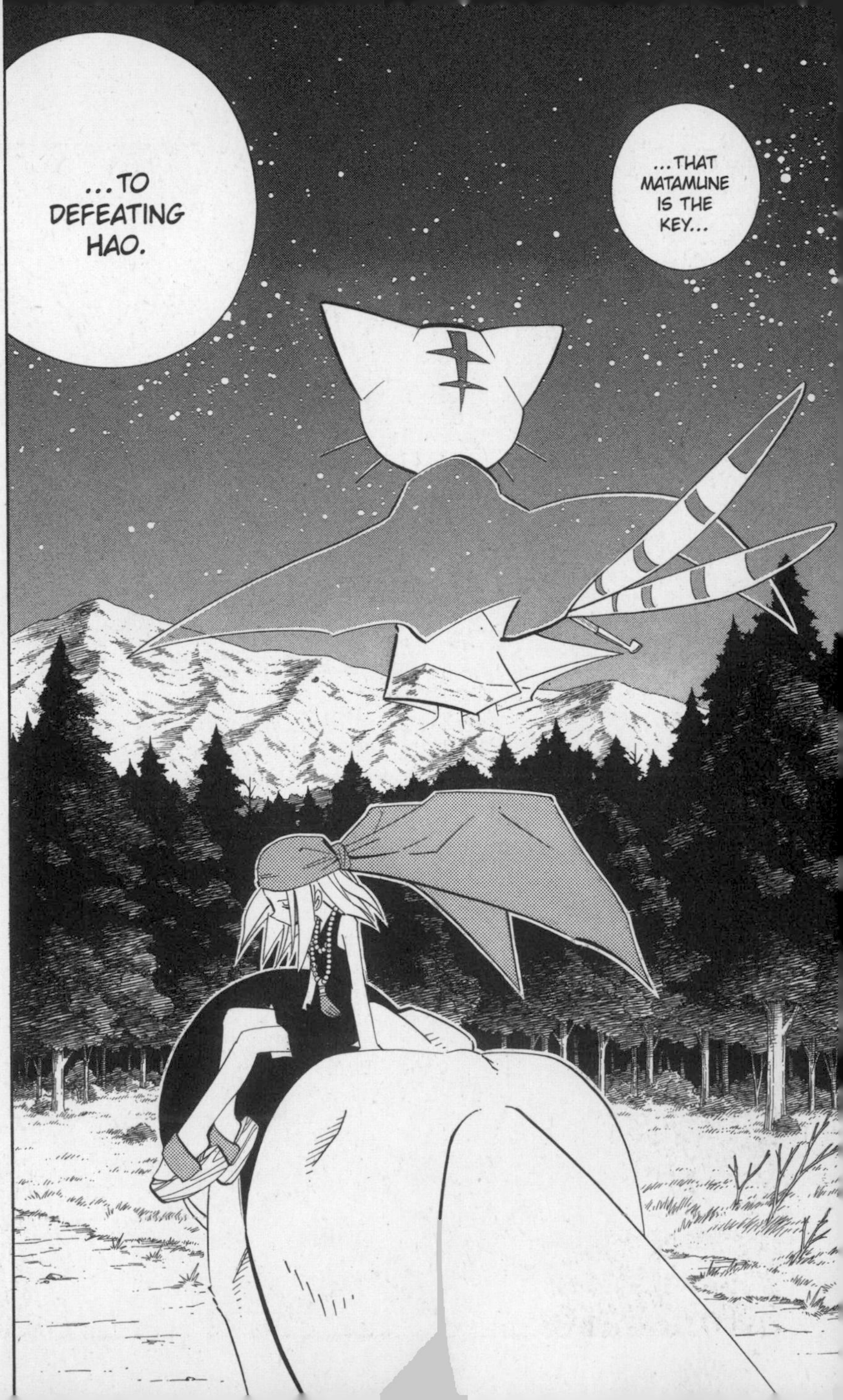
...THAT MATAMUNE IS THE KEY...
...TO DEFEATING HAO.

Reincarnation 199: Epilogue V: Stop

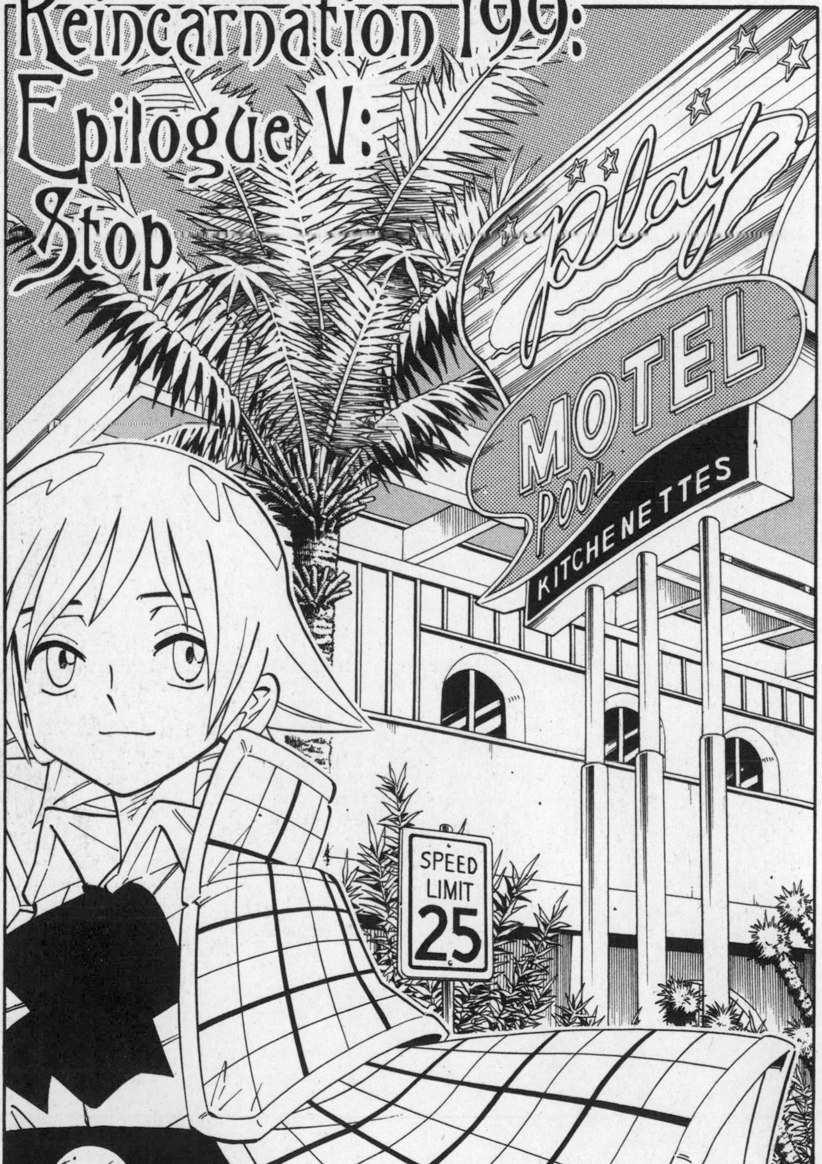
play
MOTEL
POOL
KITCHENETTES
SPEED LIMIT 25

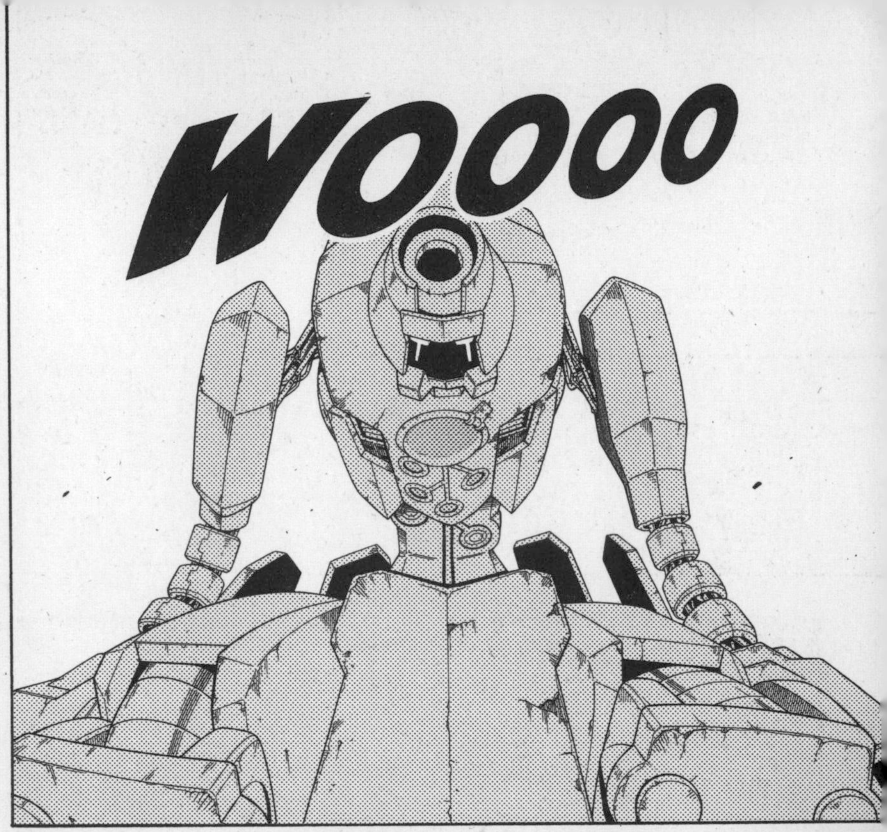
WOOOO
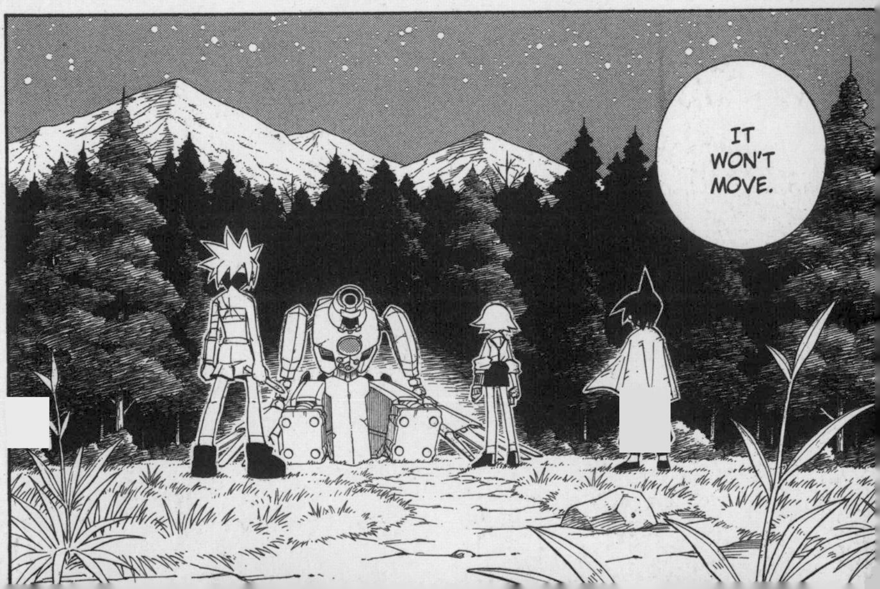
IT WON'T MOVE.

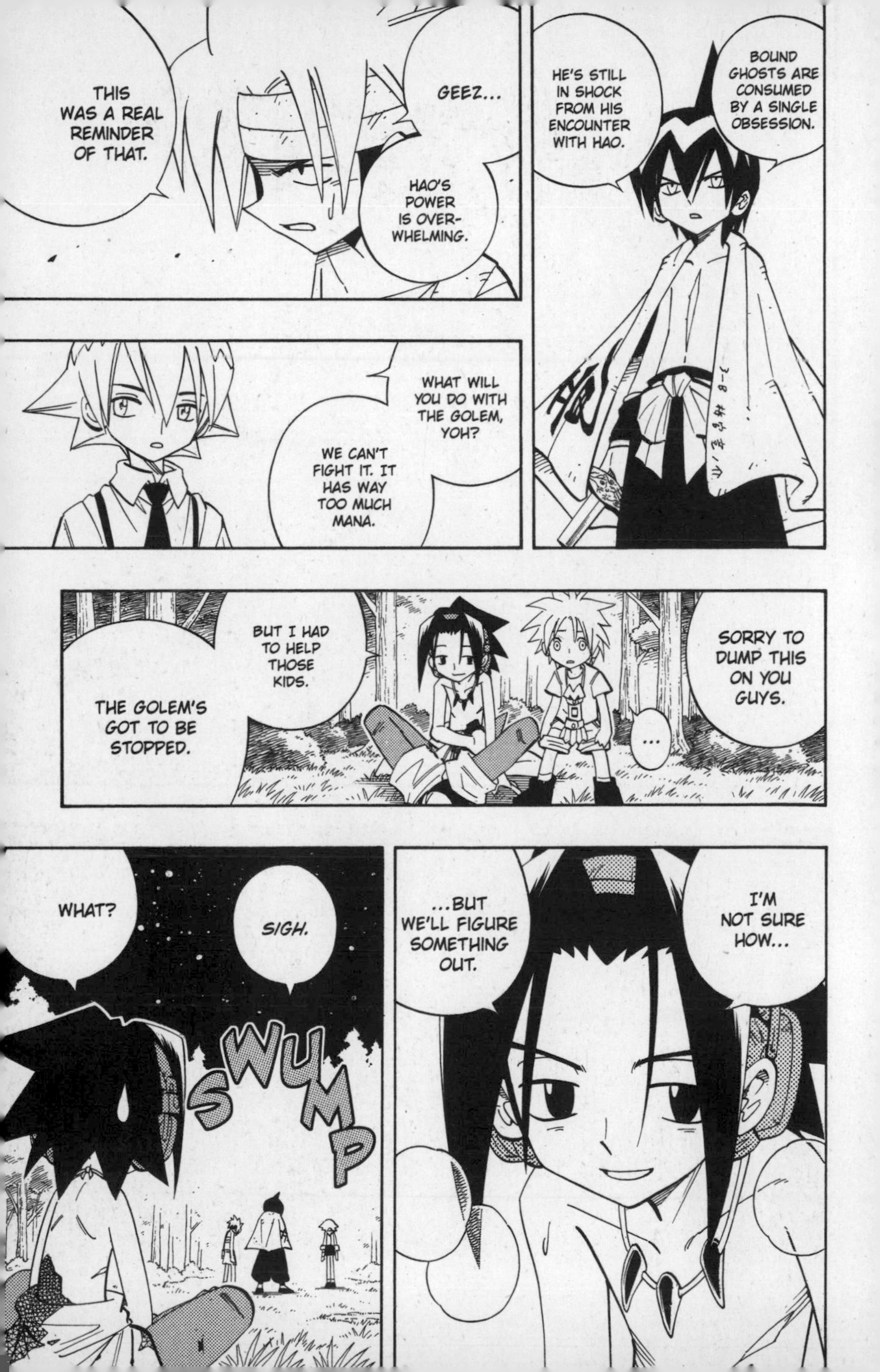
BOUND GHOSTS ARE CONSUMED BY A SINGLE OBSESSION.
HE'S STILL IN SHOCK FROM HIS ENCOUNTER WITH HAO.
GEEZ...
HAO'S POWER IS OVER-WHELMING.
THIS WAS A REAL REMINDER OF THAT.
WHAT WILL YOU DO WITH THE GOLEM, YOH?
WE CAN'T FIGHT IT. IT HAS WAY TOO MUCH MANA.
SORRY TO DUMP THIS ON YOU GUYS.
...
BUT I HAD TO HELP THOSE KIDS.
THE GOLEM'S GOT TO BE STOPPED.
I'M NOT SURE HOW...
...BUT WE'LL FIGURE SOMETHING OUT.
SIGH.
WHAT?
SWUMP

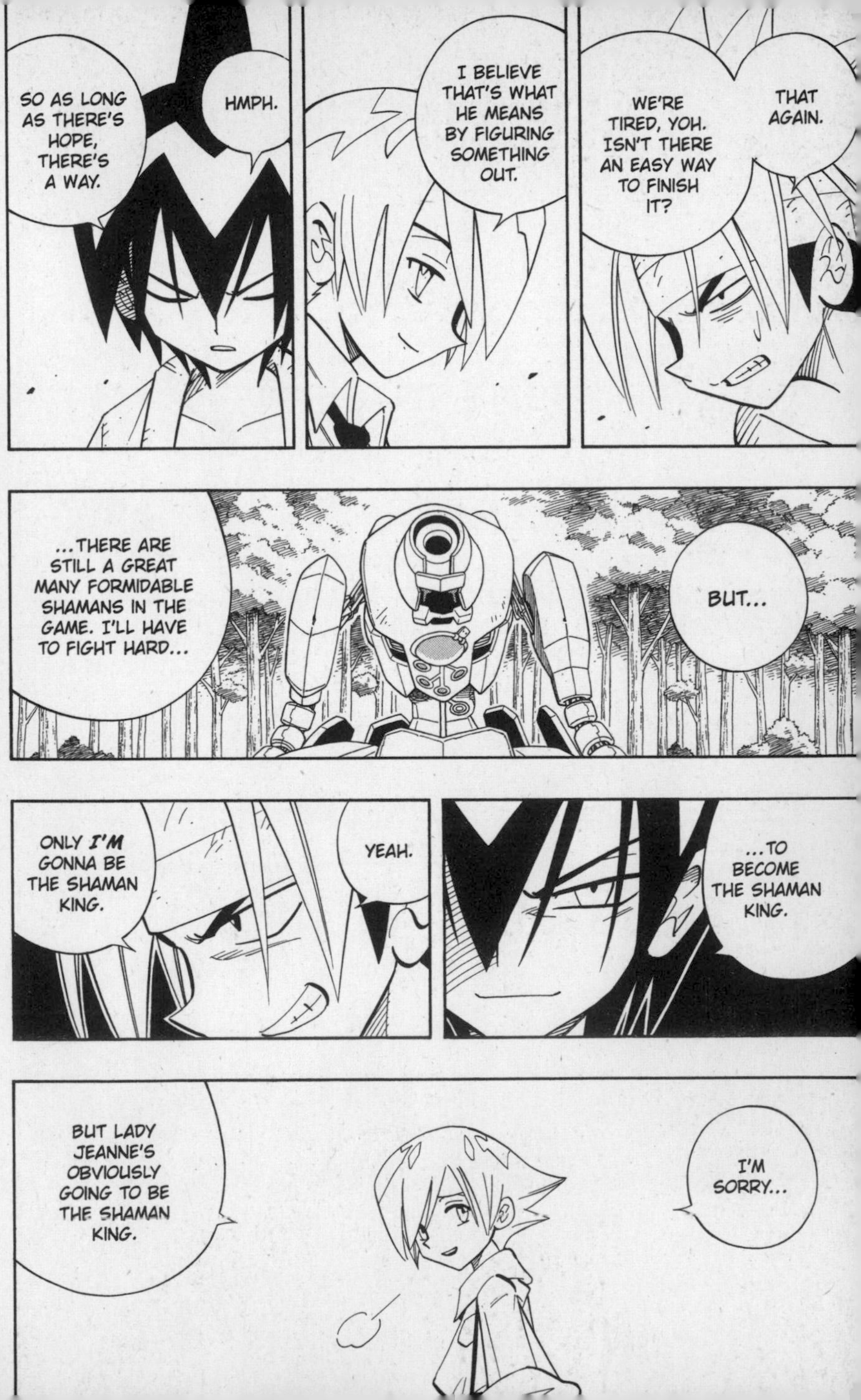
THAT AGAIN.
WE'RE TIRED, YOH. ISN'T THERE AN EASY WAY TO FINISH IT?
I BELIEVE THAT'S WHAT HE MEANS BY FIGURING SOMETHING OUT.
HMPH.
SO AS LONG AS THERE'S HOPE, THERE'S A WAY.
BUT...
...THERE ARE STILL A GREAT MANY FORMIDABLE SHAMANS IN THE GAME. I'LL HAVE TO FIGHT HARD...
...TO BECOME THE SHAMAN KING.
YEAH.
ONLY *I'M* GONNA BE THE SHAMAN KING.
I'M SORRY...
BUT LADY JEANNE'S OBVIOUSLY GOING TO BE THE SHAMAN KING.

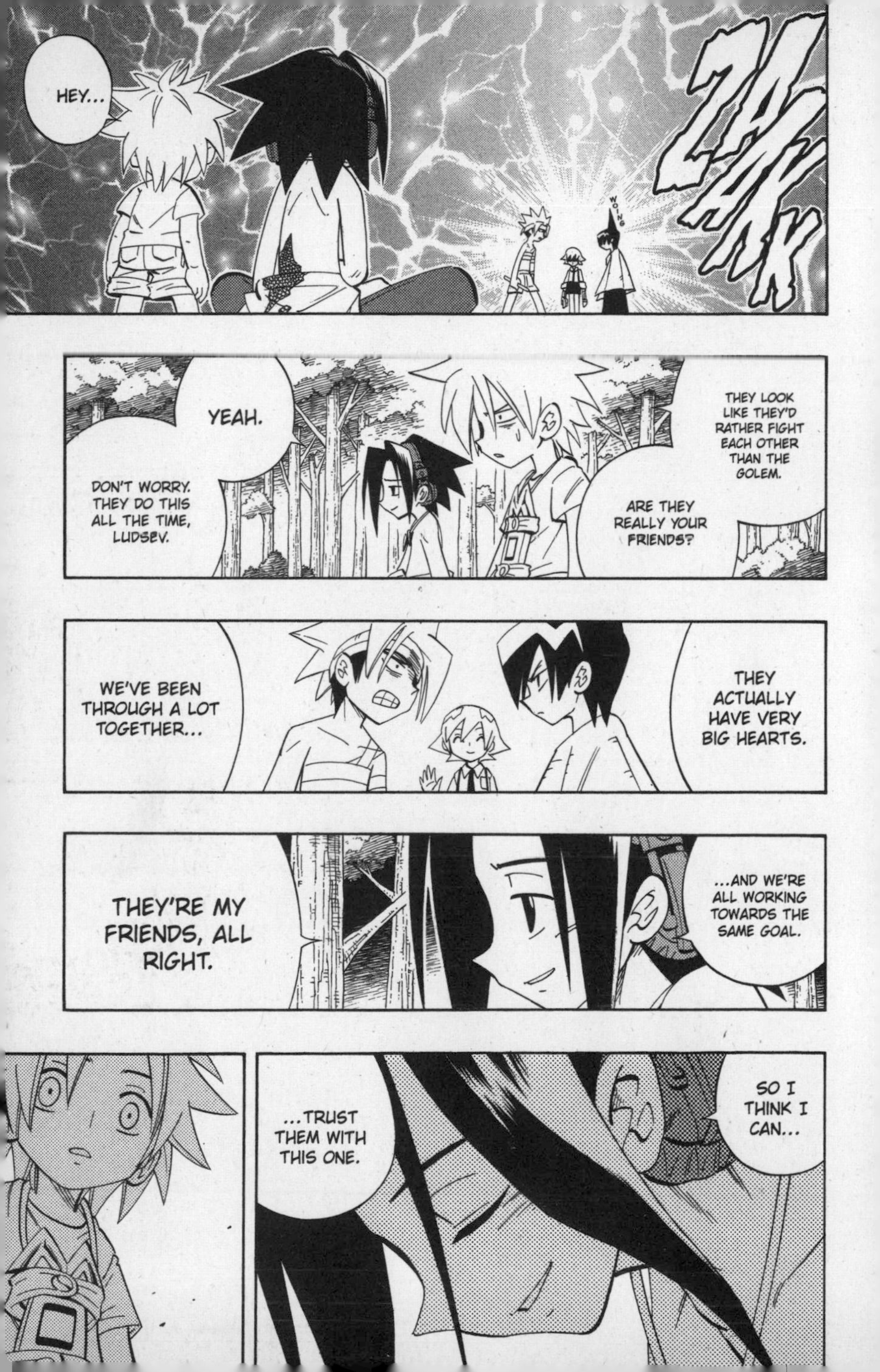
ZAKK
WOING
HEY...
THEY LOOK LIKE THEY'D RATHER FIGHT EACH OTHER THAN THE GOLEM.
ARE THEY REALLY YOUR FRIENDS?
YEAH.
DON'T WORRY. THEY DO THIS ALL THE TIME, LUDSEV.
THEY ACTUALLY HAVE VERY BIG HEARTS.
WE'VE BEEN THROUGH A LOT TOGETHER...
...AND WE'RE ALL WORKING TOWARDS THE SAME GOAL.
THEY'RE MY FRIENDS, ALL RIGHT.
SO I THINK I CAN...
...TRUST THEM WITH THIS ONE.

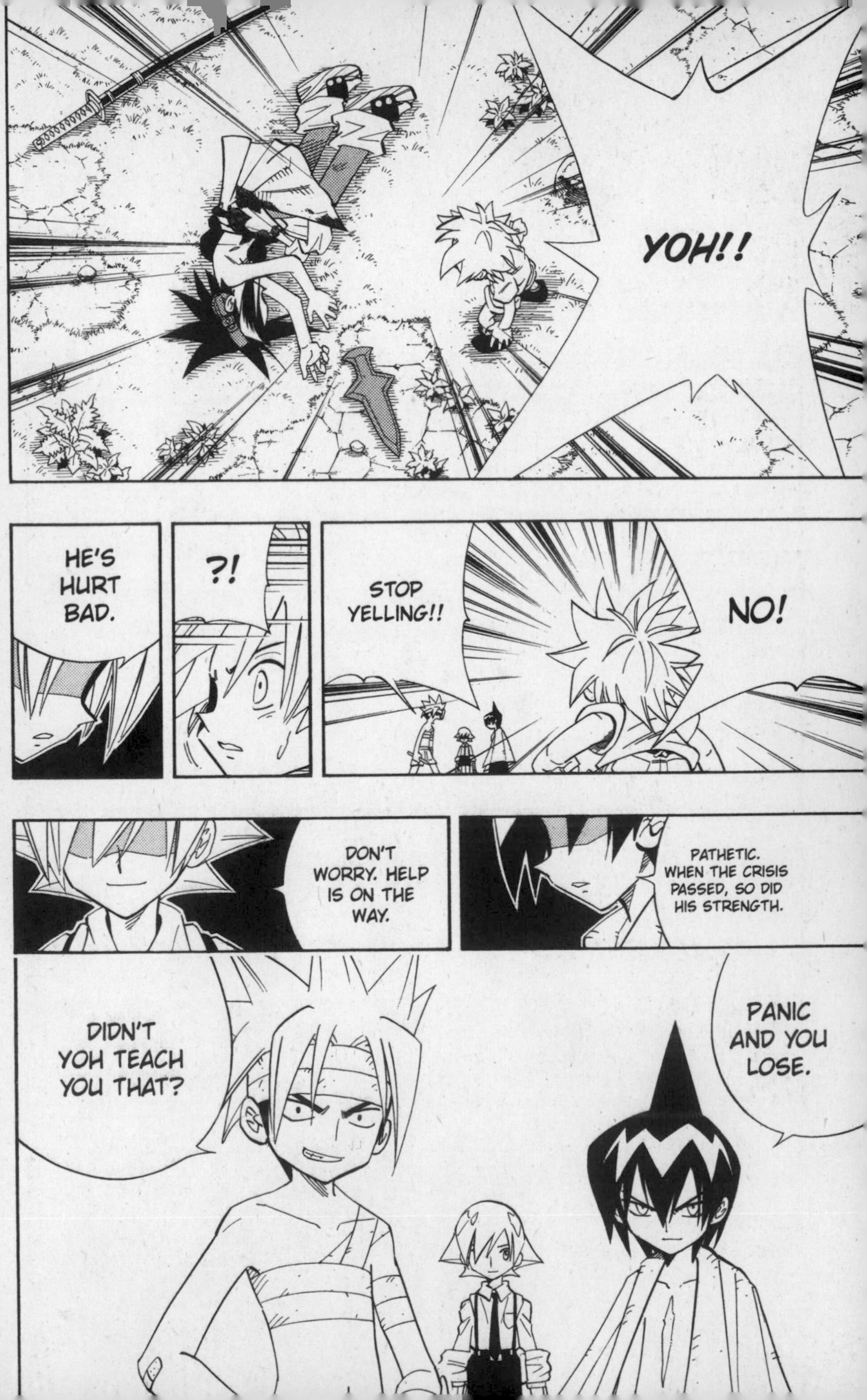
YOH!!
NO!
STOP YELLING!!
?!
HE'S HURT BAD.
PATHETIC. WHEN THE CRISIS PASSED, SO DID HIS STRENGTH.
DON'T WORRY. HELP IS ON THE WAY.
PANIC AND YOU LOSE.
DIDN'T YOH TEACH YOU THAT?

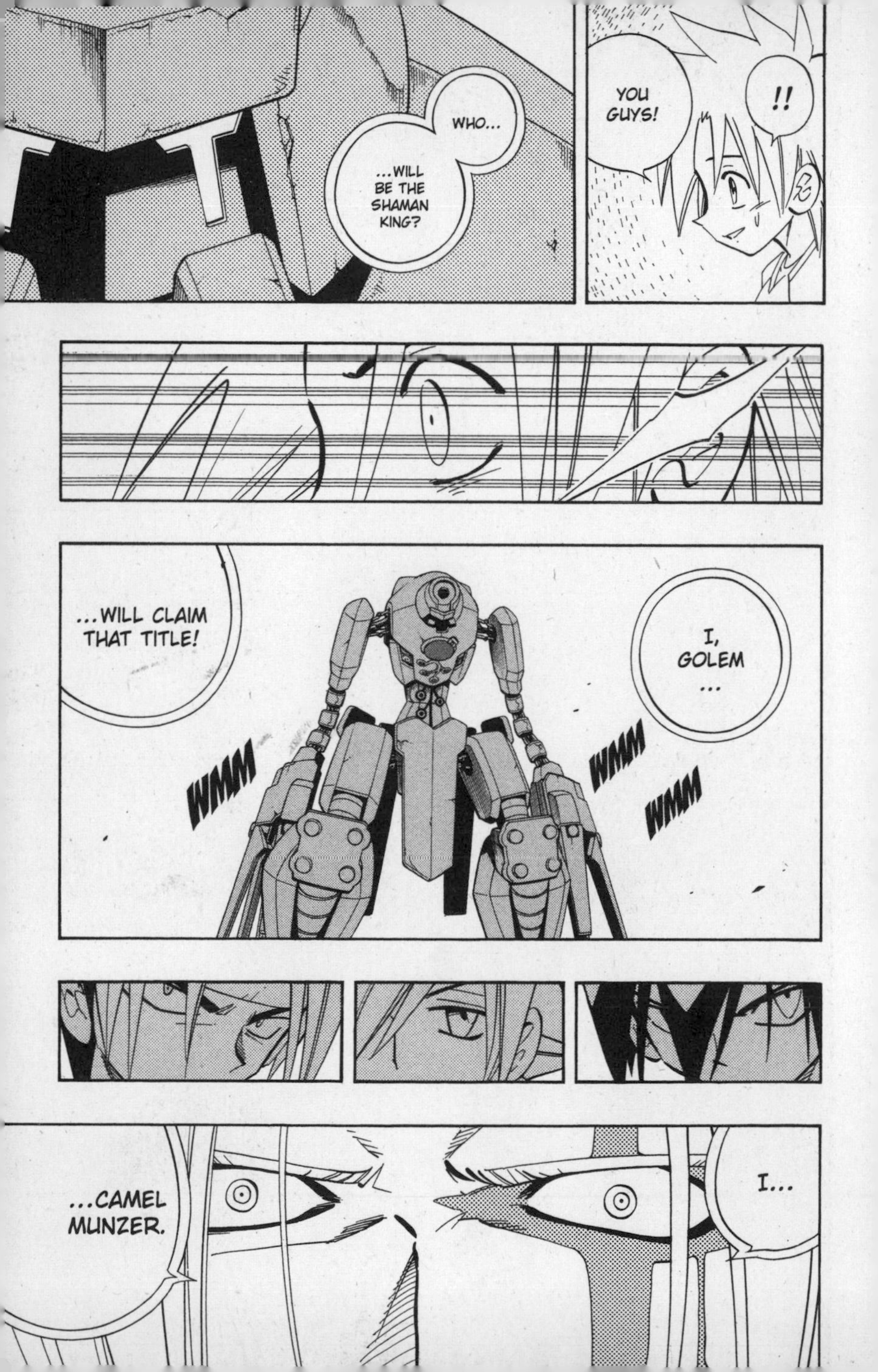
!!
YOU GUYS!
WHO...
...WILL BE THE SHAMAN KING?
I, GOLEM ...
...WILL CLAIM THAT TITLE!
WMM
WMM
WMM
I...
...CAMEL MUNZER.

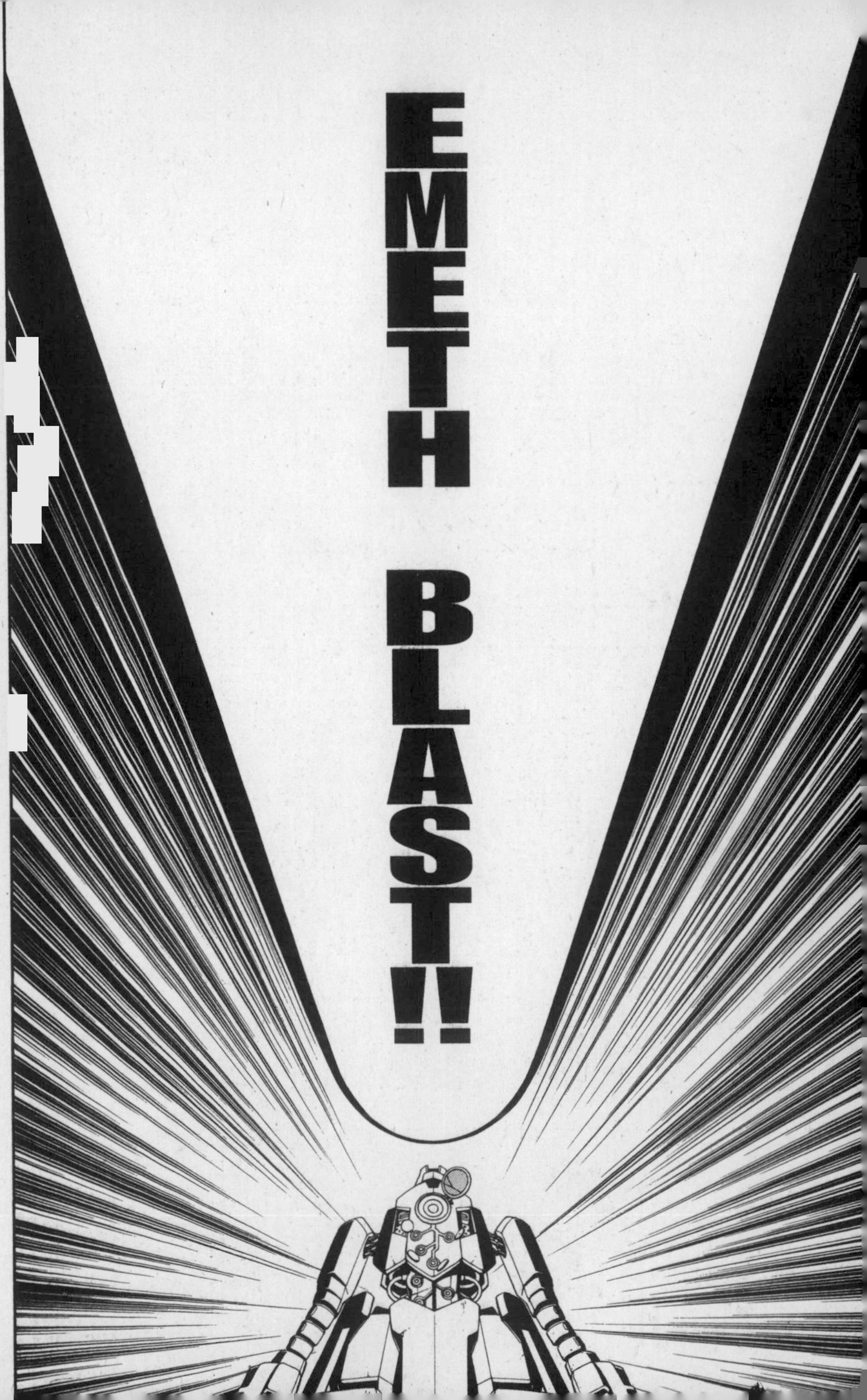
EMETH BLAST!!

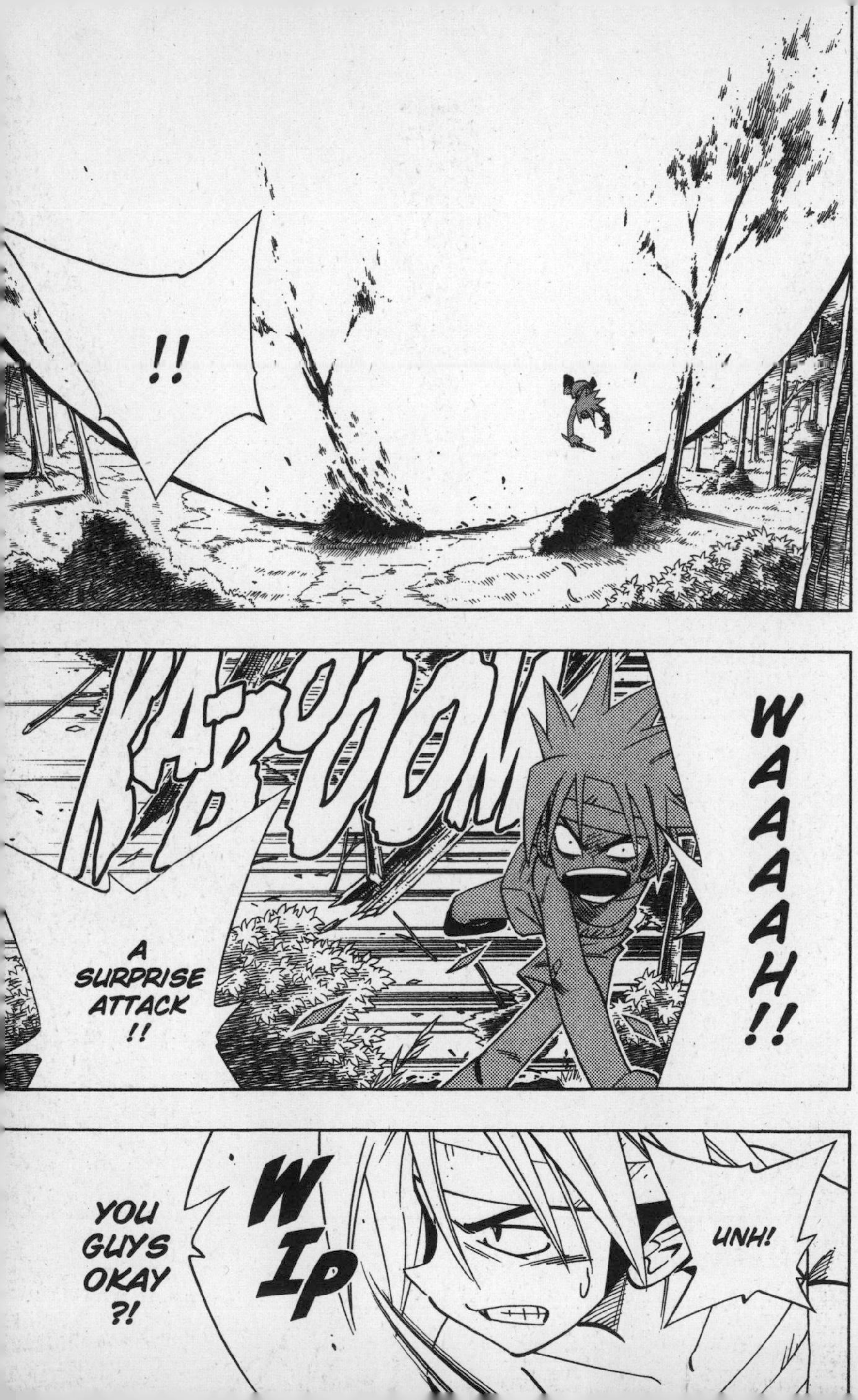
!!
WAAAAAH!!
KABOOOM
A SURPRISE ATTACK !!
UNH!
WIP
YOU GUYS OKAY ?!

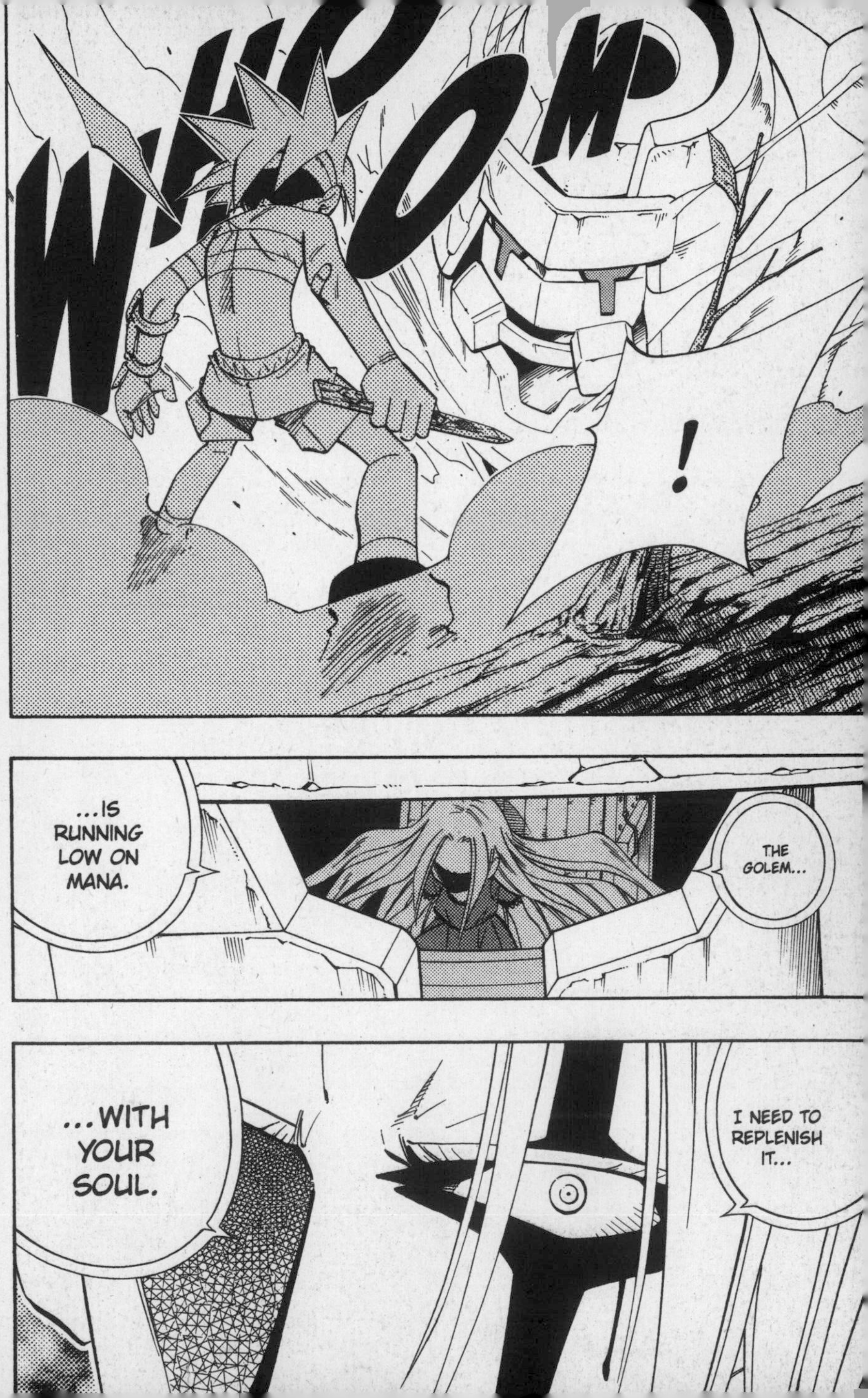
WHOOM
!
THE GOLEM...
...IS RUNNING LOW ON MANA.
I NEED TO REPLENISH IT...
...WITH YOUR SOUL.

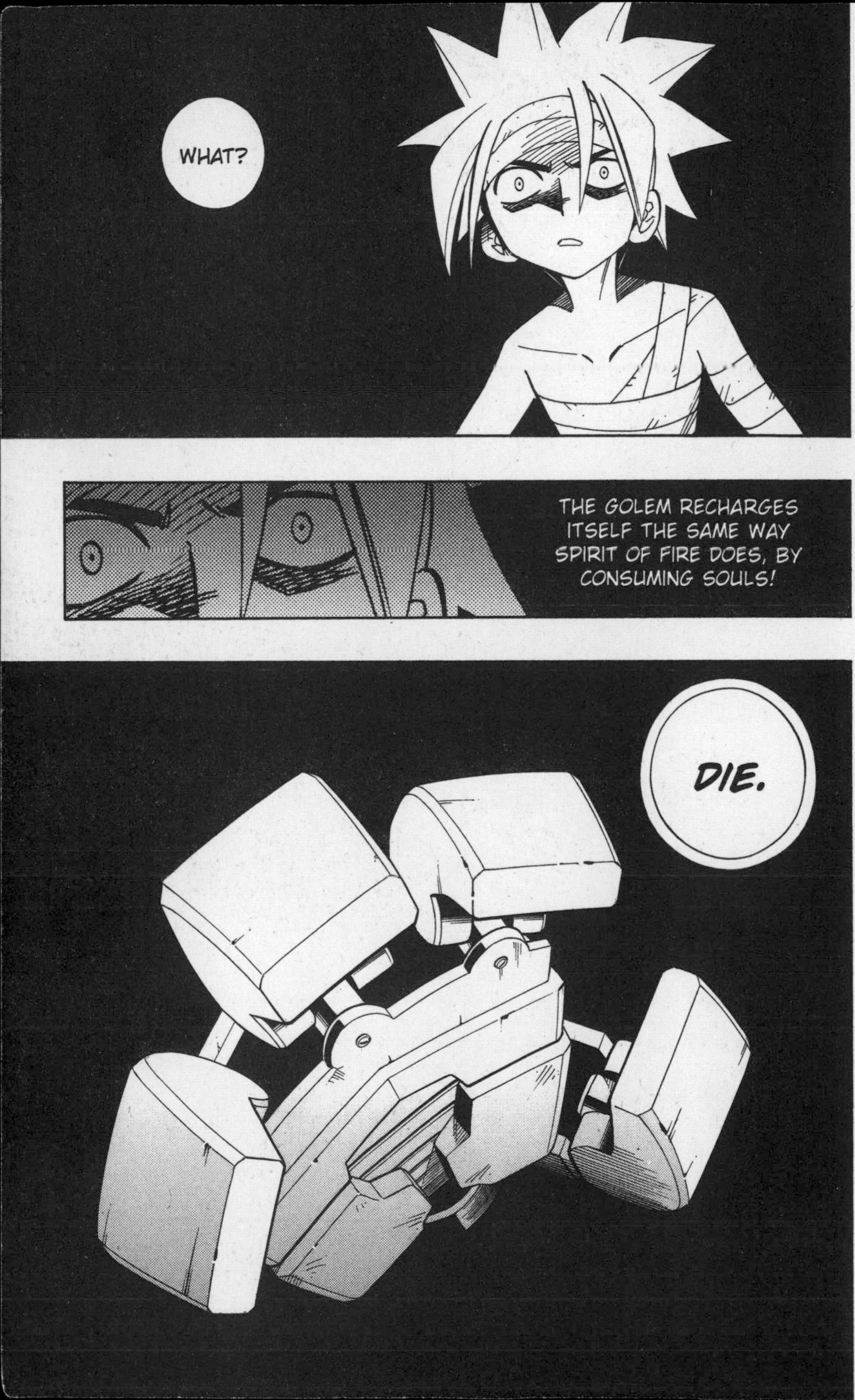
WHAT?
THE GOLEM RECHARGES ITSELF THE SAME WAY SPIRIT OF FIRE DOES, BY CONSUMING SOULS!
DIE.

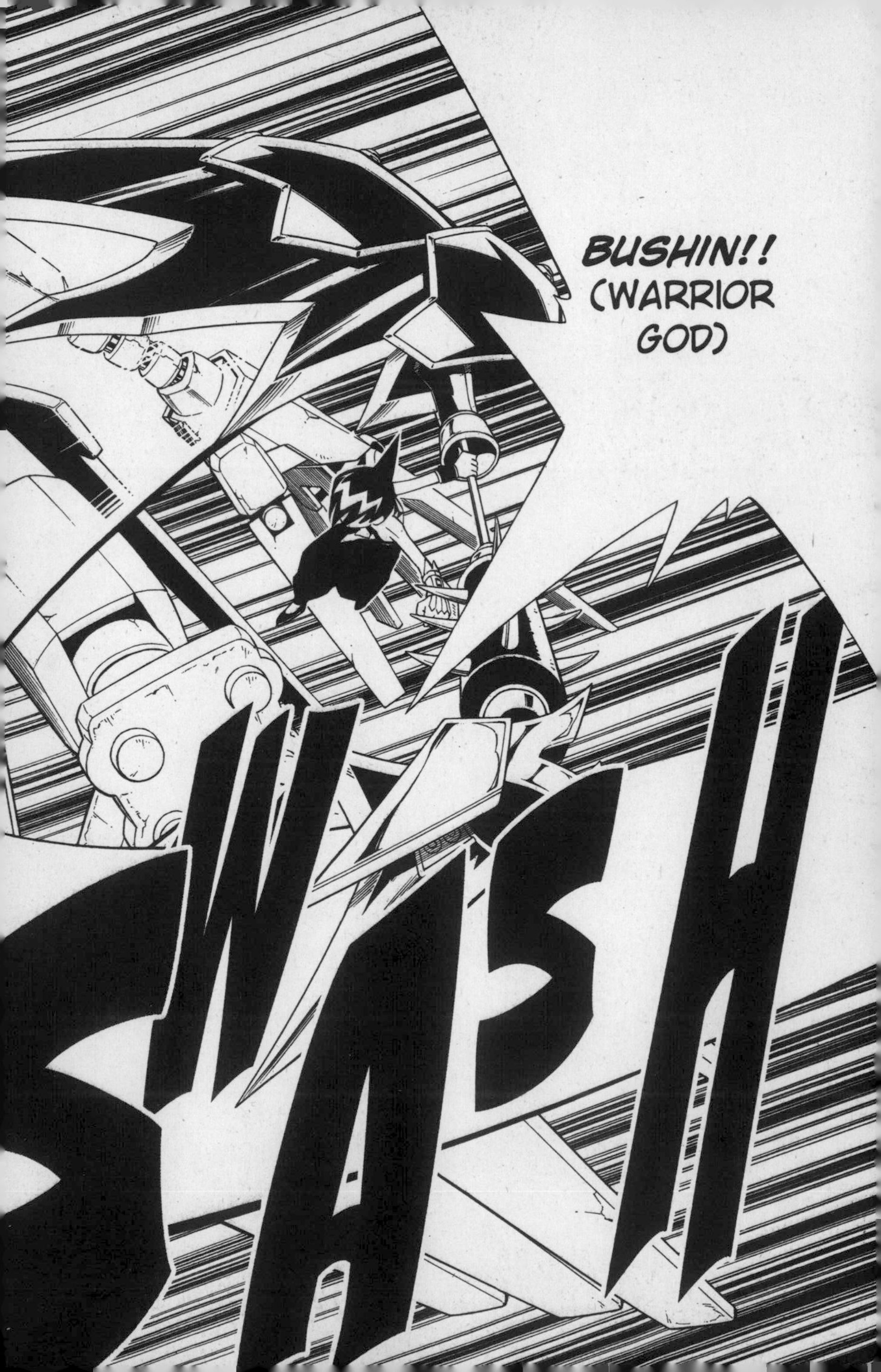
BUSHIN!!
(WARRIOR GOD)
SWASH

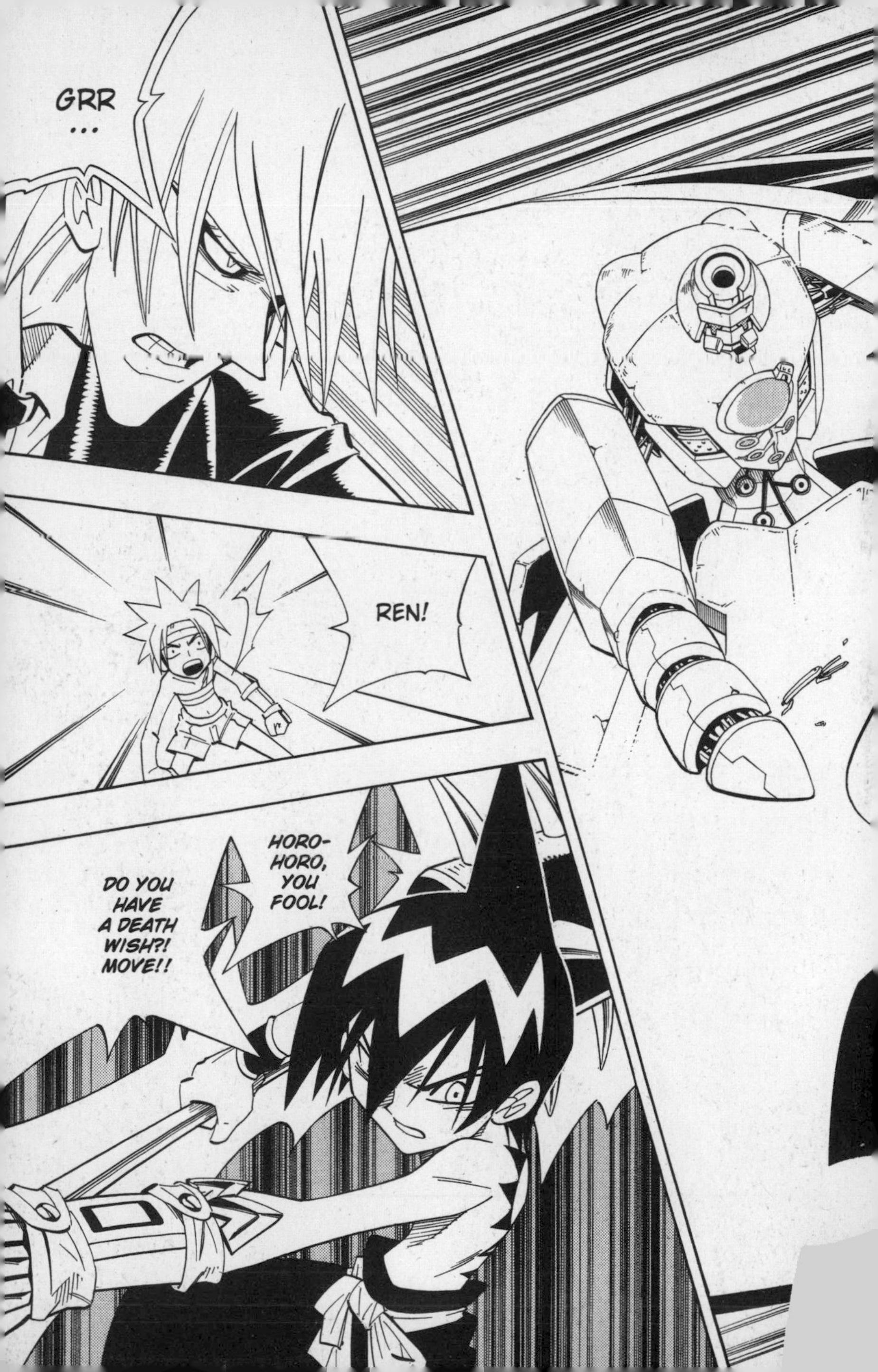
GRR ...
REN!
HORO-HORO, YOU FOOL!
DO YOU HAVE A DEATH WISH?! MOVE!!

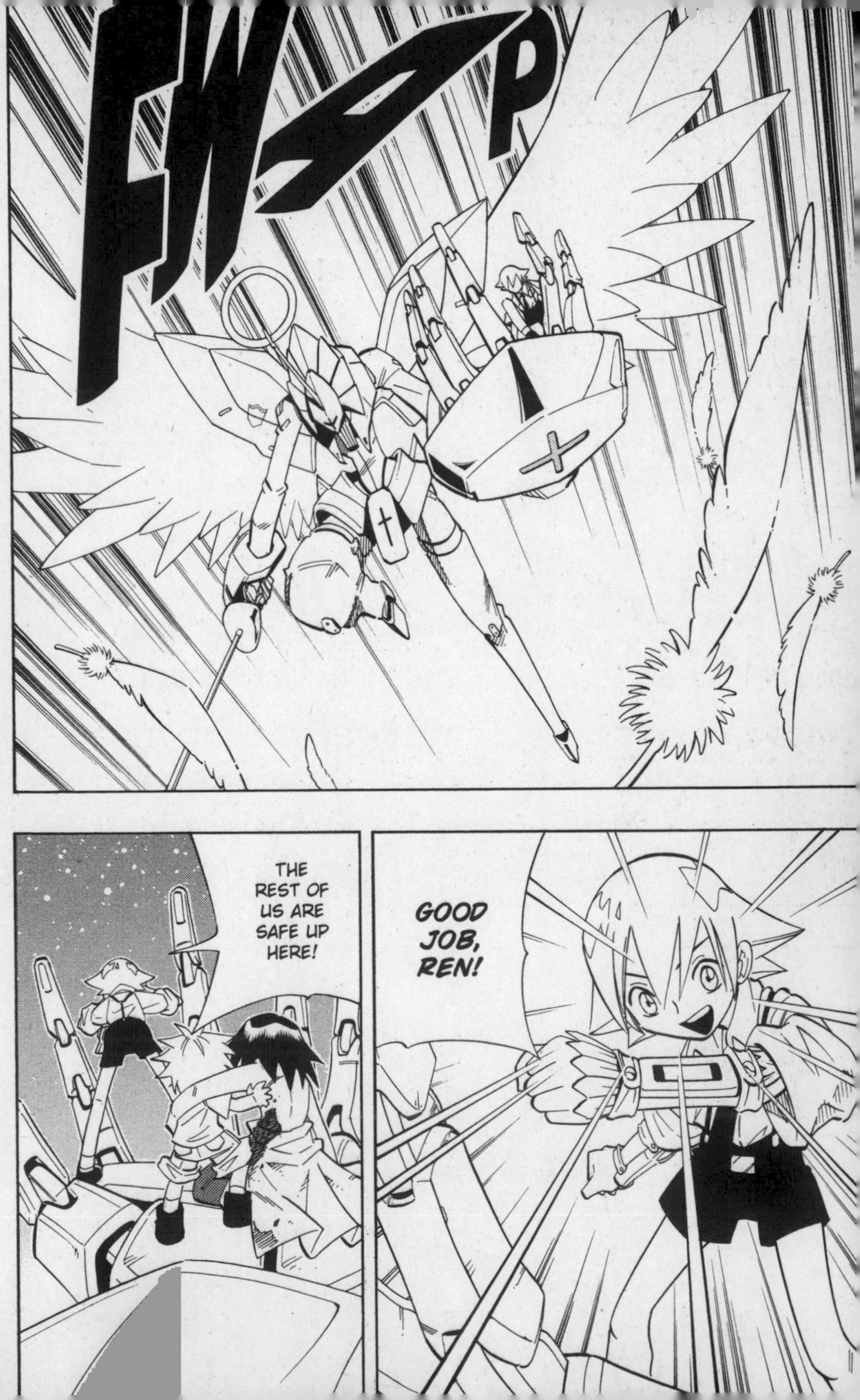
FWAP
GOOD JOB, REN!
THE REST OF US ARE SAFE UP HERE!

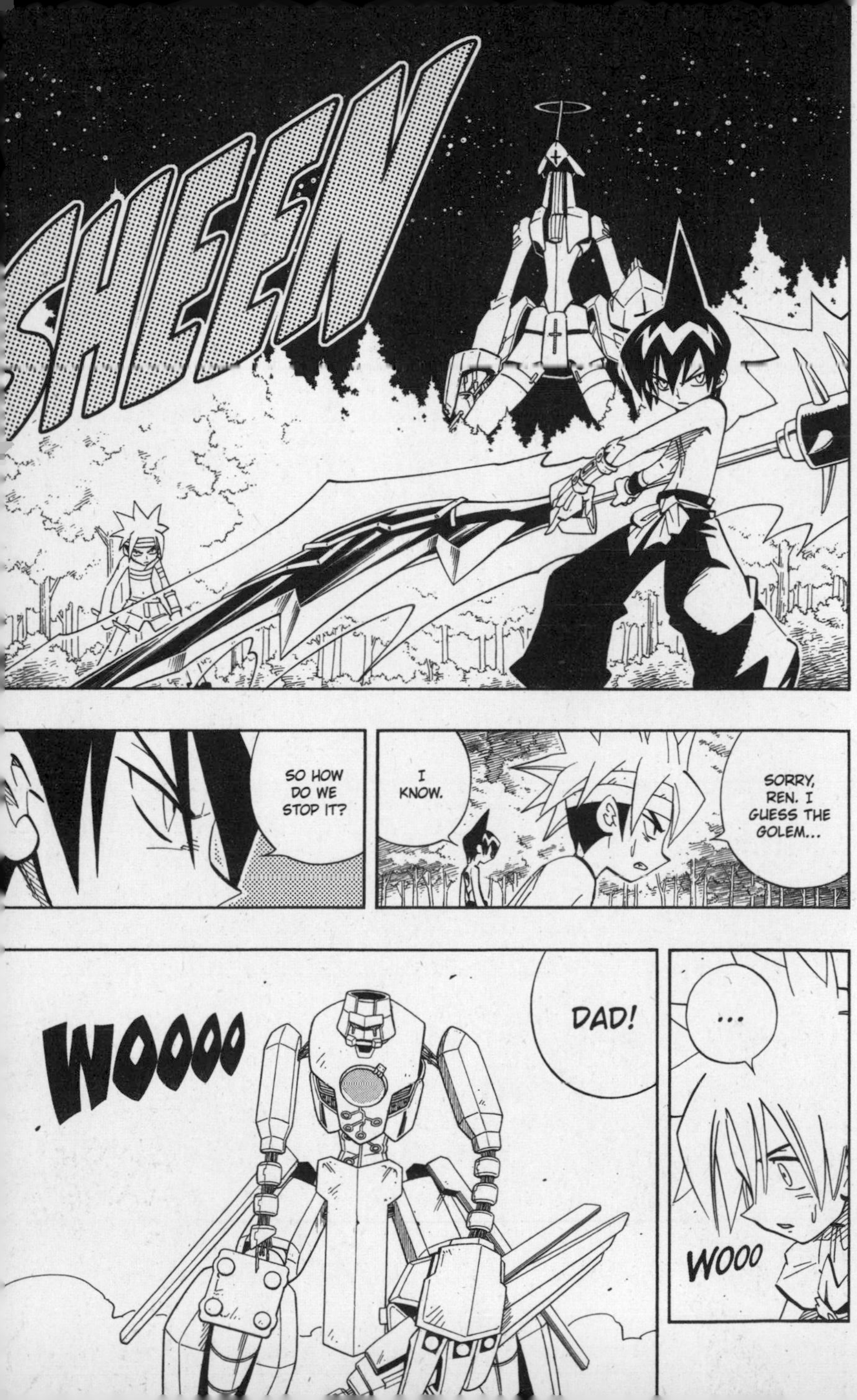
SHEEN
SORRY, REN. I GUESS THE GOLEM...
I KNOW.
SO HOW DO WE STOP IT?
...
WOOO
DAD!
WOOOO

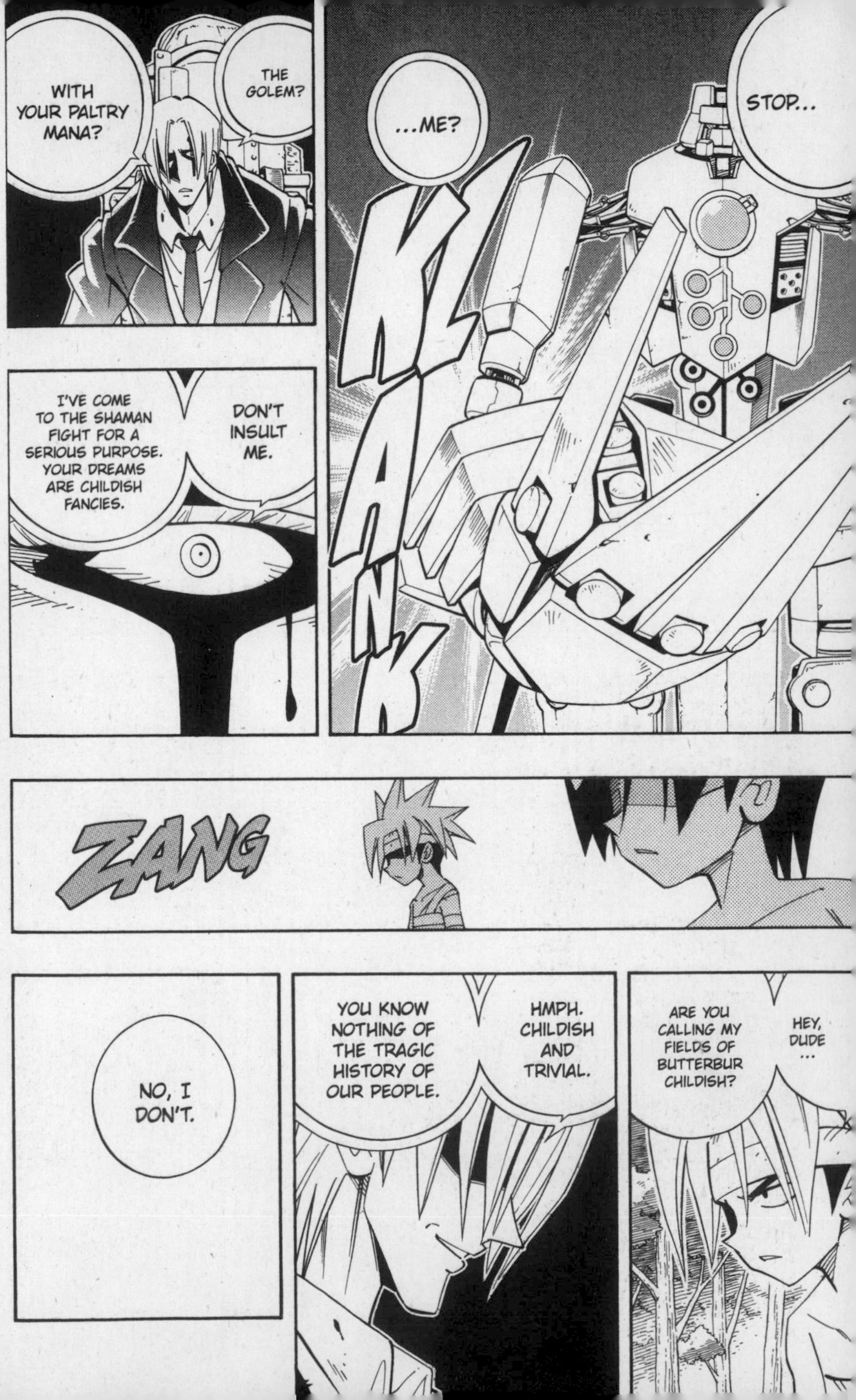
STOP...
...ME?
KLANK
THE GOLEM?
WITH YOUR PALTRY MANA?
DON'T INSULT ME.
I'VE COME TO THE SHAMAN FIGHT FOR A SERIOUS PURPOSE. YOUR DREAMS ARE CHILDISH FANCIES.
ZANG
HEY, DUDE ...
ARE YOU CALLING MY FIELDS OF BUTTERBUR CHILDISH?
HMPH. CHILDISH AND TRIVIAL.
YOU KNOW NOTHING OF THE TRAGIC HISTORY OF OUR PEOPLE.
NO, I DON'T.

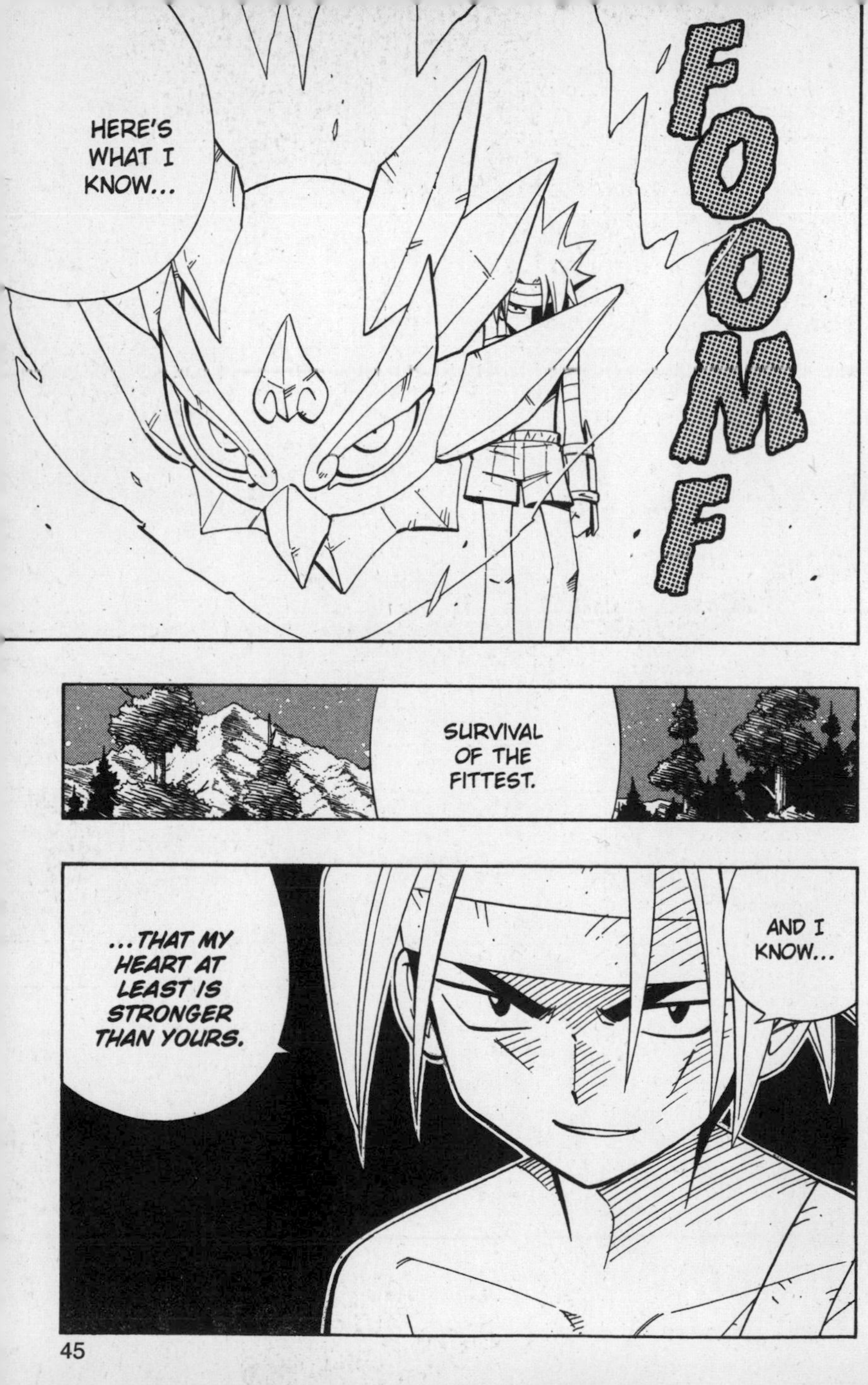
FOOMF
HERE'S WHAT I KNOW...
SURVIVAL OF THE FITTEST.
AND I KNOW...
...THAT MY HEART AT LEAST IS STRONGER THAN YOURS.

SHAMAN KING ITEM FILE No.58

2001
(JAN)

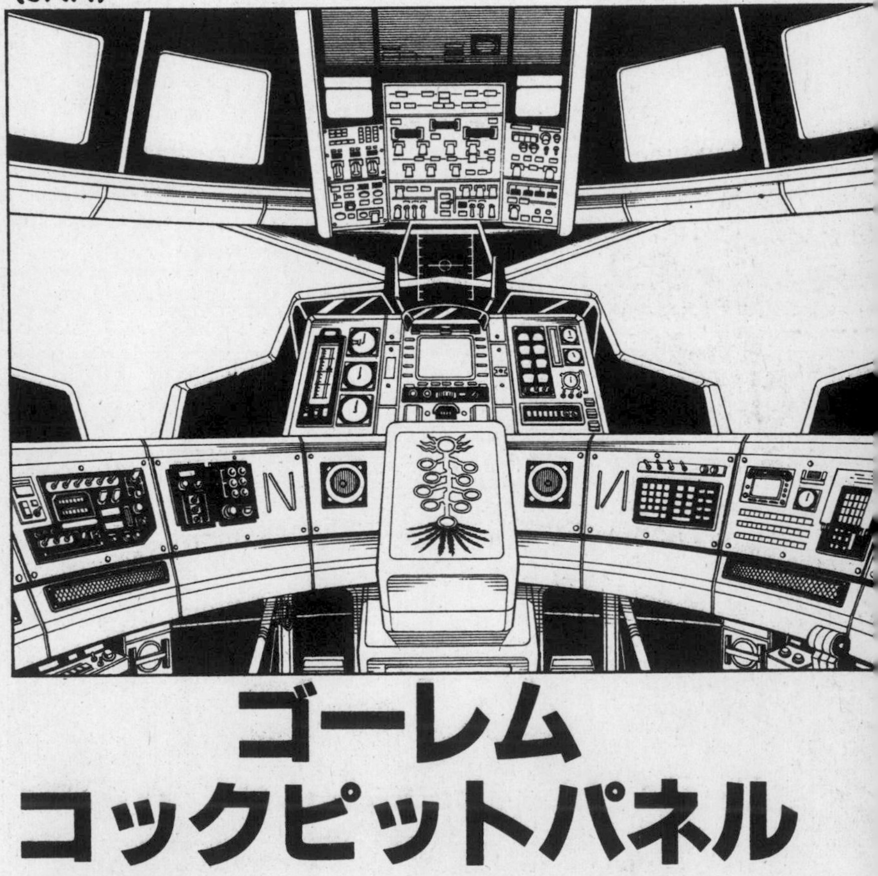

ゴーレム
コックピットパネル

GOLEM
COCKPIT
PANELS

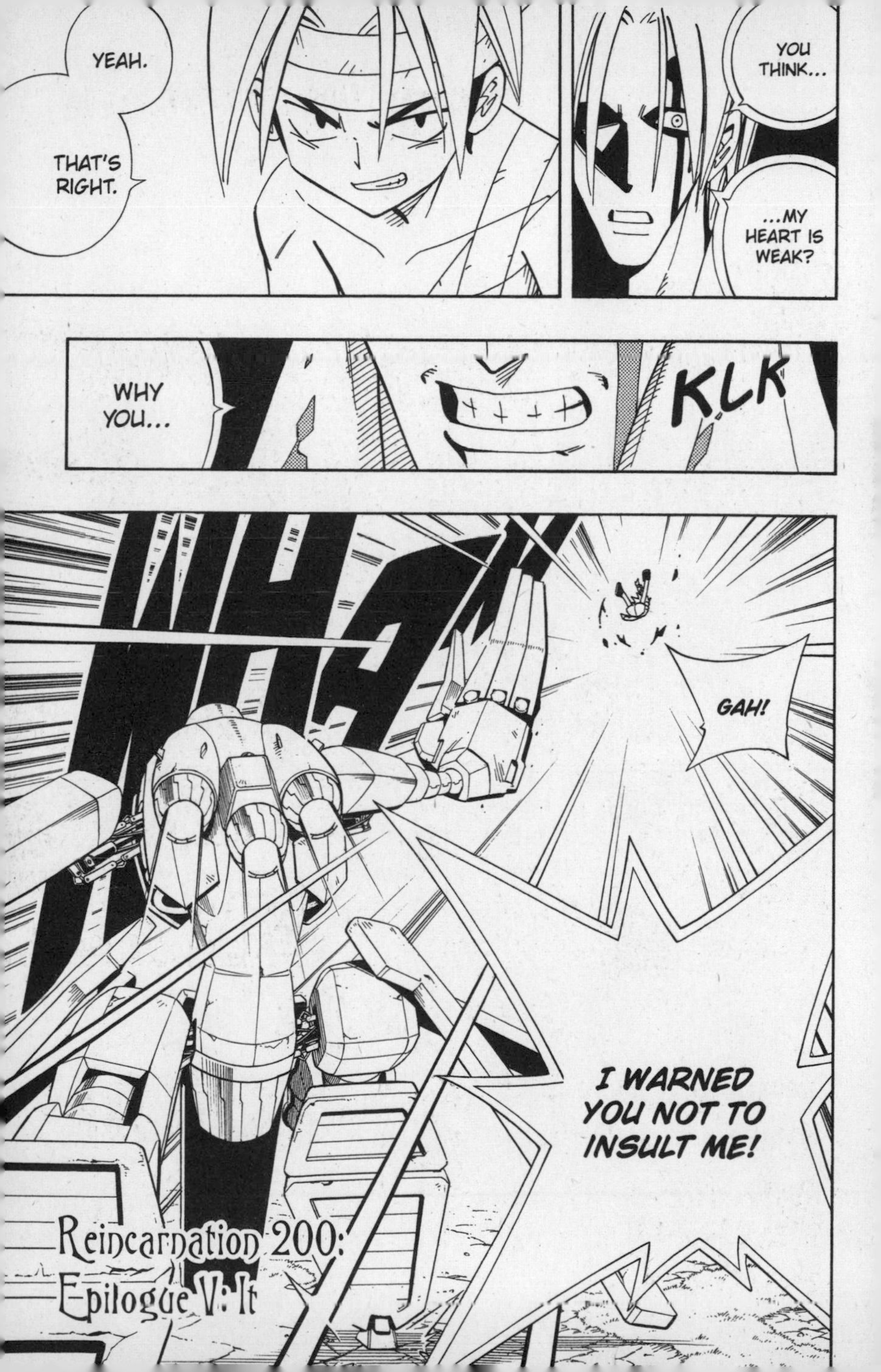
YOU THINK...
...MY HEART IS WEAK?
YEAH.
THAT'S RIGHT.
KLK
WHY YOU...
GAH!
I WARNED YOU NOT TO INSULT ME!
Reincarnation 200:
Epilogue V: It

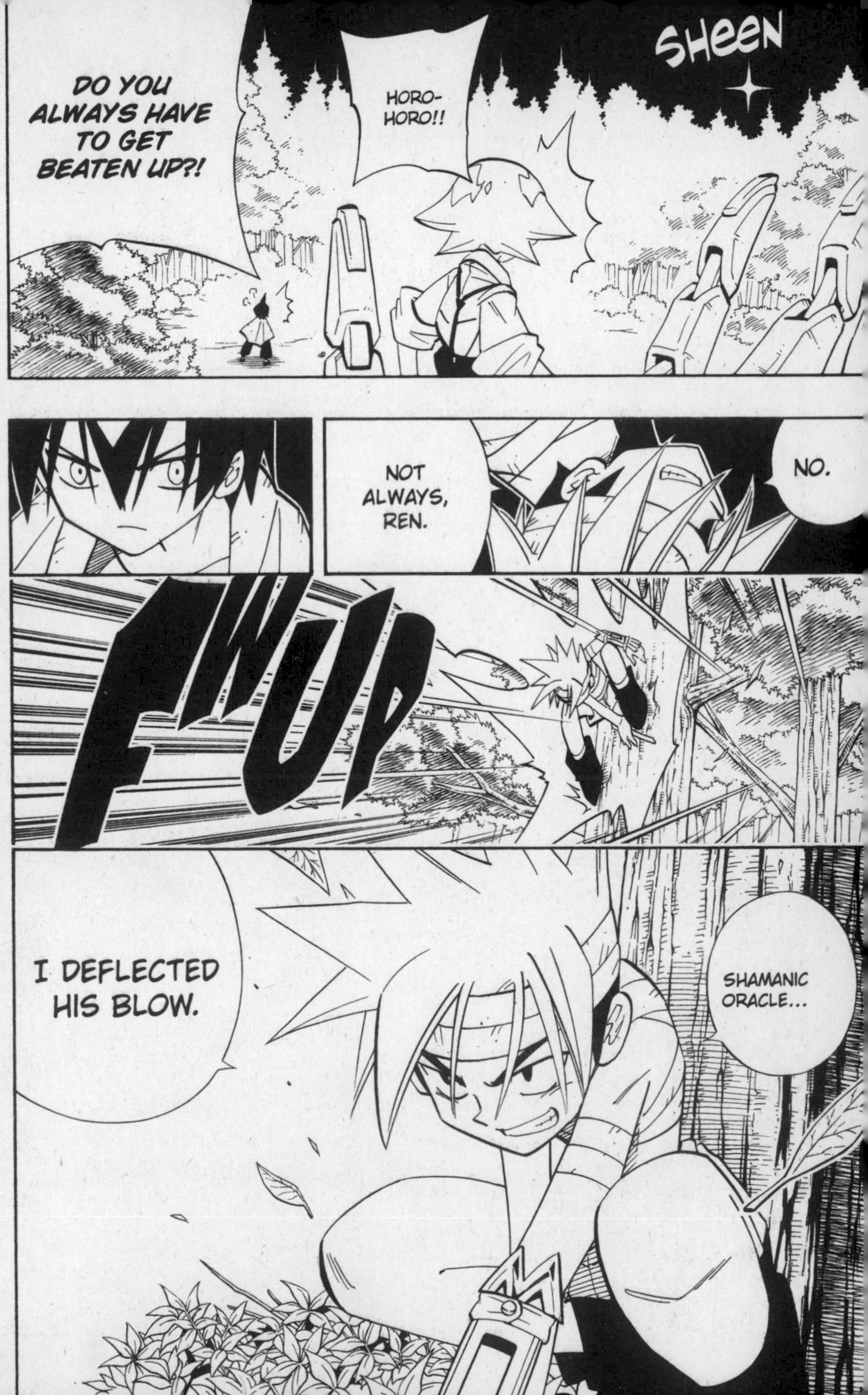
SHEEN
HORO-HORO!!
DO YOU ALWAYS HAVE TO GET BEATEN UP?!
NO.
NOT ALWAYS, REN.
FWUD
SHAMANIC ORACLE...
I DEFLECTED HIS BLOW.

Reincarnation 200: Epilogue V: It

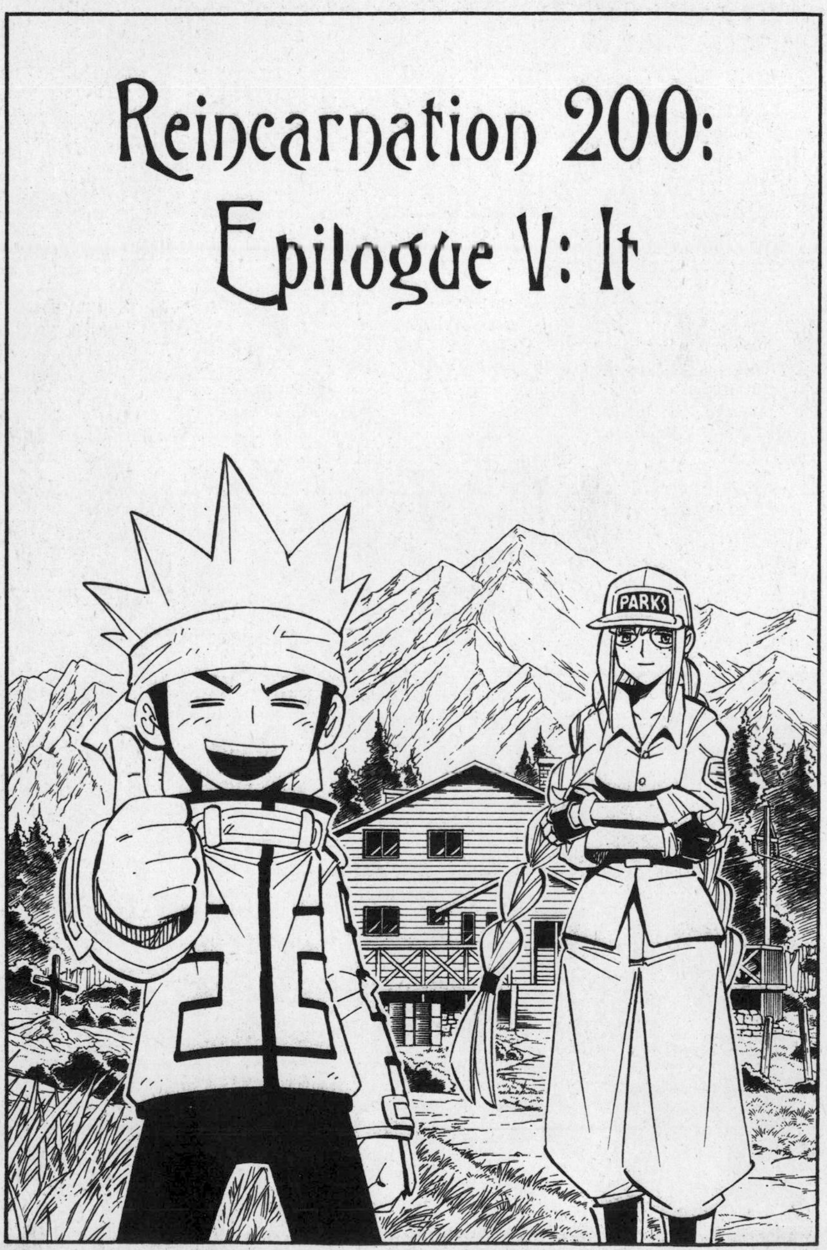
PARKS

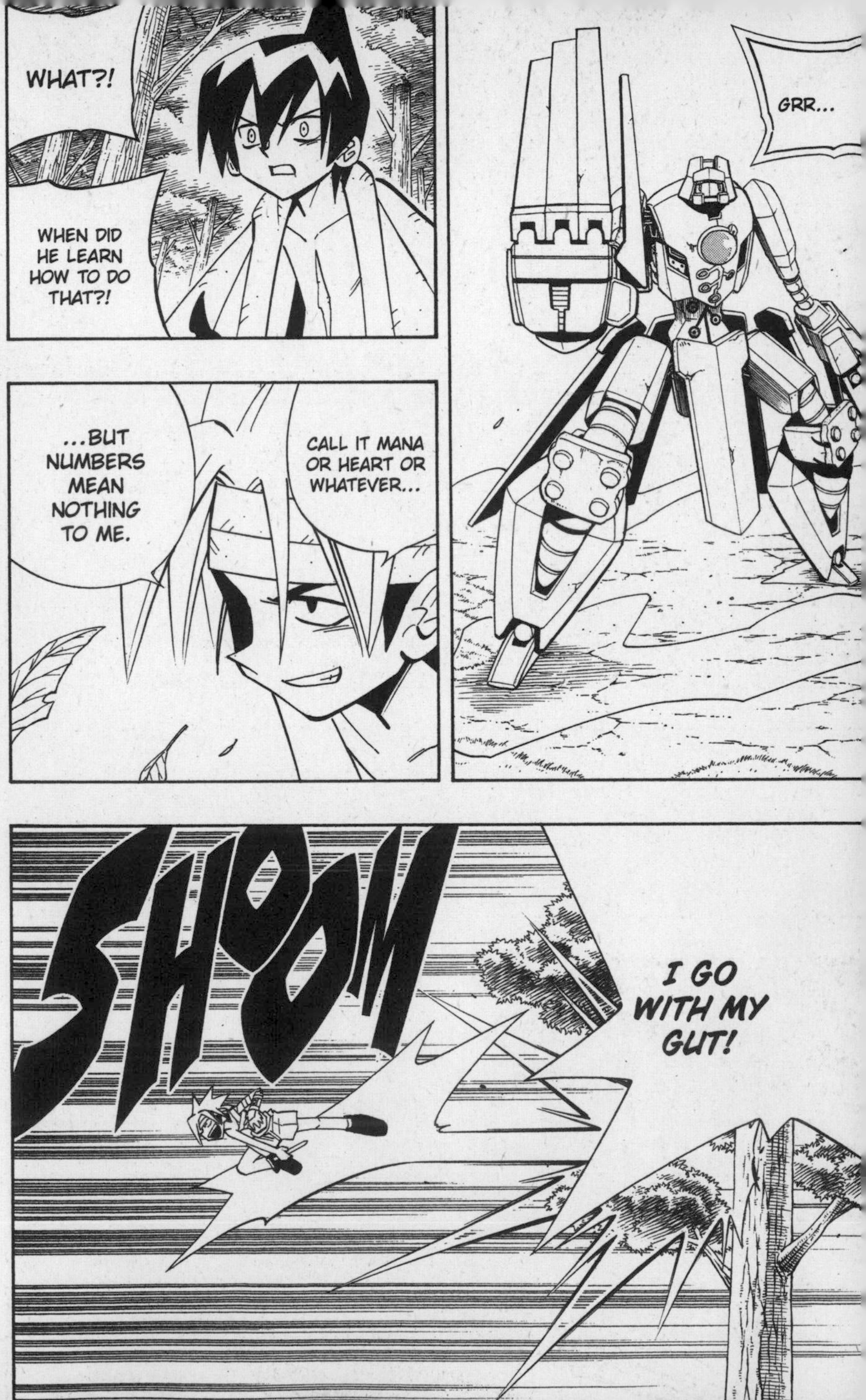
GRR...
WHAT?!
WHEN DID HE LEARN HOW TO DO THAT?!
CALL IT MANA OR HEART OR WHATEVER...
...BUT NUMBERS MEAN NOTHING TO ME.
I GO WITH MY GUT!
SHOOM

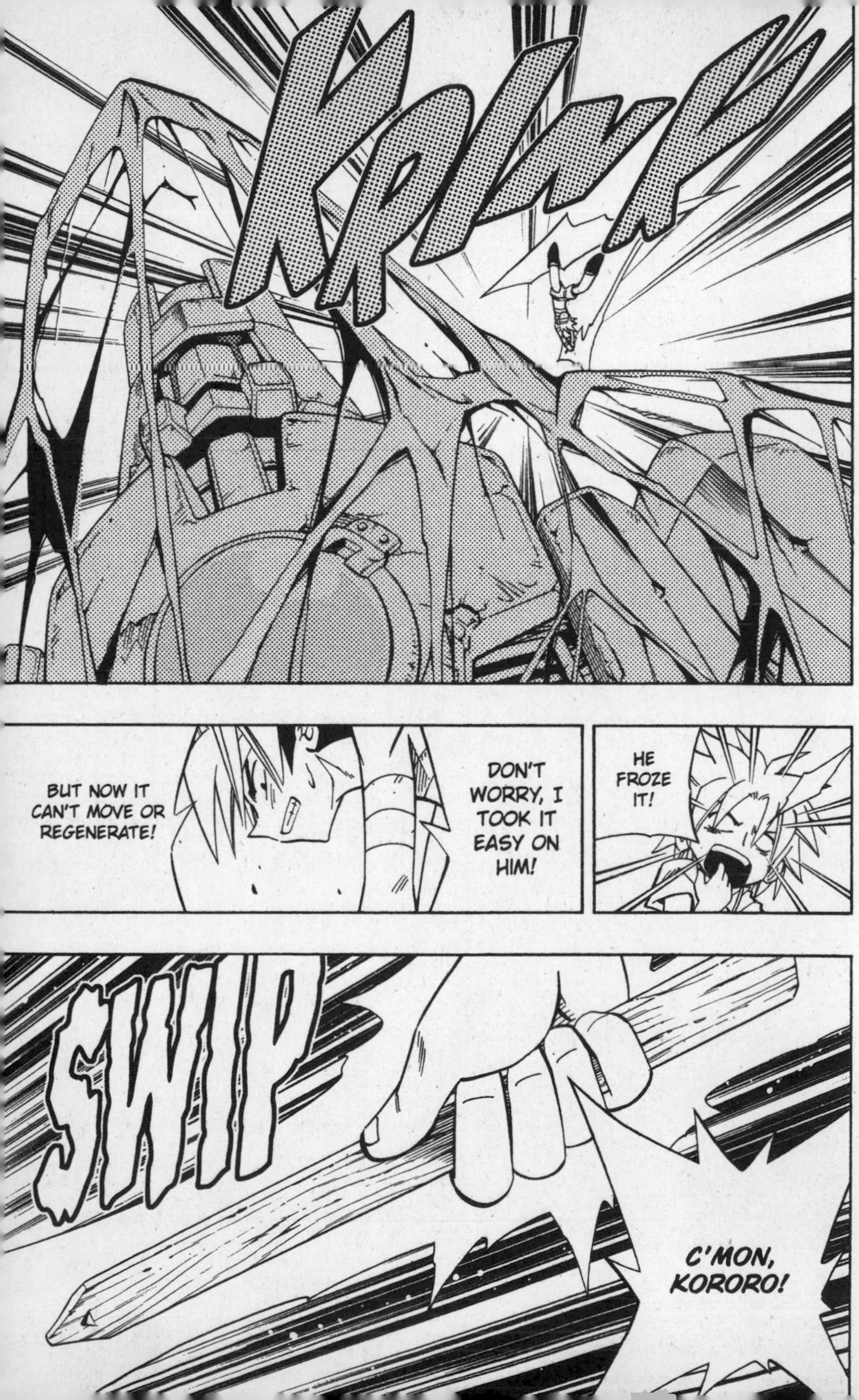
HE FROZE IT!
DON'T WORRY, I TOOK IT EASY ON HIM!
BUT NOW IT CAN'T MOVE OR REGENERATE!
SWIP
C'MON, KORORO!

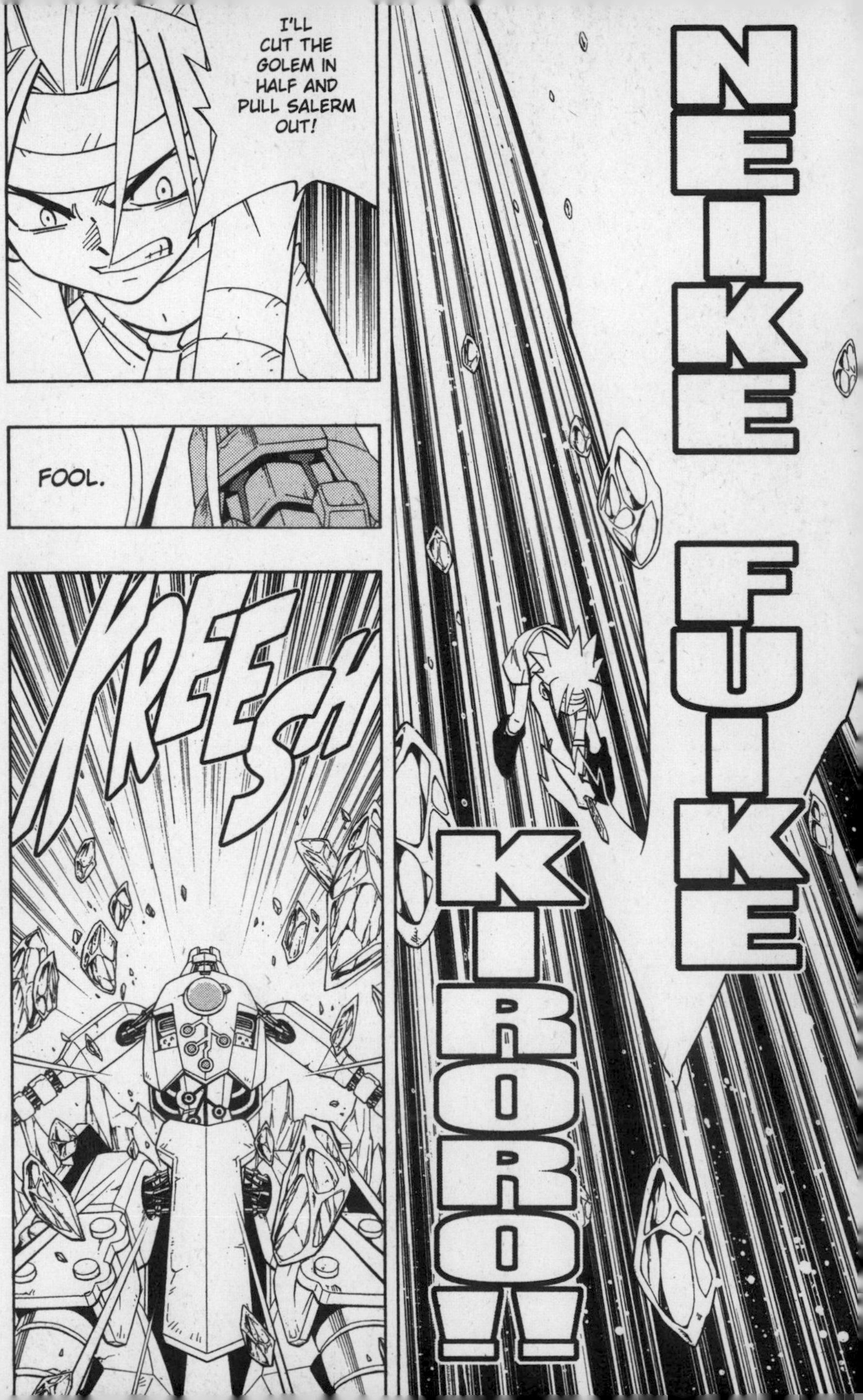
NEIKE FUKE
KIRORO!!
I'LL CUT THE GOLEM IN HALF AND PULL SALERM OUT!
FOOL.
KREESH

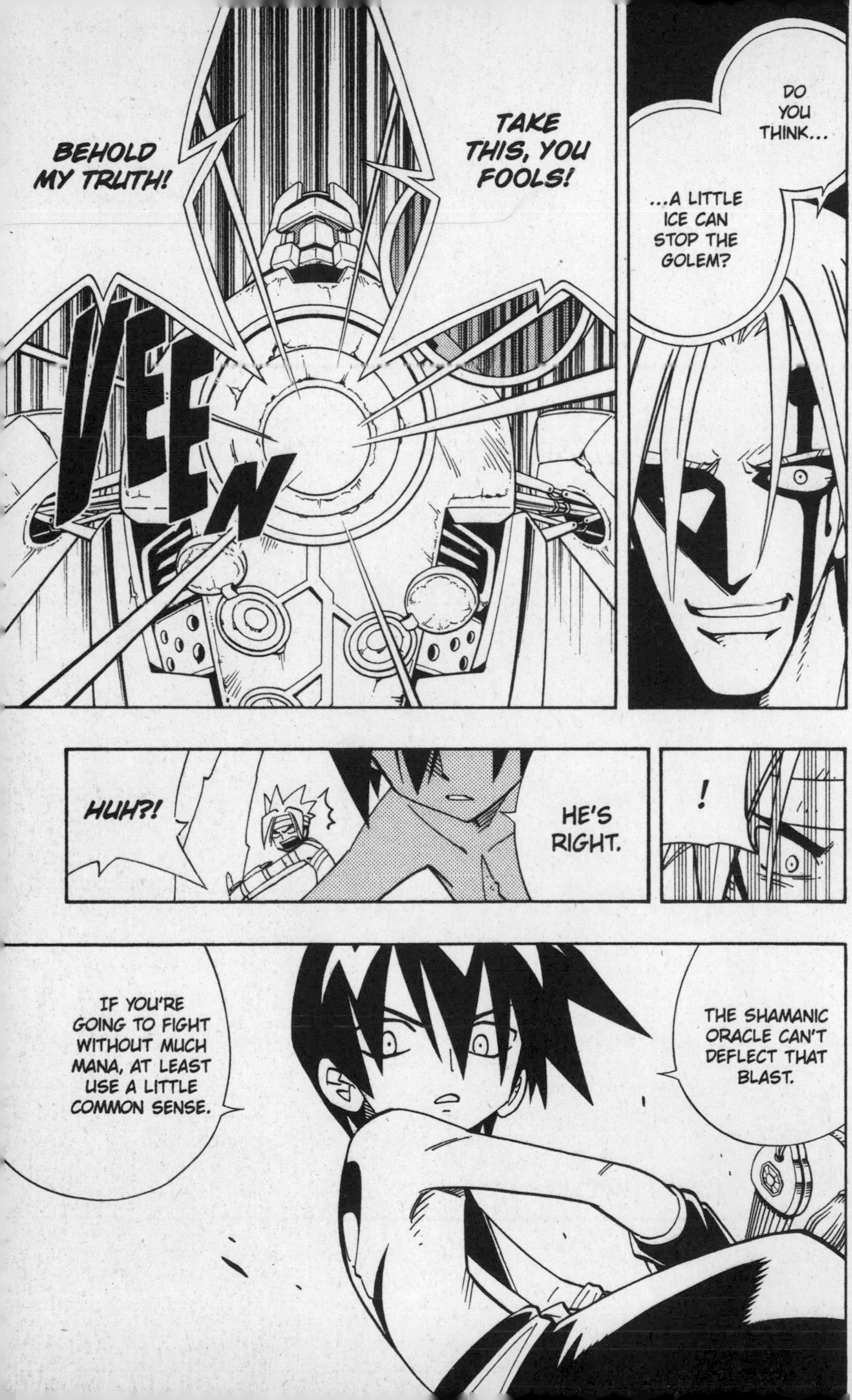
DO YOU THINK...
...A LITTLE ICE CAN STOP THE GOLEM?
TAKE THIS, YOU FOOLS!
BEHOLD MY TRUTH!
VEEN
!
HE'S RIGHT.
HUH?!
THE SHAMANIC ORACLE CAN'T DEFLECT THAT BLAST.
IF YOU'RE GOING TO FIGHT WITHOUT MUCH MANA, AT LEAST USE A LITTLE COMMON SENSE.

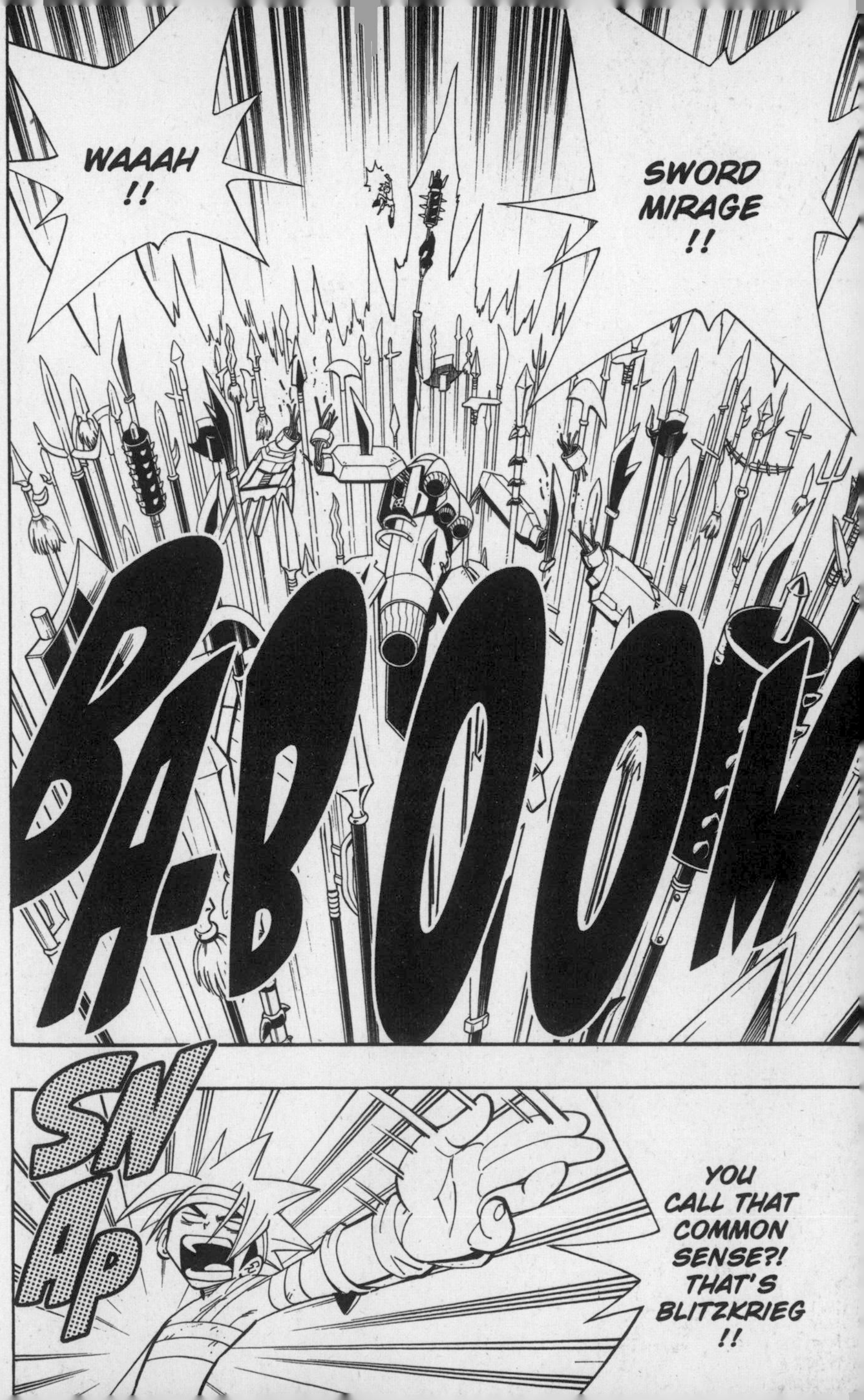
SWORD MIRAGE !!
WAAAH !!
BA-BOOM
YOU CALL THAT COMMON SENSE?! THAT'S BLITZKRIEG !!
SNAP

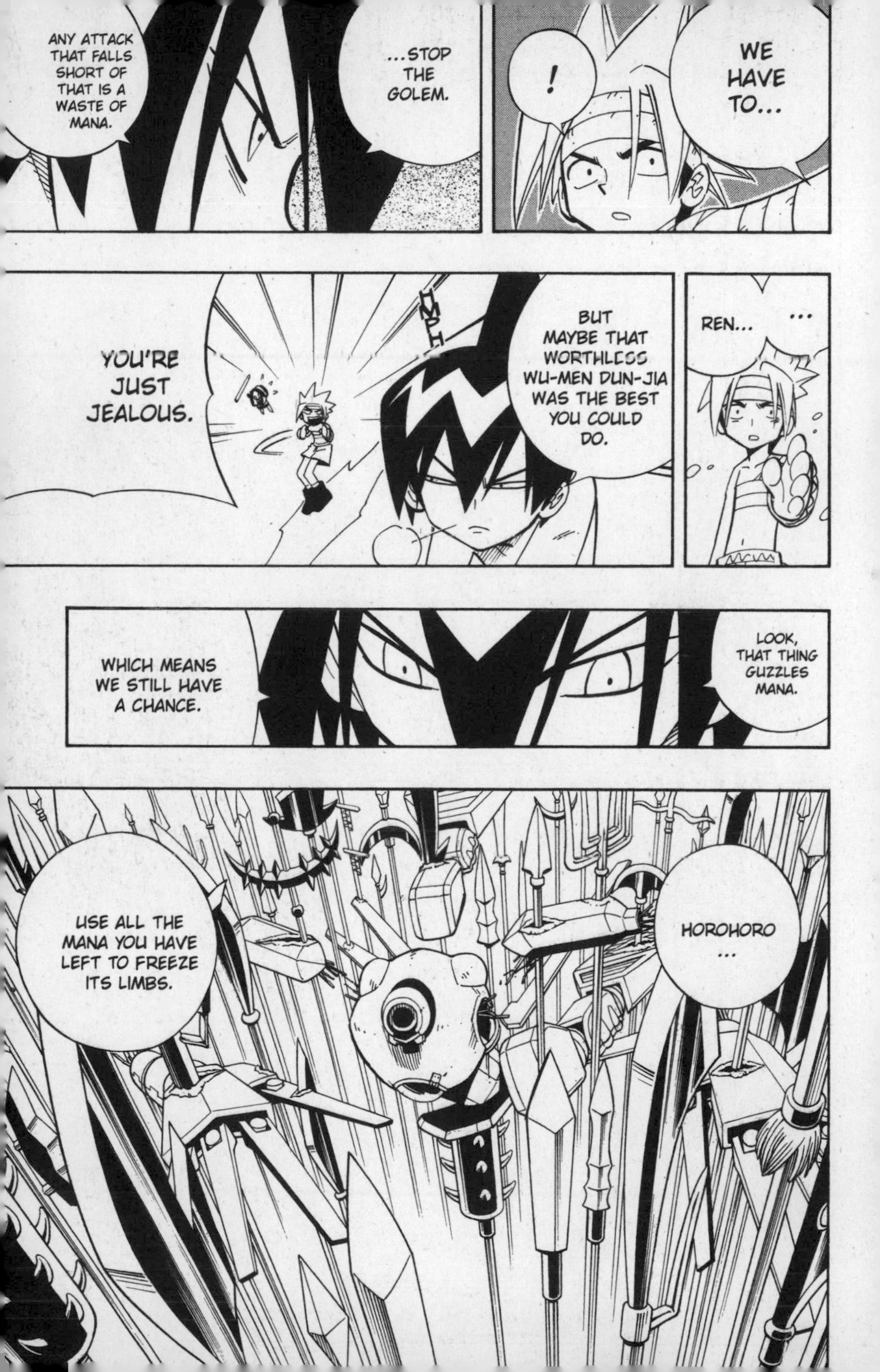
WE HAVE TO...
!
...STOP THE GOLEM.
ANY ATTACK THAT FALLS SHORT OF THAT IS A WASTE OF MANA.
...
REN...
BUT MAYBE THAT WORTHLESS WU-MEN DUN-JIA WAS THE BEST YOU COULD DO.
HMPH
YOU'RE JUST JEALOUS.
LOOK, THAT THING GUZZLES MANA.
WHICH MEANS WE STILL HAVE A CHANCE.
HOROHORO ...
USE ALL THE MANA YOU HAVE LEFT TO FREEZE ITS LIMBS.

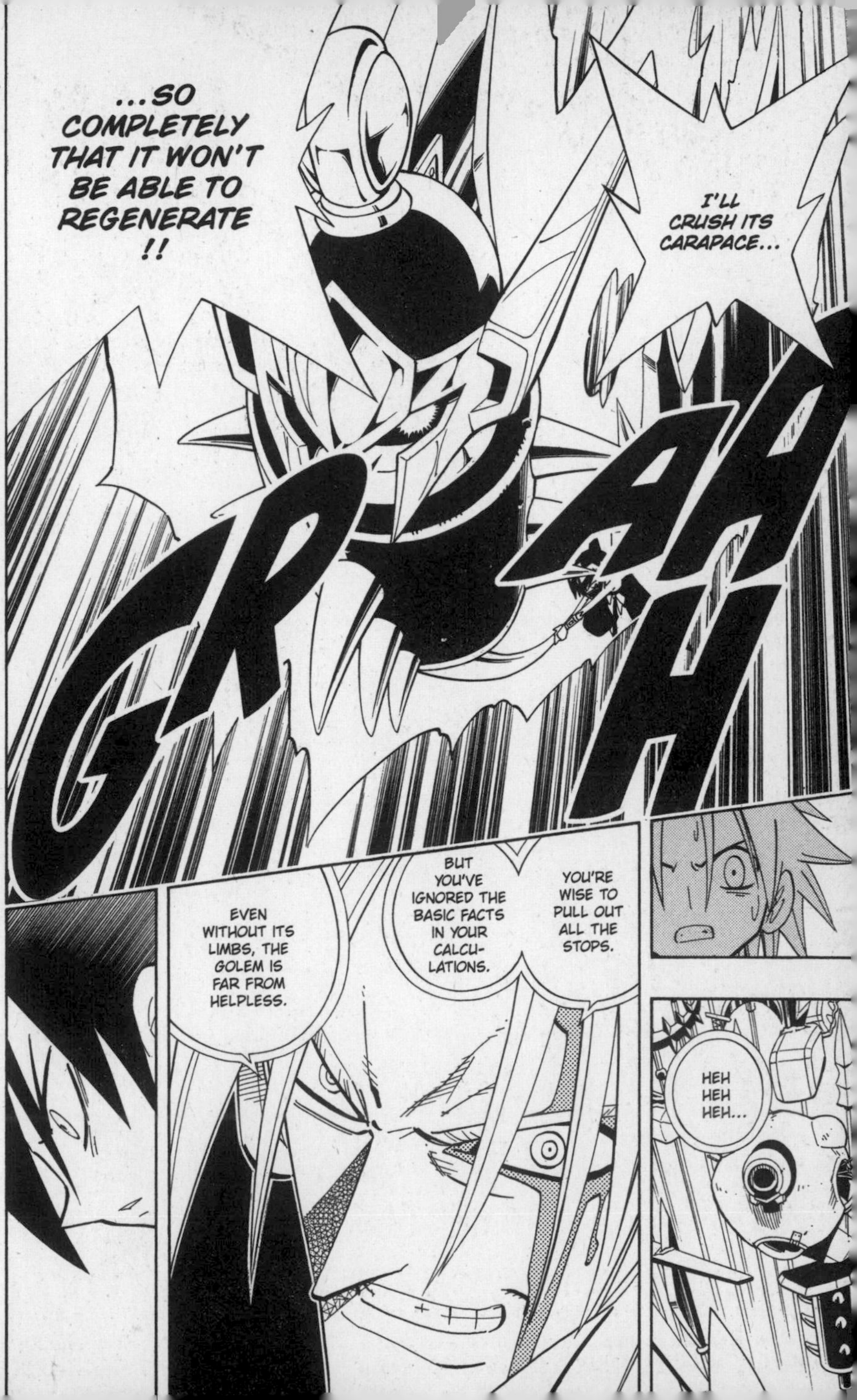
I'LL CRUSH ITS CARAPACE...
...SO COMPLETELY THAT IT WON'T BE ABLE TO REGENERATE !!
HEH HEH HEH...
YOU'RE WISE TO PULL OUT ALL THE STOPS.
BUT YOU'VE IGNORED THE BASIC FACTS IN YOUR CALCULATIONS.
EVEN WITHOUT ITS LIMBS, THE GOLEM IS FAR FROM HELPLESS.

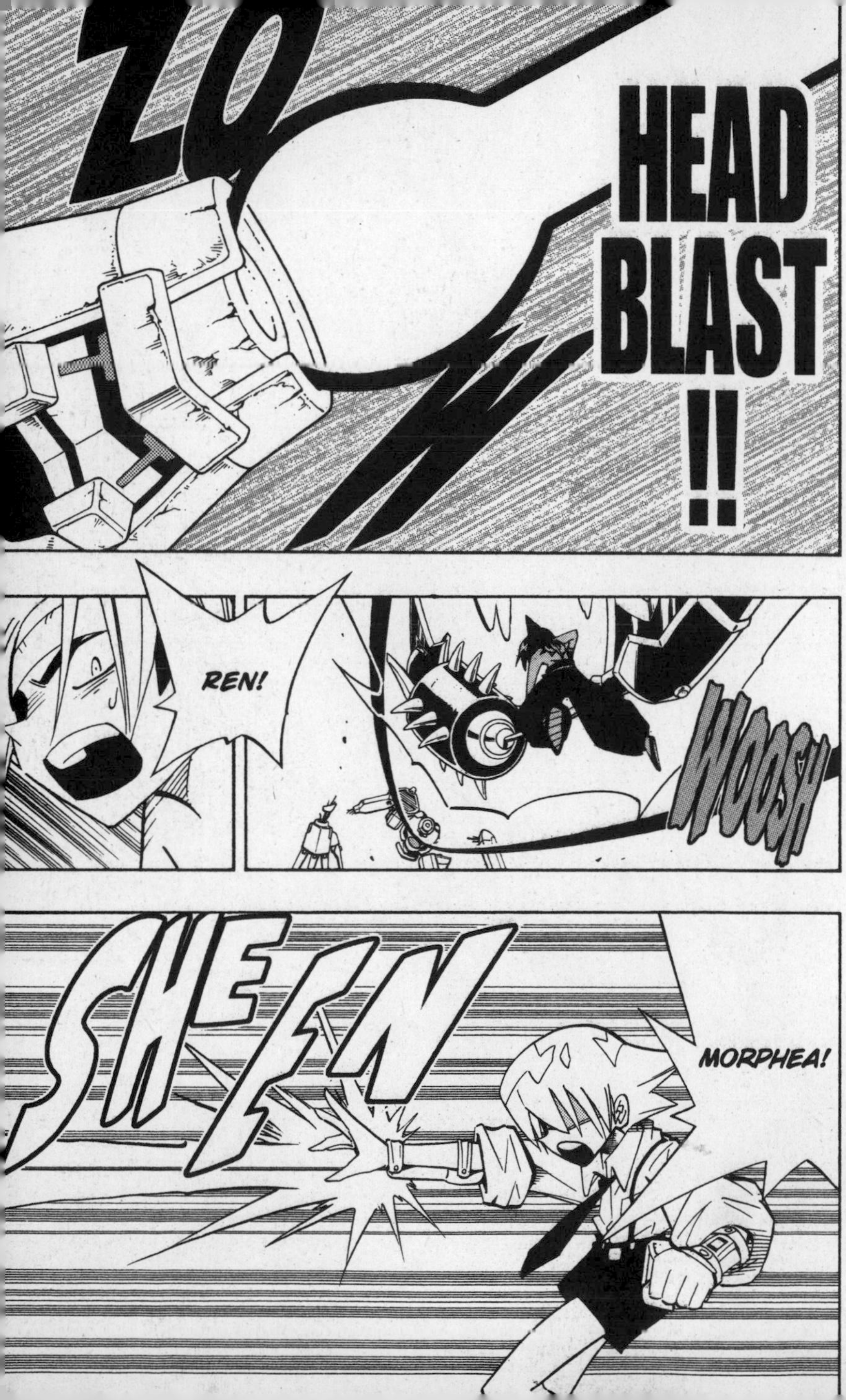
HEAD BLAST!!
WOOSH
REN!
SHEEN
MORPHEA!

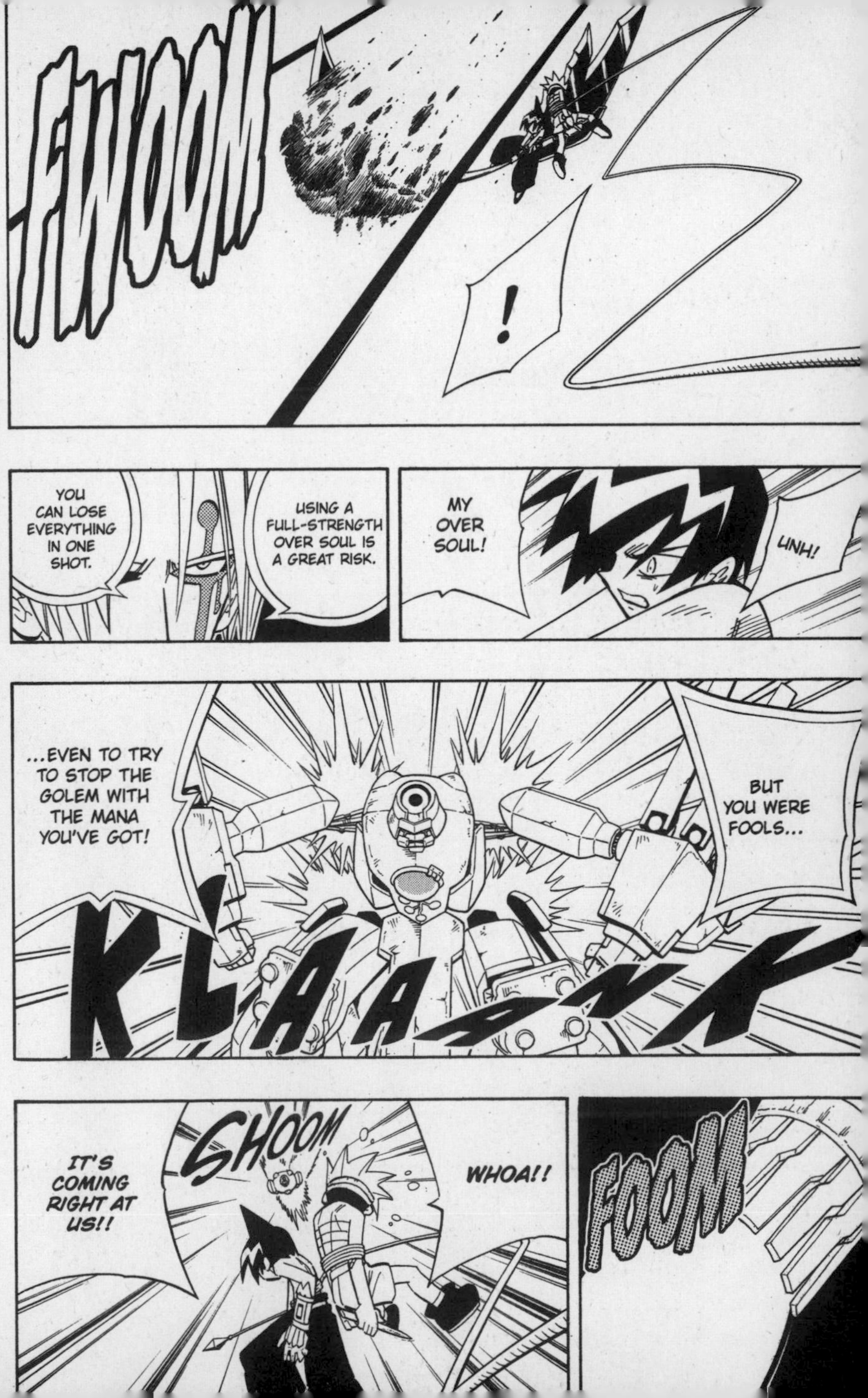
!
FWOOM
UNH!
MY OVER SOUL!
USING A FULL-STRENGTH OVER SOUL IS A GREAT RISK.
YOU CAN LOSE EVERYTHING IN ONE SHOT.
BUT YOU WERE FOOLS...
...EVEN TO TRY TO STOP THE GOLEM WITH THE MANA YOU'VE GOT!
KLAAANK
FOOM
WHOA!!
SHOOM
IT'S COMING RIGHT AT US!!

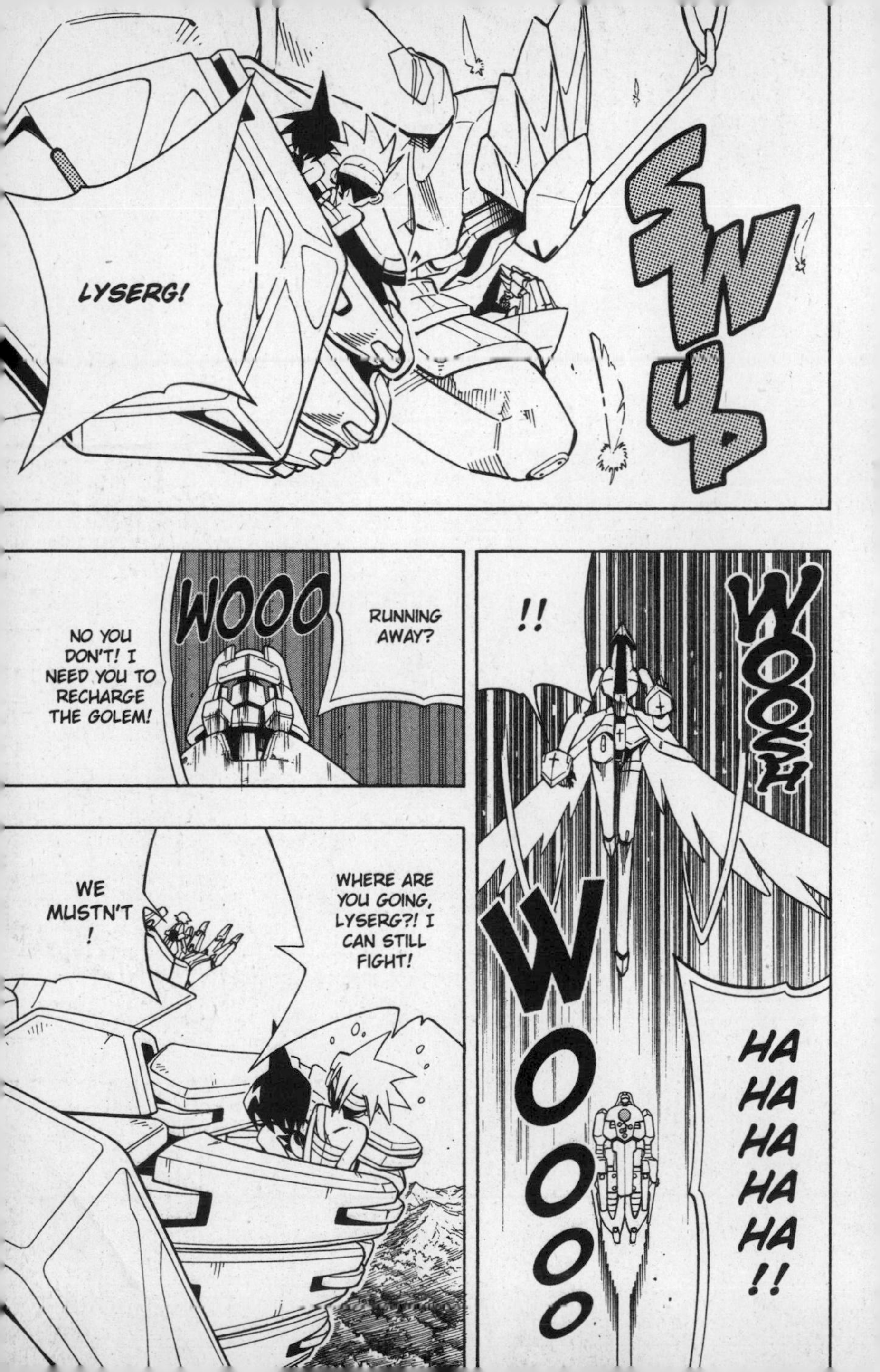
SWUP
LYSERG!
WOOOSH
!!
WOOOOO
HA HA HA HA HA HA!!
RUNNING AWAY?
WOOO
NO YOU DON'T! I NEED YOU TO RECHARGE THE GOLEM!
WHERE ARE YOU GOING, LYSERG?! I CAN STILL FIGHT!
WE MUSTN'T!

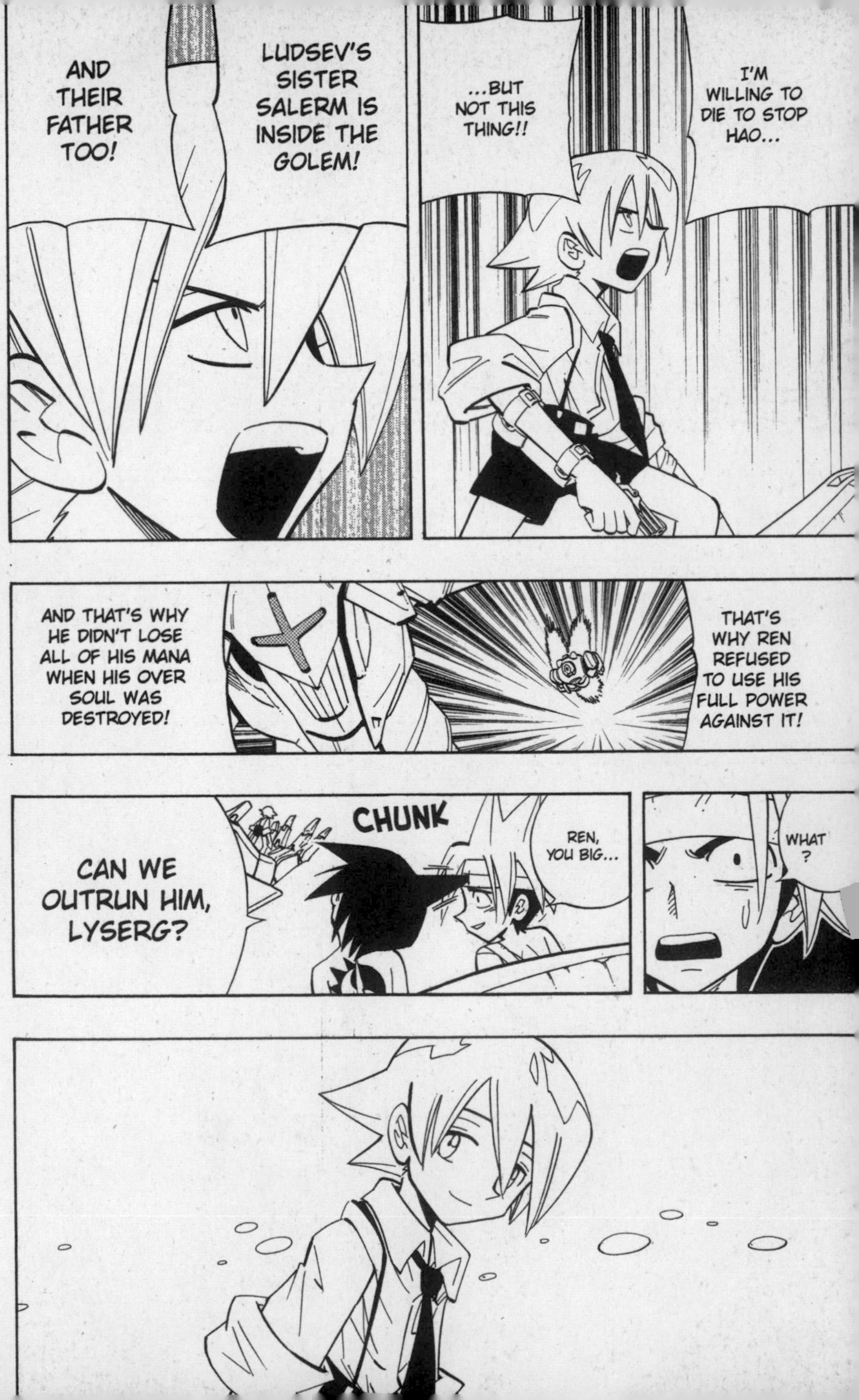

I'M WILLING TO DIE TO STOP HAO...
...BUT NOT THIS THING!!
LUDSEV'S SISTER SALERM IS INSIDE THE GOLEM!
AND THEIR FATHER TOO!
THAT'S WHY REN REFUSED TO USE HIS FULL POWER AGAINST IT!
AND THAT'S WHY HE DIDN'T LOSE ALL OF HIS MANA WHEN HIS OVER SOUL WAS DESTROYED!
WHAT ?
REN, YOU BIG...
CHUNK
CAN WE OUTRUN HIM, LYSERG?

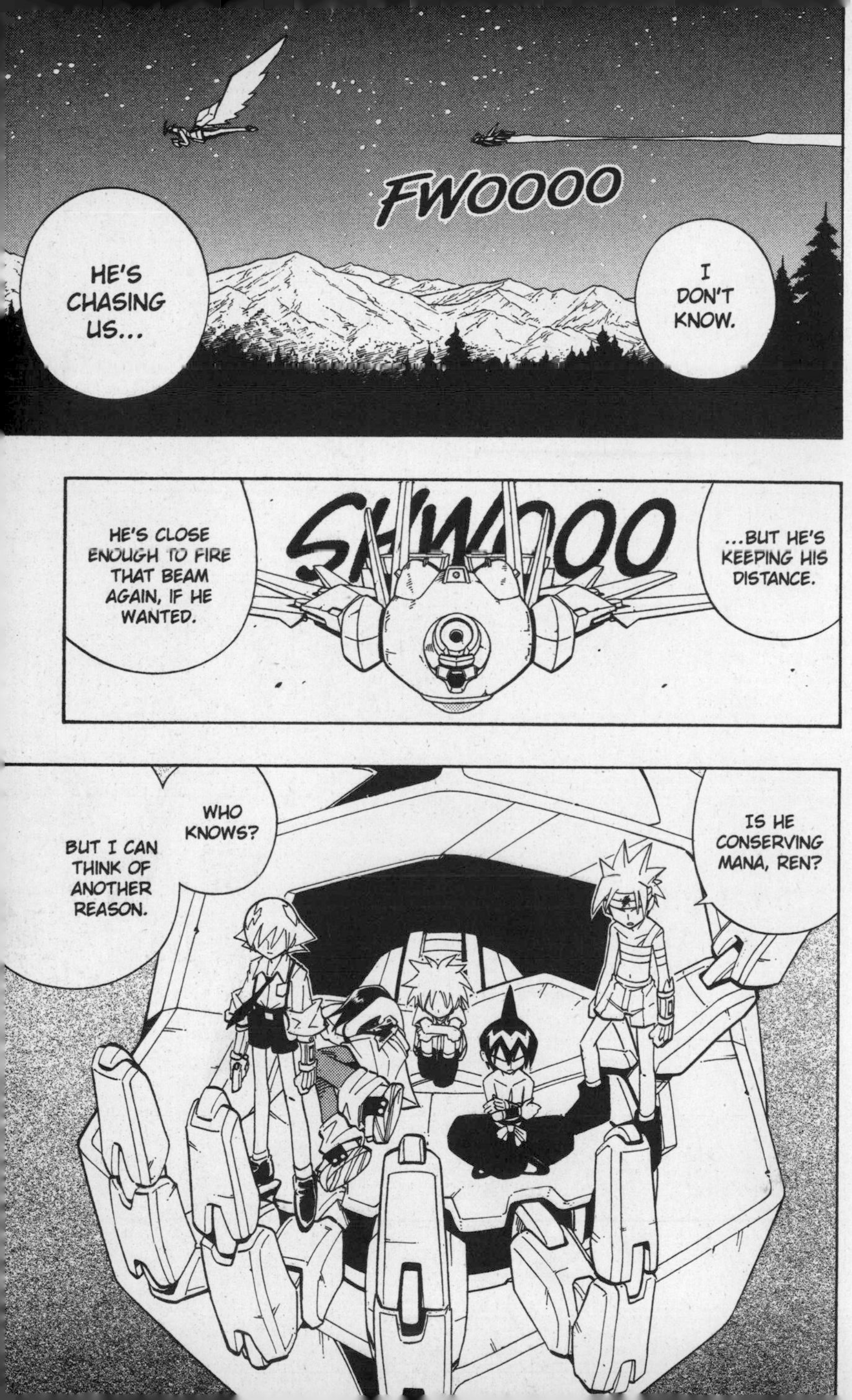
FWOOOO
I DON'T KNOW.
HE'S CHASING US...
SHWOOO
HE'S CLOSE ENOUGH TO FIRE THAT BEAM AGAIN, IF HE WANTED.
...BUT HE'S KEEPING HIS DISTANCE.
IS HE CONSERVING MANA, REN?
WHO KNOWS?
BUT I CAN THINK OF ANOTHER REASON.

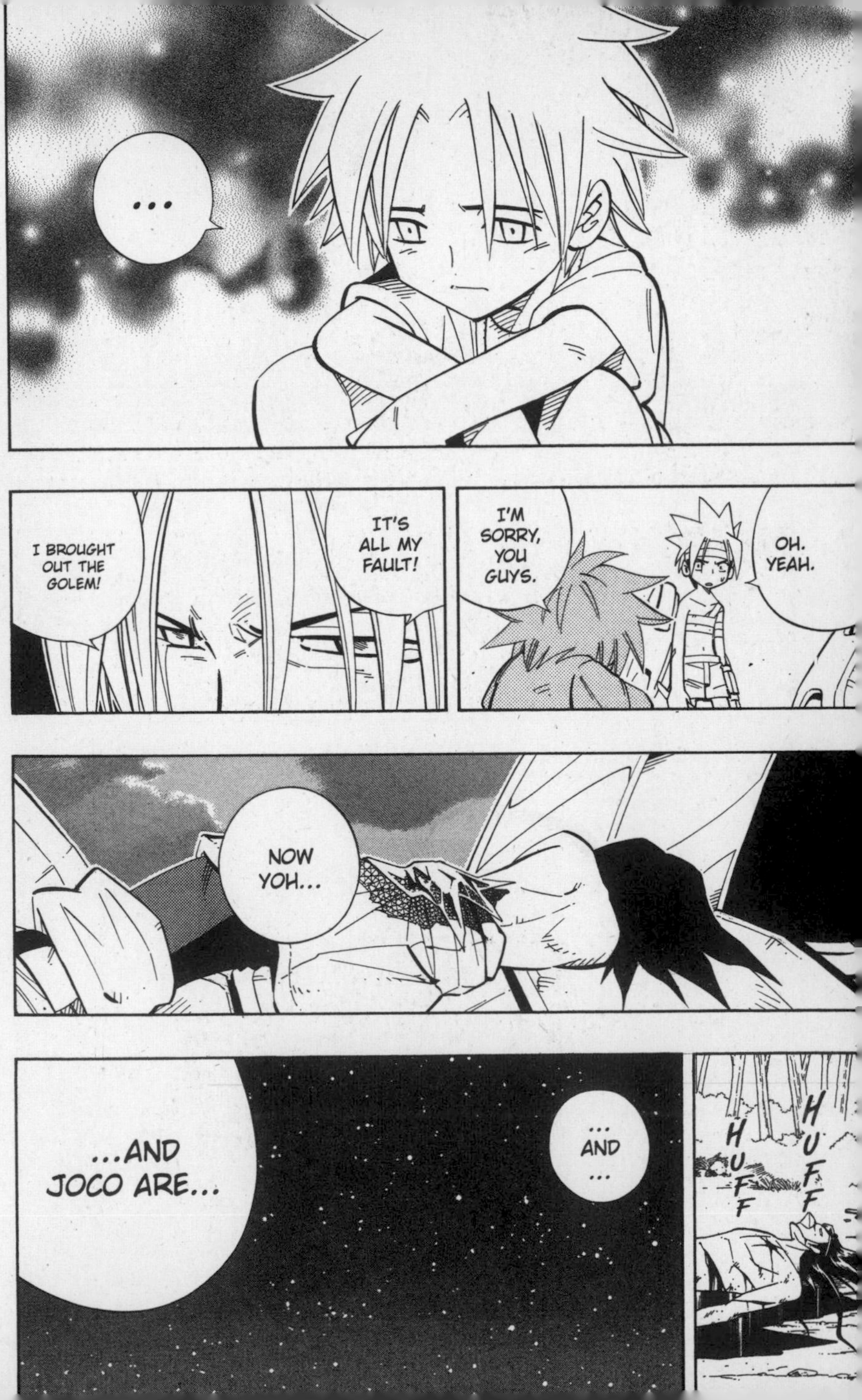
...
OH. YEAH.
I'M SORRY, YOU GUYS.
IT'S ALL MY FAULT!
I BROUGHT OUT THE GOLEM!
NOW YOH...
HUFF
HUFF
... AND ...
...AND JOCO ARE...

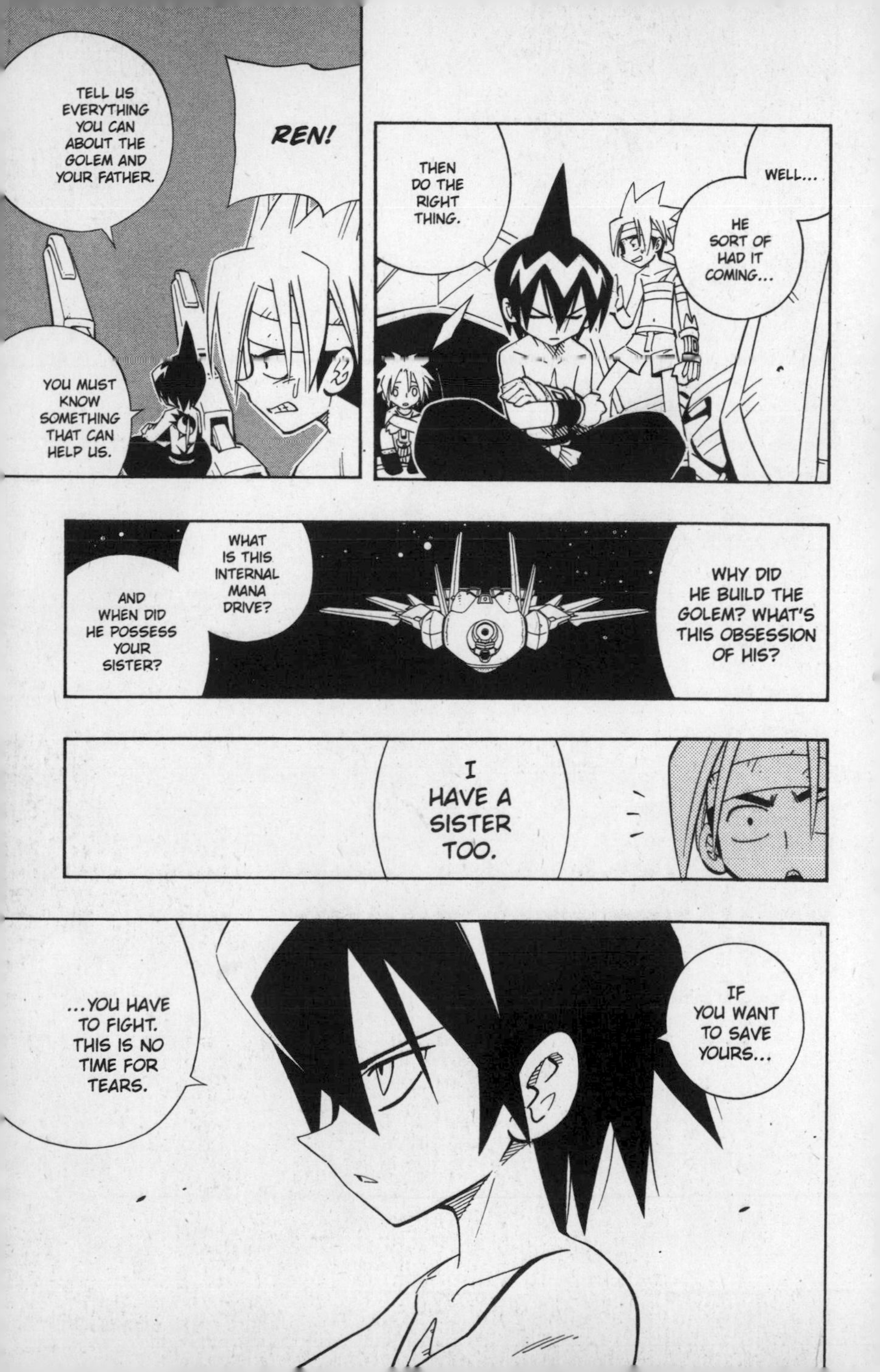
WELL...
HE SORT OF HAD IT COMING...
THEN DO THE RIGHT THING.
REN!
TELL US EVERYTHING YOU CAN ABOUT THE GOLEM AND YOUR FATHER.
YOU MUST KNOW SOMETHING THAT CAN HELP US.
WHY DID HE BUILD THE GOLEM? WHAT'S THIS OBSESSION OF HIS?
WHAT IS THIS INTERNAL MANA DRIVE?
AND WHEN DID HE POSSESS YOUR SISTER?
I HAVE A SISTER TOO.
IF YOU WANT TO SAVE YOURS...
...YOU HAVE TO FIGHT. THIS IS NO TIME FOR TEARS.

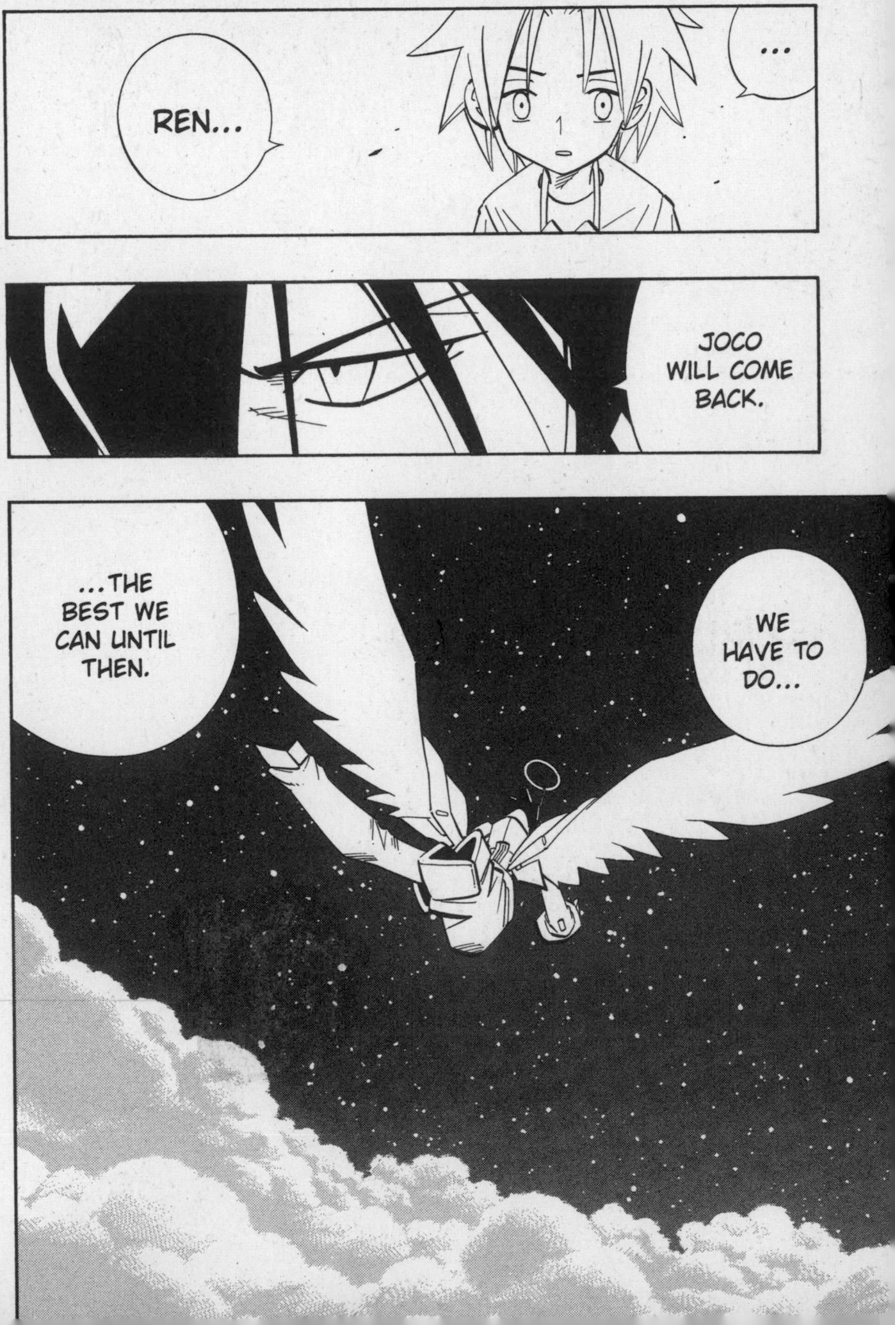
...
REN...
JOCO WILL COME BACK.
WE HAVE TO DO...
...THE BEST WE CAN UNTIL THEN.

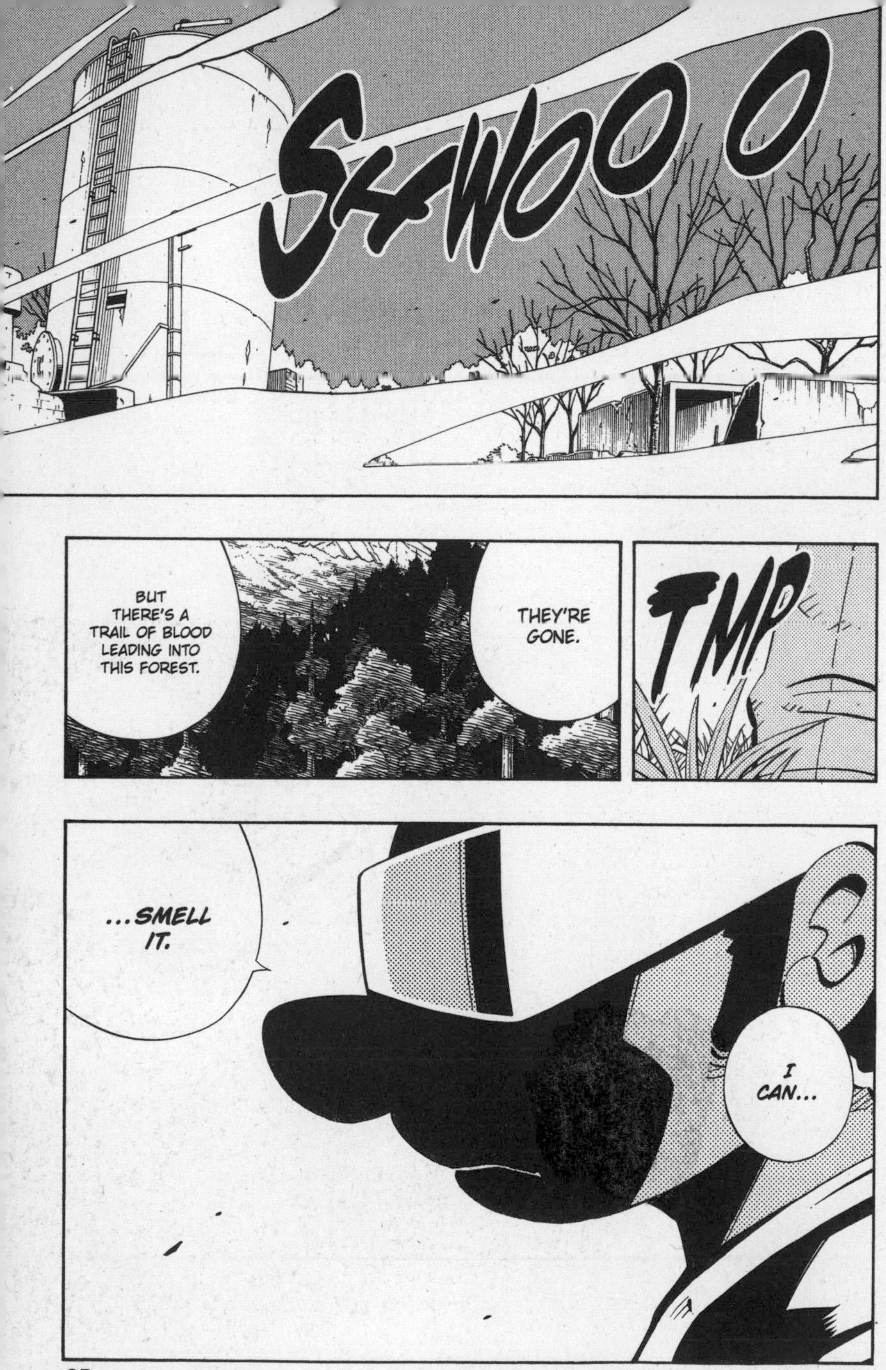
SWOOO
TMP
THEY'RE GONE.
BUT THERE'S A TRAIL OF BLOOD LEADING INTO THIS FOREST.
I CAN...
...SMELL IT.

SHAMAN KING CHARACTER FILE No.123

2001
(JAN)

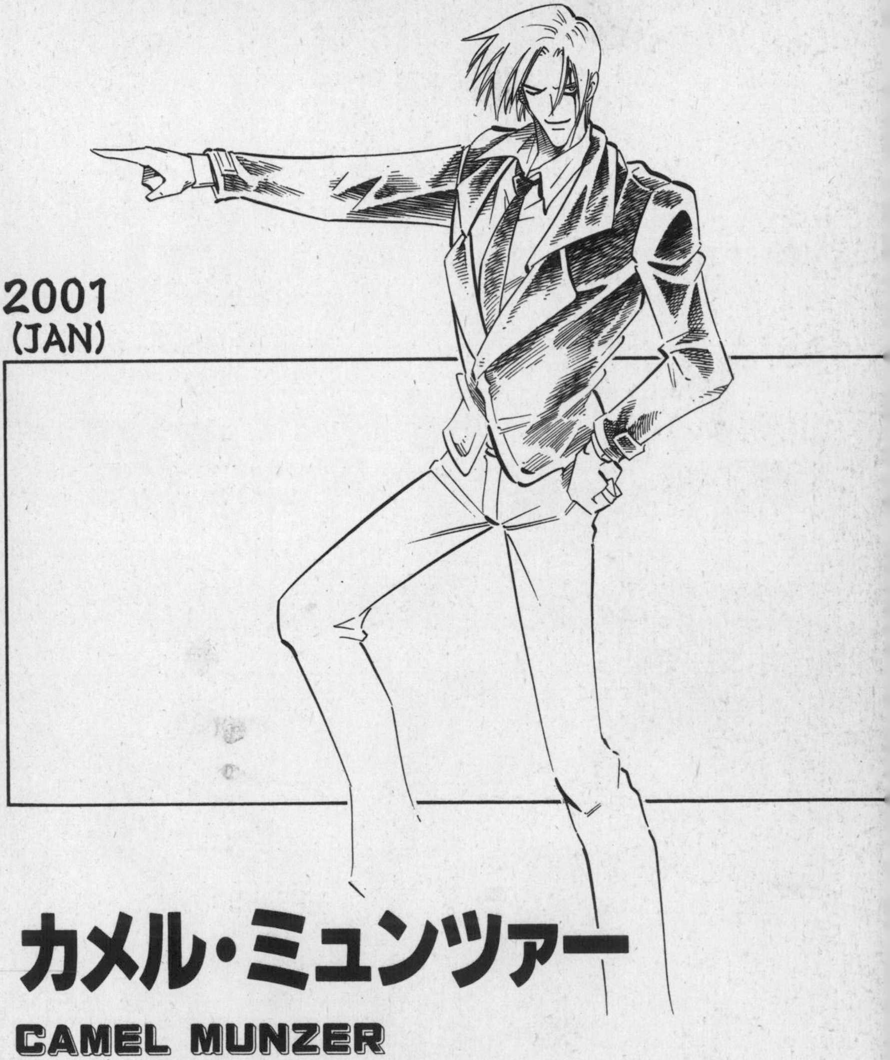

カメル・ミュンツァー

CAMEL MUNZER

BIRTHDAY: MAY 29, 1962

ASTROLOGICAL SIGN: GEMINI

BLOOD TYPE: O

36 YEARS OLD AT DEATH

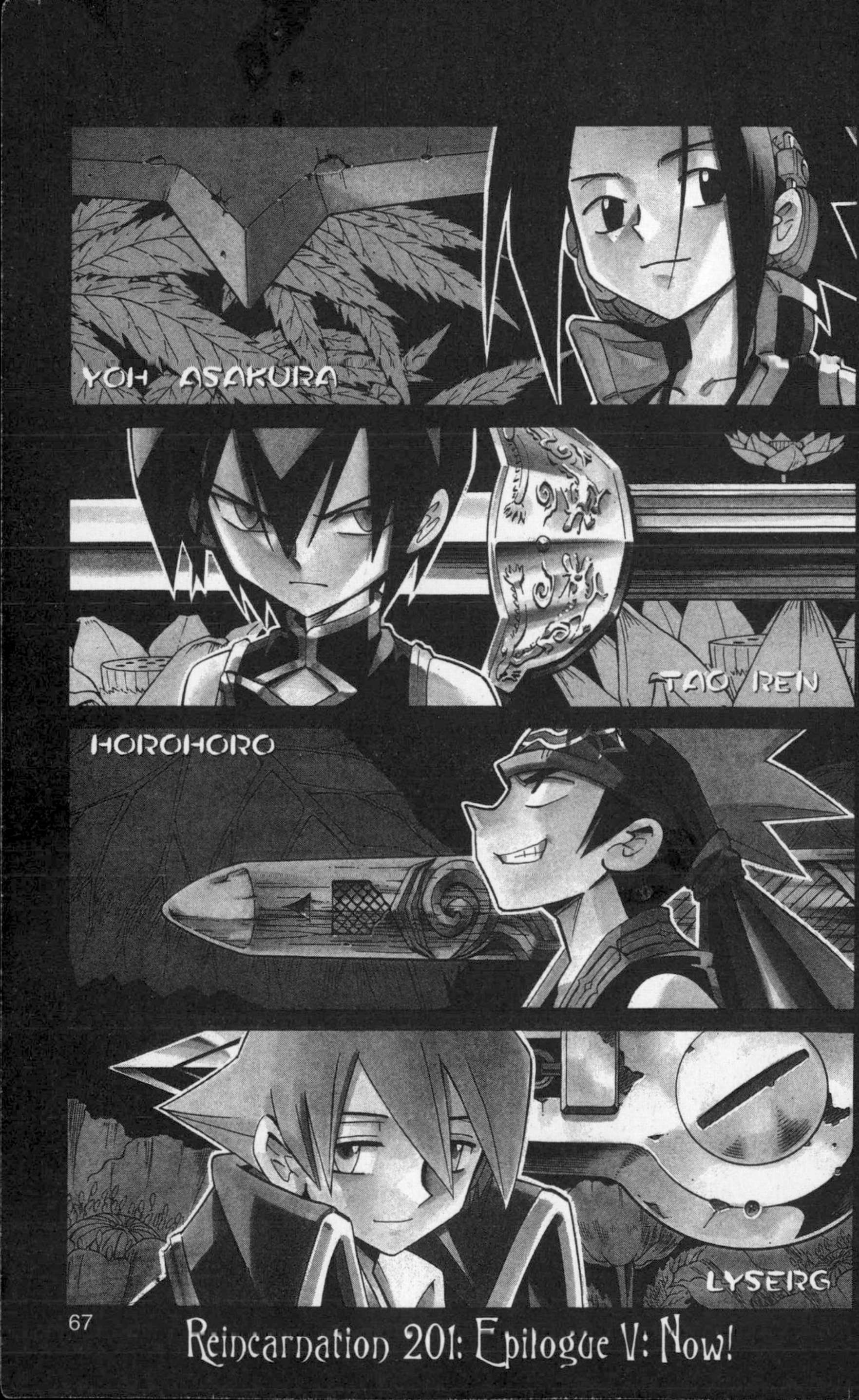
YOH ASAKURA
TAO REN
HOROHORO
LYSERG

Reincarnation 201: Epilogue V: Now!

Reincarnation 201: Epilogue V: Now!

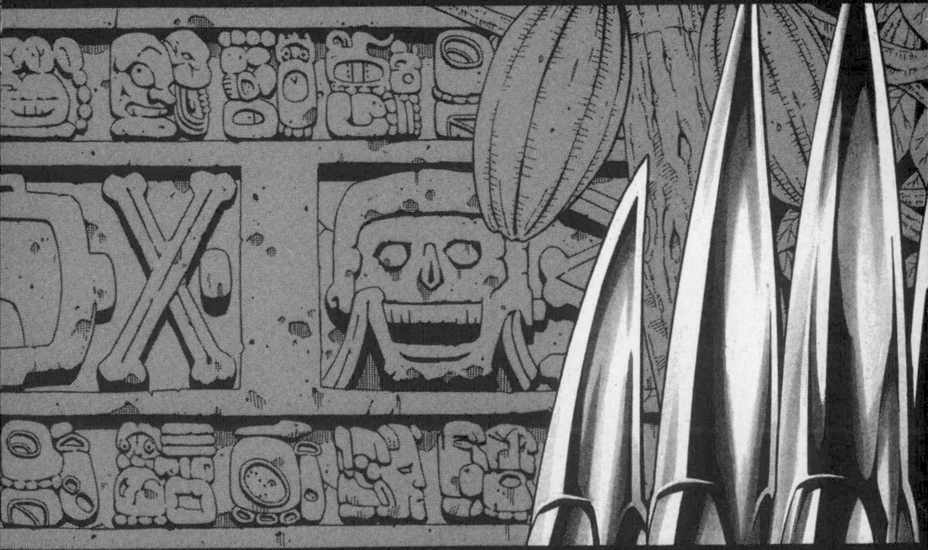

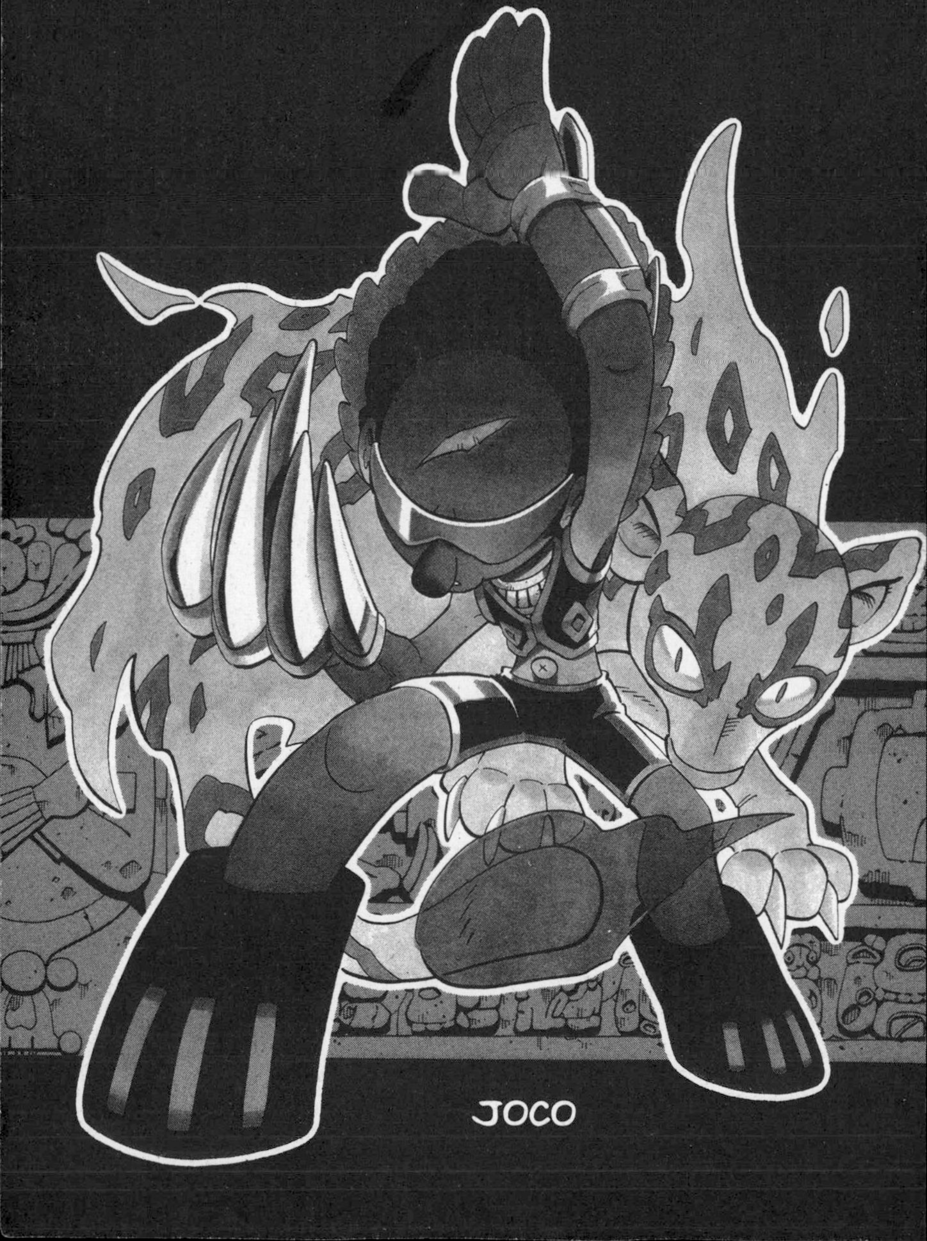

JOCO

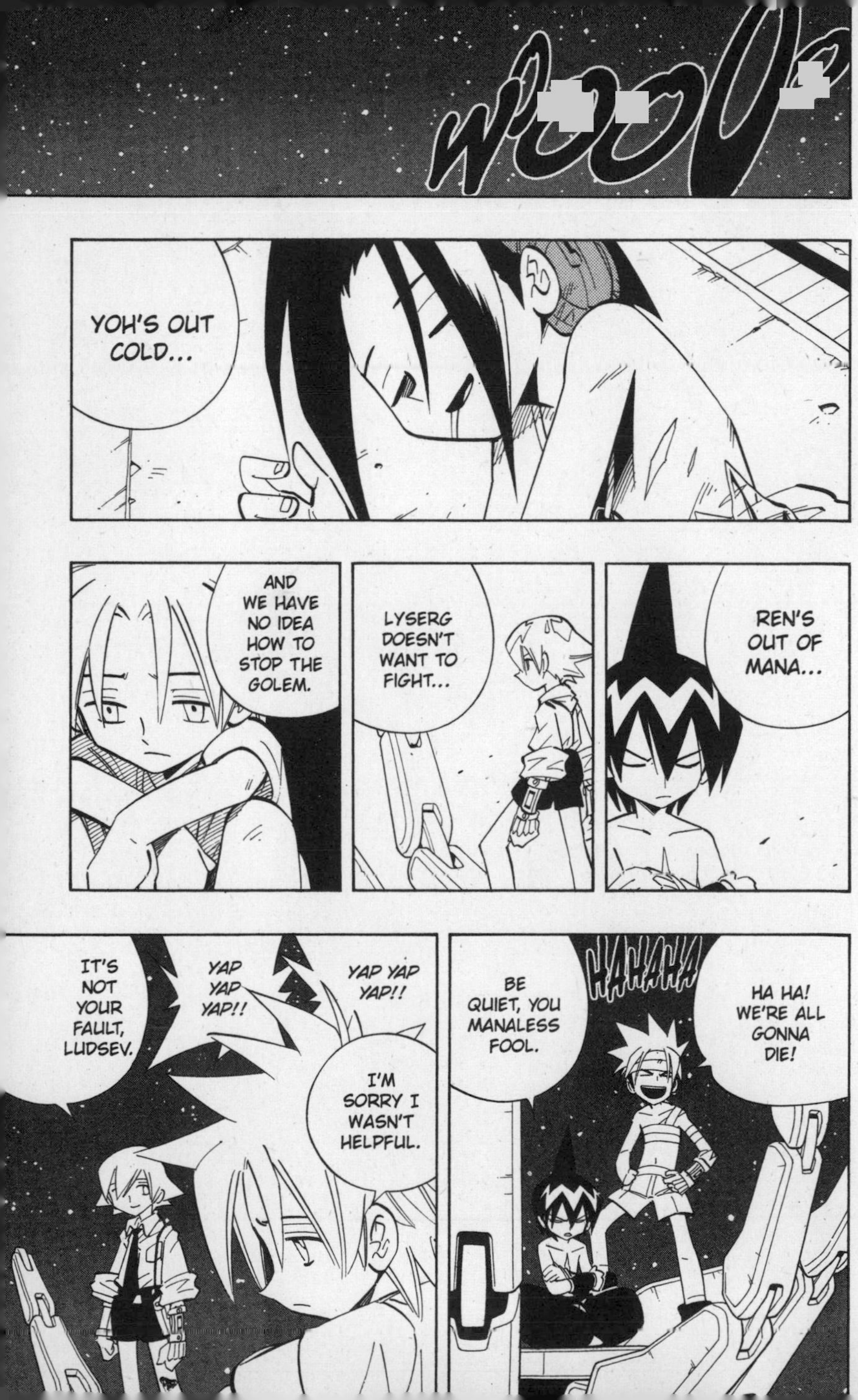
YOH'S OUT COLD...
REN'S OUT OF MANA...
LYSERG DOESN'T WANT TO FIGHT...
AND WE HAVE NO IDEA HOW TO STOP THE GOLEM.
HAHAHA
HA HA! WE'RE ALL GONNA DIE!
BE QUIET, YOU MANALESS FOOL.
YAP YAP YAP!!
YAP YAP YAP!!
I'M SORRY I WASN'T HELPFUL.
IT'S NOT YOUR FAULT, LUDSEV.

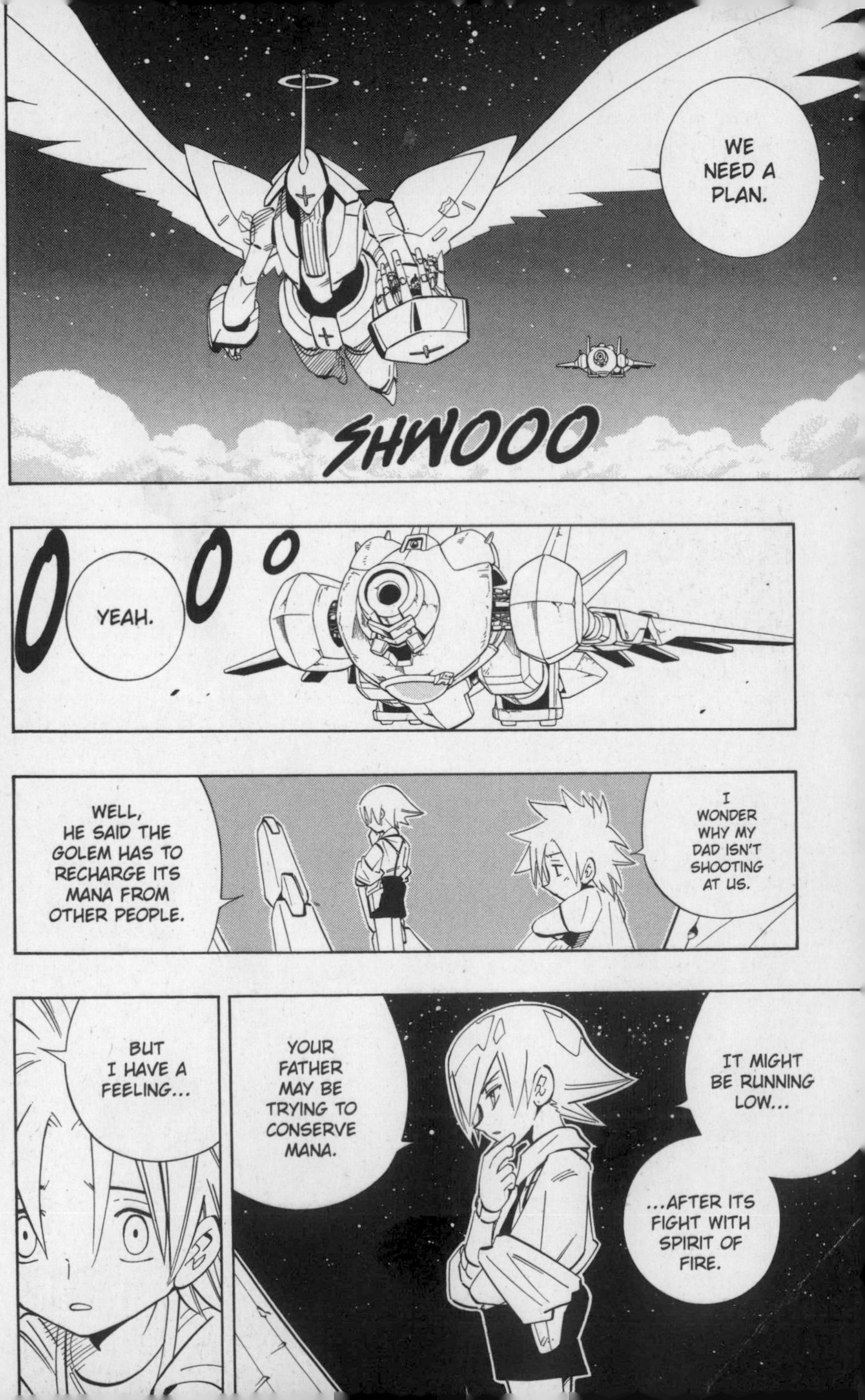
WE NEED A PLAN.
SHWOOO
OOO
YEAH.
I WONDER WHY MY DAD ISN'T SHOOTING AT US.
WELL, HE SAID THE GOLEM HAS TO RECHARGE ITS MANA FROM OTHER PEOPLE.
IT MIGHT BE RUNNING LOW...
...AFTER ITS FIGHT WITH SPIRIT OF FIRE.
YOUR FATHER MAY BE TRYING TO CONSERVE MANA.
BUT I HAVE A FEELING...

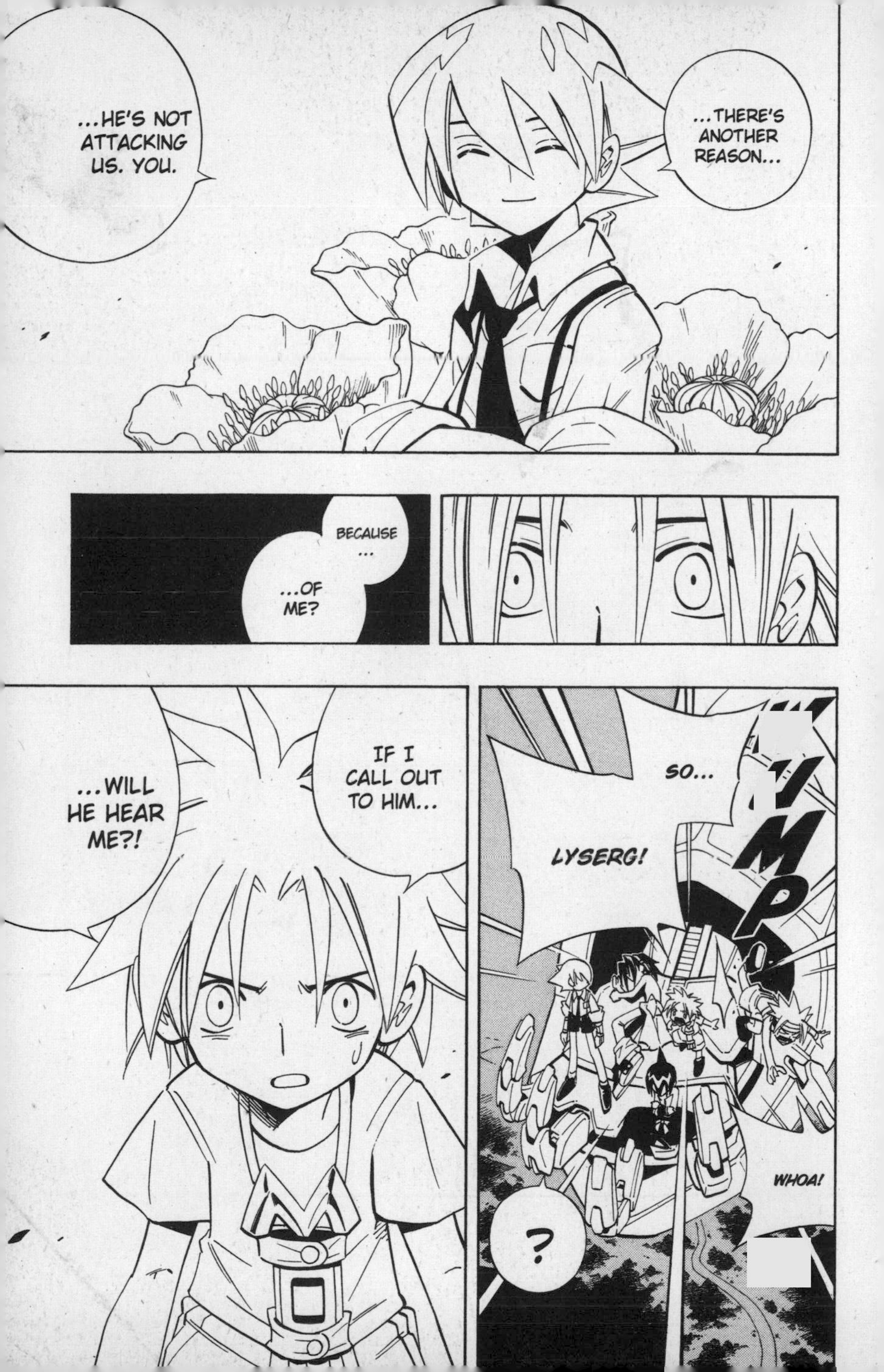
...THERE'S ANOTHER REASON...
...HE'S NOT ATTACKING US. YOU.
BECAUSE ...
...OF ME?
SO...
LYSERG!
WHOA!
?
IF I CALL OUT TO HIM...
...WILL HE HEAR ME?!

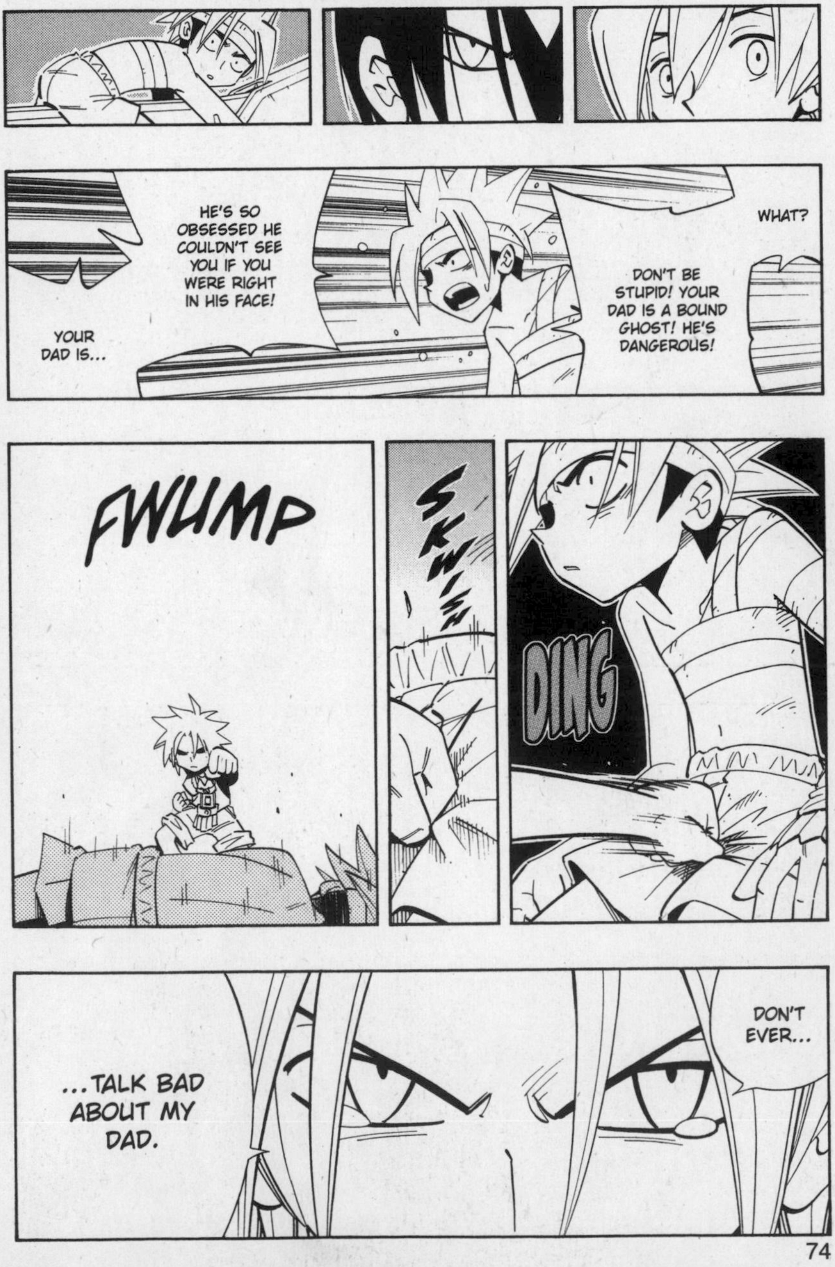

WHAT?
DON'T BE STUPID! YOUR DAD IS A BOUND GHOST! HE'S DANGEROUS!
HE'S SO OBSESSED HE COULDN'T SEE YOU IF YOU WERE RIGHT IN HIS FACE!
YOUR DAD IS...
DING
SKWISH
FWUMP
DON'T EVER...
...TALK BAD ABOUT MY DAD.

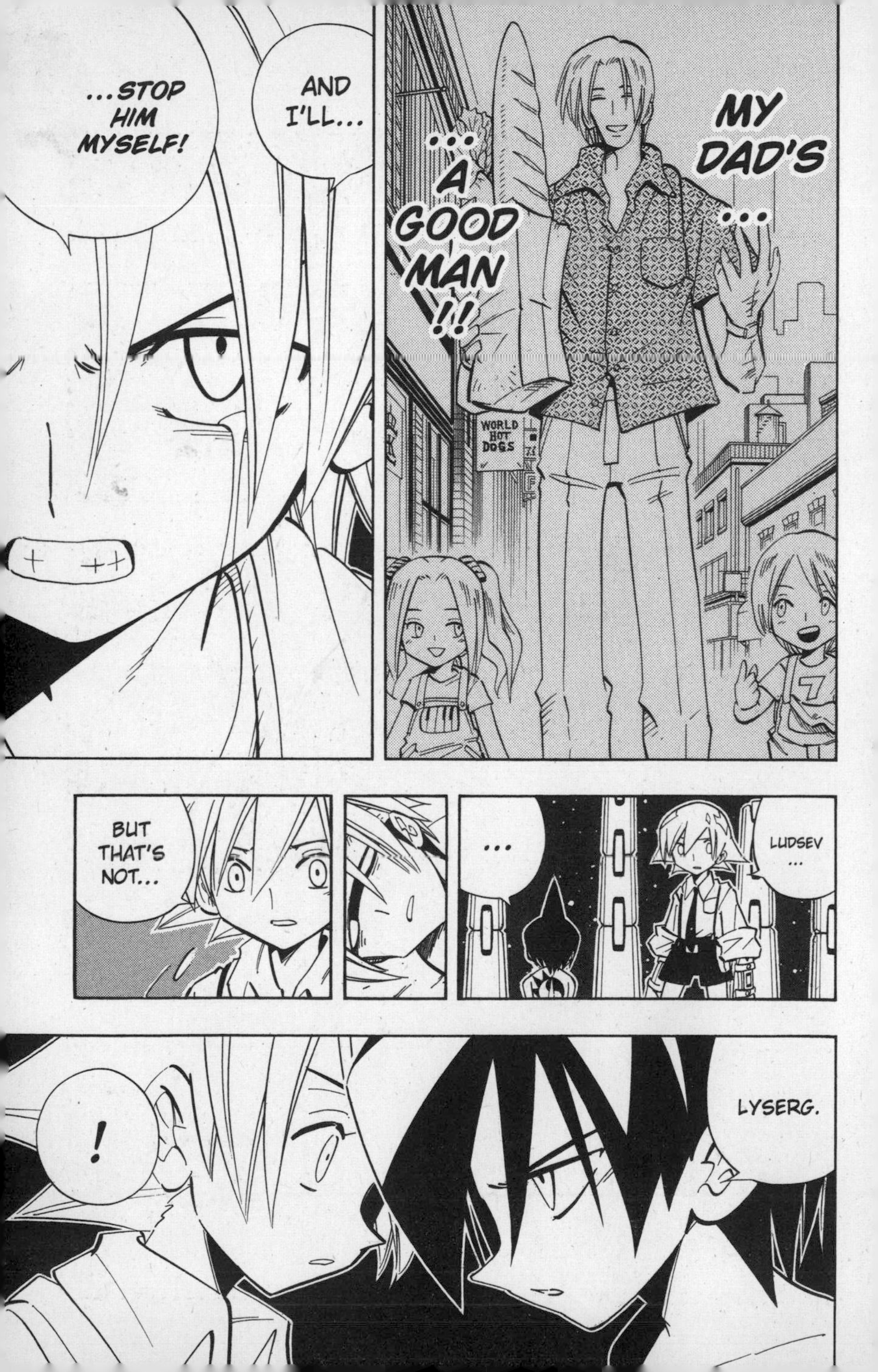

MY DAD'S...
...A GOOD MAN!!
AND I'LL...
...STOP HIM MYSELF!
LUDSEV...
...
BUT THAT'S NOT...
LYSERG.
!

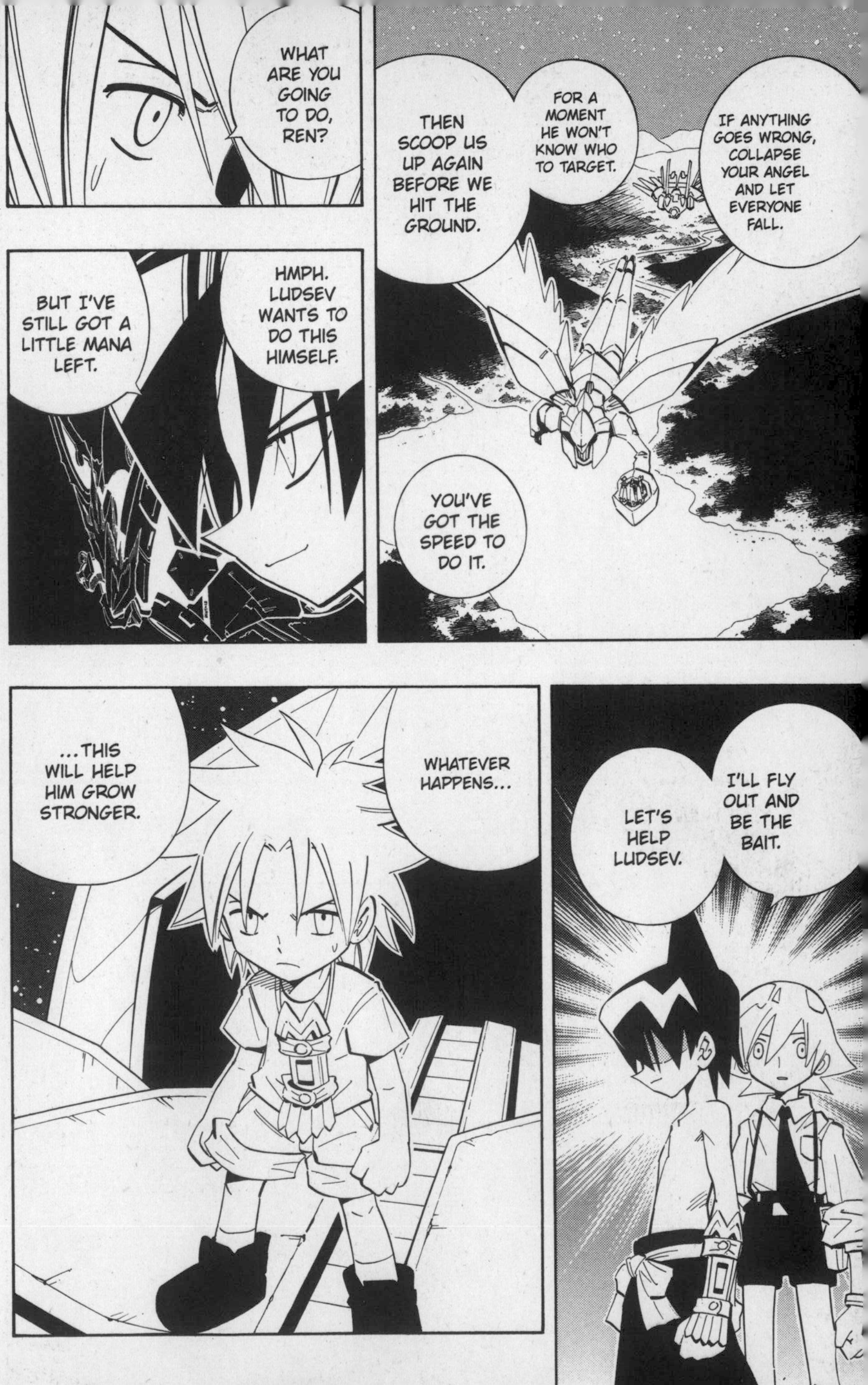
IF ANYTHING GOES WRONG, COLLAPSE YOUR ANGEL AND LET EVERYONE FALL.
FOR A MOMENT HE WON'T KNOW WHO TO TARGET.
THEN SCOOP US UP AGAIN BEFORE WE HIT THE GROUND.
YOU'VE GOT THE SPEED TO DO IT.
WHAT ARE YOU GOING TO DO, REN?
HMPH. LUDSEV WANTS TO DO THIS HIMSELF.
BUT I'VE STILL GOT A LITTLE MANA LEFT.
I'LL FLY OUT AND BE THE BAIT.
LET'S HELP LUDSEV.
WHATEVER HAPPENS...
...THIS WILL HELP HIM GROW STRONGER.

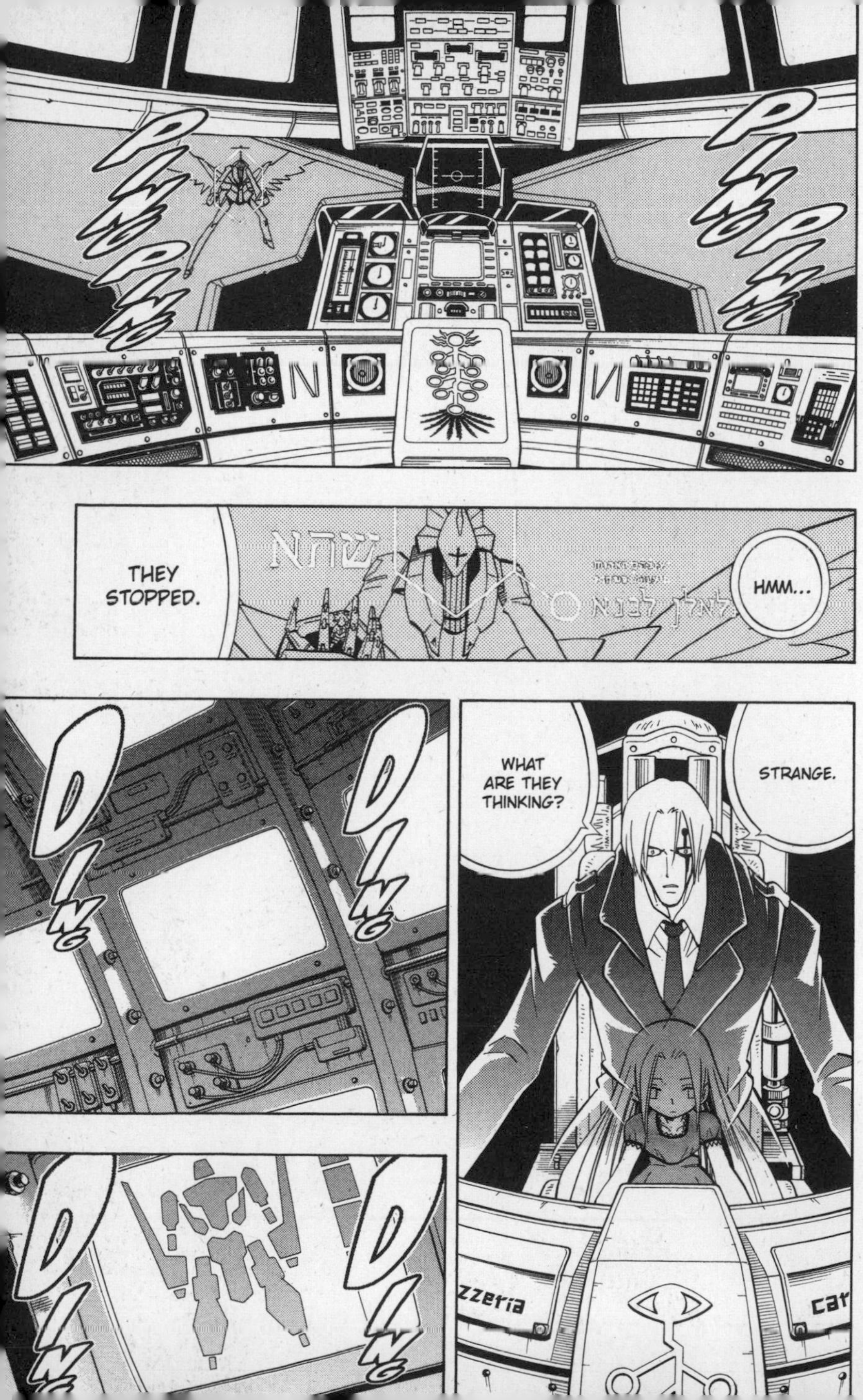
PIMPOMPIMPOM
PIMPOMPIMPOM
HMM...
THEY STOPPED.
STRANGE.
WHAT ARE THEY THINKING?
DING
DING
DING
DING

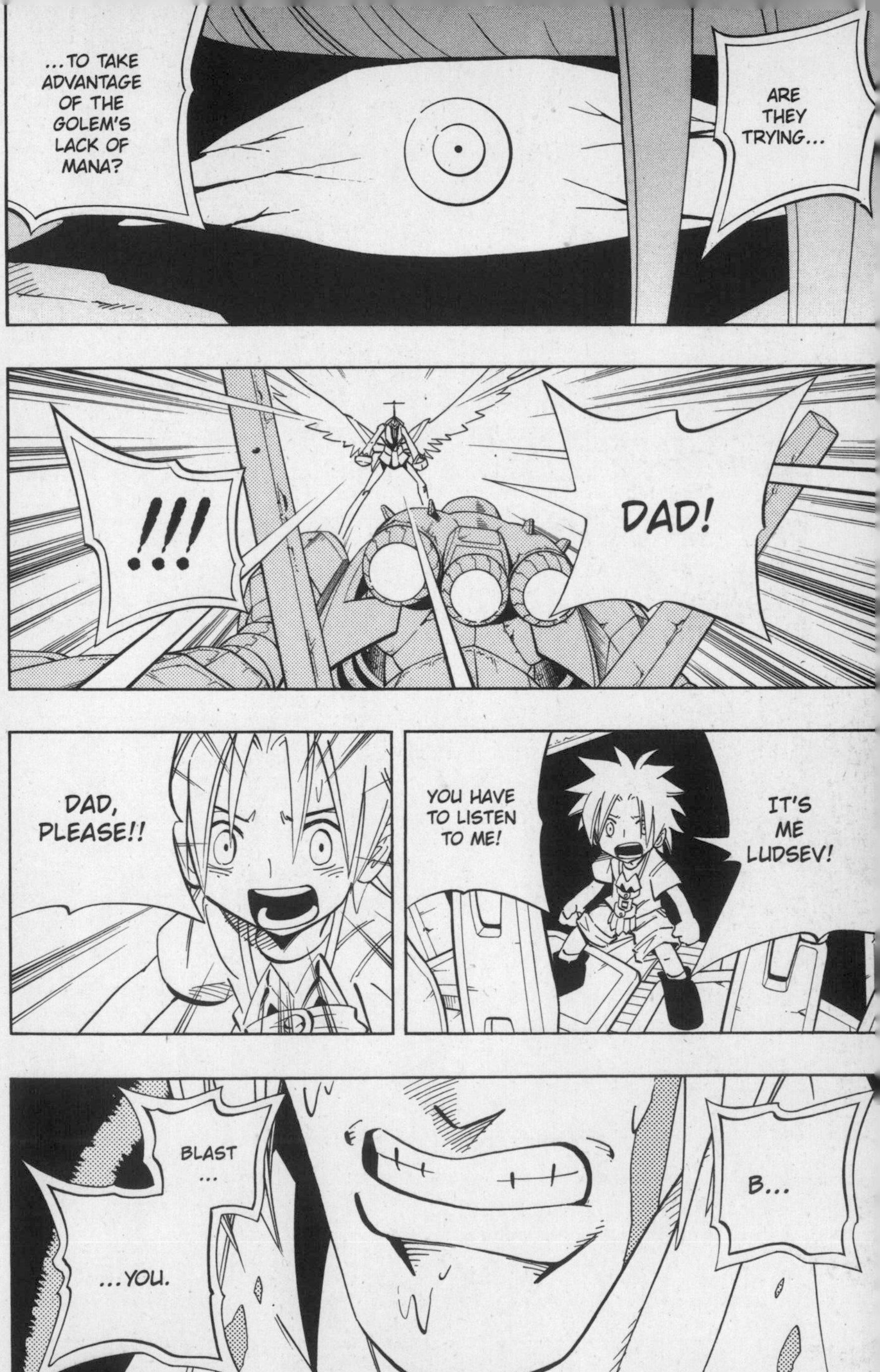
ARE THEY TRYING...
...TO TAKE ADVANTAGE OF THE GOLEM'S LACK OF MANA?
DAD!
!!!
IT'S ME LUDSEV!
YOU HAVE TO LISTEN TO ME!
DAD, PLEASE!!
B...
BLAST ...
...YOU.

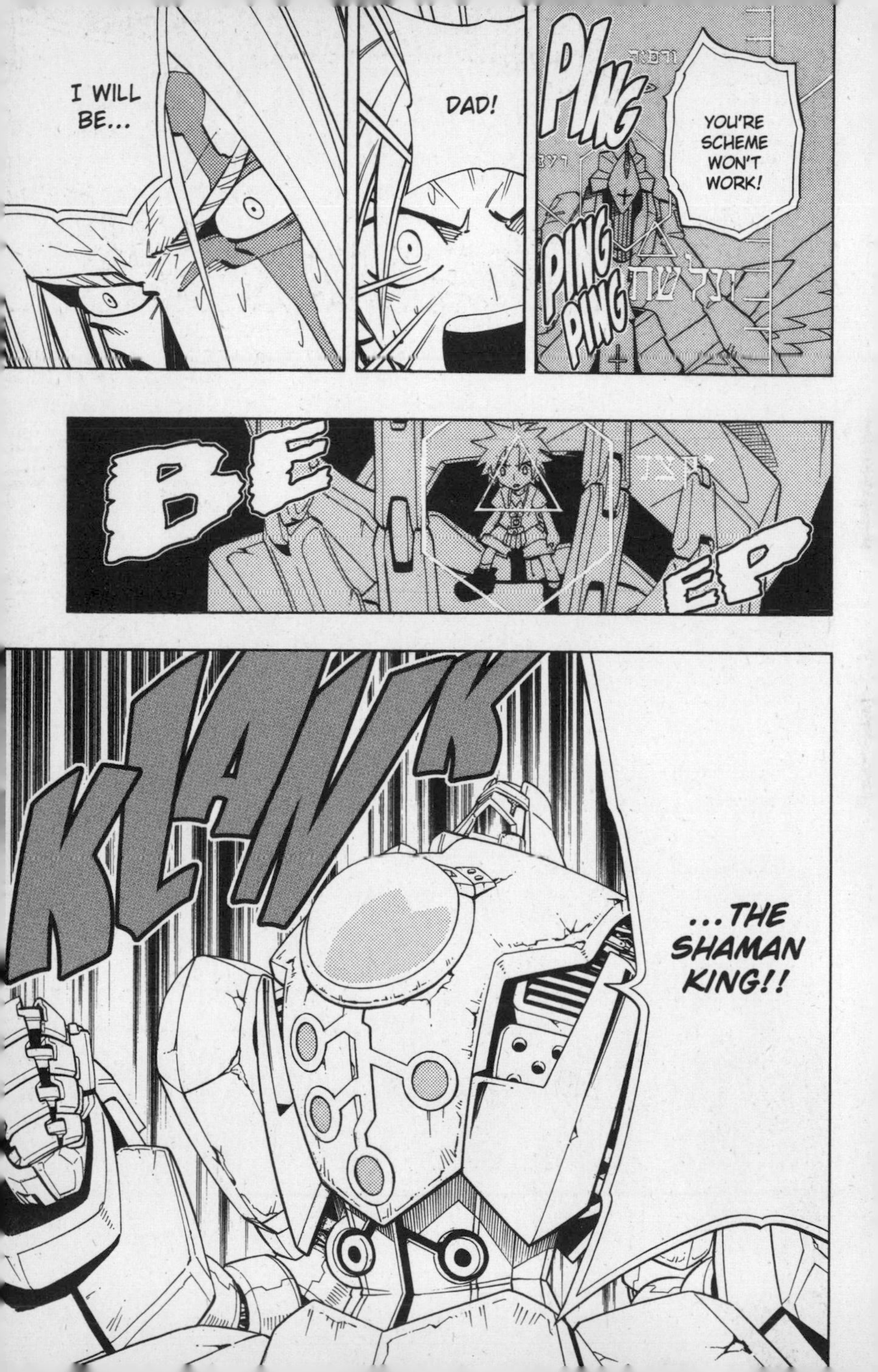
YOU'RE SCHEME WON'T WORK!
PING
PING PING
DAD!
I WILL BE...
BEEP
KLANK
...THE SHAMAN KING!!

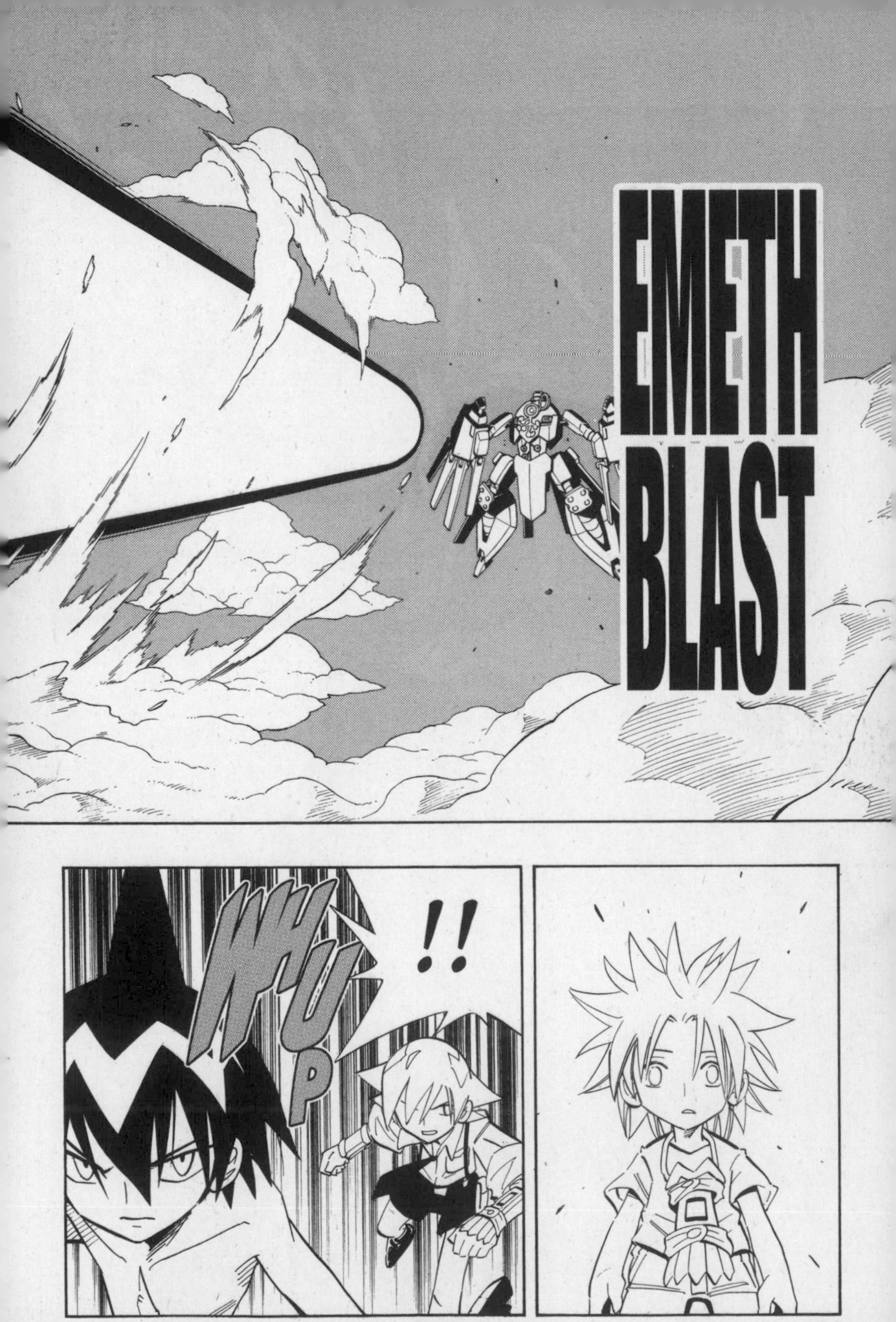
EMETH BLAST
!!
WHUP

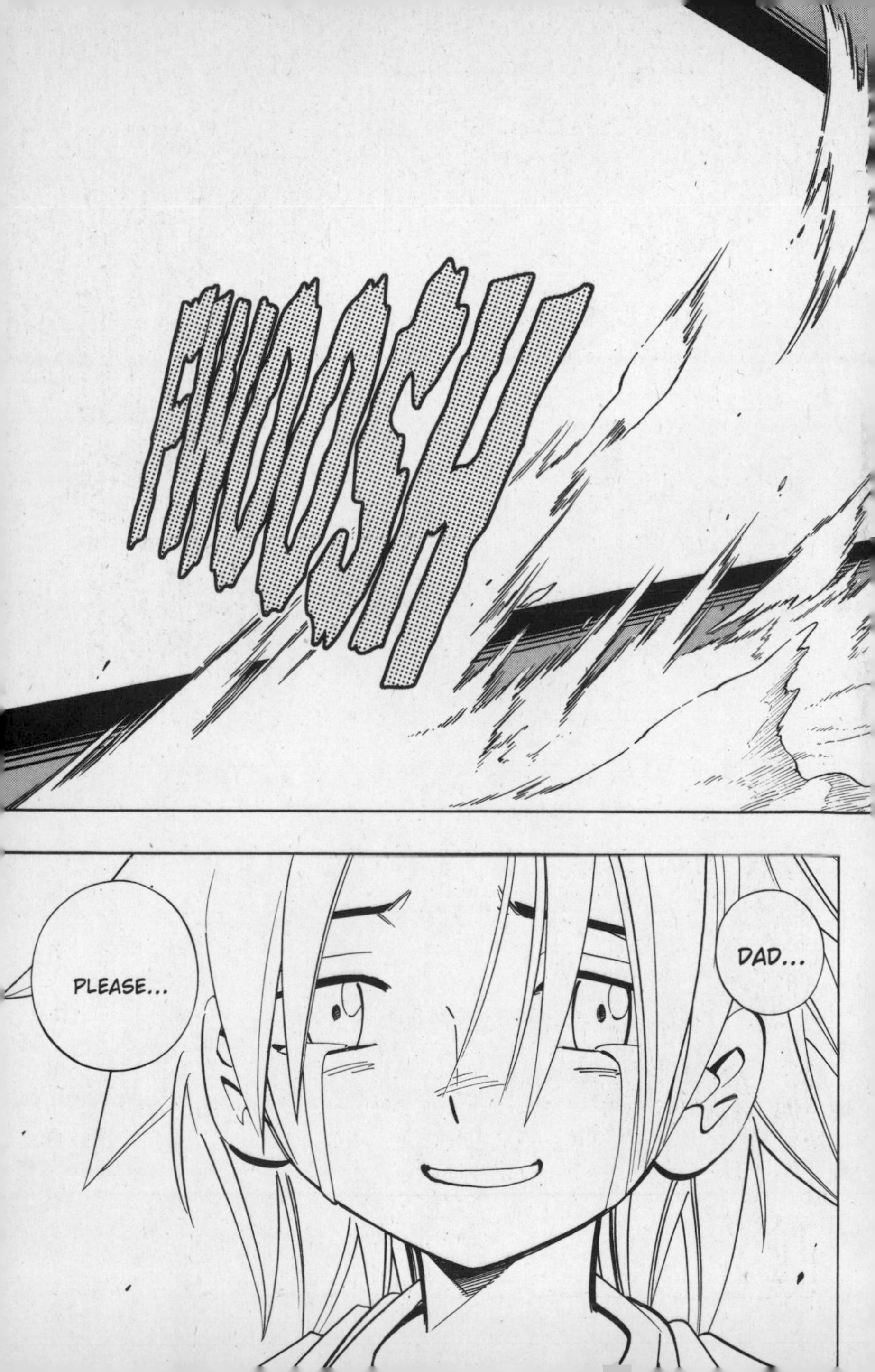
FWOOSH
DAD...
PLEASE...

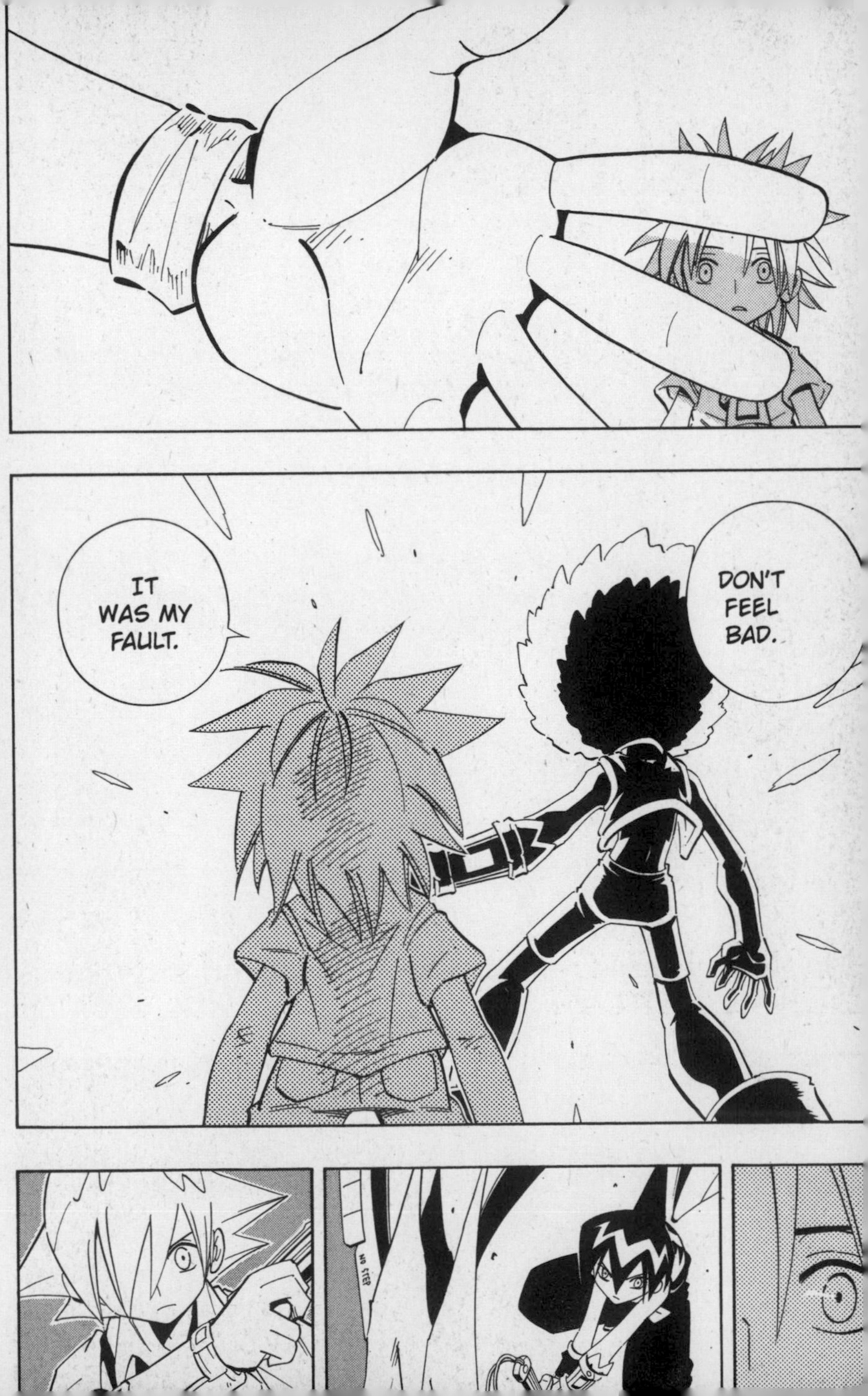
DON'T FEEL BAD.
IT WAS MY FAULT.

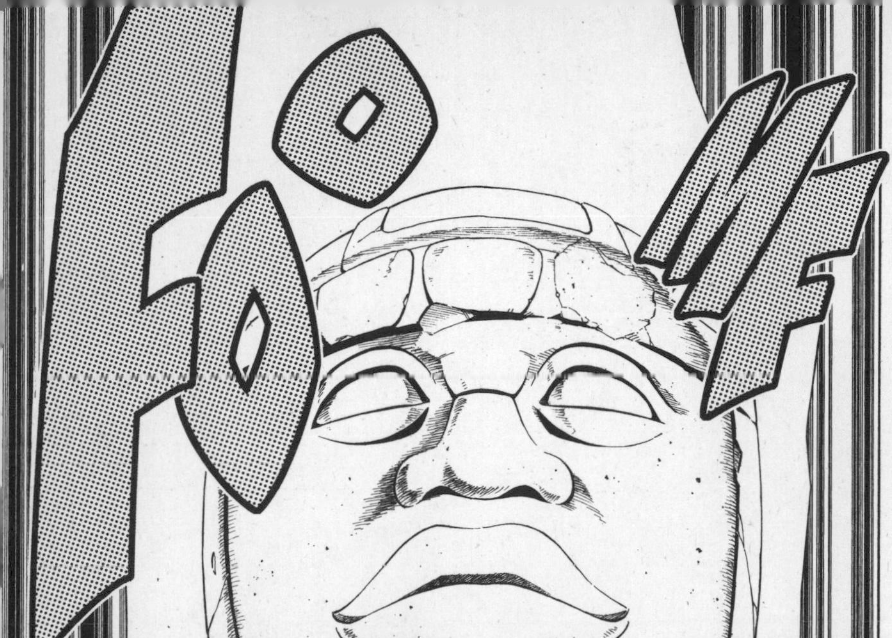
FOOMF

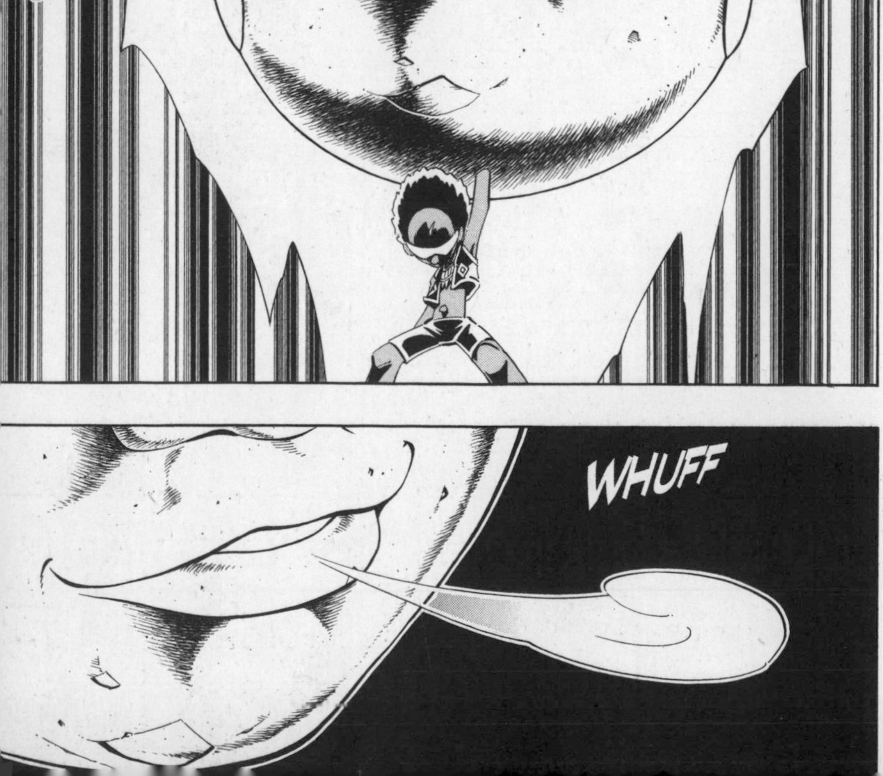
WHUFF

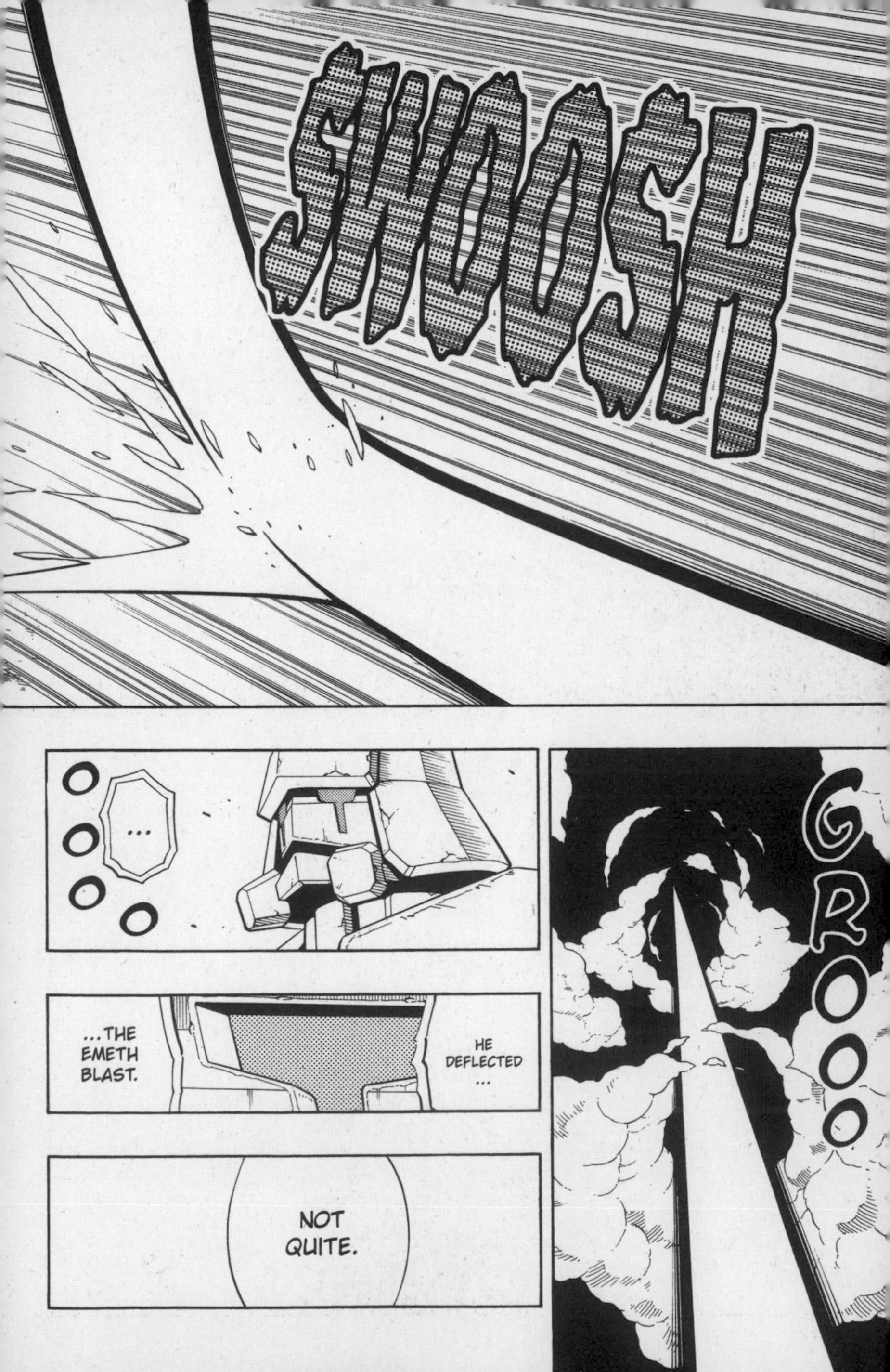
SWOOSH
GROOOO
OOOO
...
HE DEFLECTED...
...THE EMETH BLAST.
NOT QUITE.

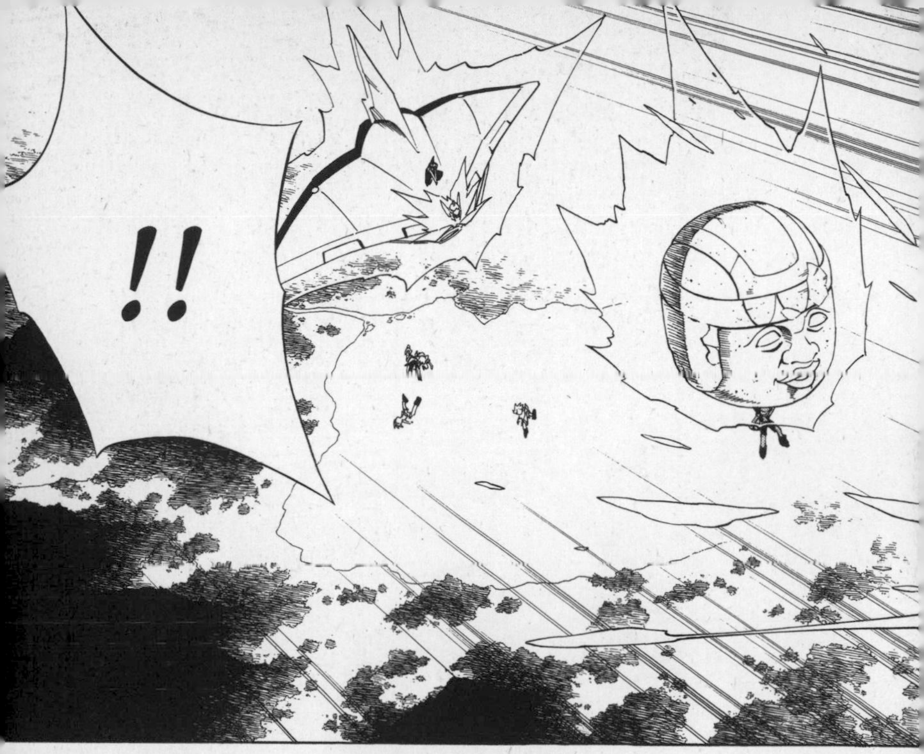
!!

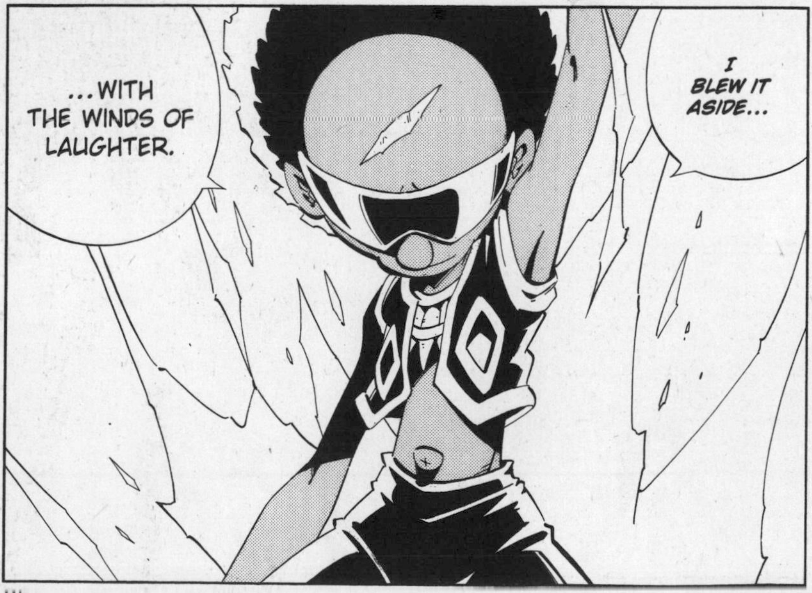
I BLEW IT ASIDE...
...WITH THE WINDS OF LAUGHTER.

SHAMAN KING CHARACTER FILE No.124

2001
(JAN)

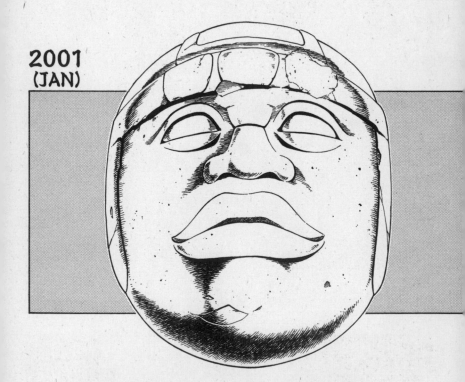

オーバーソウル
O.S.オルメカ
OVER SOUL: OLMEC

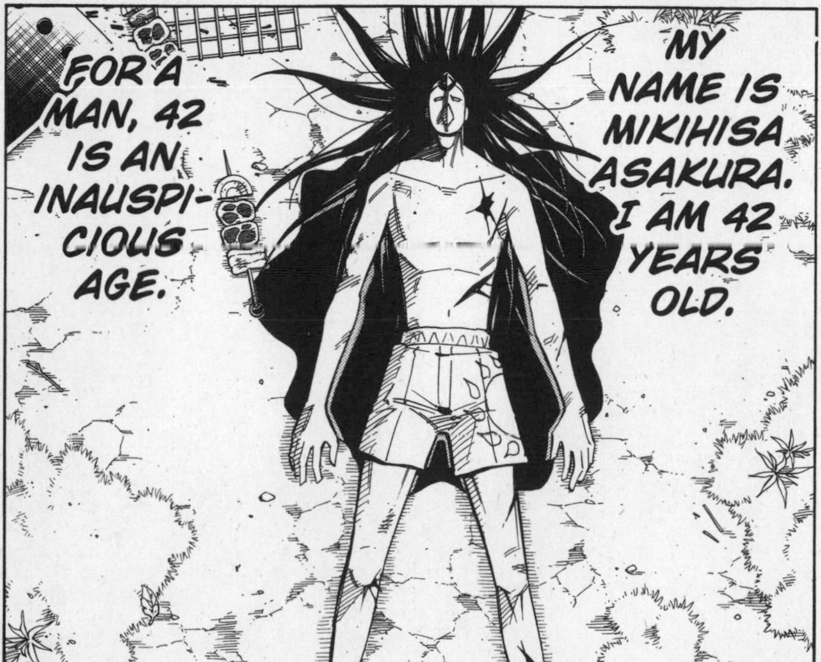
MY NAME IS MIKIHISA ASAKURA. I AM 42 YEARS OLD.
FOR A MAN, 42 IS AN INAUSPICIOUS AGE.
Reincarnation 202:
Epilogue V: Forbidden Finland

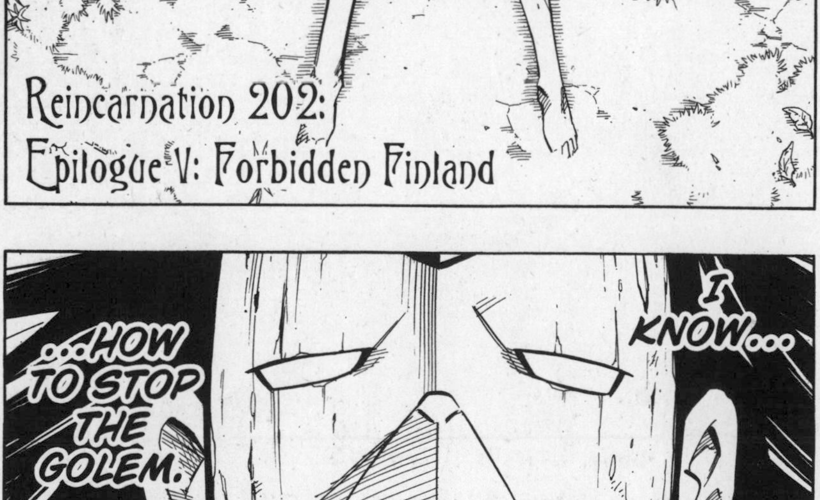
I KNOW...
...HOW TO STOP THE GOLEM.

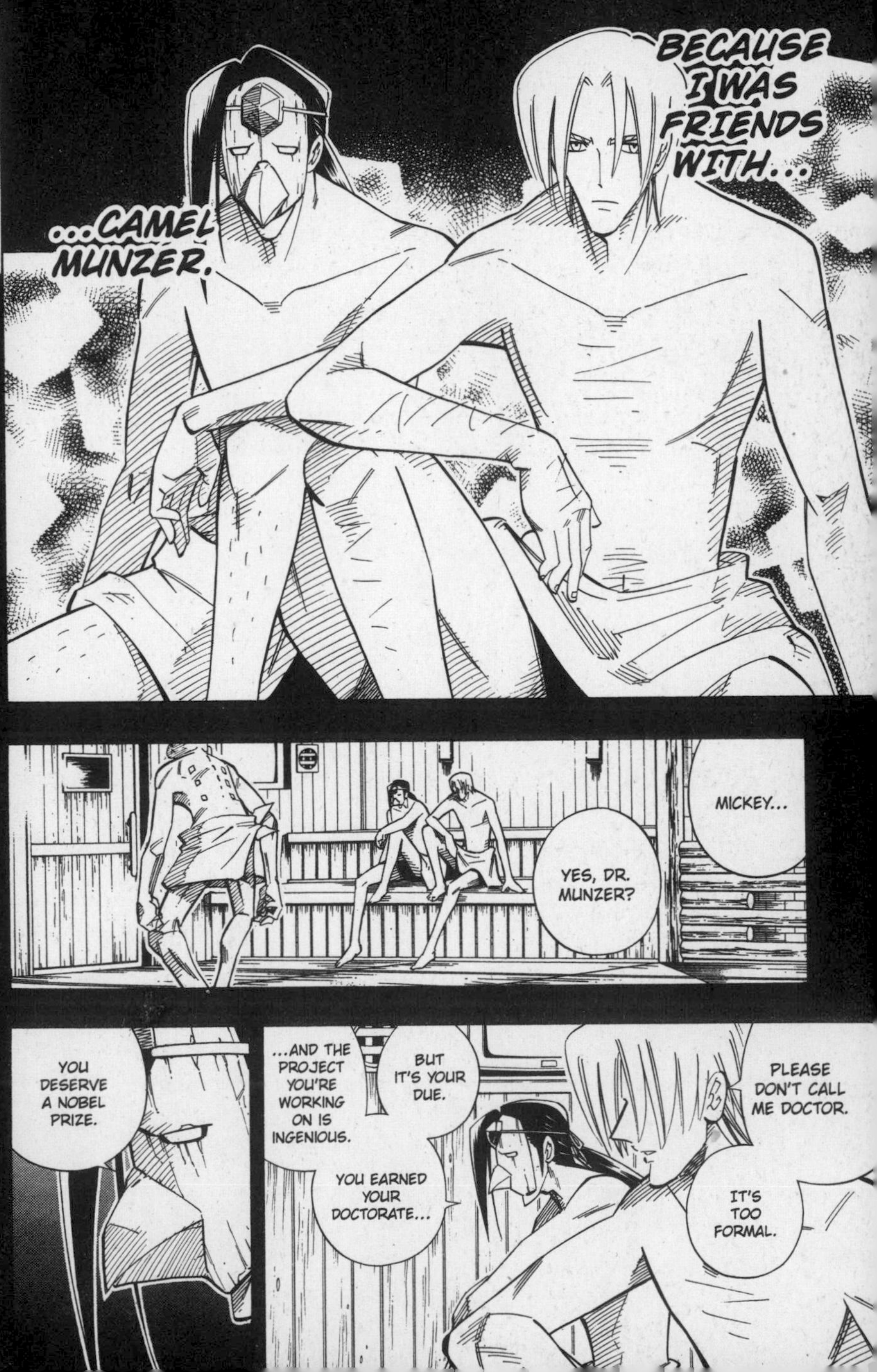
BECAUSE I WAS FRIENDS WITH...
...CAMEL MUNZER.
MICKEY...
YES, DR. MUNZER?
PLEASE DON'T CALL ME DOCTOR.
IT'S TOO FORMAL.
BUT IT'S YOUR DUE.
YOU EARNED YOUR DOCTORATE...
...AND THE PROJECT YOU'RE WORKING ON IS INGENIOUS.
YOU DESERVE A NOBEL PRIZE.

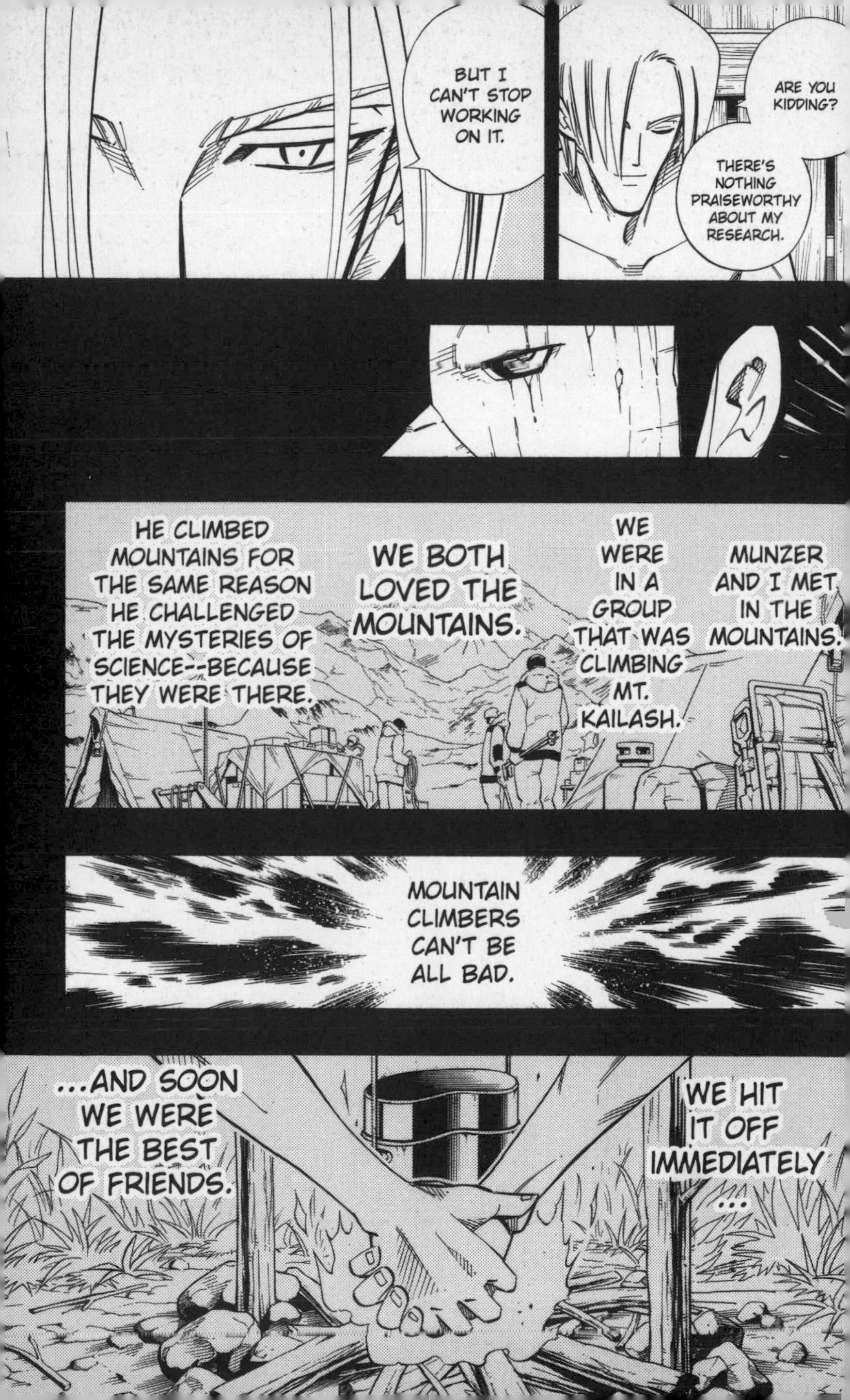
ARE YOU KIDDING?
THERE'S NOTHING PRAISEWORTHY ABOUT MY RESEARCH.
BUT I CAN'T STOP WORKING ON IT.
MUNZER AND I MET IN THE MOUNTAINS.
WE WERE IN A GROUP THAT WAS CLIMBING MT. KAILASH.
WE BOTH LOVED THE MOUNTAINS.
HE CLIMBED MOUNTAINS FOR THE SAME REASON HE CHALLENGED THE MYSTERIES OF SCIENCE--BECAUSE THEY WERE THERE.
MOUNTAIN CLIMBERS CAN'T BE ALL BAD.
WE HIT IT OFF IMMEDIATELY...
...AND SOON WE WERE THE BEST OF FRIENDS.

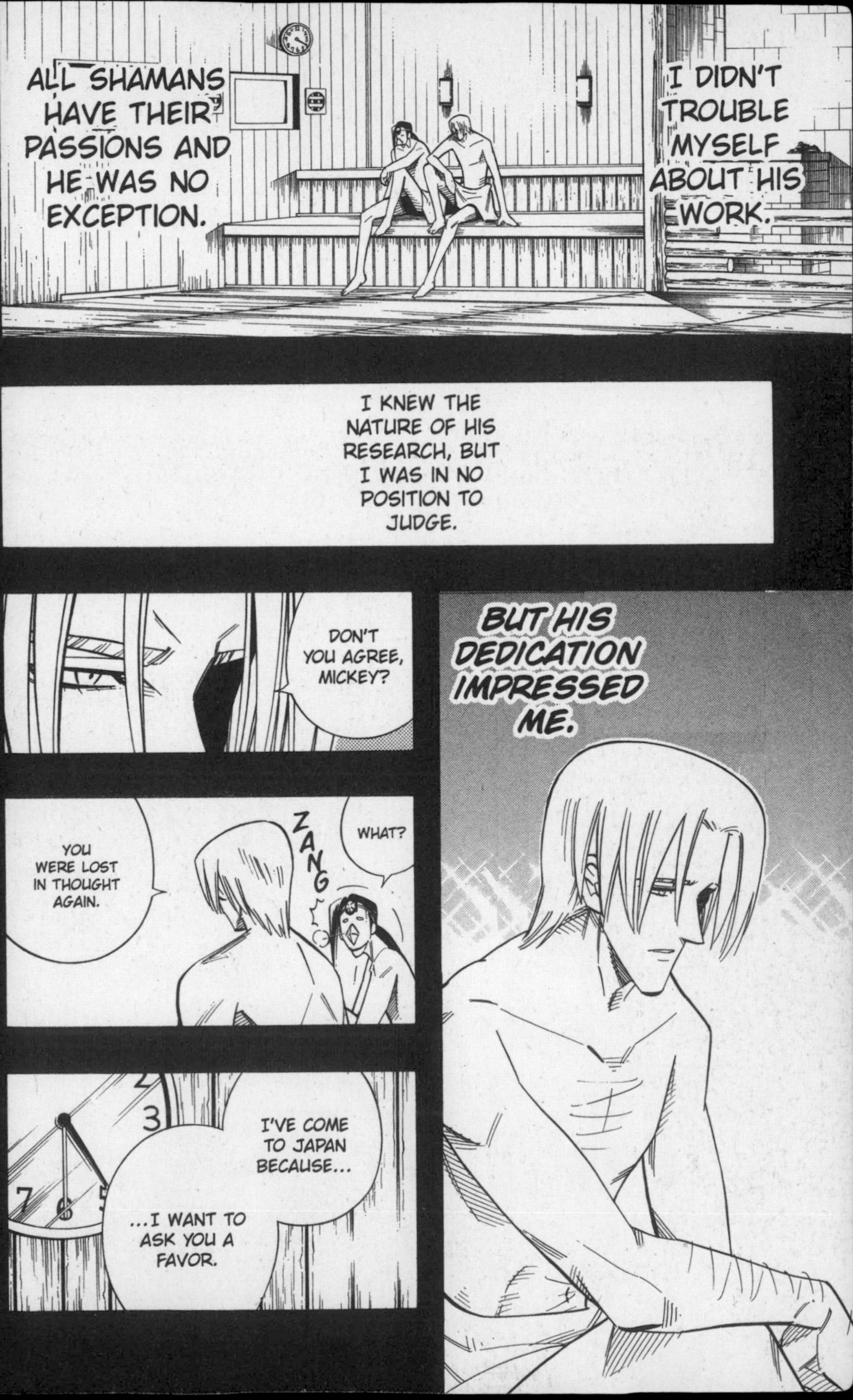
I DIDN'T TROUBLE MYSELF ABOUT HIS WORK.
ALL SHAMANS HAVE THEIR PASSIONS AND HE WAS NO EXCEPTION.
I KNEW THE NATURE OF HIS RESEARCH, BUT I WAS IN NO POSITION TO JUDGE.
BUT HIS DEDICATION IMPRESSED ME.
DON'T YOU AGREE, MICKEY?
WHAT?
ZANG
YOU WERE LOST IN THOUGHT AGAIN.
I'VE COME TO JAPAN BECAUSE...
...I WANT TO ASK YOU A FAVOR.

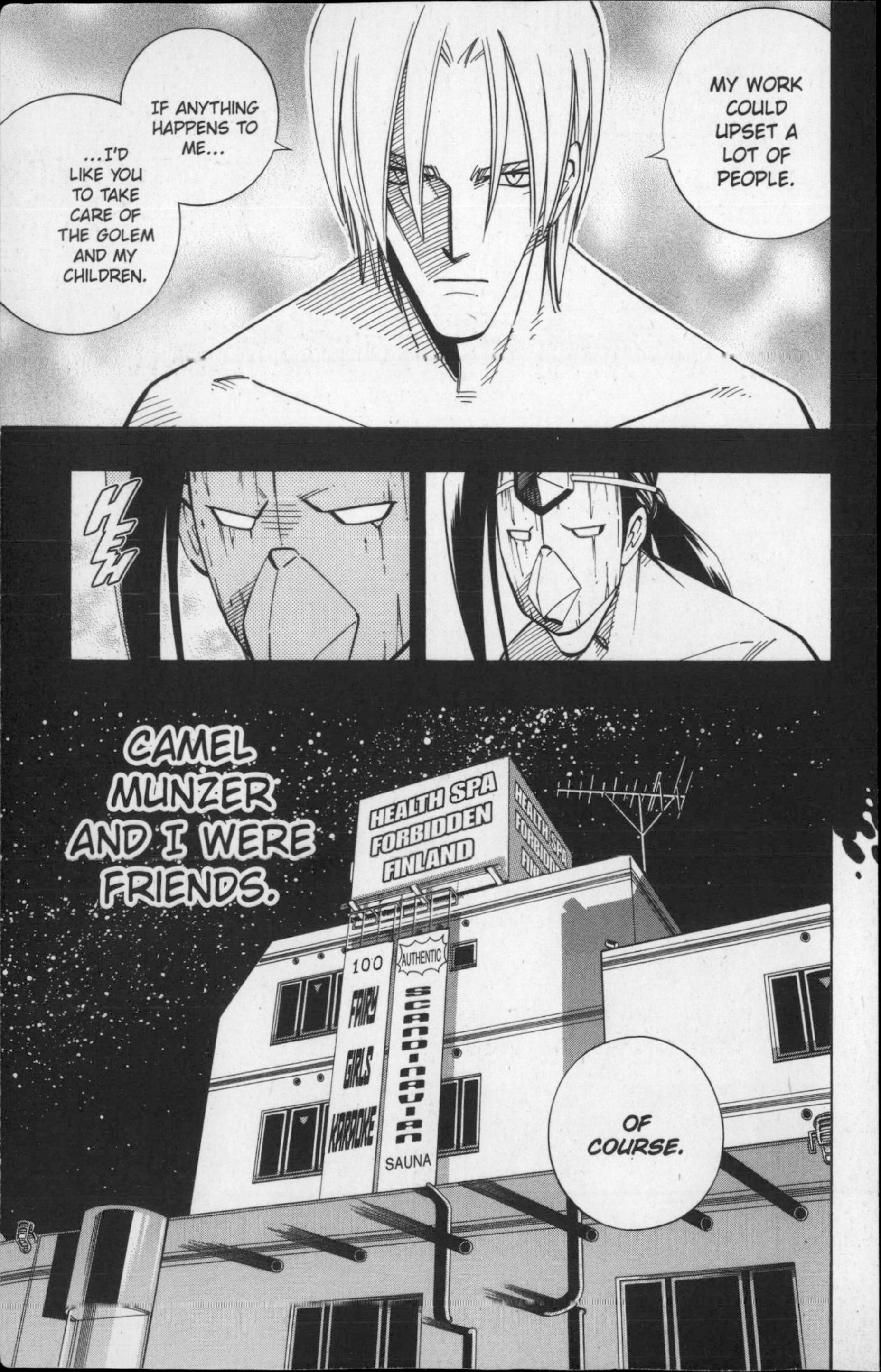
MY WORK COULD UPSET A LOT OF PEOPLE.
IF ANYTHING HAPPENS TO ME...
...I'D LIKE YOU TO TAKE CARE OF THE GOLEM AND MY CHILDREN.
HEH
HEALTH SPA FORBIDDEN FINLAND
OF COURSE.
CAMEL MUNZER AND I WERE FRIENDS.
AUTHENTIC SCANDINAVIAN SAUNA
100 FAIRY GIRLS KARAOKE

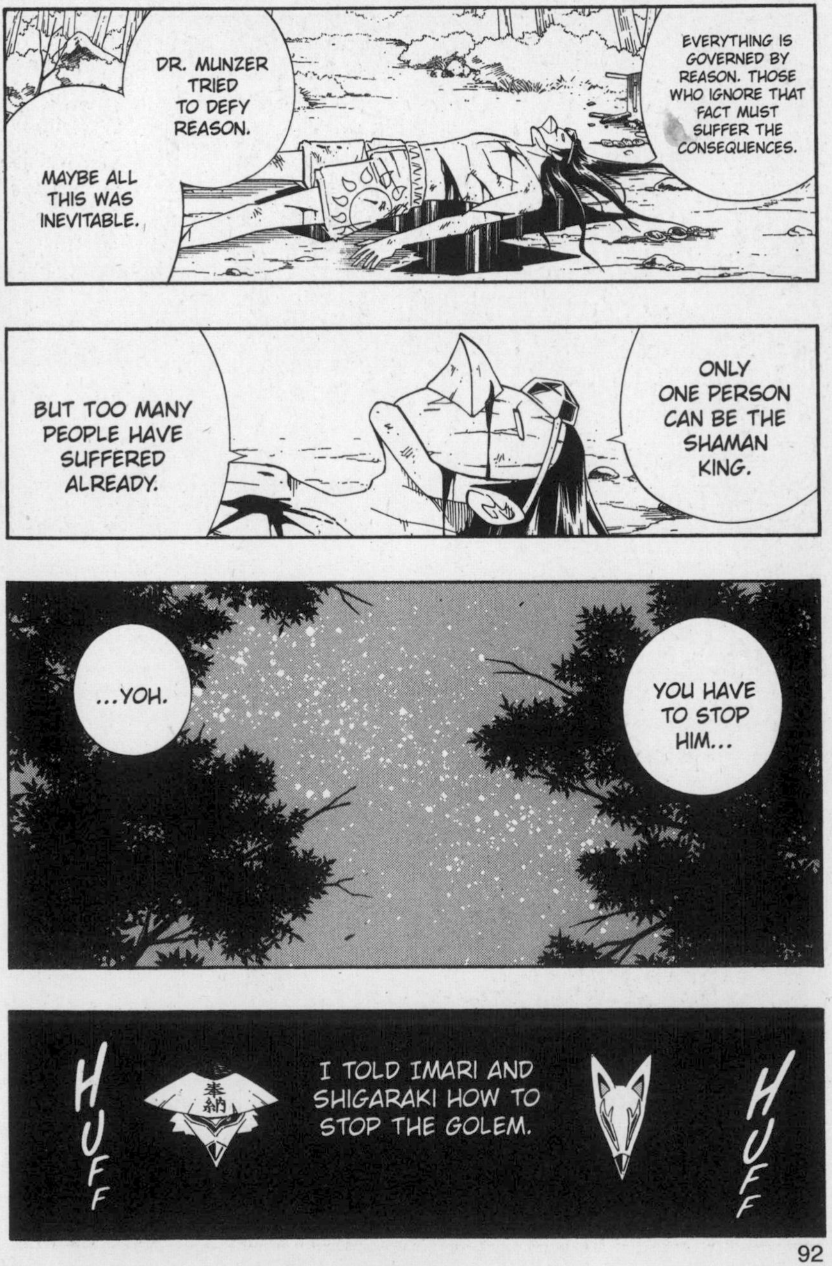
EVERYTHING IS GOVERNED BY REASON. THOSE WHO IGNORE THAT FACT MUST SUFFER THE CONSEQUENCES.
DR. MUNZER TRIED TO DEFY REASON.
MAYBE ALL THIS WAS INEVITABLE.
ONLY ONE PERSON CAN BE THE SHAMAN KING.
BUT TOO MANY PEOPLE HAVE SUFFERED ALREADY.
YOU HAVE TO STOP HIM...
...YOH.
HUFF
I TOLD IMARI AND SHIGARAKI HOW TO STOP THE GOLEM.
奉納
HUFF

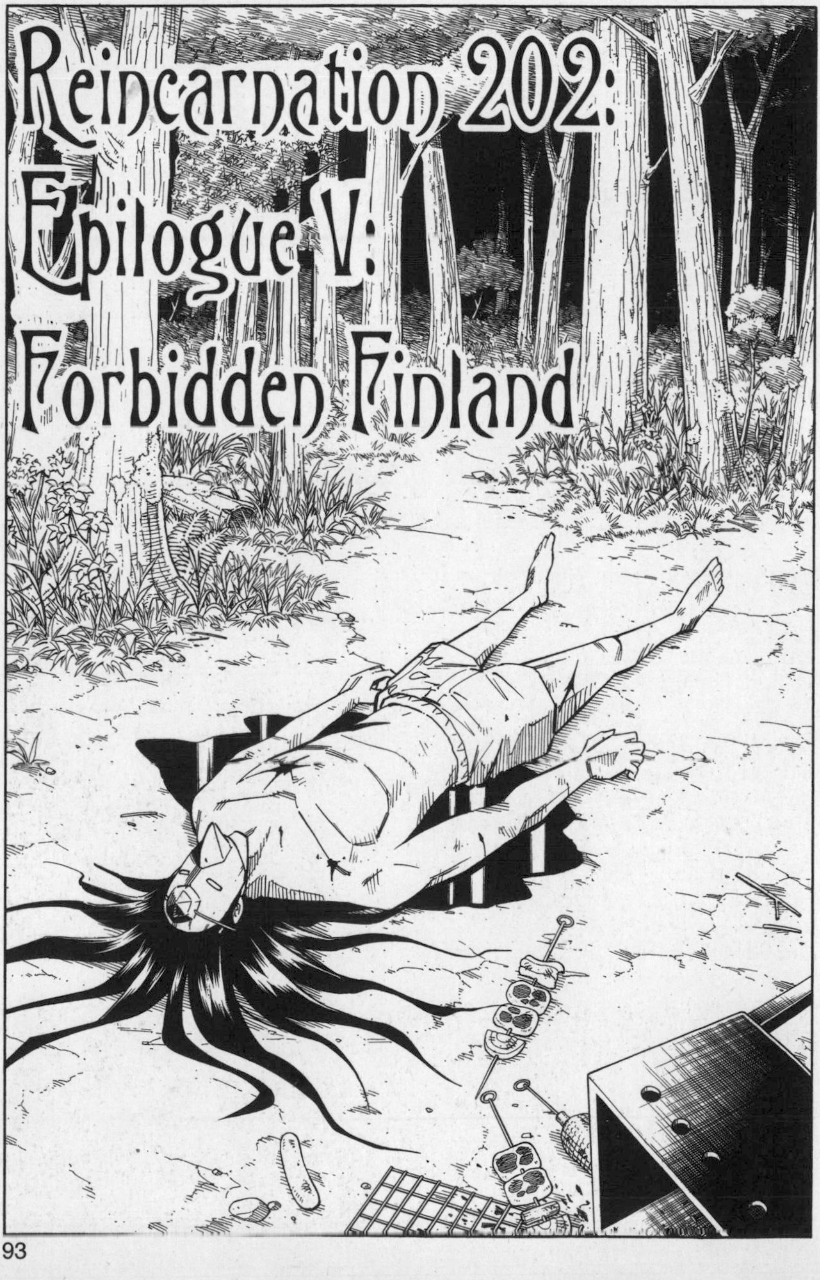
Reincarnation 202:
Epilogue V:
Forbidden Finland

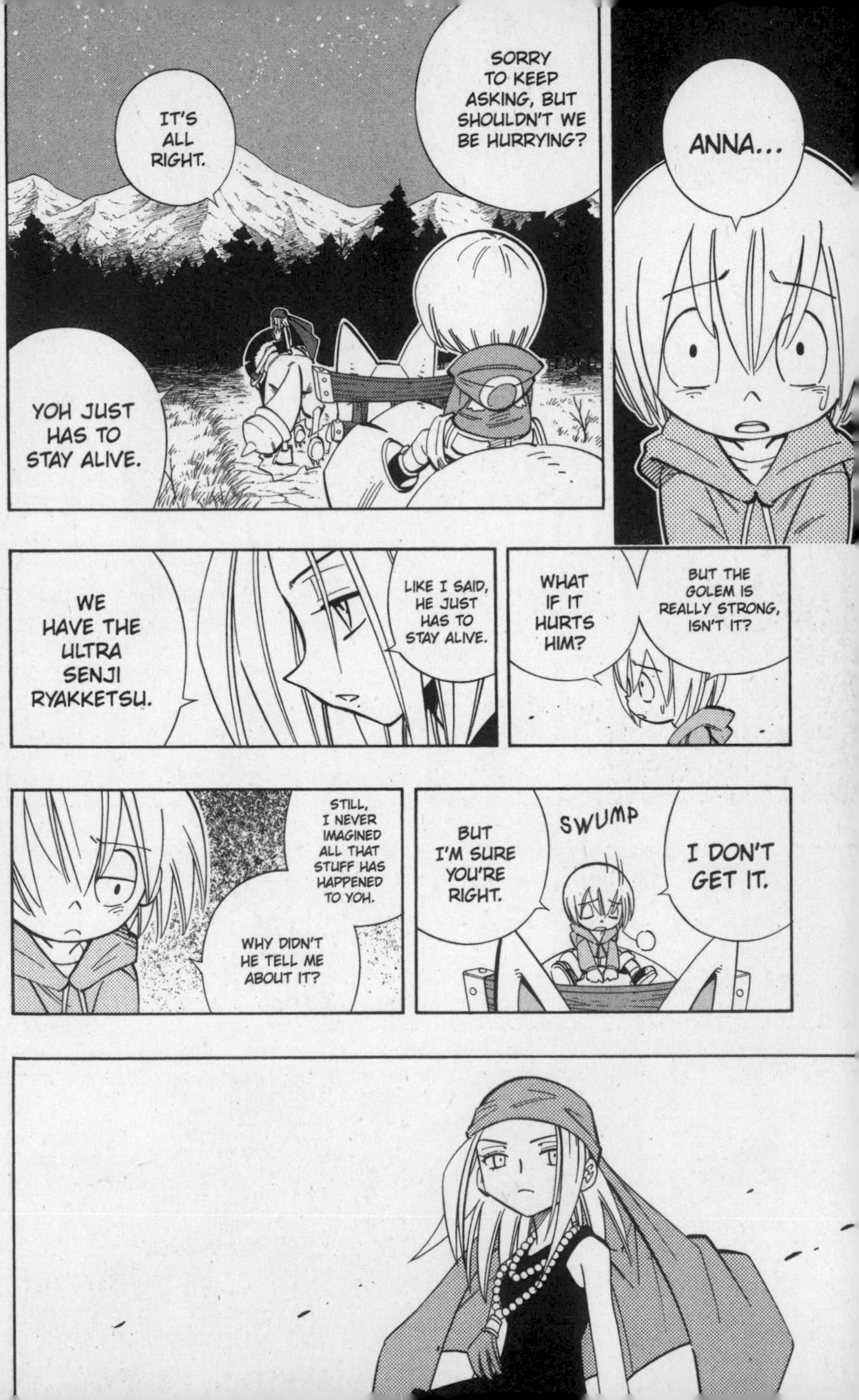
ANNA...
SORRY TO KEEP ASKING, BUT SHOULDN'T WE BE HURRYING?
IT'S ALL RIGHT.
YOH JUST HAS TO STAY ALIVE.
BUT THE GOLEM IS REALLY STRONG, ISN'T IT?
WHAT IF IT HURTS HIM?
LIKE I SAID, HE JUST HAS TO STAY ALIVE.
WE HAVE THE ULTRA SENJI RYAKKETSU.
I DON'T GET IT.
SWUMP
BUT I'M SURE YOU'RE RIGHT.
STILL, I NEVER IMAGINED ALL THAT STUFF HAS HAPPENED TO YOH.
WHY DIDN'T HE TELL ME ABOUT IT?

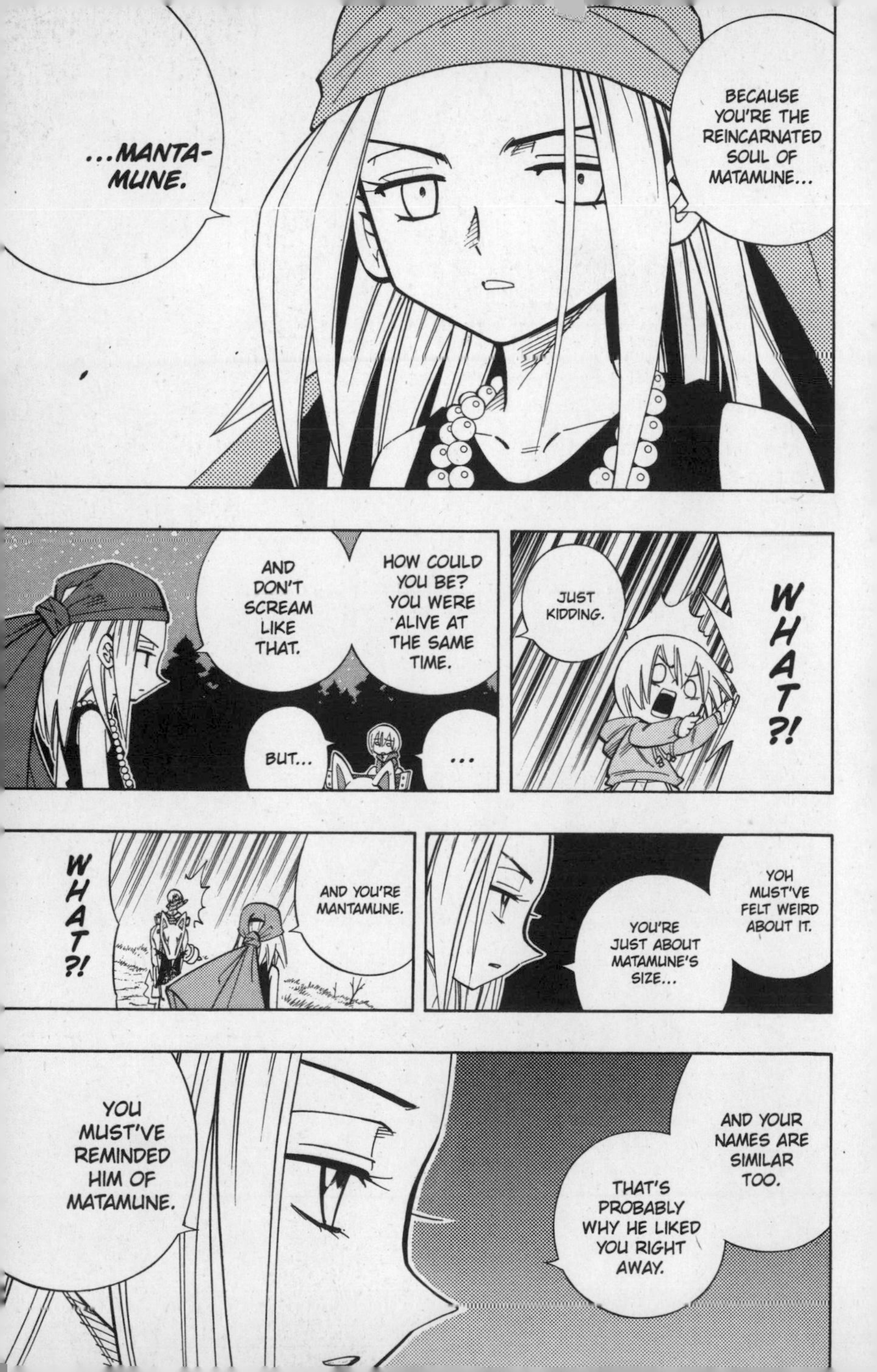
BECAUSE YOU'RE THE REINCARNATED SOUL OF MATAMUNE...
...MANTA-MUNE.
WHAT?!
JUST KIDDING.
HOW COULD YOU BE? YOU WERE ALIVE AT THE SAME TIME.
AND DON'T SCREAM LIKE THAT.
...
BUT...
YOH MUST'VE FELT WEIRD ABOUT IT.
YOU'RE JUST ABOUT MATAMUNE'S SIZE...
AND YOU'RE MANTAMUNE.
WHAT?!
AND YOUR NAMES ARE SIMILAR TOO.
THAT'S PROBABLY WHY HE LIKED YOU RIGHT AWAY.
YOU MUST'VE REMINDED HIM OF MATAMUNE.

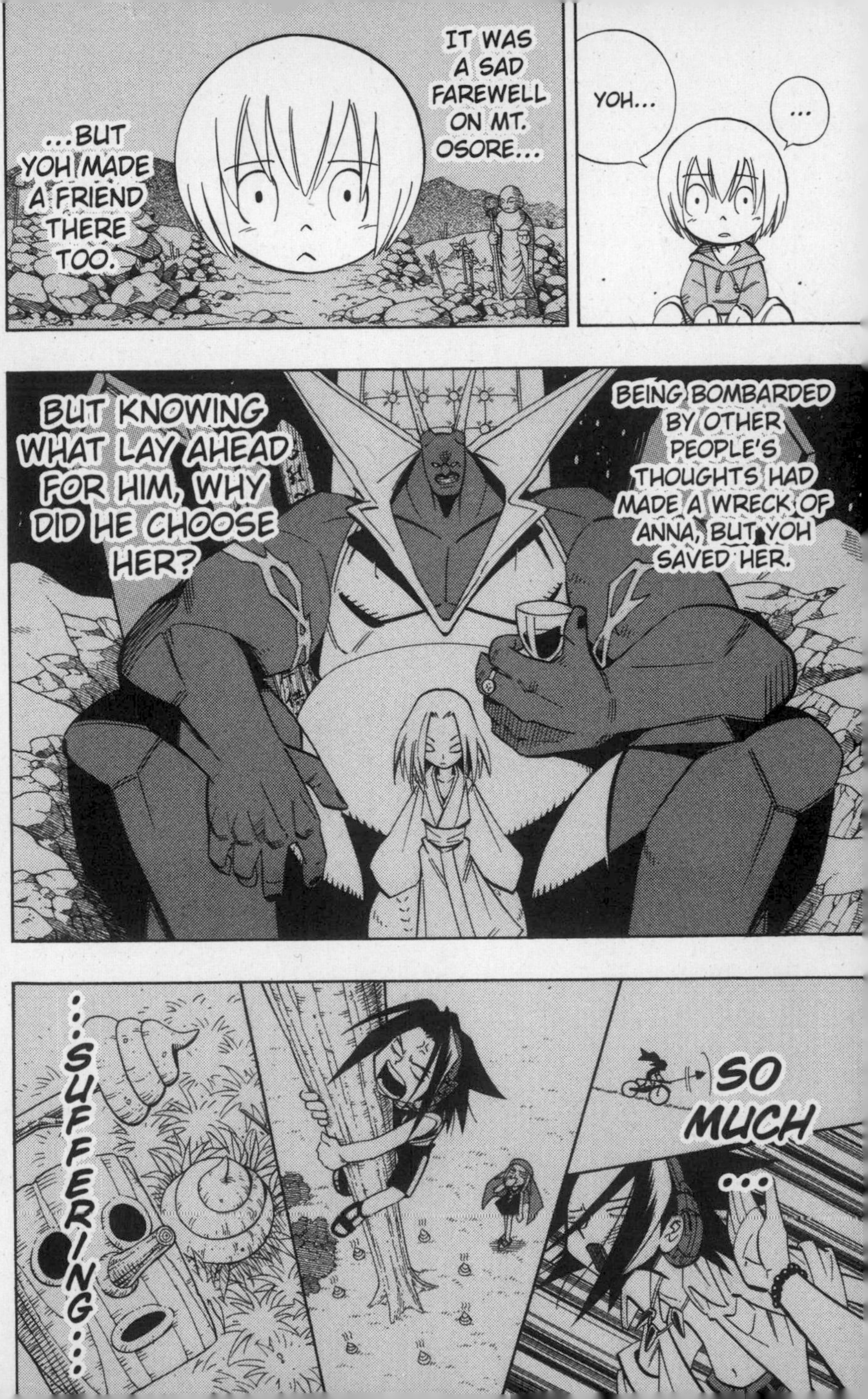
YOH...
...
IT WAS A SAD FAREWELL ON MT. OSORE...
...BUT YOH MADE A FRIEND THERE TOO.
BEING BOMBARDED BY OTHER PEOPLE'S THOUGHTS HAD MADE A WRECK OF ANNA, BUT YOH SAVED HER.
BUT KNOWING WHAT LAY AHEAD FOR HIM, WHY DID HE CHOOSE HER?
SO MUCH...
...SUFFERING...

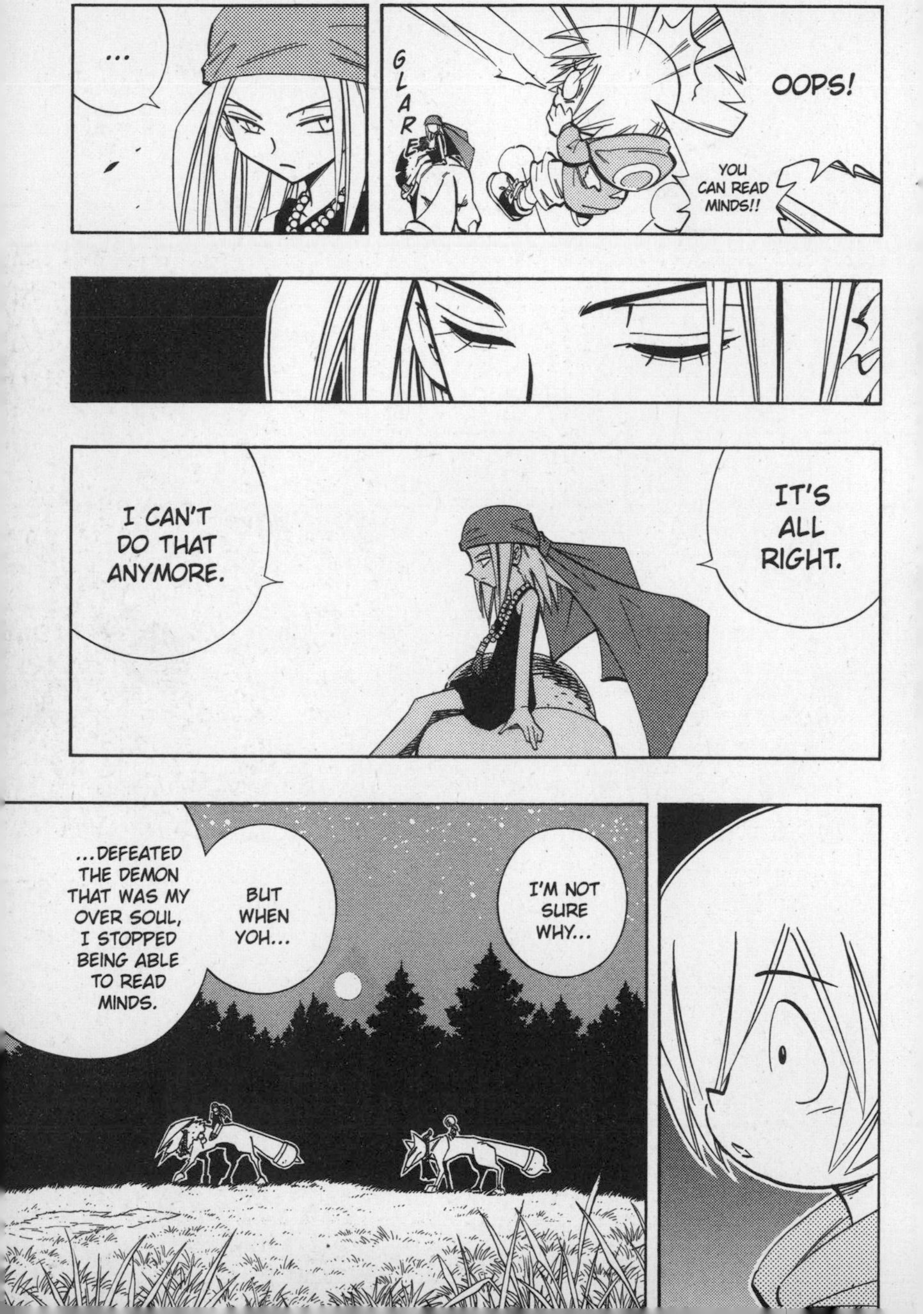
OOPS!
YOU CAN READ MINDS!!
GLARE
...
IT'S ALL RIGHT.
I CAN'T DO THAT ANYMORE.
I'M NOT SURE WHY...
BUT WHEN YOH...
...DEFEATED THE DEMON THAT WAS MY OVER SOUL, I STOPPED BEING ABLE TO READ MINDS.

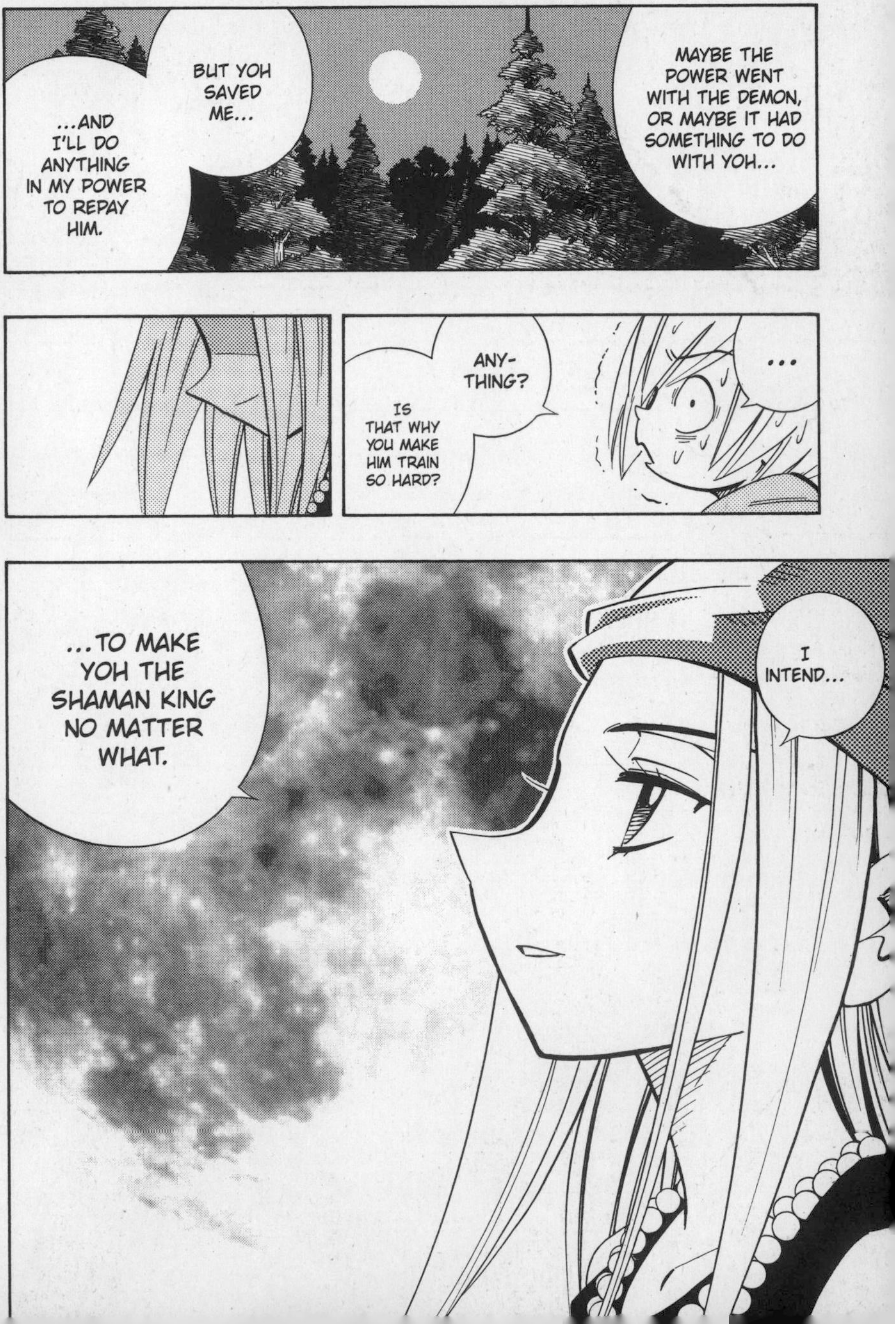
MAYBE THE POWER WENT WITH THE DEMON, OR MAYBE IT HAD SOMETHING TO DO WITH YOH...
BUT YOH SAVED ME...
...AND I'LL DO ANYTHING IN MY POWER TO REPAY HIM.
...
ANY-THING?
IS THAT WHY YOU MAKE HIM TRAIN SO HARD?
I INTEND...
...TO MAKE YOH THE SHAMAN KING NO MATTER WHAT.

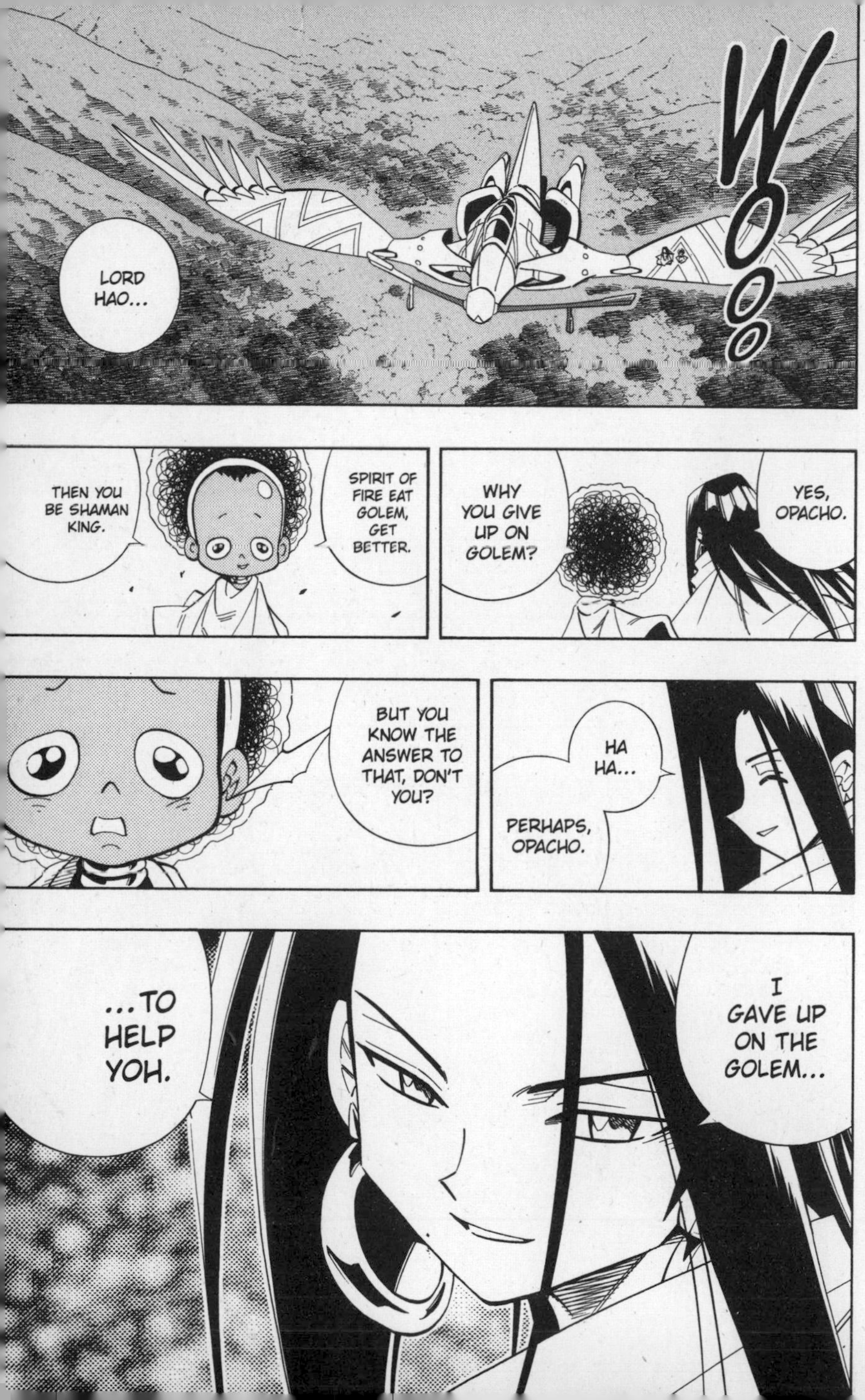
WOOOOO
LORD HAO...
YES, OPACHO.
WHY YOU GIVE UP ON GOLEM?
SPIRIT OF FIRE EAT GOLEM, GET BETTER.
THEN YOU BE SHAMAN KING.
HA HA...
PERHAPS, OPACHO.
BUT YOU KNOW THE ANSWER TO THAT, DON'T YOU?
I GAVE UP ON THE GOLEM...
...TO HELP YOH.

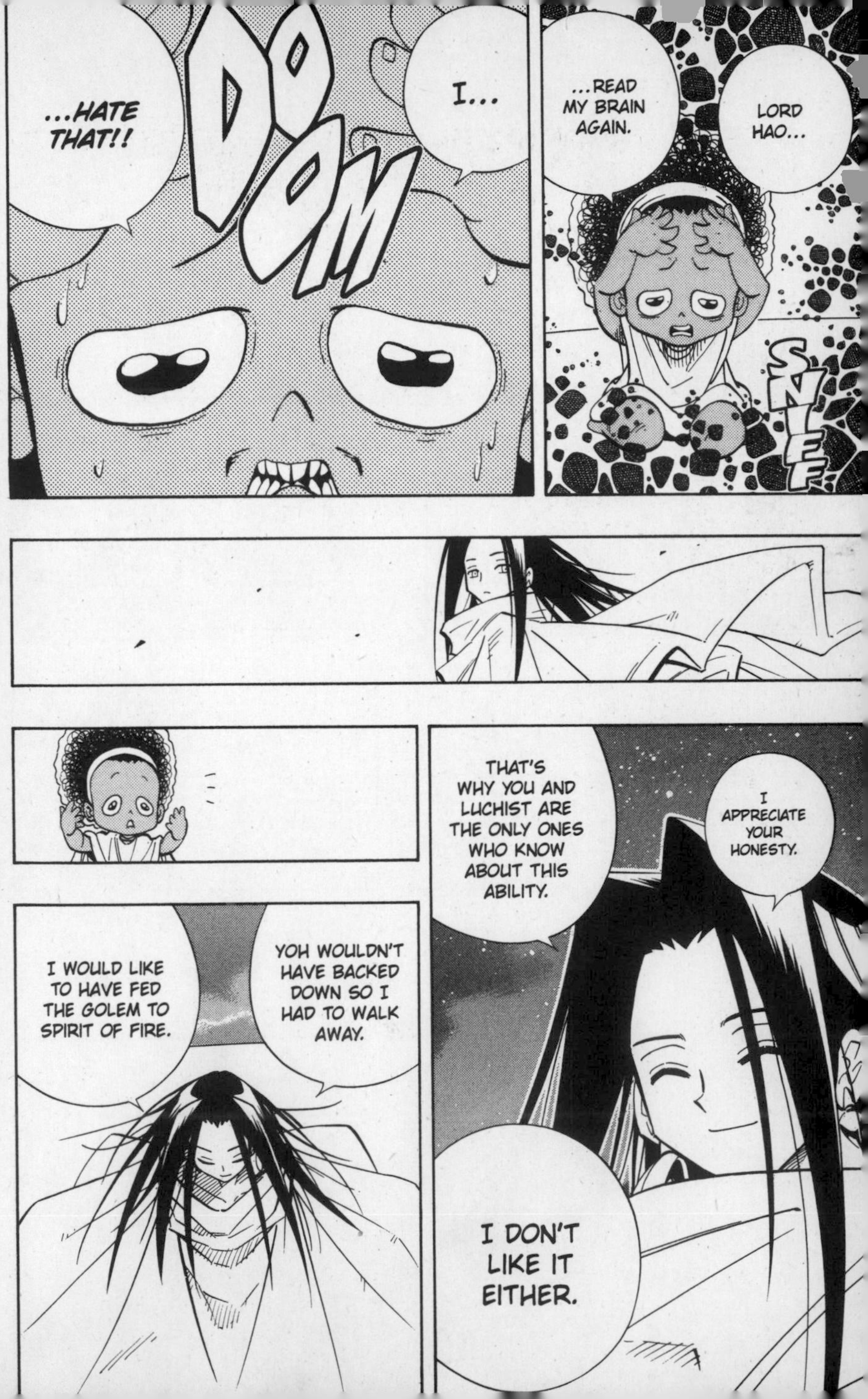
LORD HAO...
...READ MY BRAIN AGAIN.
SNIFF
I...
DOOM
...HATE THAT!!
I APPRECIATE YOUR HONESTY.
THAT'S WHY YOU AND LUCHIST ARE THE ONLY ONES WHO KNOW ABOUT THIS ABILITY.
I DON'T LIKE IT EITHER.
YOH WOULDN'T HAVE BACKED DOWN SO I HAD TO WALK AWAY.
I WOULD LIKE TO HAVE FED THE GOLEM TO SPIRIT OF FIRE.

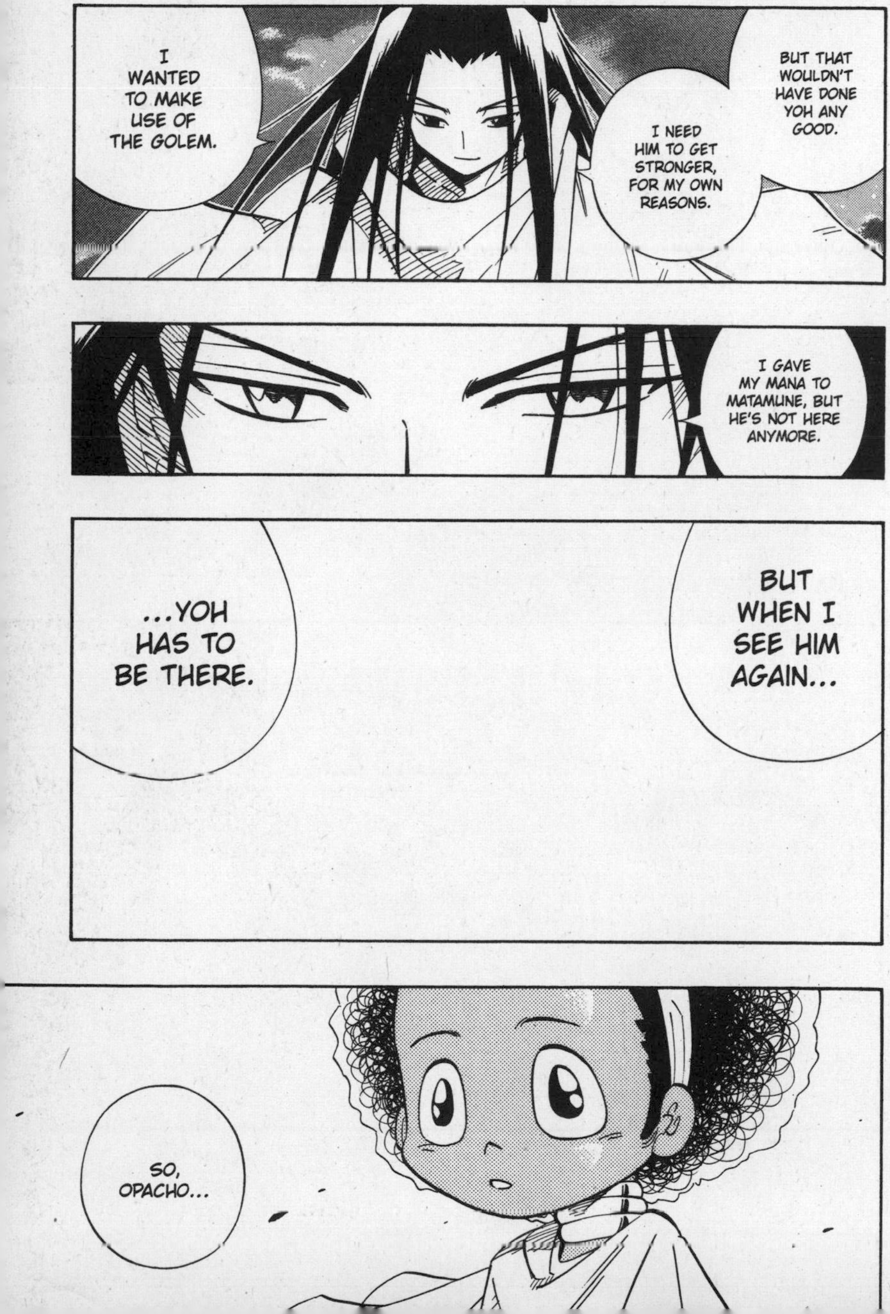
BUT THAT WOULDN'T HAVE DONE YOH ANY GOOD.
I NEED HIM TO GET STRONGER, FOR MY OWN REASONS.
I WANTED TO MAKE USE OF THE GOLEM.
I GAVE MY MANA TO MATAMUNE, BUT HE'S NOT HERE ANYMORE.
BUT WHEN I SEE HIM AGAIN...
...YOH HAS TO BE THERE.
SO, OPACHO...

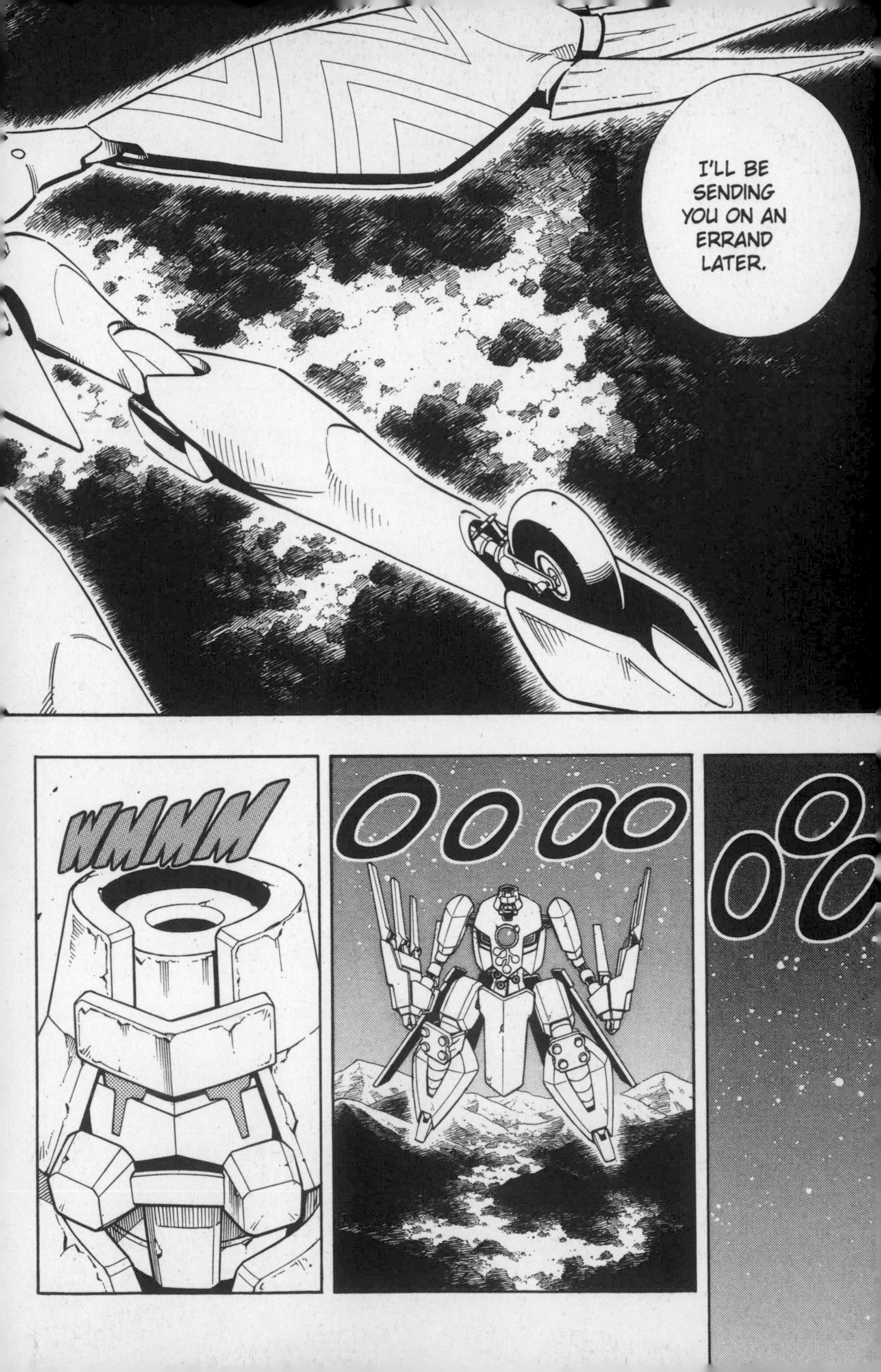
I'LL BE SENDING YOU ON AN ERRAND LATER.
WMMM

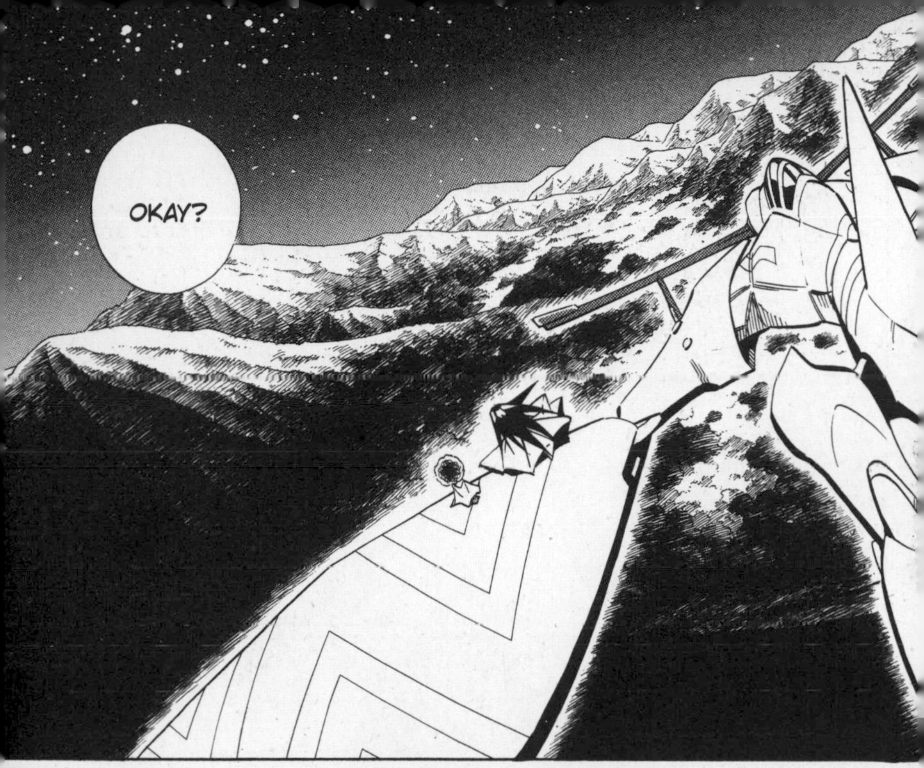
OKAY?

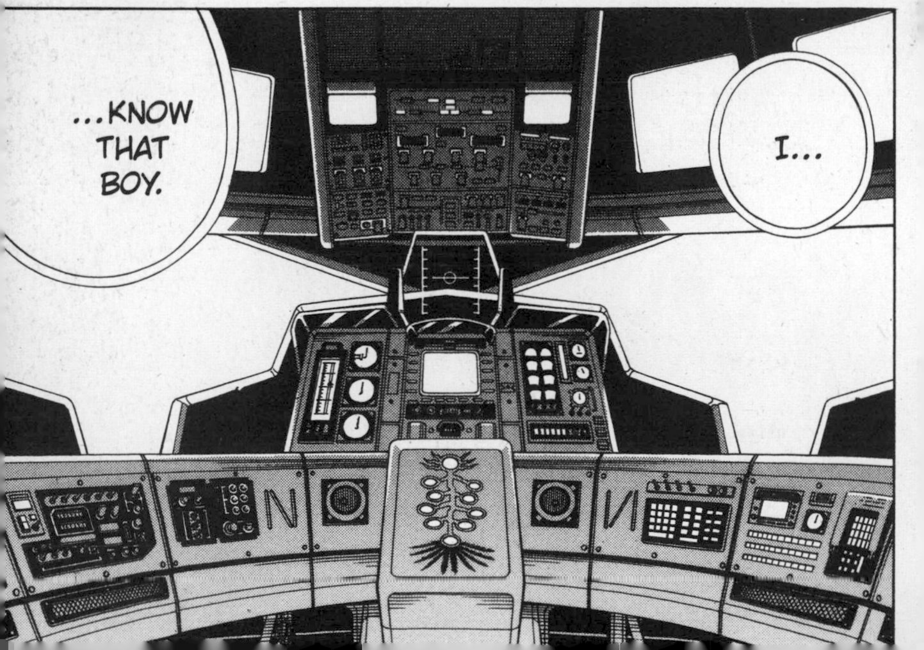
I...
...KNOW THAT BOY.

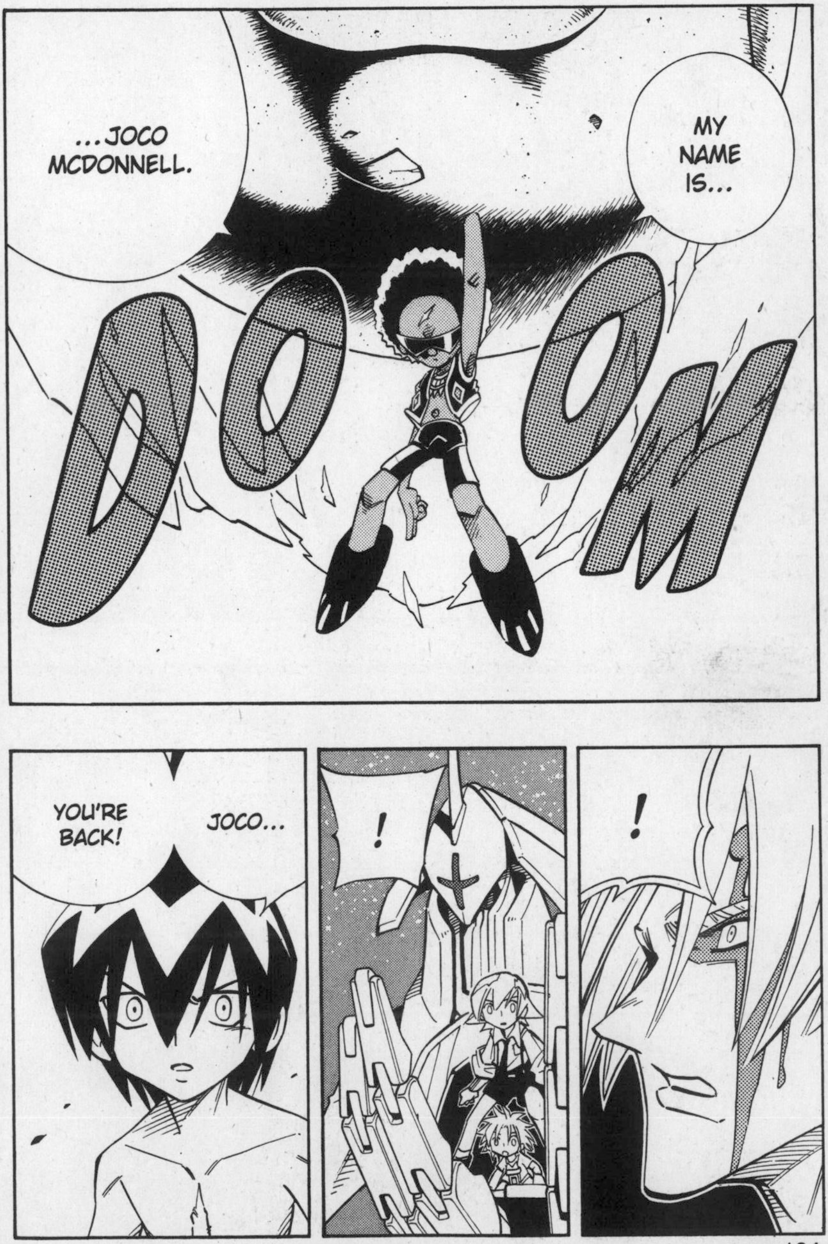
MY NAME IS...
...JOCO MCDONNELL.
DOOM
!
!
JOCO...
YOU'RE BACK!

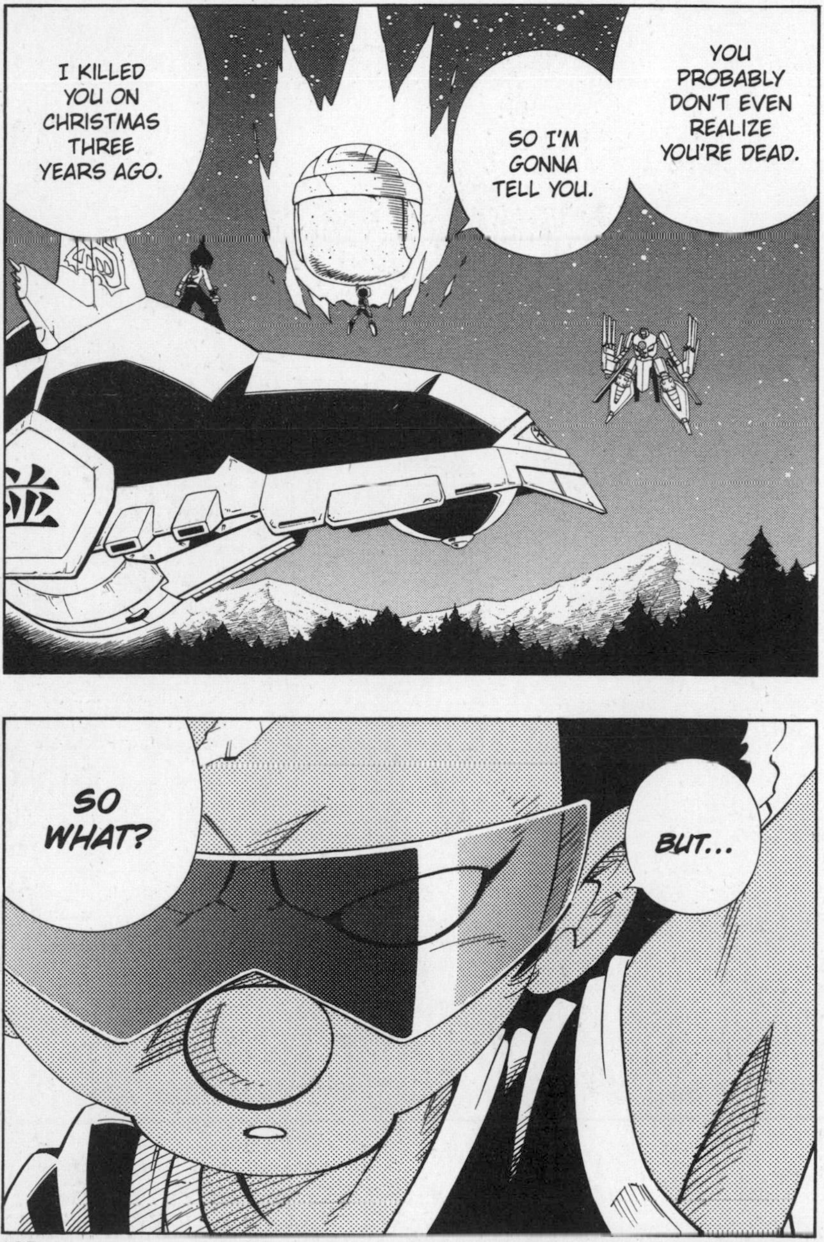
YOU PROBABLY DON'T EVEN REALIZE YOU'RE DEAD.
SO I'M GONNA TELL YOU.
I KILLED YOU ON CHRISTMAS THREE YEARS AGO.
BUT...
SO WHAT?

SHAMAN KING ITEM FILE No.59

2001
(JAN)

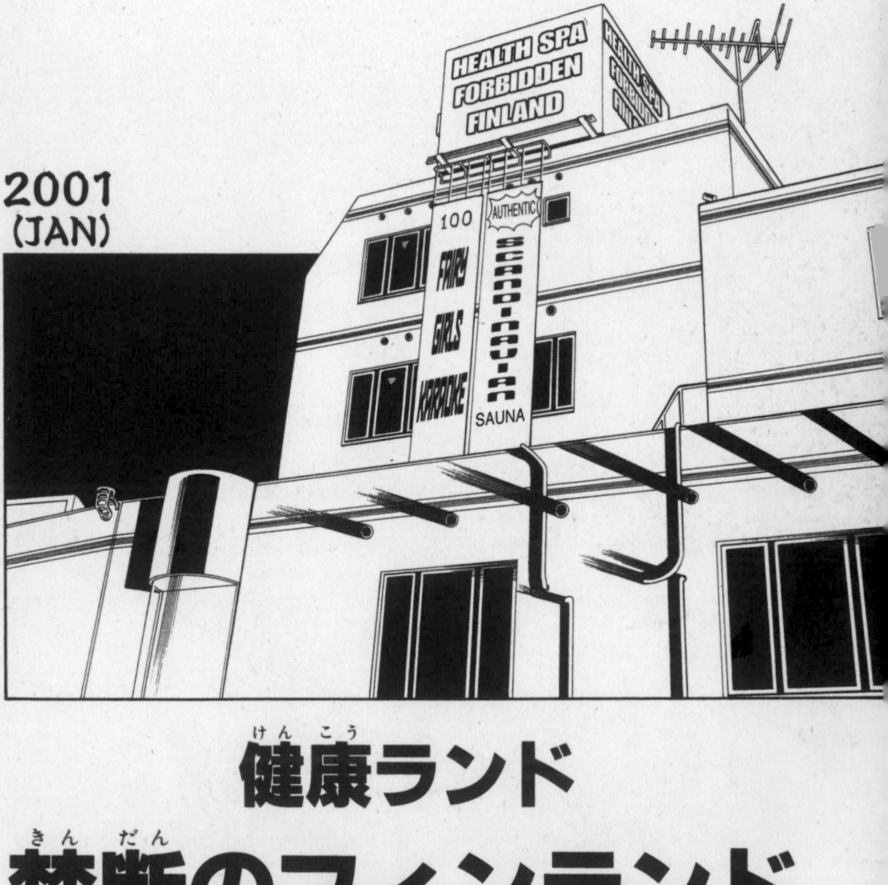
HEALTH SPA
FORBIDDEN
FINLAND
100
FAIRY
GIRLS
KARAOKE
AUTHENTIC
SCANDINAVIAN
SAUNA

健康ランド
禁断のフィンランド

HEALTH SPA

FORBIDDEN FINLAND

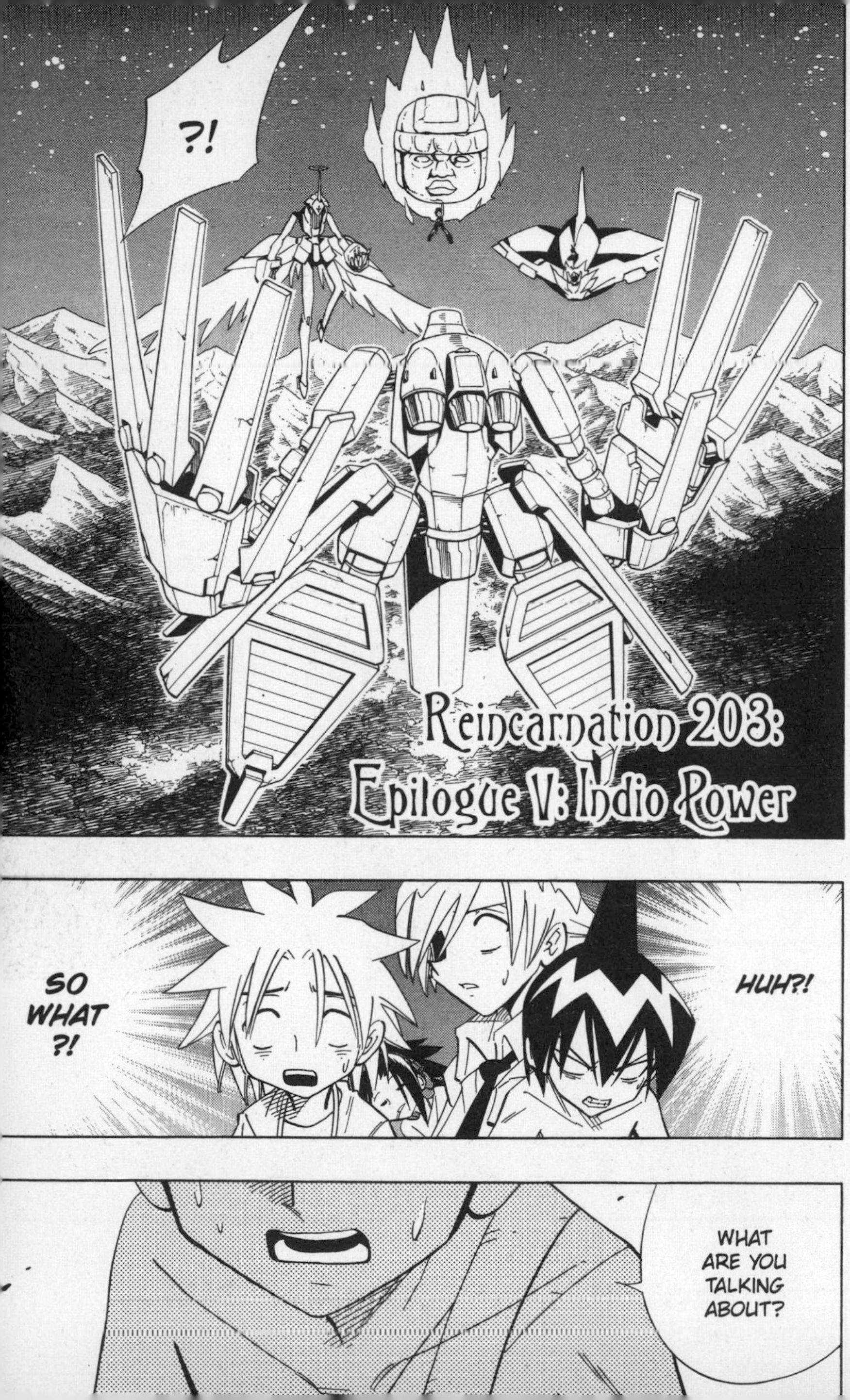
?!
Reincarnation 203:
Epilogue V: Indio Power
HUH?!
SO WHAT ?!
WHAT ARE YOU TALKING ABOUT?

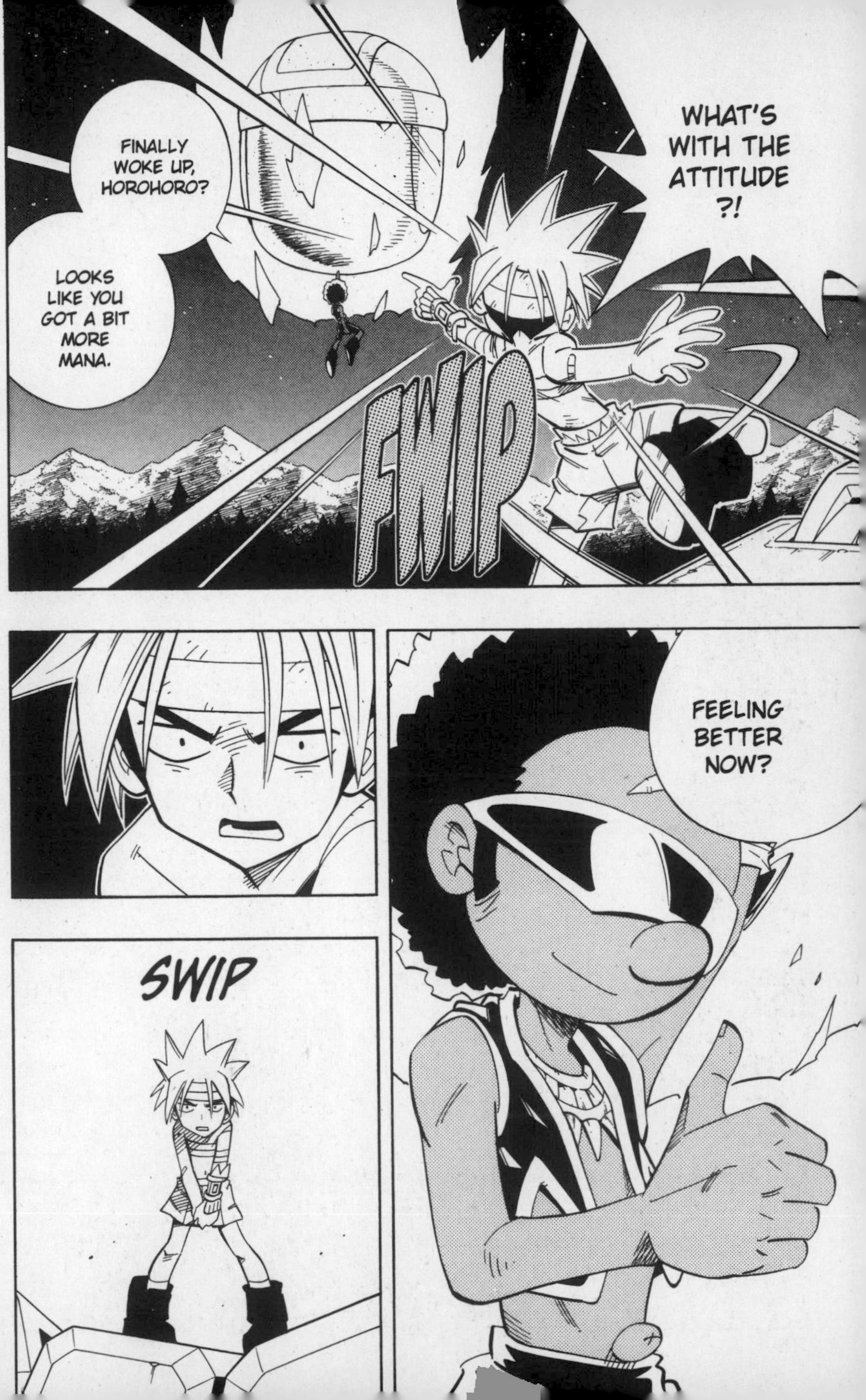
WHAT'S WITH THE ATTITUDE ?!
FINALLY WOKE UP, HOROHORO?
LOOKS LIKE YOU GOT A BIT MORE MANA.
FWIP
FEELING BETTER NOW?
SWIP

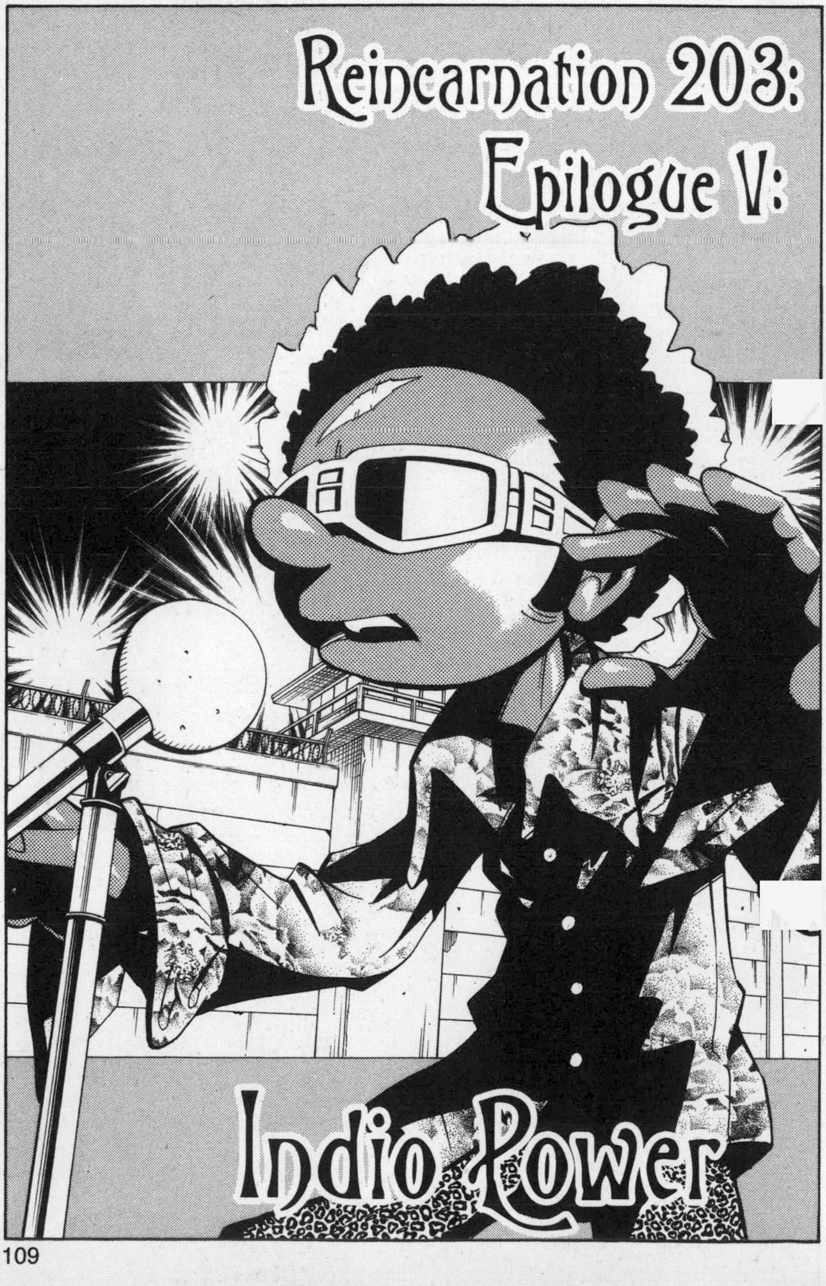
Reincarnation 203:
Epilogue V:
Indio Power

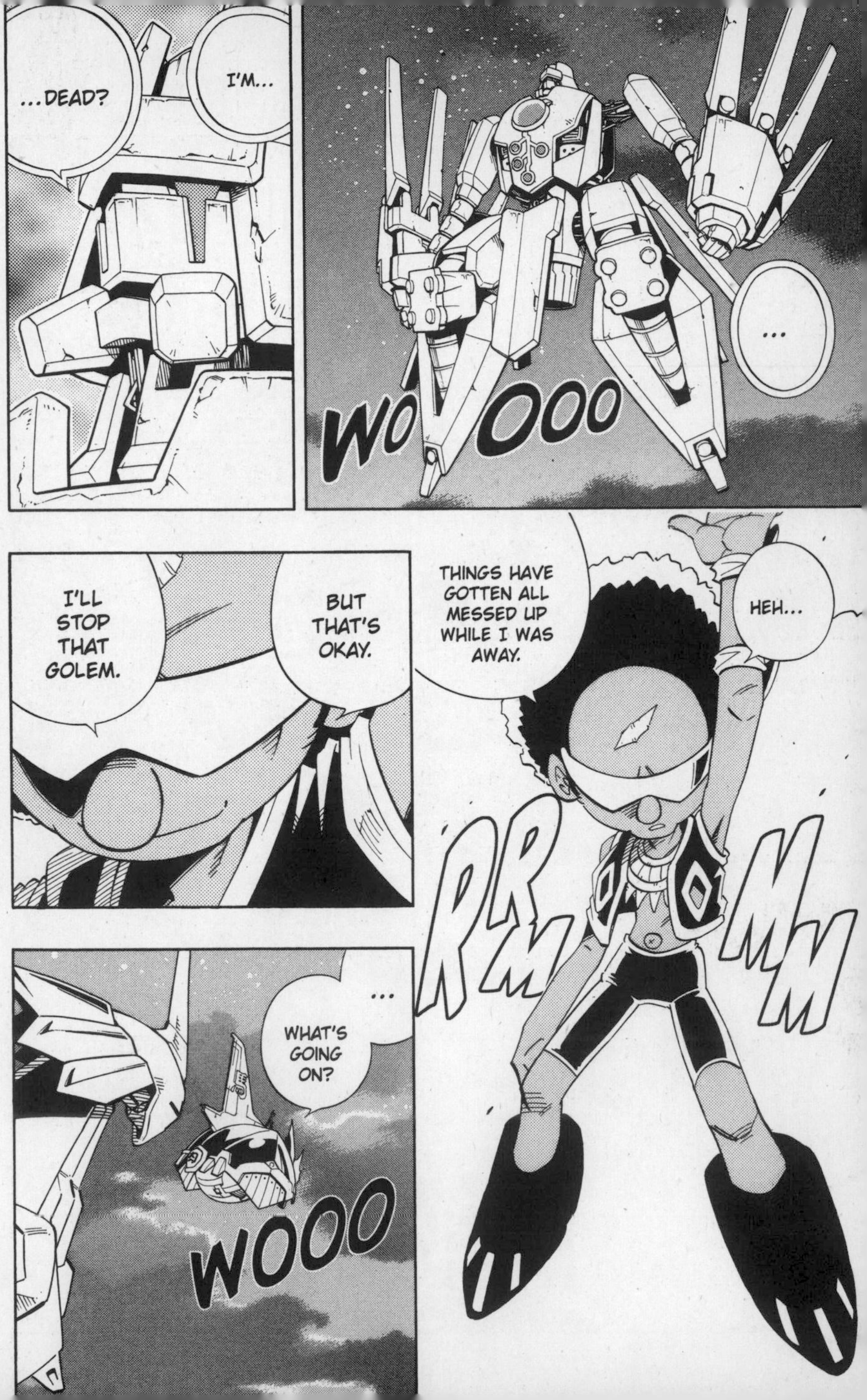
...
WO OOO
I'M...
...DEAD?
HEH...
THINGS HAVE GOTTEN ALL MESSED UP WHILE I WAS AWAY.
RRMMMMM
BUT THAT'S OKAY.
I'LL STOP THAT GOLEM.
...
WHAT'S GOING ON?
WOOO

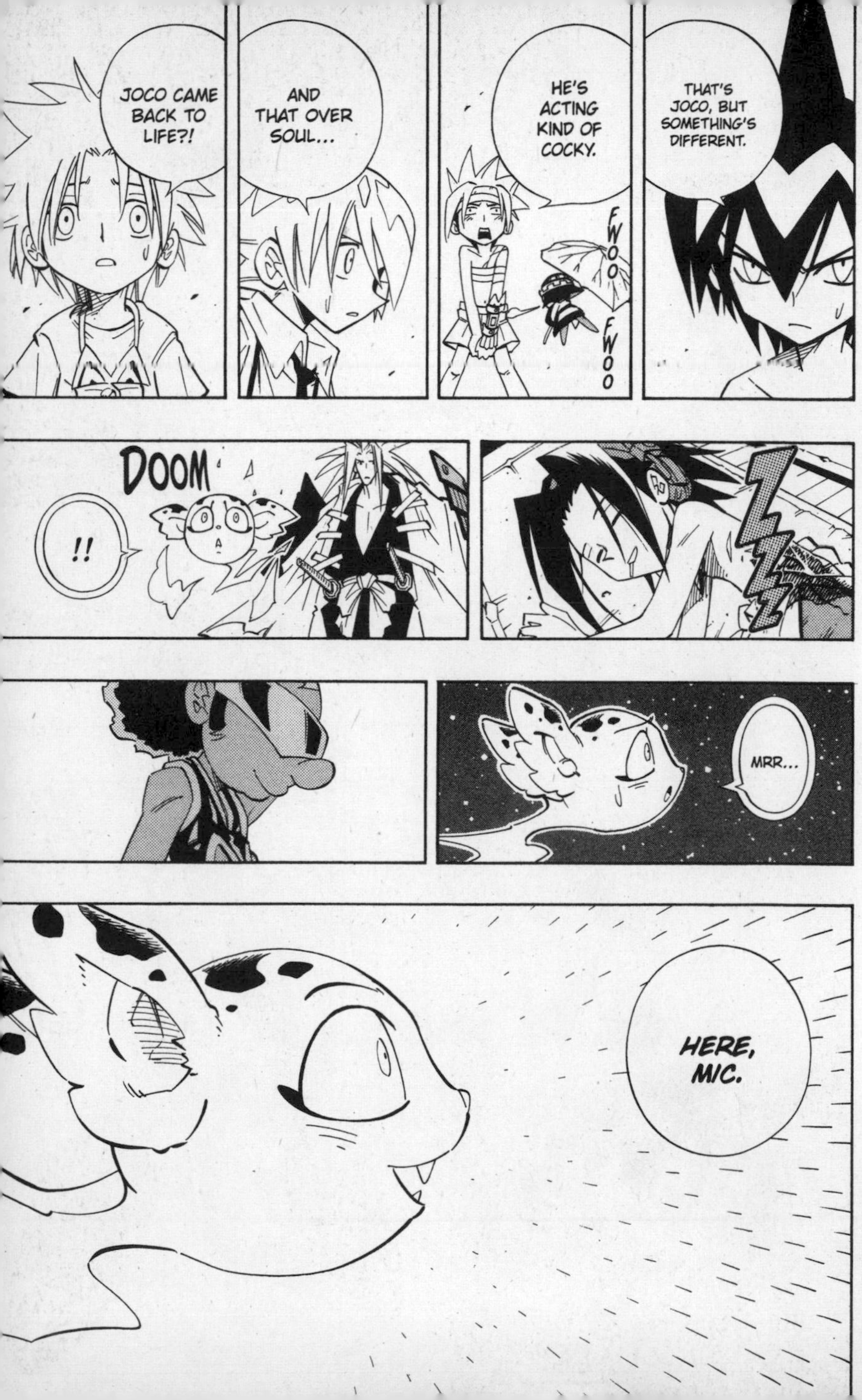
THAT'S JOCO, BUT SOMETHING'S DIFFERENT.
HE'S ACTING KIND OF COCKY.
FWOO FWOO
AND THAT OVER SOUL...
JOCO CAME BACK TO LIFE?!
DOOM
!!
MRR...
HERE, MIC.

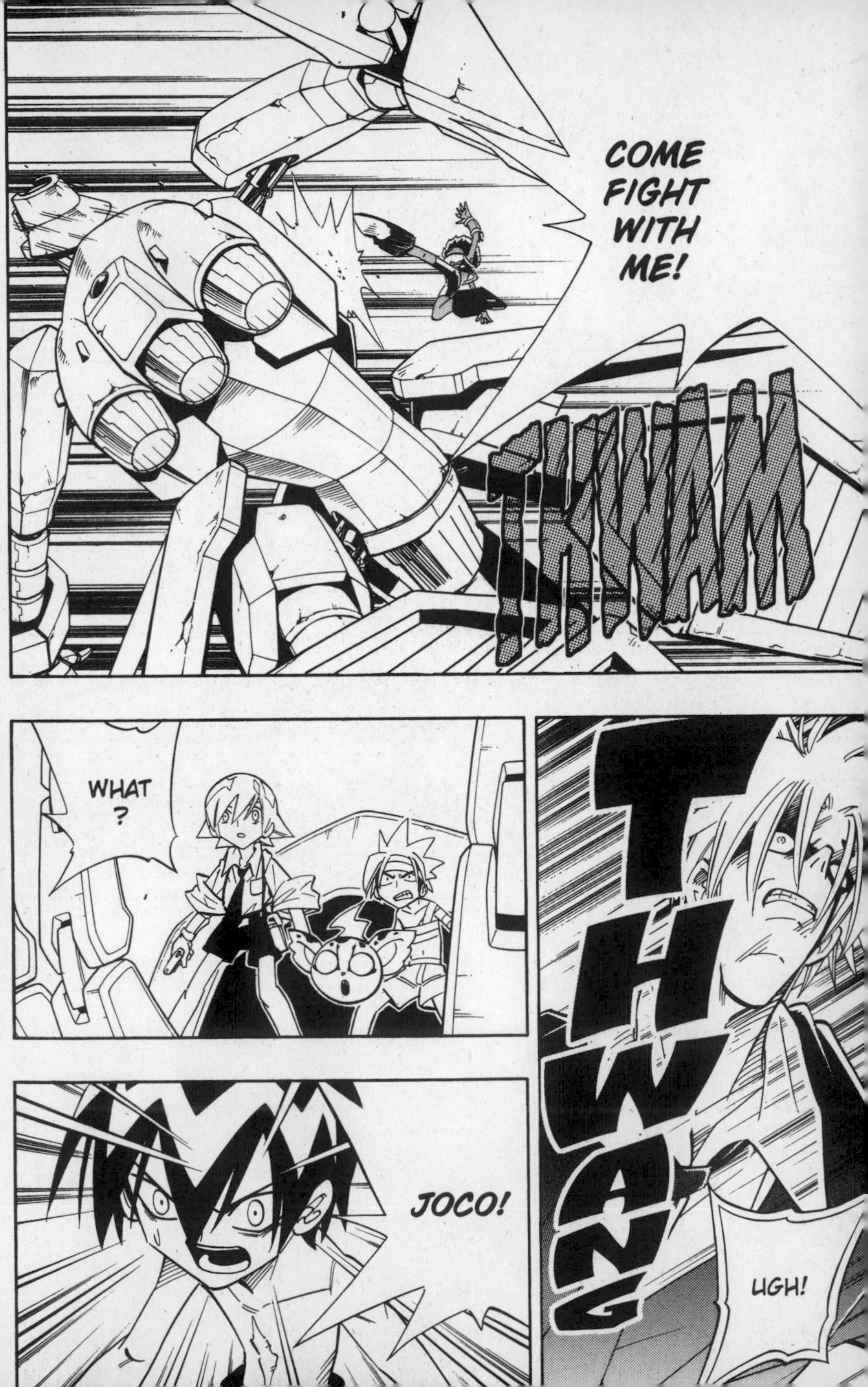
COME FIGHT WITH ME!
THWAM
THWANG
UGH!
WHAT ?
JOCO!

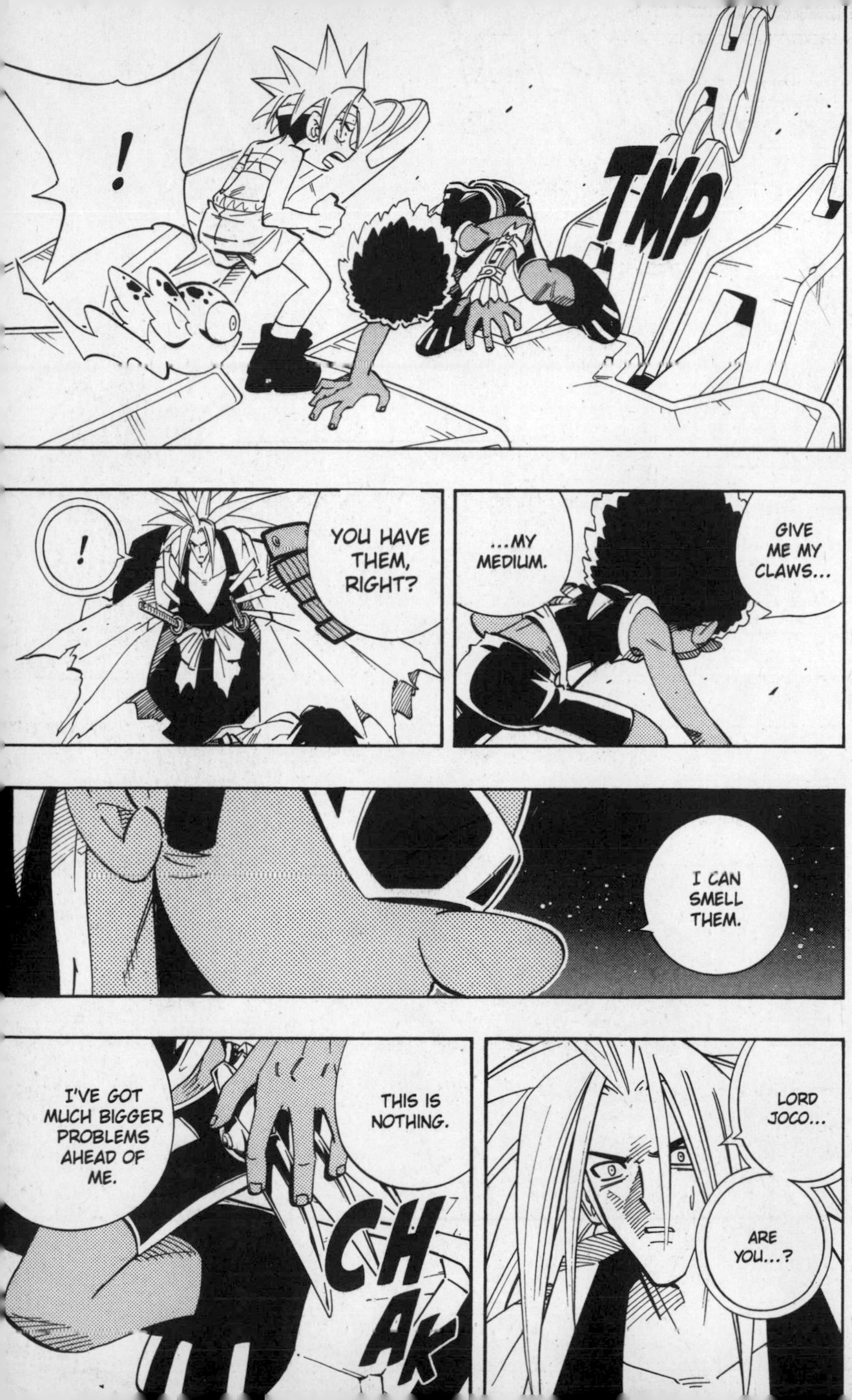
TMP
!
GIVE ME MY CLAWS...
...MY MEDIUM.
YOU HAVE THEM, RIGHT?
!
I CAN SMELL THEM.
LORD JOCO...
ARE YOU...?
THIS IS NOTHING.
I'VE GOT MUCH BIGGER PROBLEMS AHEAD OF ME.
CHAK

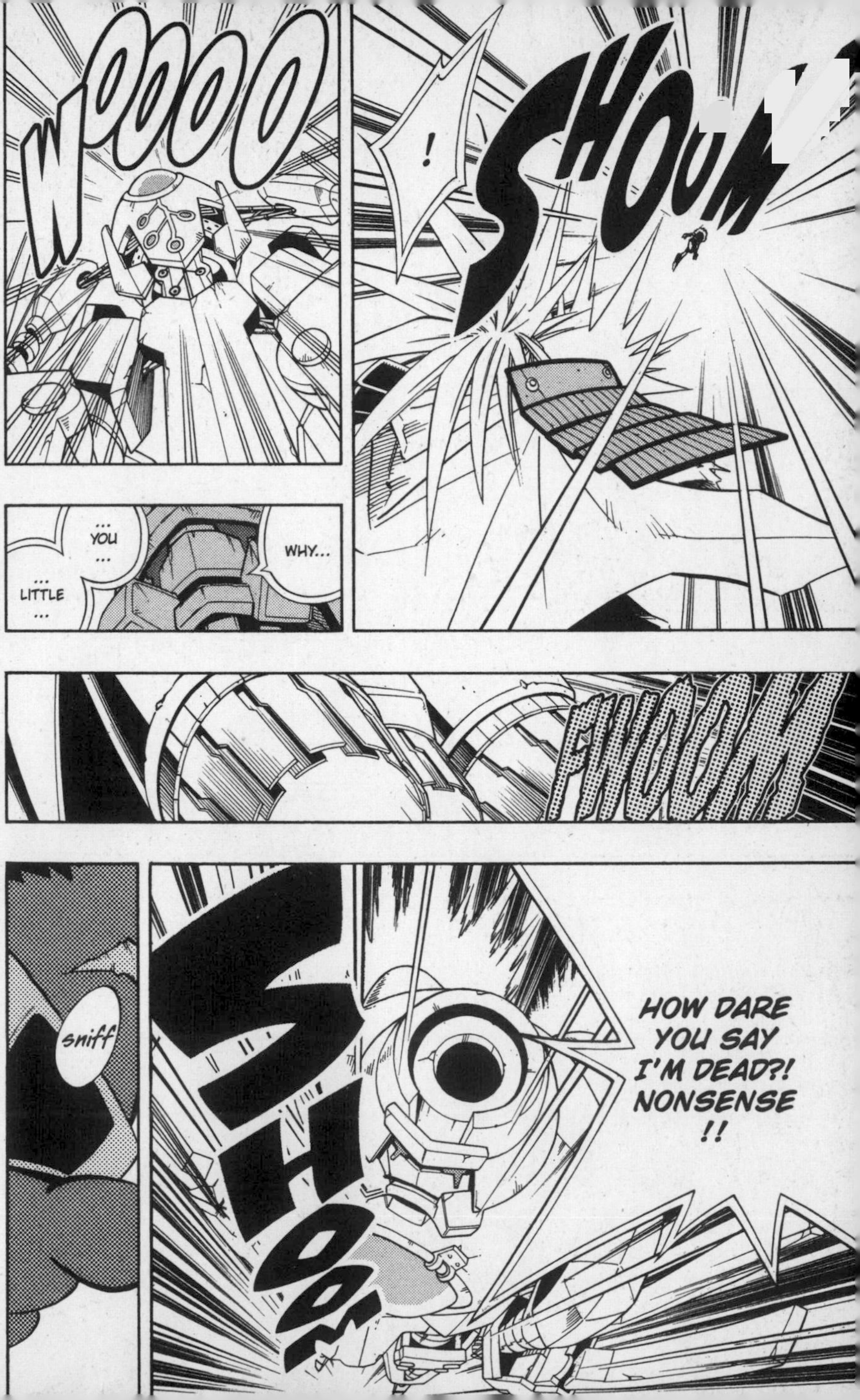
SHOOM
!
WOOOO
WHY...
...YOU...
...LITTLE...
FWOOM
SHOOO
HOW DARE YOU SAY I'M DEAD?! NONSENSE !!
sniff

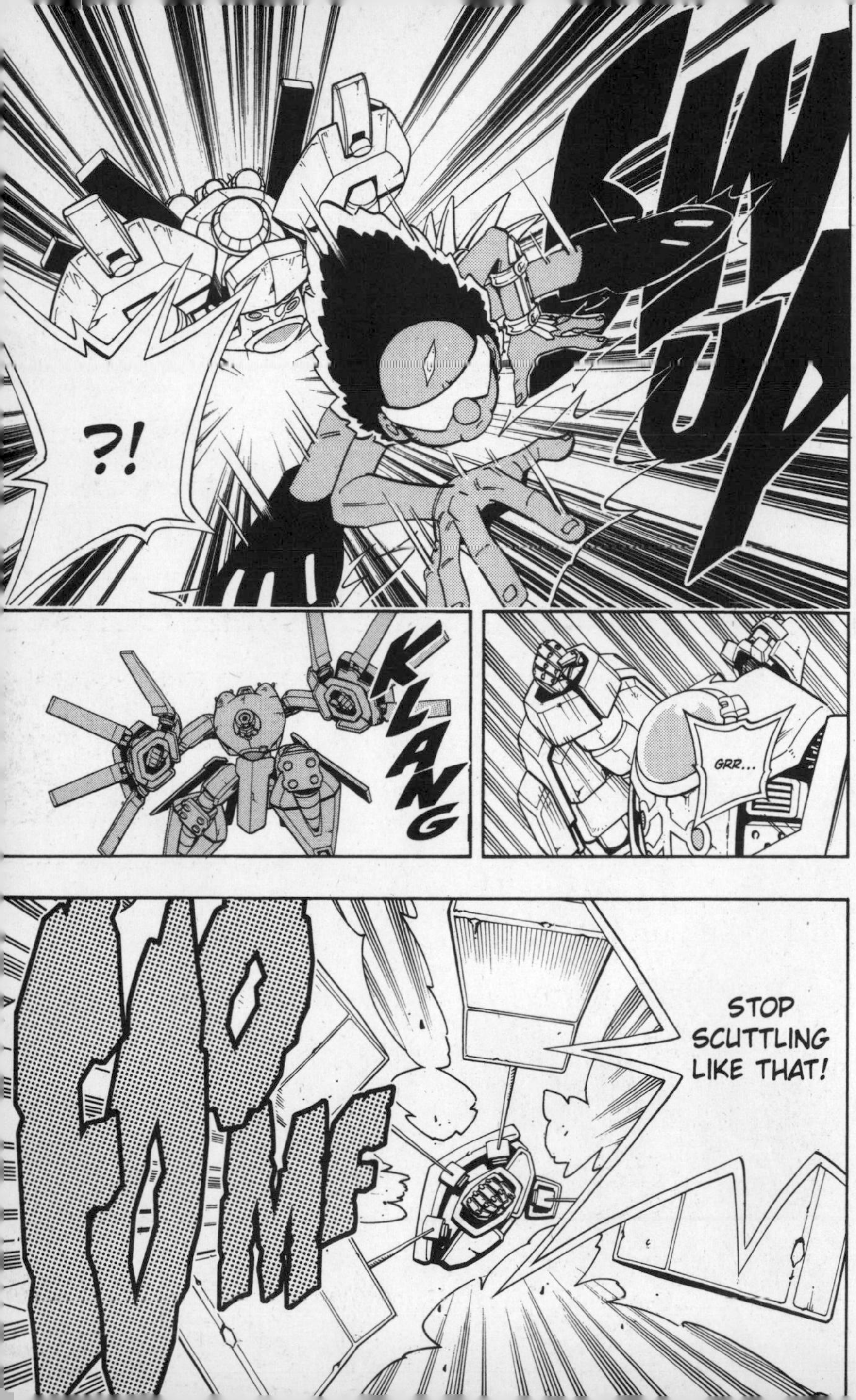
?!
GRR...
KLANG
STOP SCUTTLING LIKE THAT!

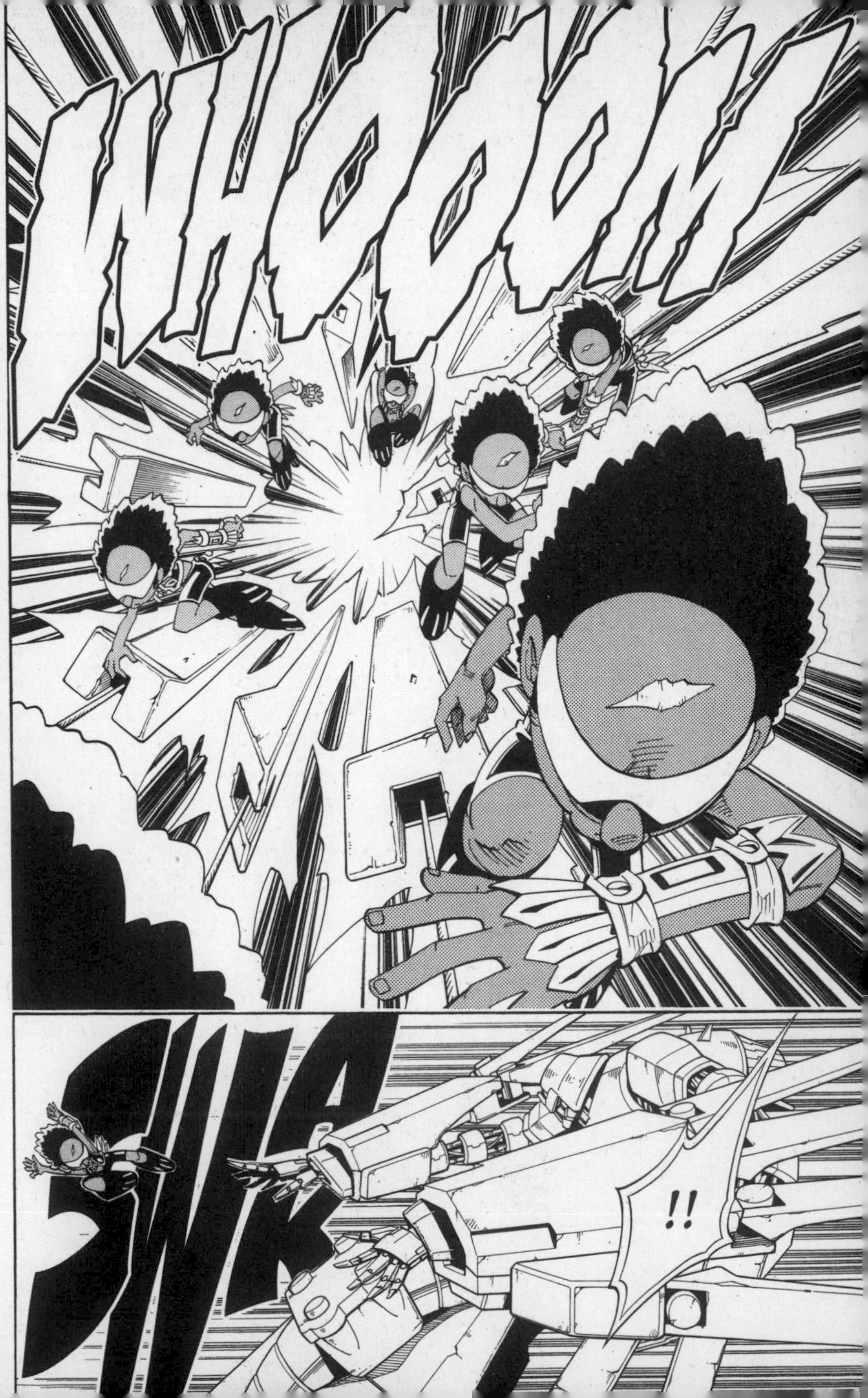
WHOOM
!!

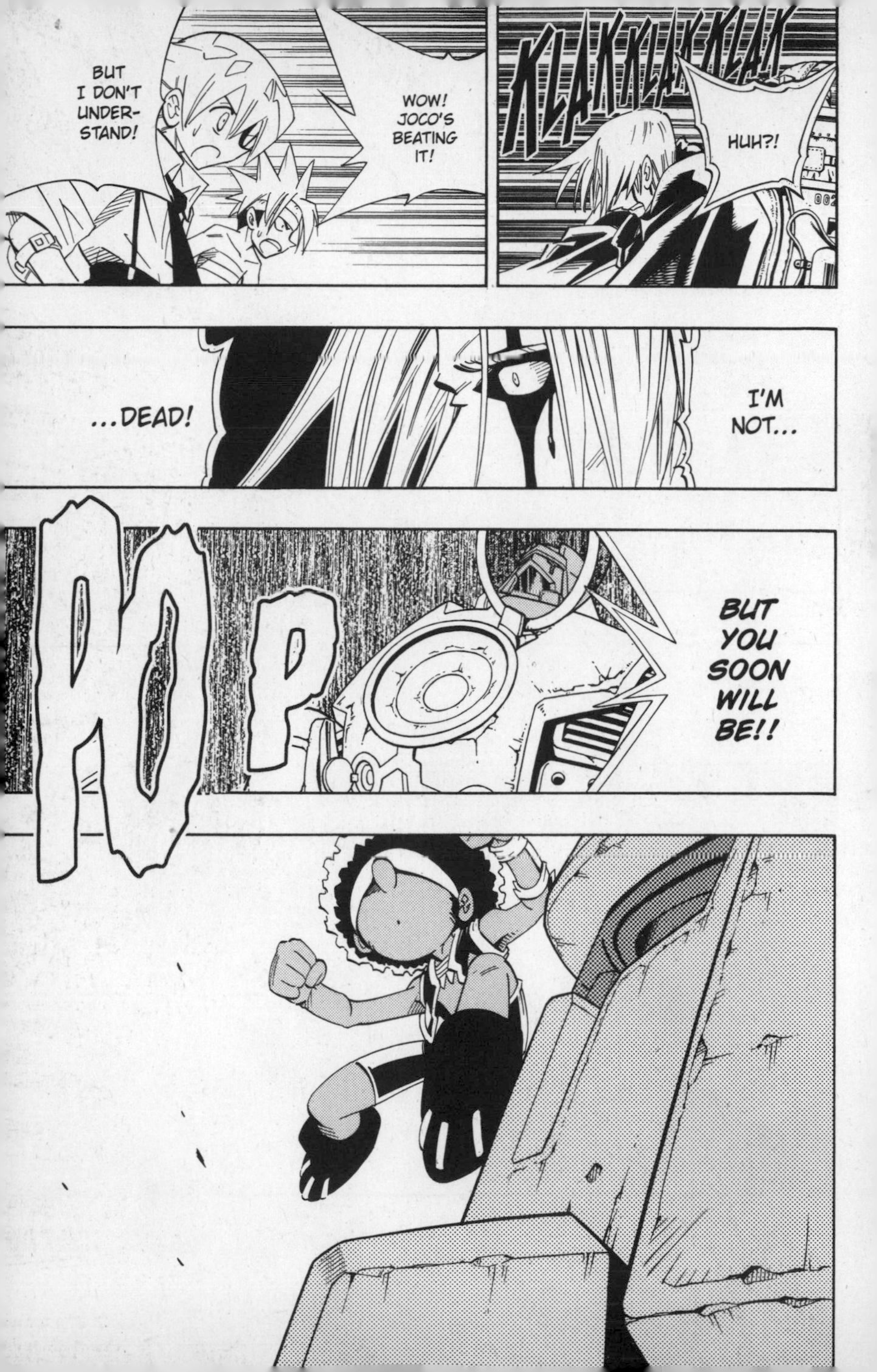
KLAK KLAK KLAK
HUH?!
WOW! JOCO'S BEATING IT!
BUT I DON'T UNDER-STAND!
I'M NOT...
...DEAD!
BUT YOU SOON WILL BE!!
HOP

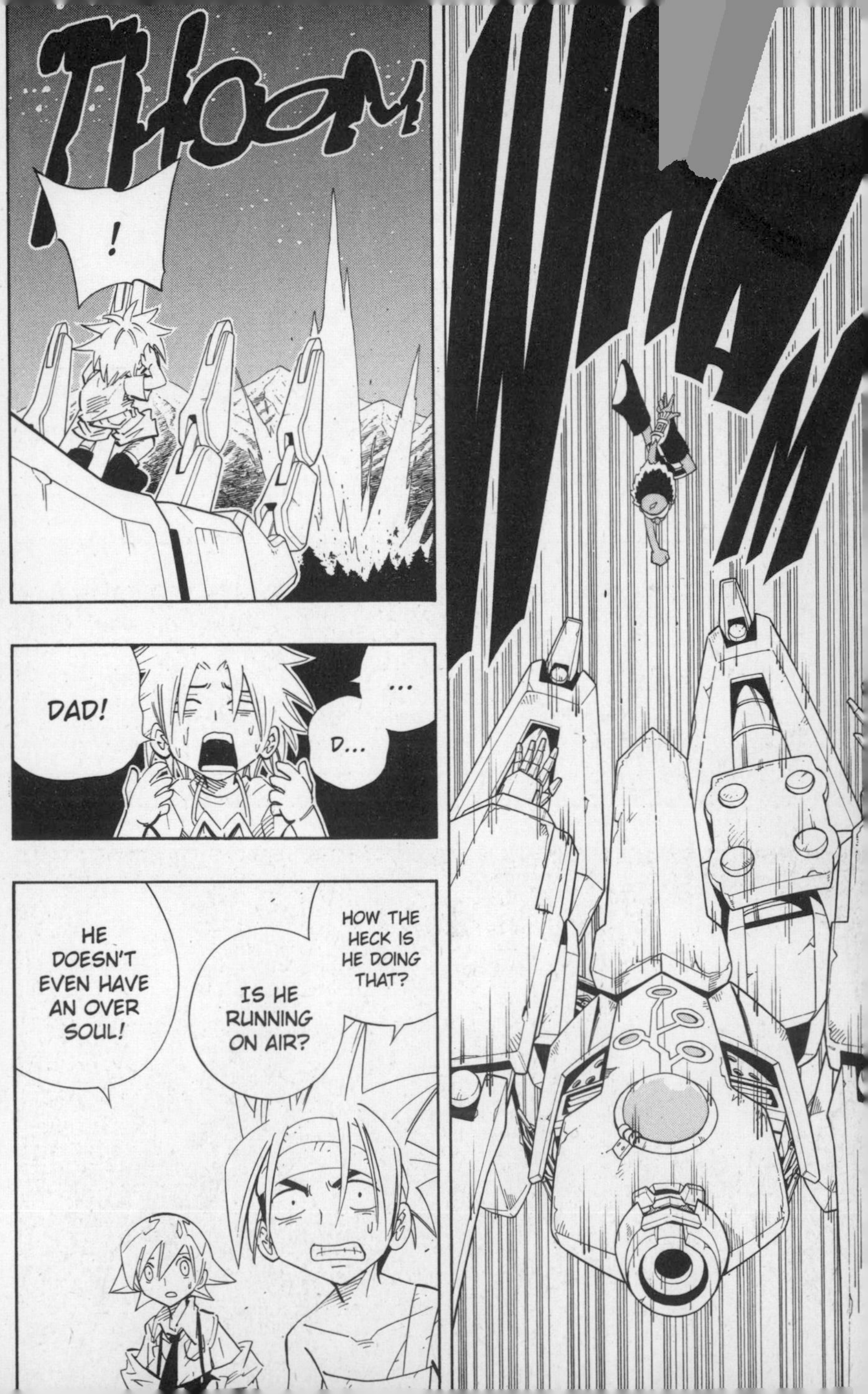
WHAM
THOOM
!
...
D...
DAD!
HOW THE HECK IS HE DOING THAT?
IS HE RUNNING ON AIR?
HE DOESN'T EVEN HAVE AN OVER SOUL!

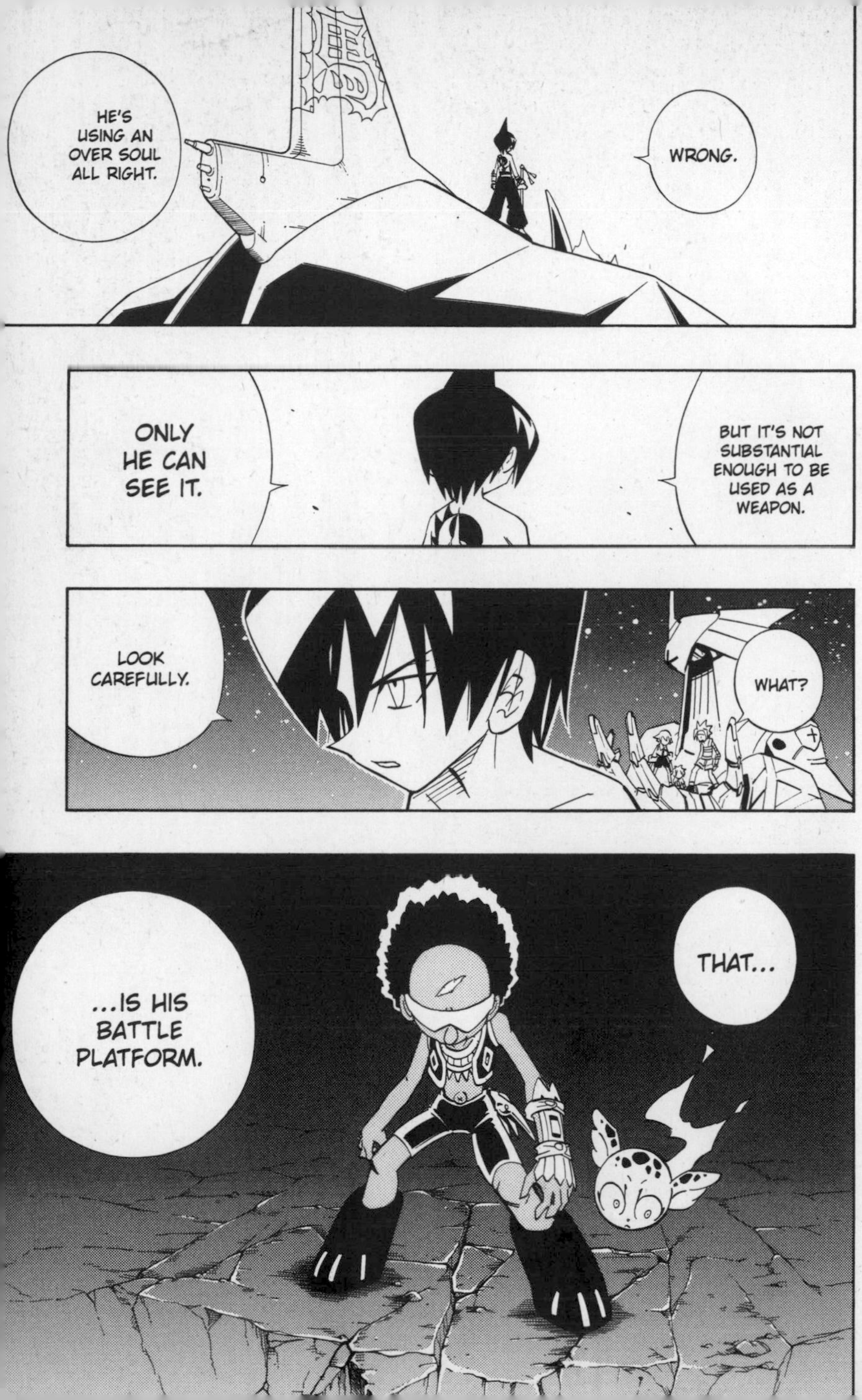
WRONG.
HE'S USING AN OVER SOUL ALL RIGHT.
BUT IT'S NOT SUBSTANTIAL ENOUGH TO BE USED AS A WEAPON.
ONLY HE CAN SEE IT.
WHAT?
LOOK CAREFULLY.
THAT...
...IS HIS BATTLE PLATFORM.

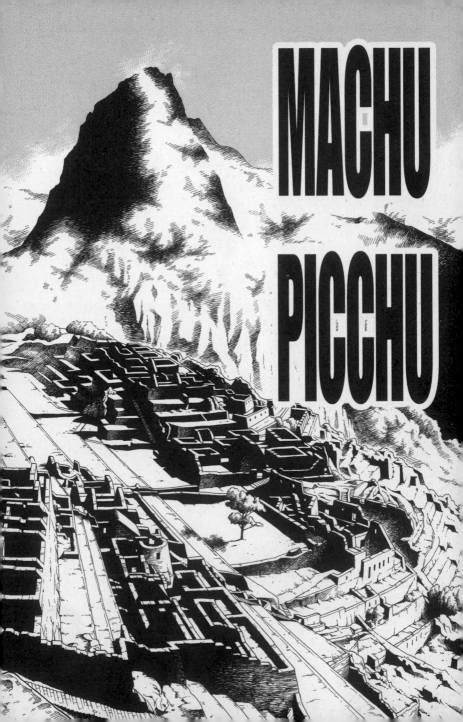

MACHU

PICCHU

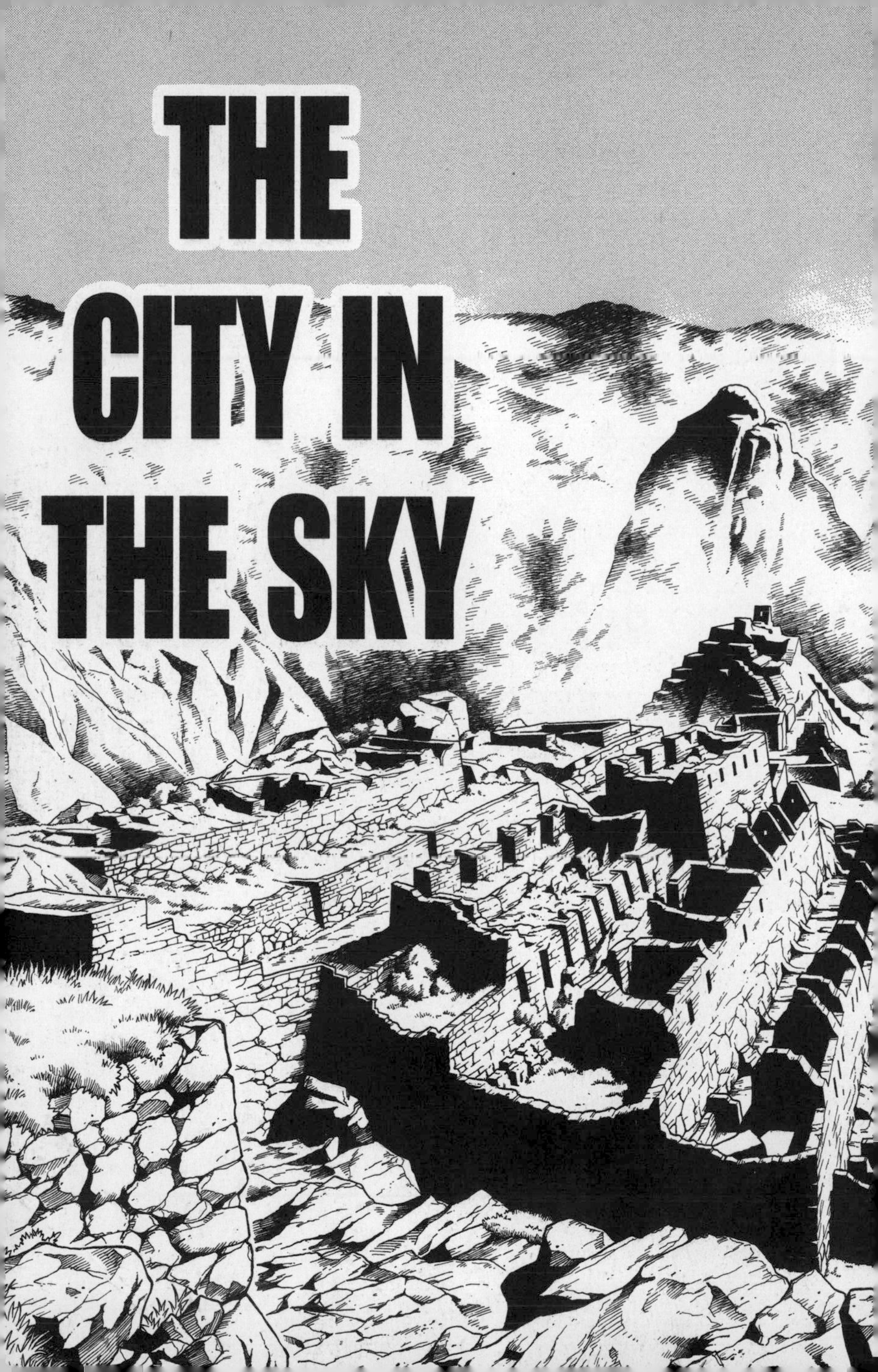
THE CITY IN THE SKY

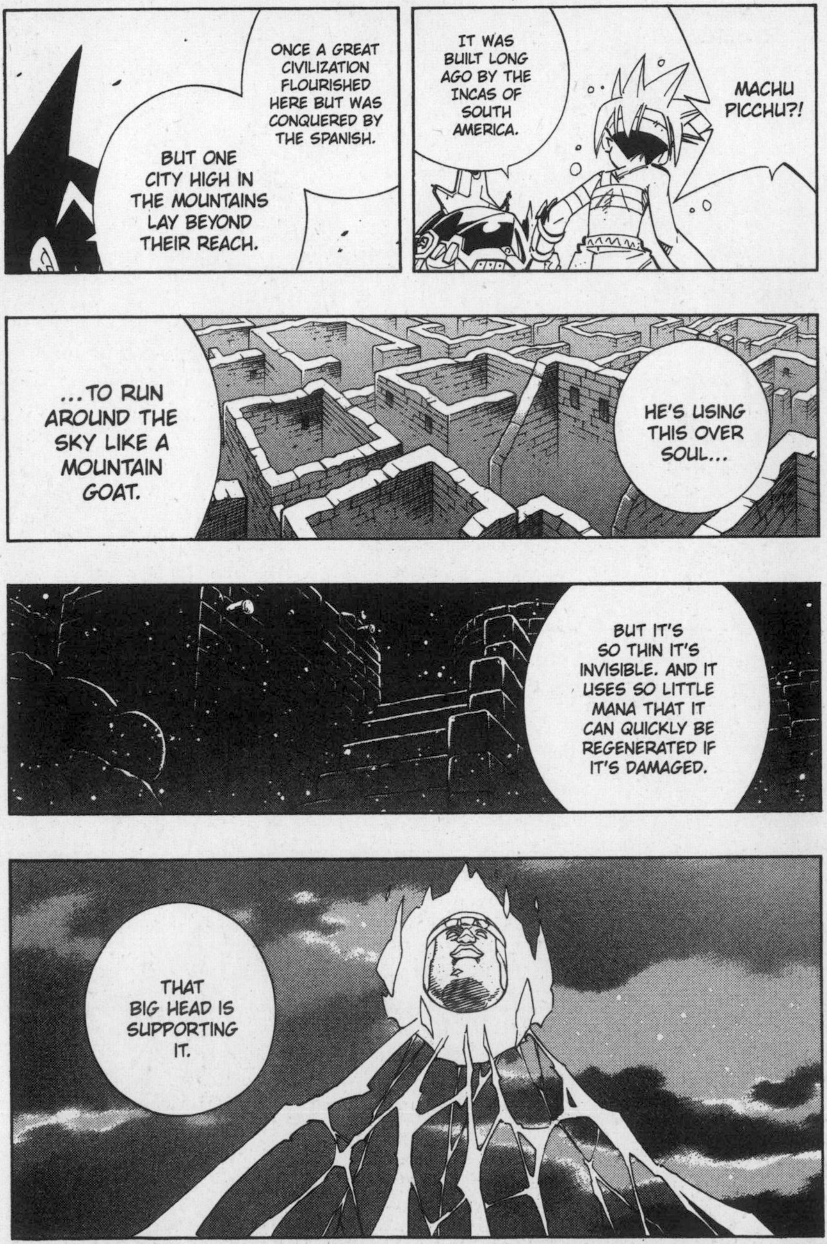
MACHU PICCHU?!
IT WAS BUILT LONG AGO BY THE INCAS OF SOUTH AMERICA.
ONCE A GREAT CIVILIZATION FLOURISHED HERE BUT WAS CONQUERED BY THE SPANISH.
BUT ONE CITY HIGH IN THE MOUNTAINS LAY BEYOND THEIR REACH.
HE'S USING THIS OVER SOUL...
...TO RUN AROUND THE SKY LIKE A MOUNTAIN GOAT.
BUT IT'S SO THIN IT'S INVISIBLE. AND IT USES SO LITTLE MANA THAT IT CAN QUICKLY BE REGENERATED IF IT'S DAMAGED.
THAT BIG HEAD IS SUPPORTING IT.

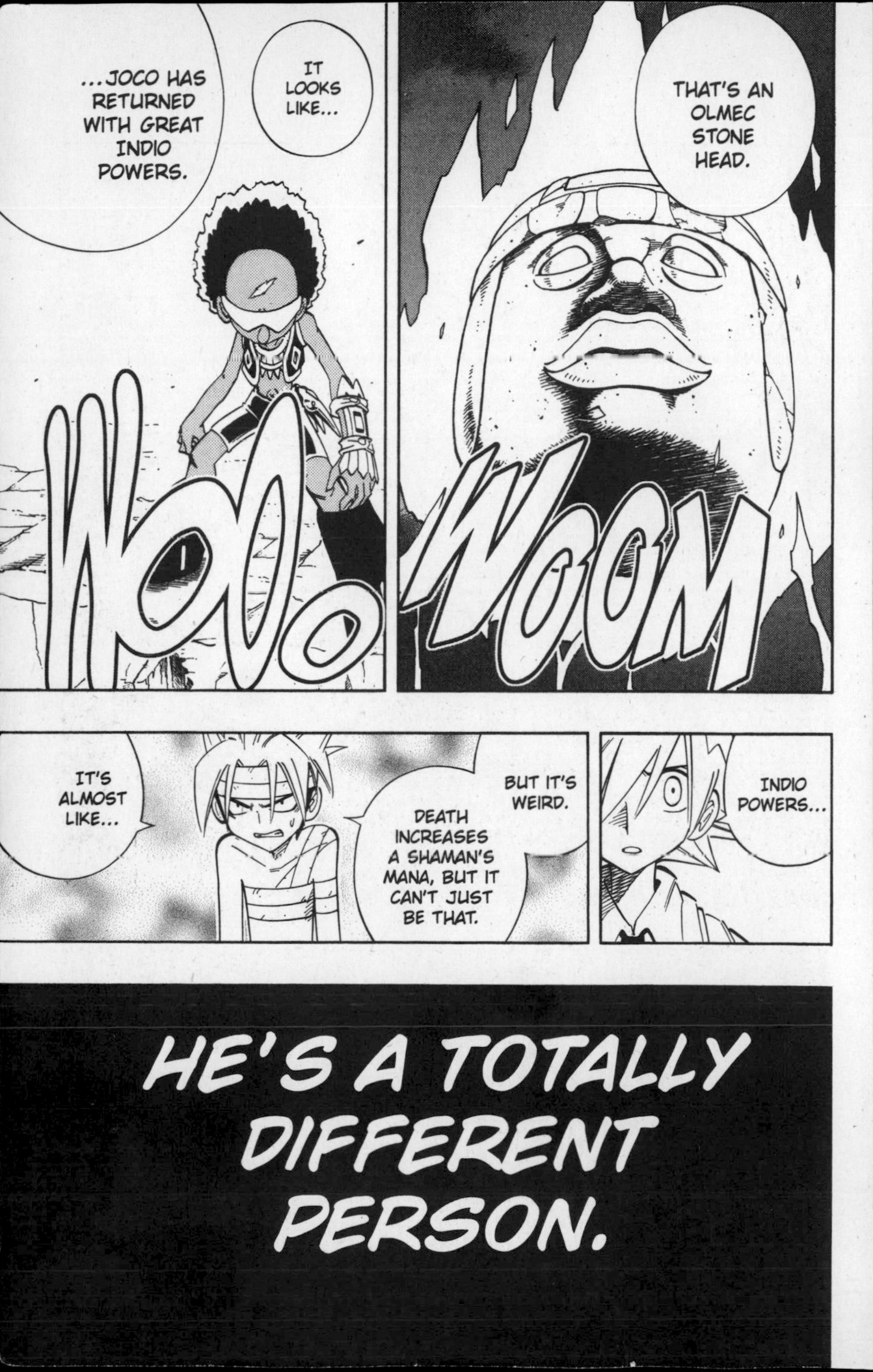
THAT'S AN OLMEC STONE HEAD.
IT LOOKS LIKE...
...JOCO HAS RETURNED WITH GREAT INDIO POWERS.
WOOOWOOM
INDIO POWERS...
BUT IT'S WEIRD.
DEATH INCREASES A SHAMAN'S MANA, BUT IT CAN'T JUST BE THAT.
IT'S ALMOST LIKE...
HE'S A TOTALLY DIFFERENT PERSON.

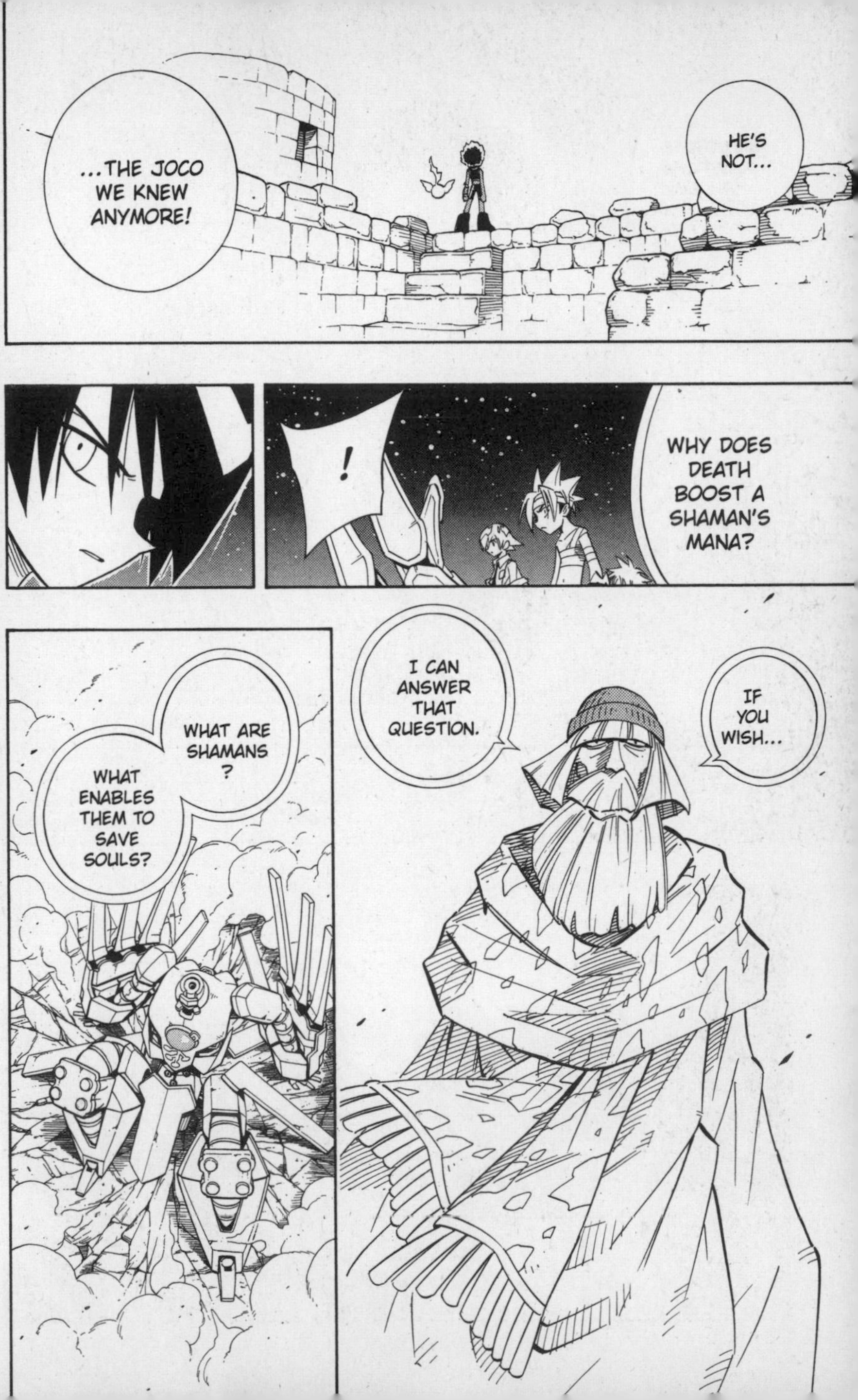
HE'S NOT...
...THE JOCO WE KNEW ANYMORE!
WHY DOES DEATH BOOST A SHAMAN'S MANA?
!
IF YOU WISH...
I CAN ANSWER THAT QUESTION.
WHAT ARE SHAMANS?
WHAT ENABLES THEM TO SAVE SOULS?

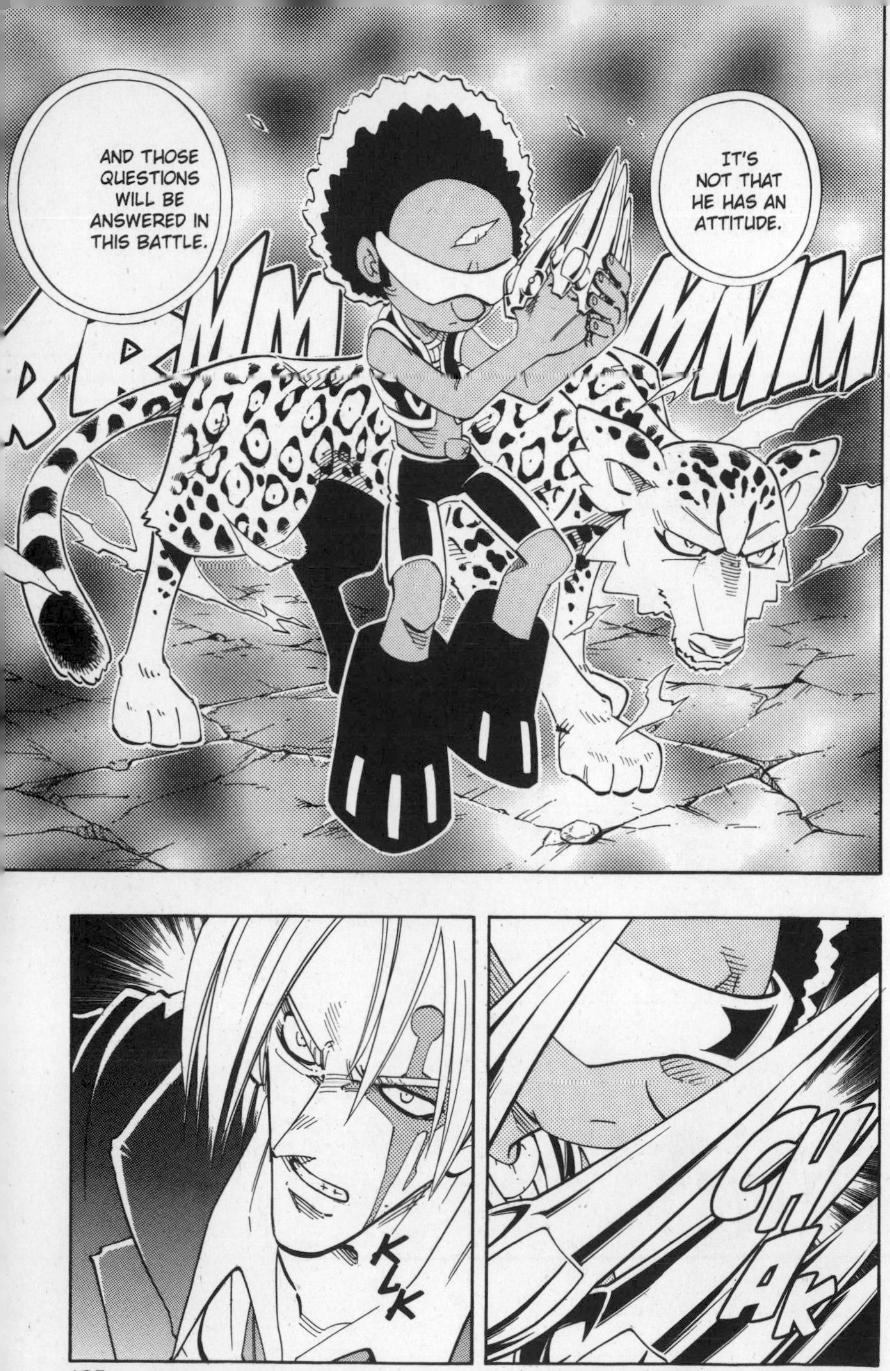
IT'S NOT THAT HE HAS AN ATTITUDE.
AND THOSE QUESTIONS WILL BE ANSWERED IN THIS BATTLE.
CHAK
KLK

SHAMAN KING ITEM FILE No.60

2001
(JAN)

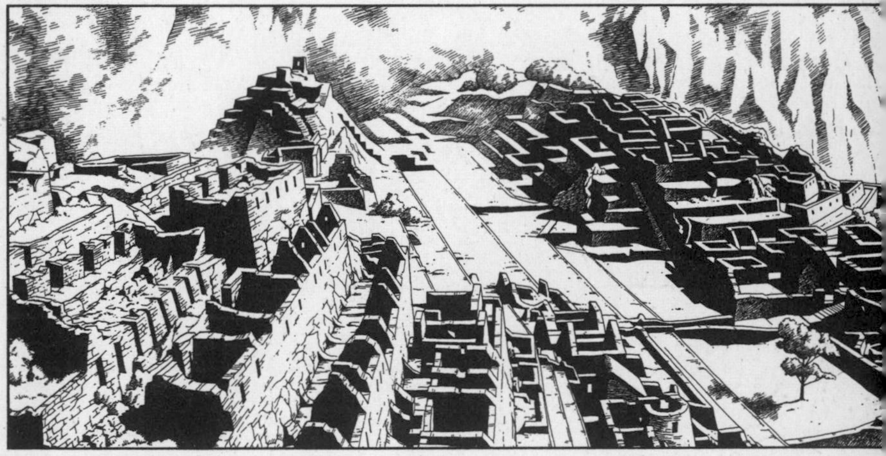

マチュピチュ遺跡(いせき)

THE RUINS OF MACHU PICCHU

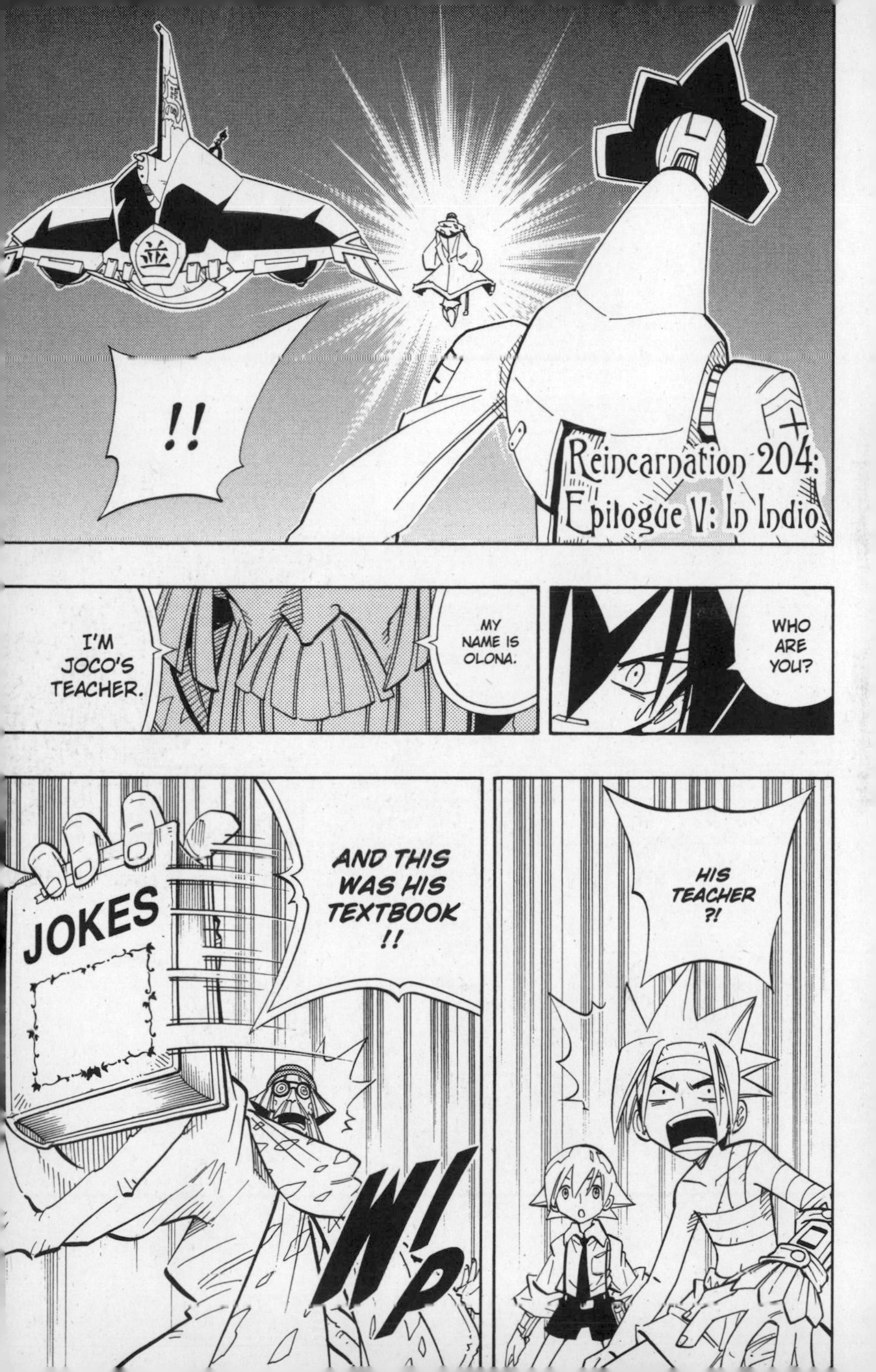
Reincarnation 204: Epilogue V: In Indio
!!
WHO ARE YOU?
MY NAME IS OLONA.
I'M JOCO'S TEACHER.
HIS TEACHER ?!
AND THIS WAS HIS TEXTBOOK !!
JOKES

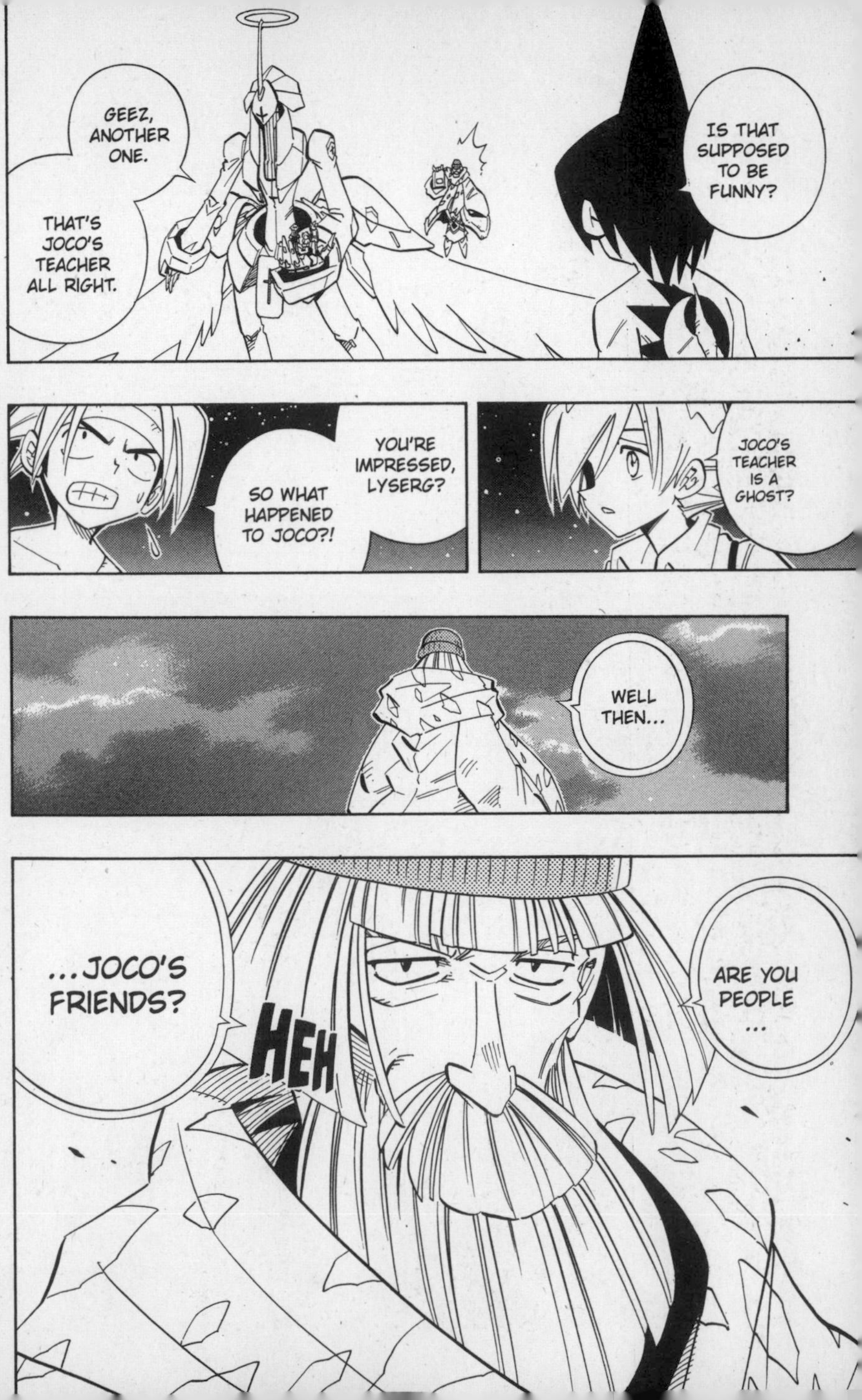
IS THAT SUPPOSED TO BE FUNNY?
GEEZ, ANOTHER ONE.
THAT'S JOCO'S TEACHER ALL RIGHT.
JOCO'S TEACHER IS A GHOST?
YOU'RE IMPRESSED, LYSERG?
SO WHAT HAPPENED TO JOCO?!
WELL THEN...
ARE YOU PEOPLE ...
HEH
...JOCO'S FRIENDS?

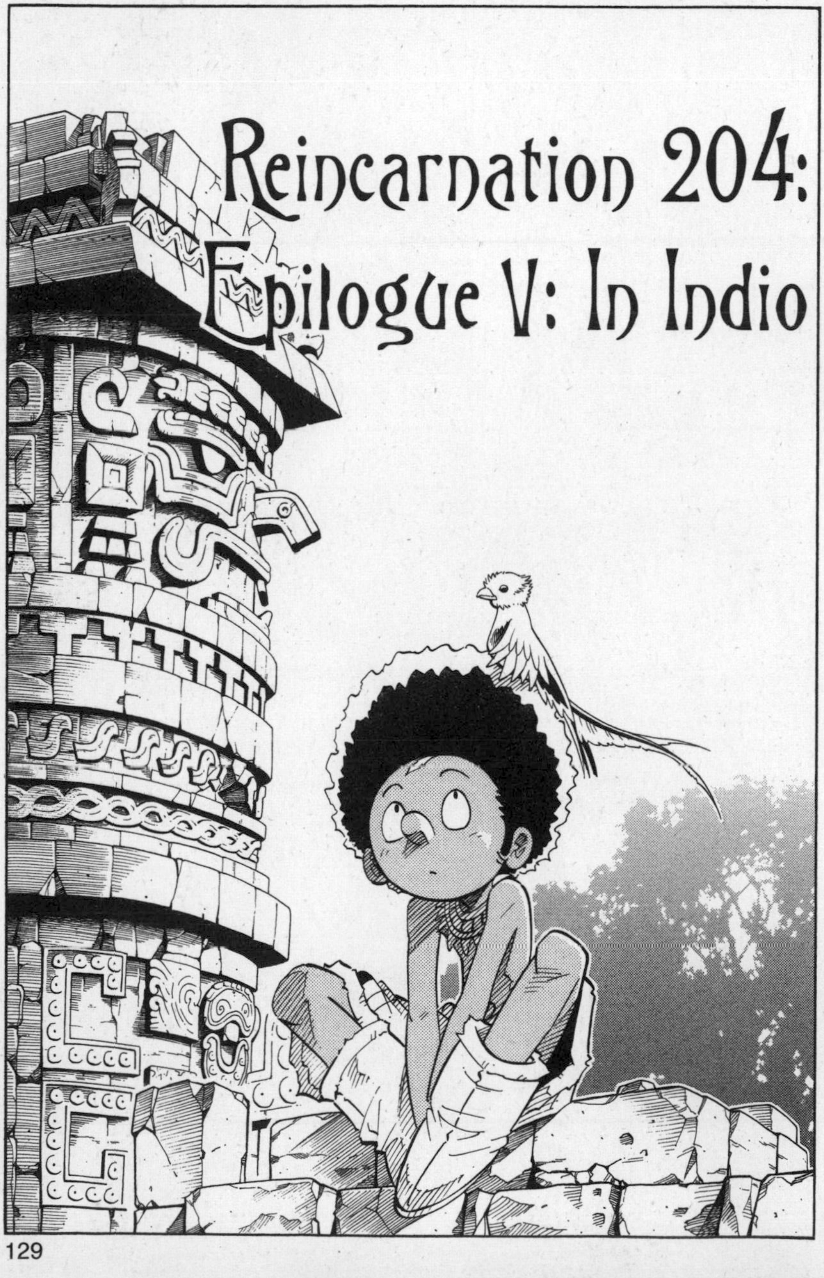
Reincarnation 204:
Epilogue V: In Indio

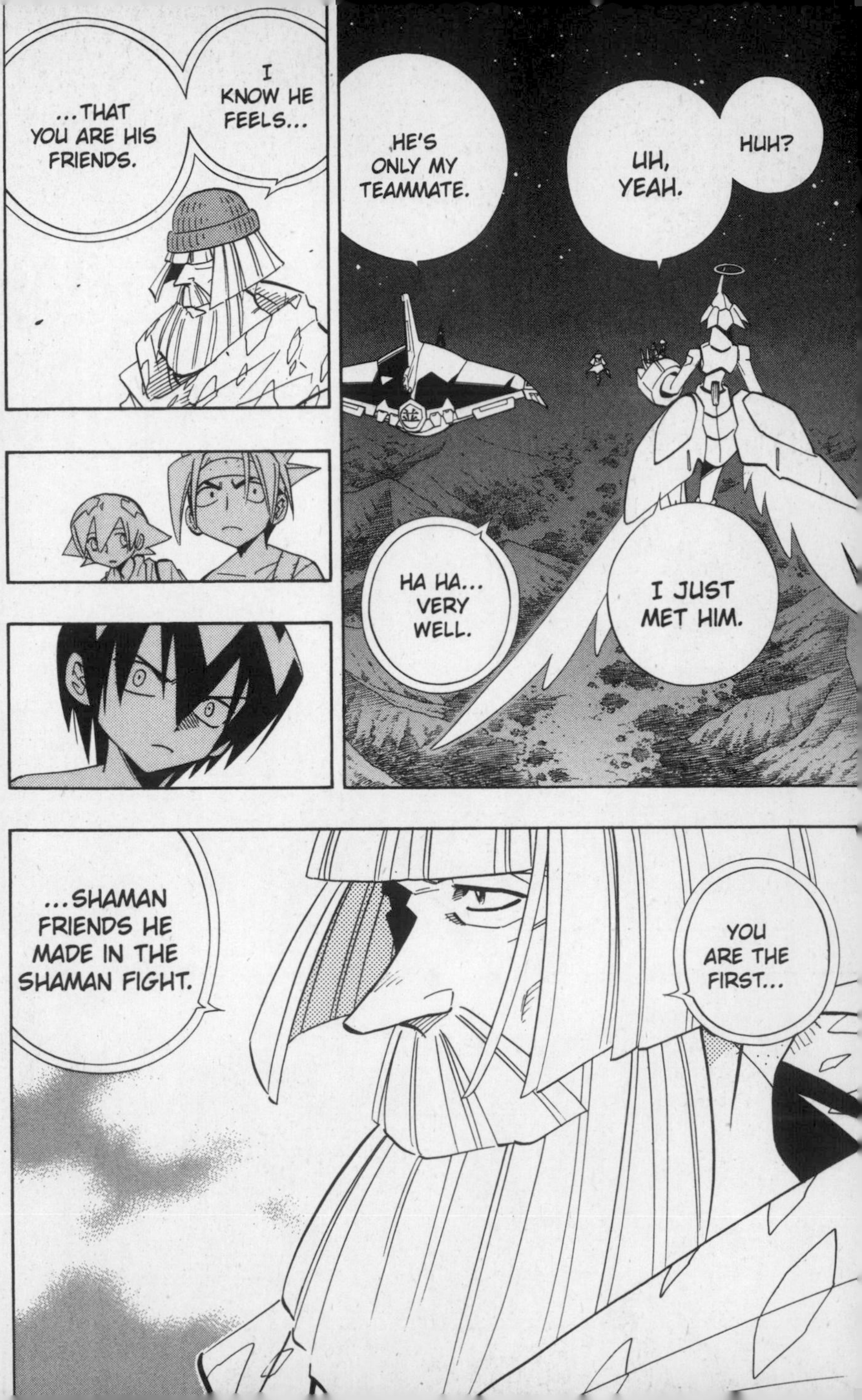
HUH?
UH, YEAH.
HE'S ONLY MY TEAMMATE.
I JUST MET HIM.
HA HA... VERY WELL.
I KNOW HE FEELS...
...THAT YOU ARE HIS FRIENDS.
YOU ARE THE FIRST...
...SHAMAN FRIENDS HE MADE IN THE SHAMAN FIGHT.

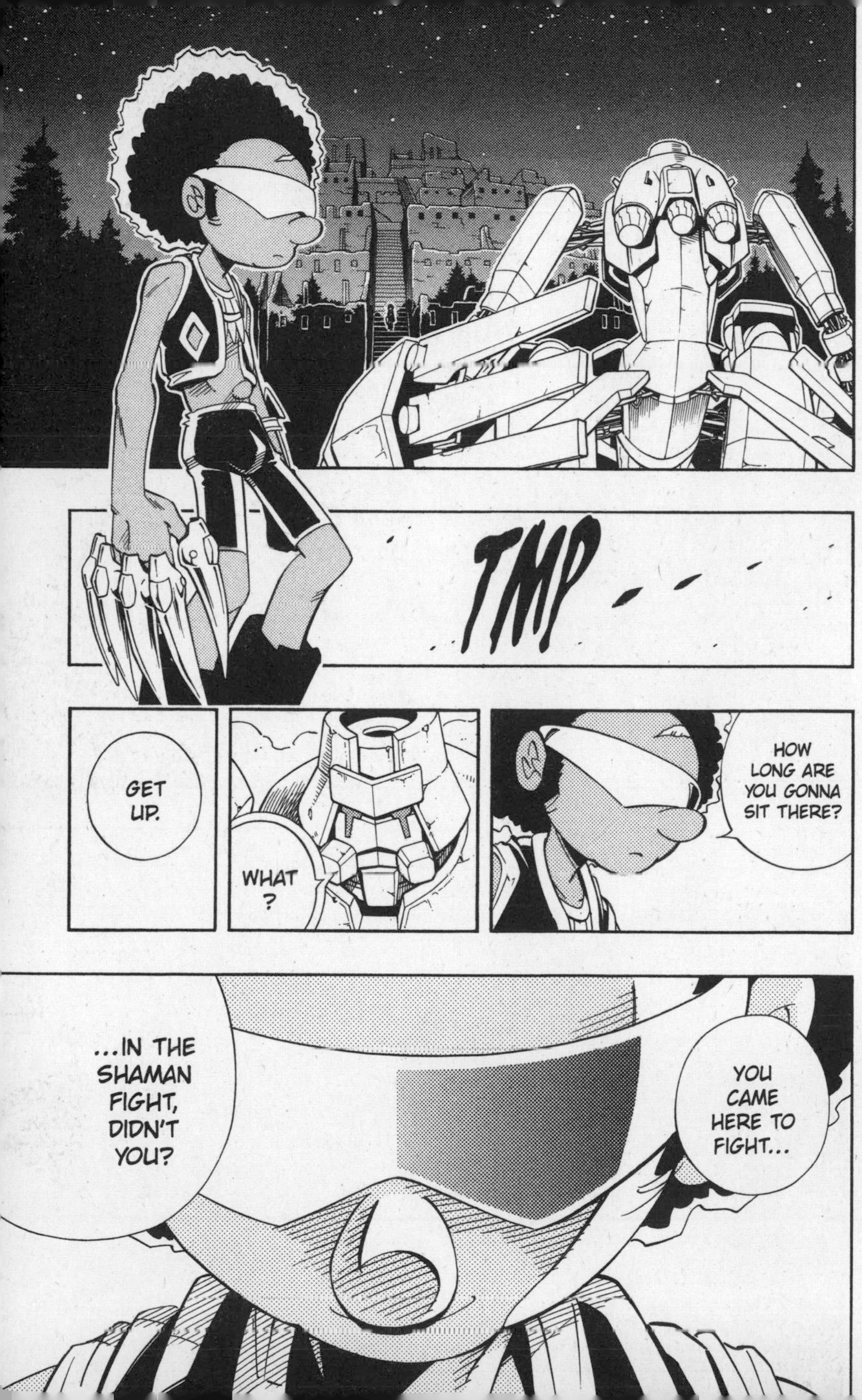
TMP
HOW LONG ARE YOU GONNA SIT THERE?
WHAT?
GET UP.
YOU CAME HERE TO FIGHT...
...IN THE SHAMAN FIGHT, DIDN'T YOU?

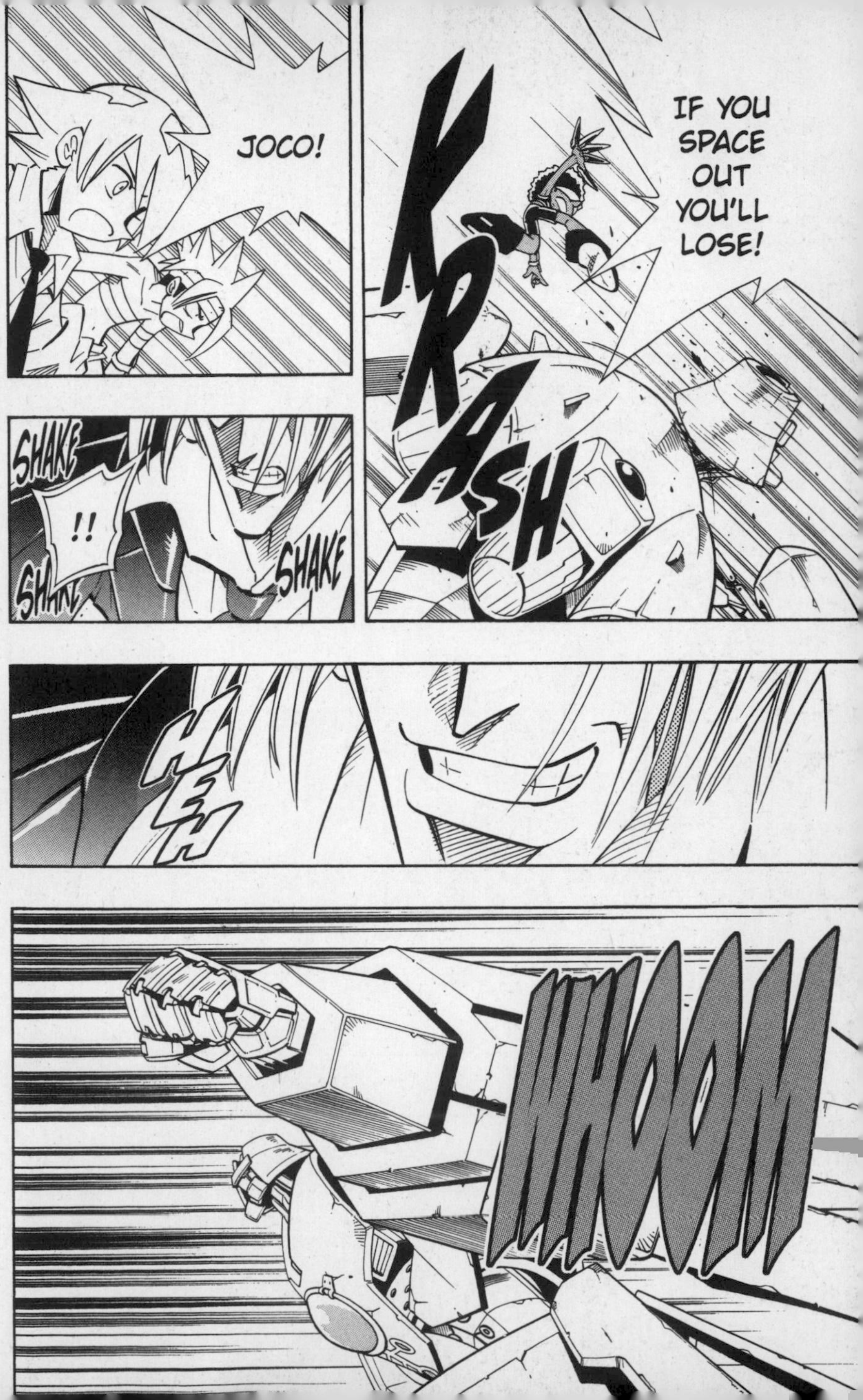
IF YOU SPACE OUT YOU'LL LOSE!
KRASH
JOCO!
SHAKE
!!
SHAKE
SHAKE
HEH
WHOOM

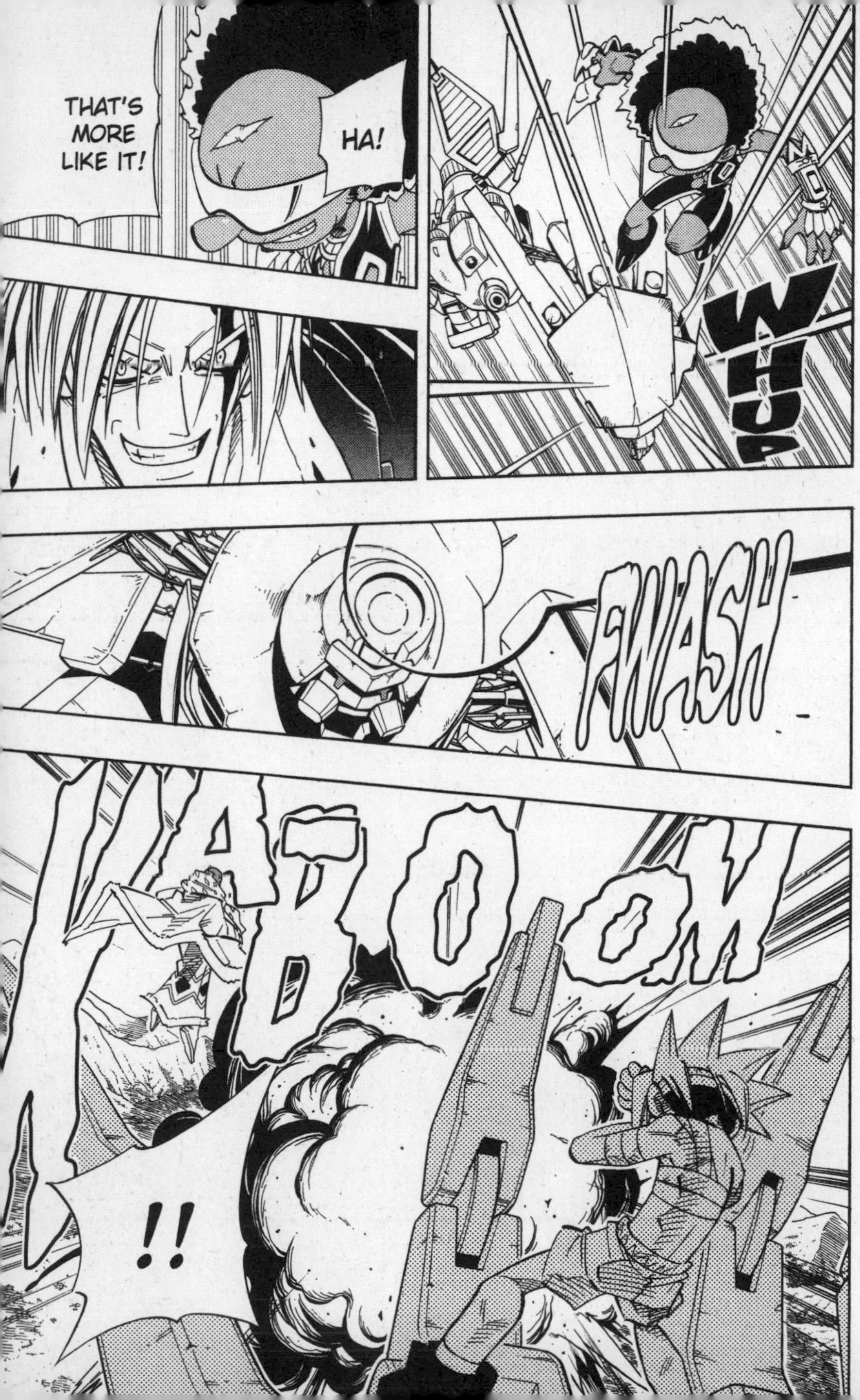
WHUP
HA!
THAT'S MORE LIKE IT!
FWASH
KABOOM
!!

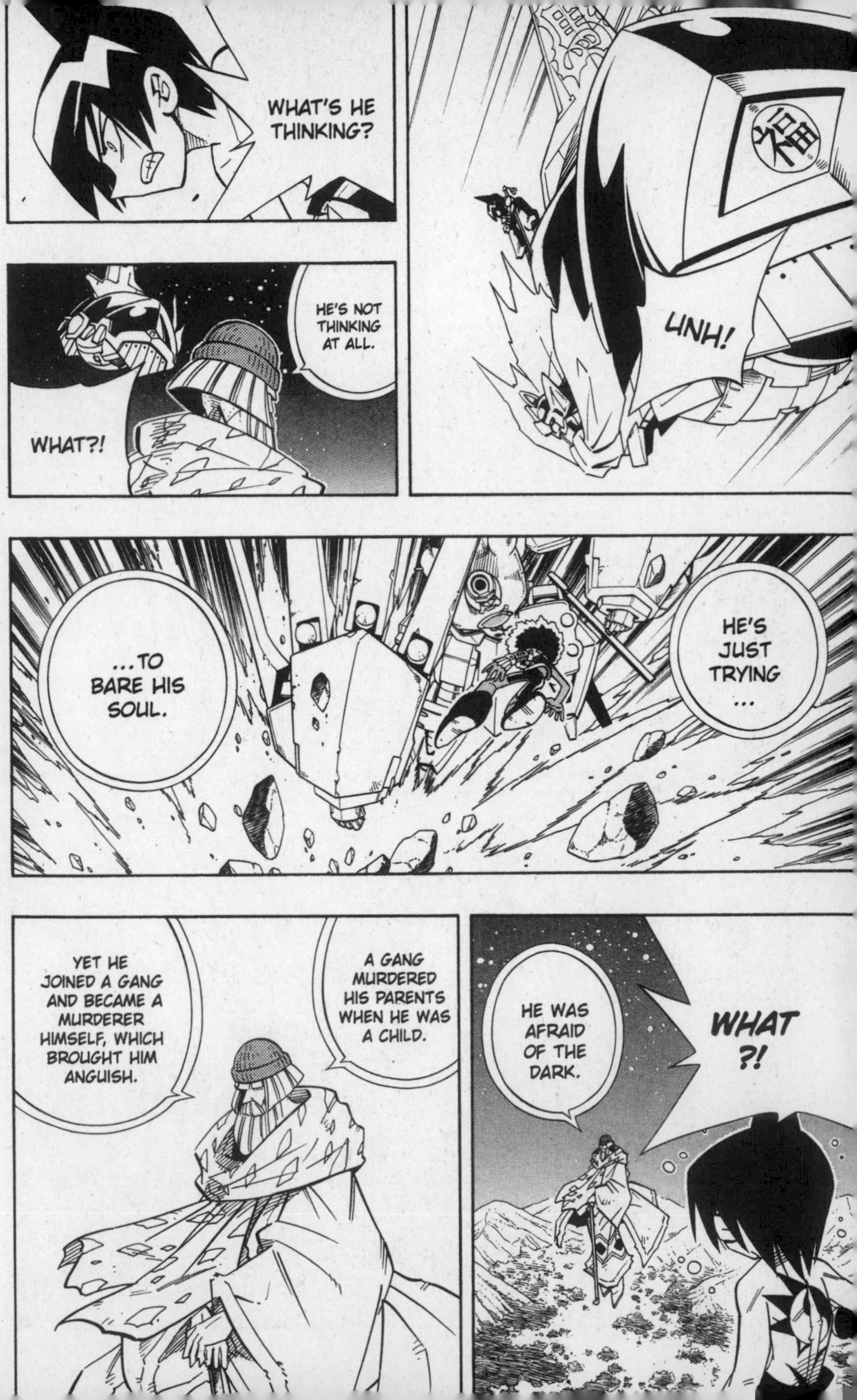
UNH!
WHAT'S HE THINKING?
HE'S NOT THINKING AT ALL.
WHAT?!
HE'S JUST TRYING ...
...TO BARE HIS SOUL.
WHAT ?!
HE WAS AFRAID OF THE DARK.
A GANG MURDERED HIS PARENTS WHEN HE WAS A CHILD.
YET HE JOINED A GANG AND BECAME A MURDERER HIMSELF, WHICH BROUGHT HIM ANGUISH.

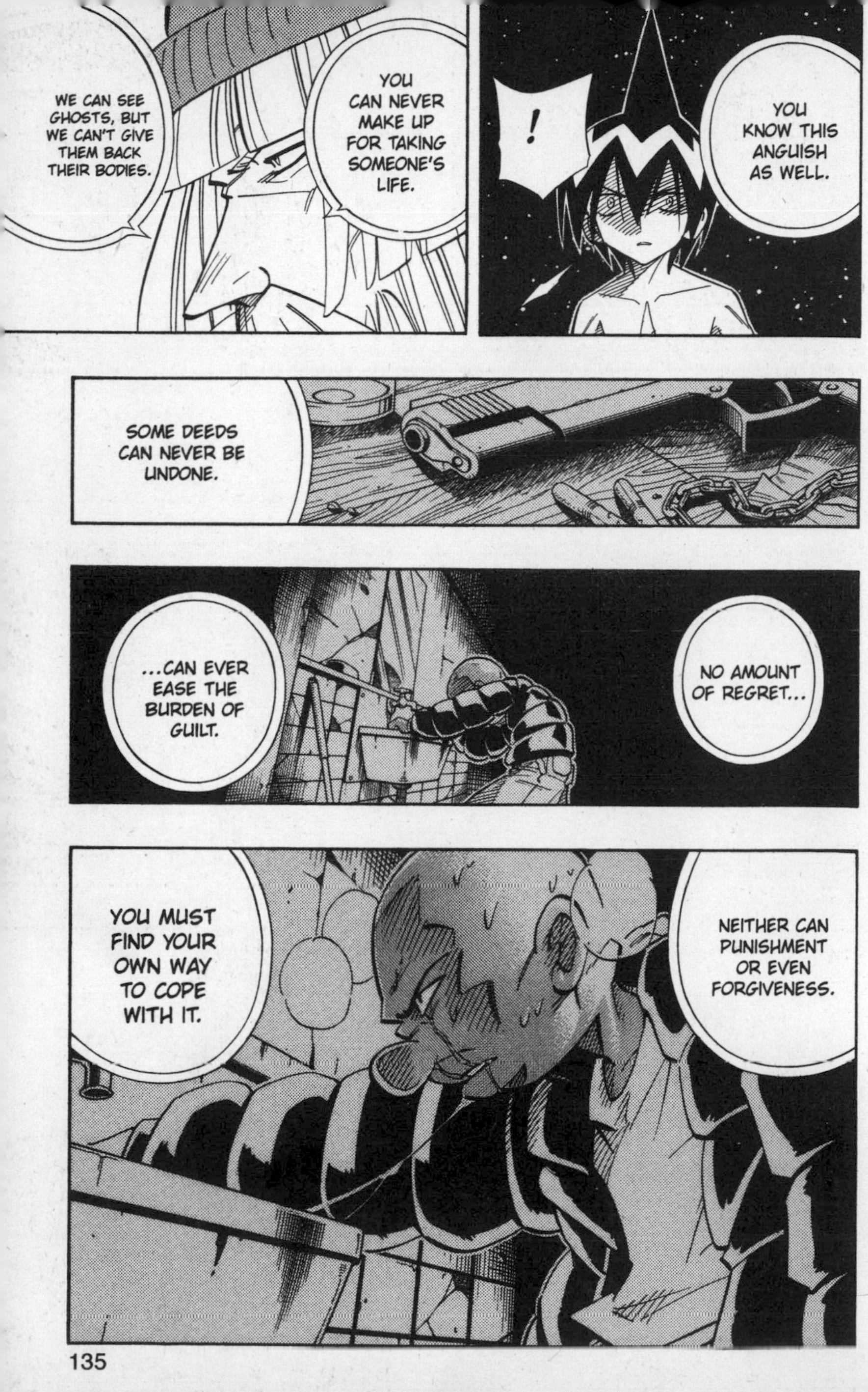
YOU KNOW THIS ANGUISH AS WELL.
!
YOU CAN NEVER MAKE UP FOR TAKING SOMEONE'S LIFE.
WE CAN SEE GHOSTS, BUT WE CAN'T GIVE THEM BACK THEIR BODIES.
SOME DEEDS CAN NEVER BE UNDONE.
NO AMOUNT OF REGRET...
...CAN EVER EASE THE BURDEN OF GUILT.
NEITHER CAN PUNISHMENT OR EVEN FORGIVENESS.
YOU MUST FIND YOUR OWN WAY TO COPE WITH IT.

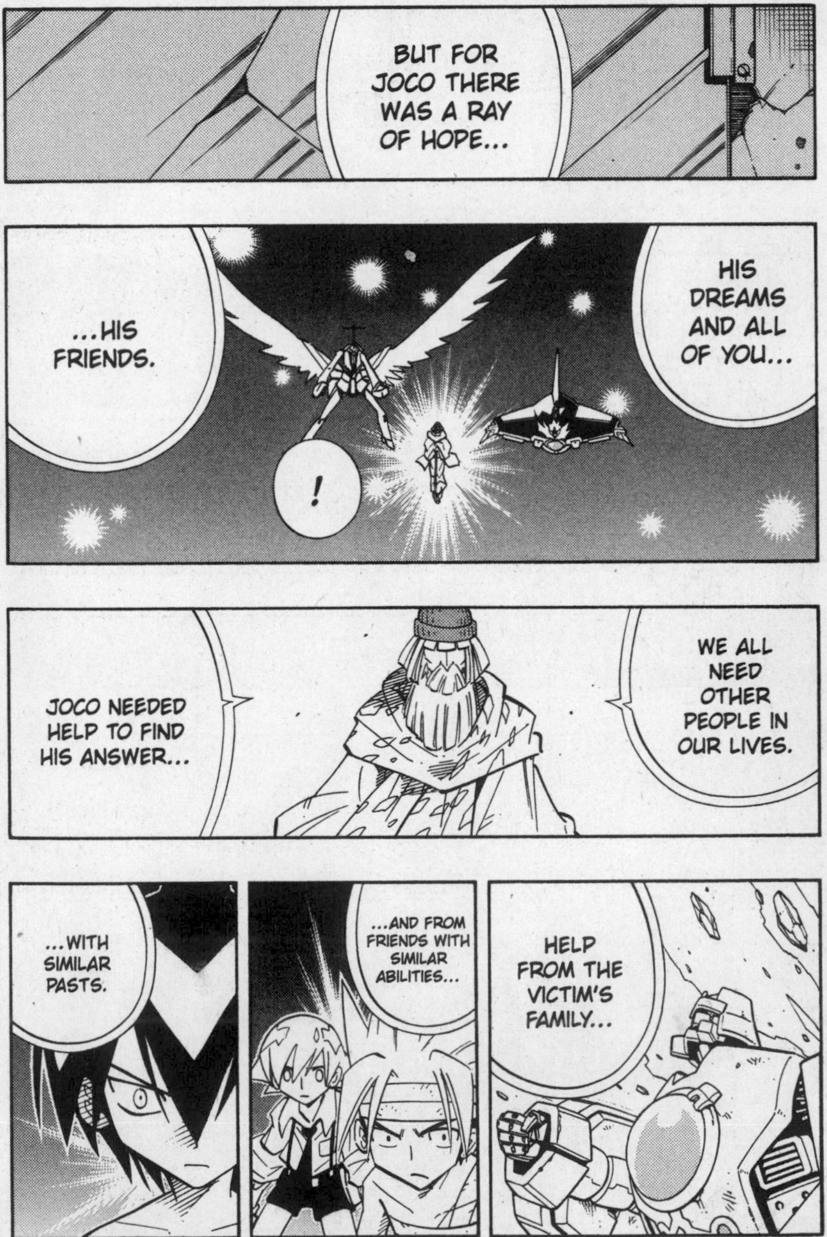
BUT FOR JOCO THERE WAS A RAY OF HOPE...
HIS DREAMS AND ALL OF YOU...
...HIS FRIENDS.
!
WE ALL NEED OTHER PEOPLE IN OUR LIVES.
JOCO NEEDED HELP TO FIND HIS ANSWER...
HELP FROM THE VICTIM'S FAMILY...
...AND FROM FRIENDS WITH SIMILAR ABILITIES...
...WITH SIMILAR PASTS.

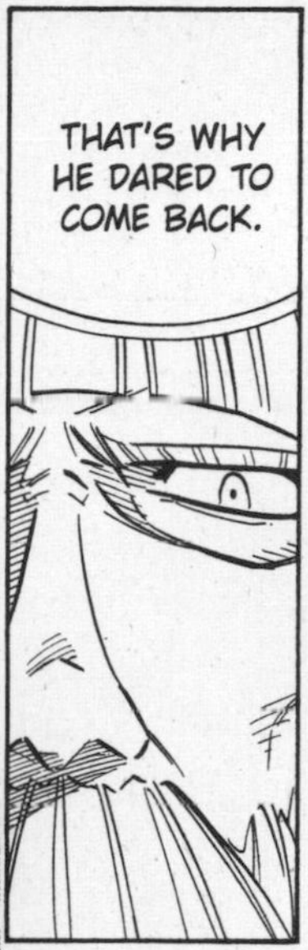

THAT'S WHY HE DARED TO COME BACK.

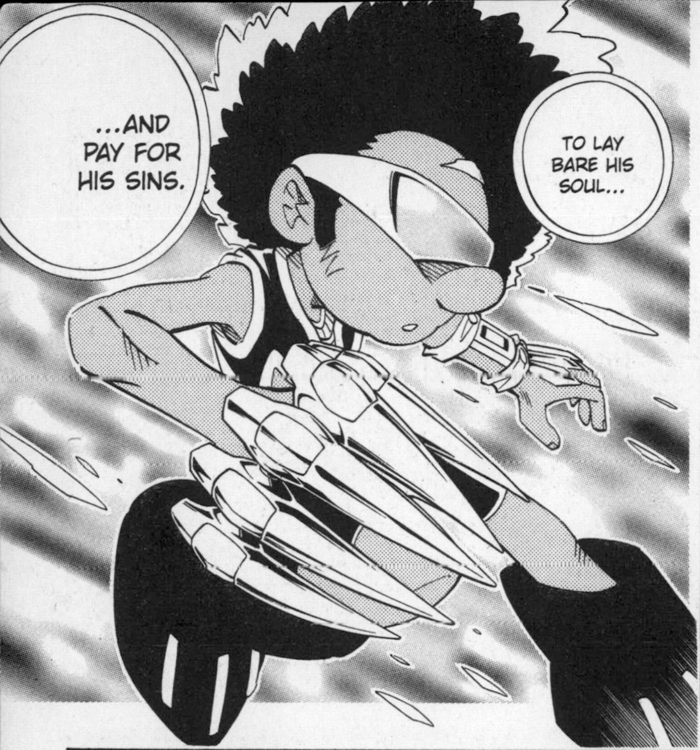

TO LAY BARE HIS SOUL...
...AND PAY FOR HIS SINS.

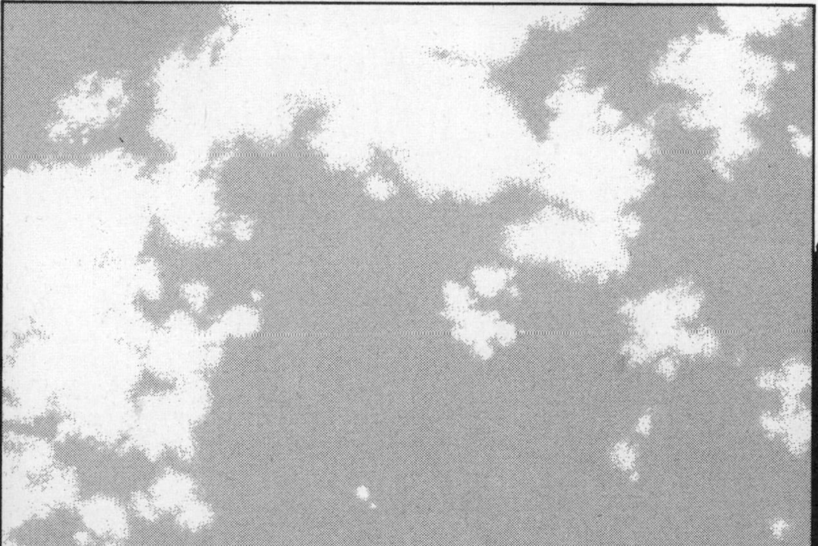

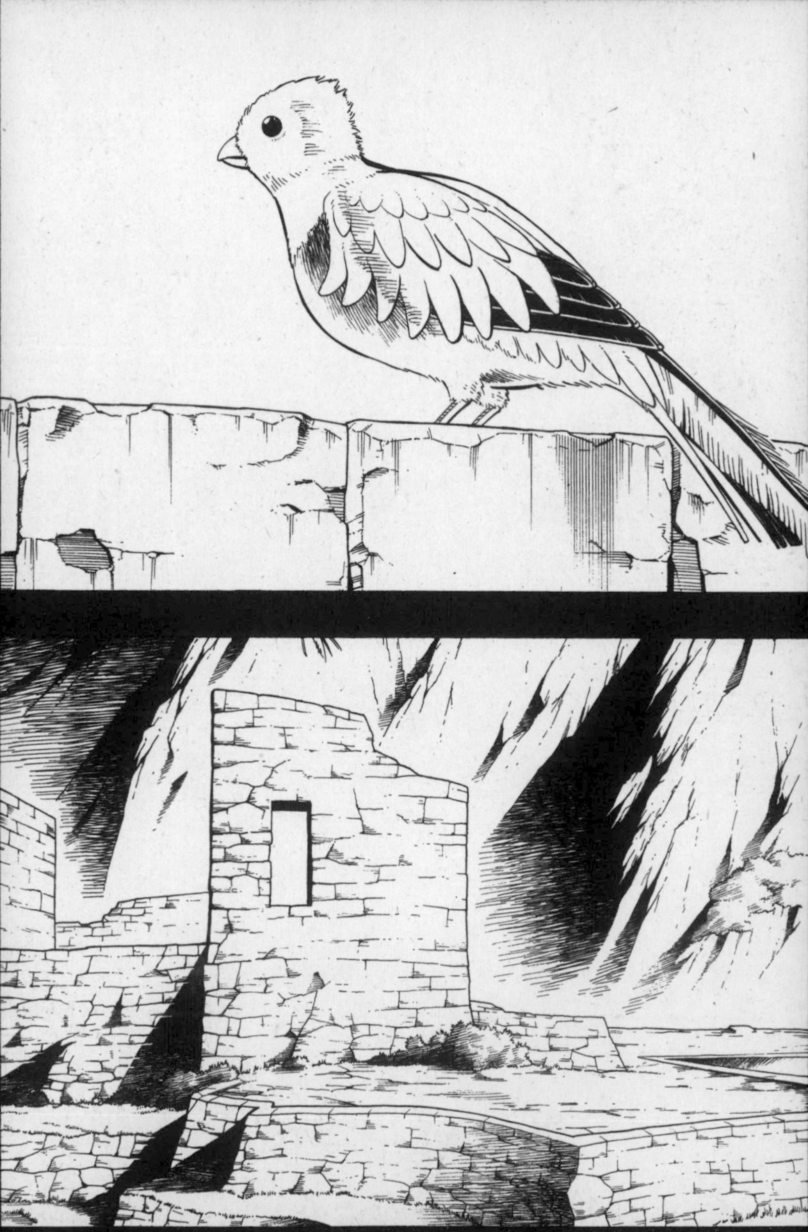

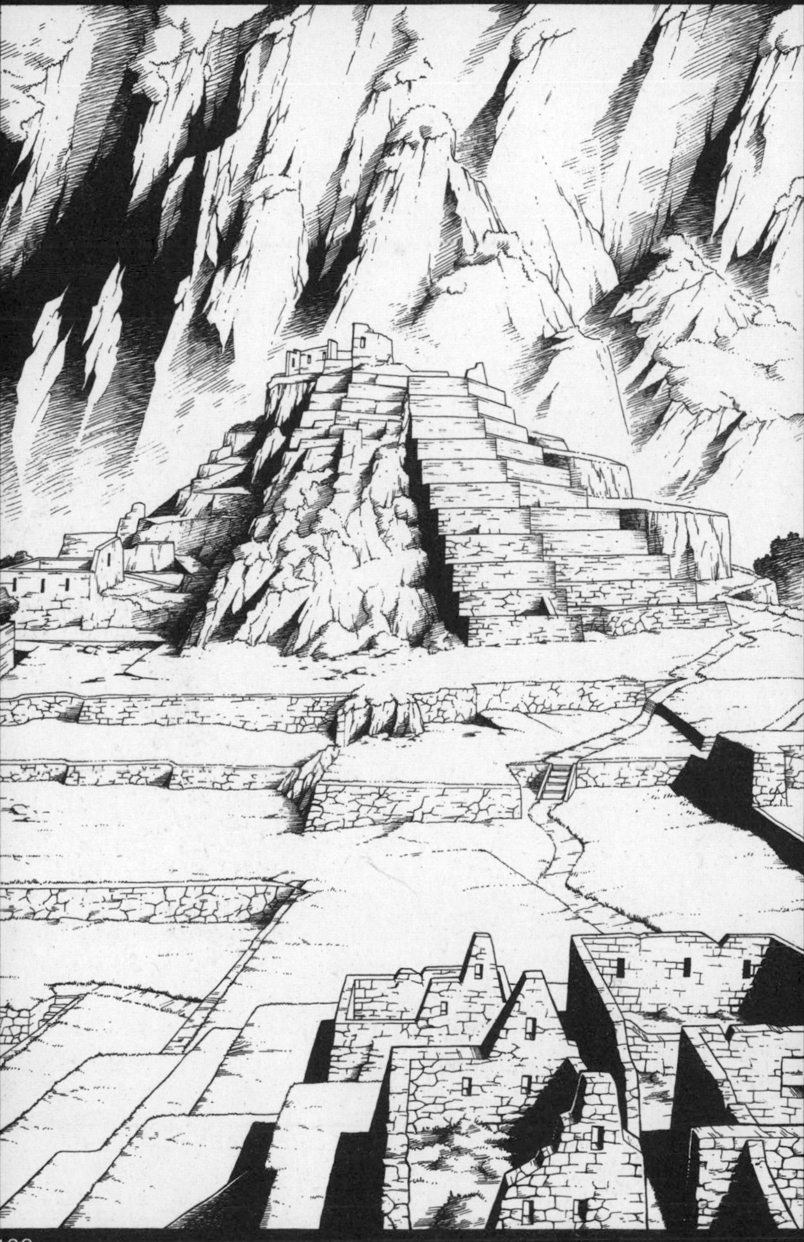

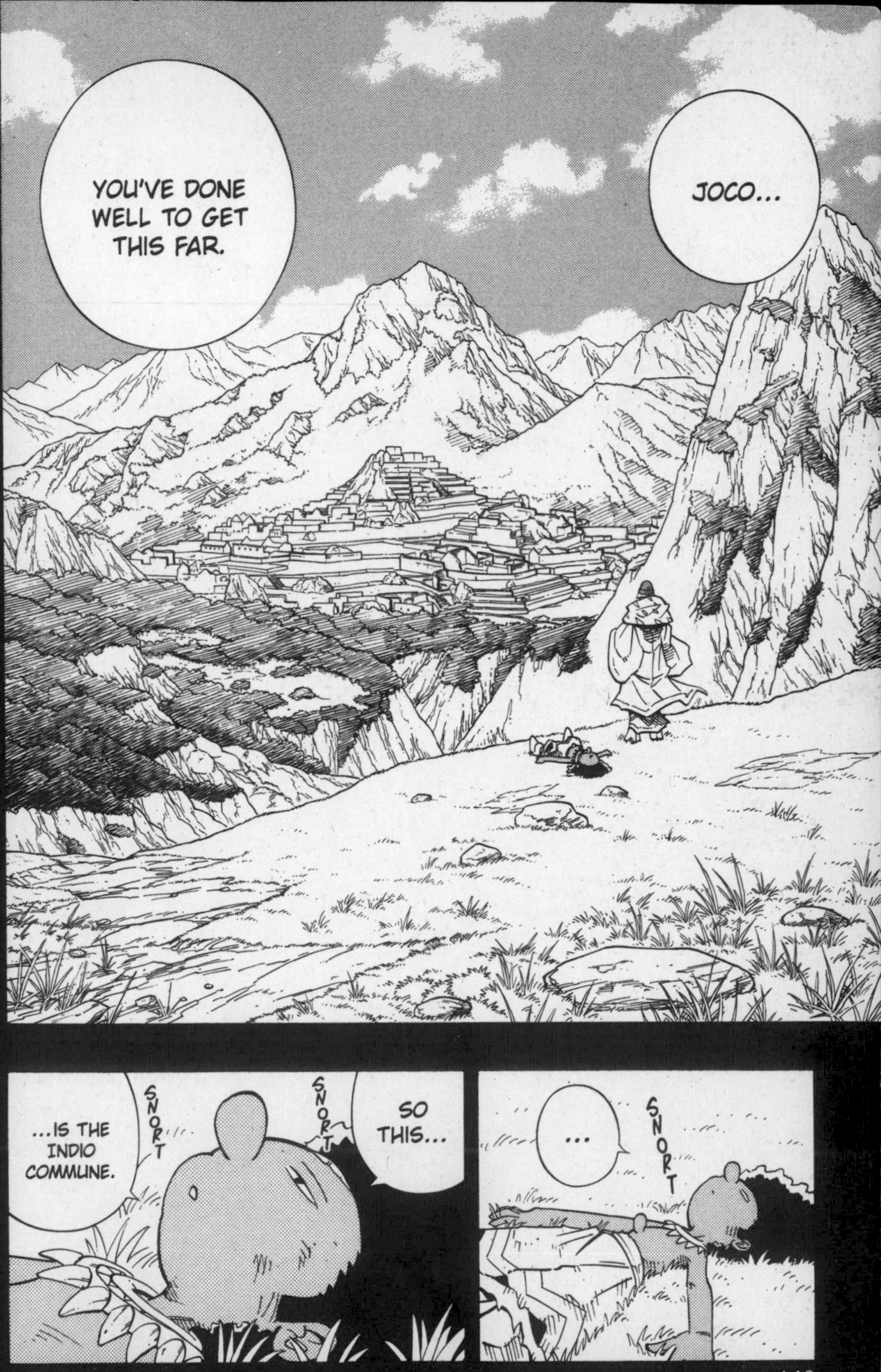
JOCO...
YOU'VE DONE WELL TO GET THIS FAR.
...
SNORT
SO THIS...
SNORT
...IS THE INDIO COMMUNE.
SNORT

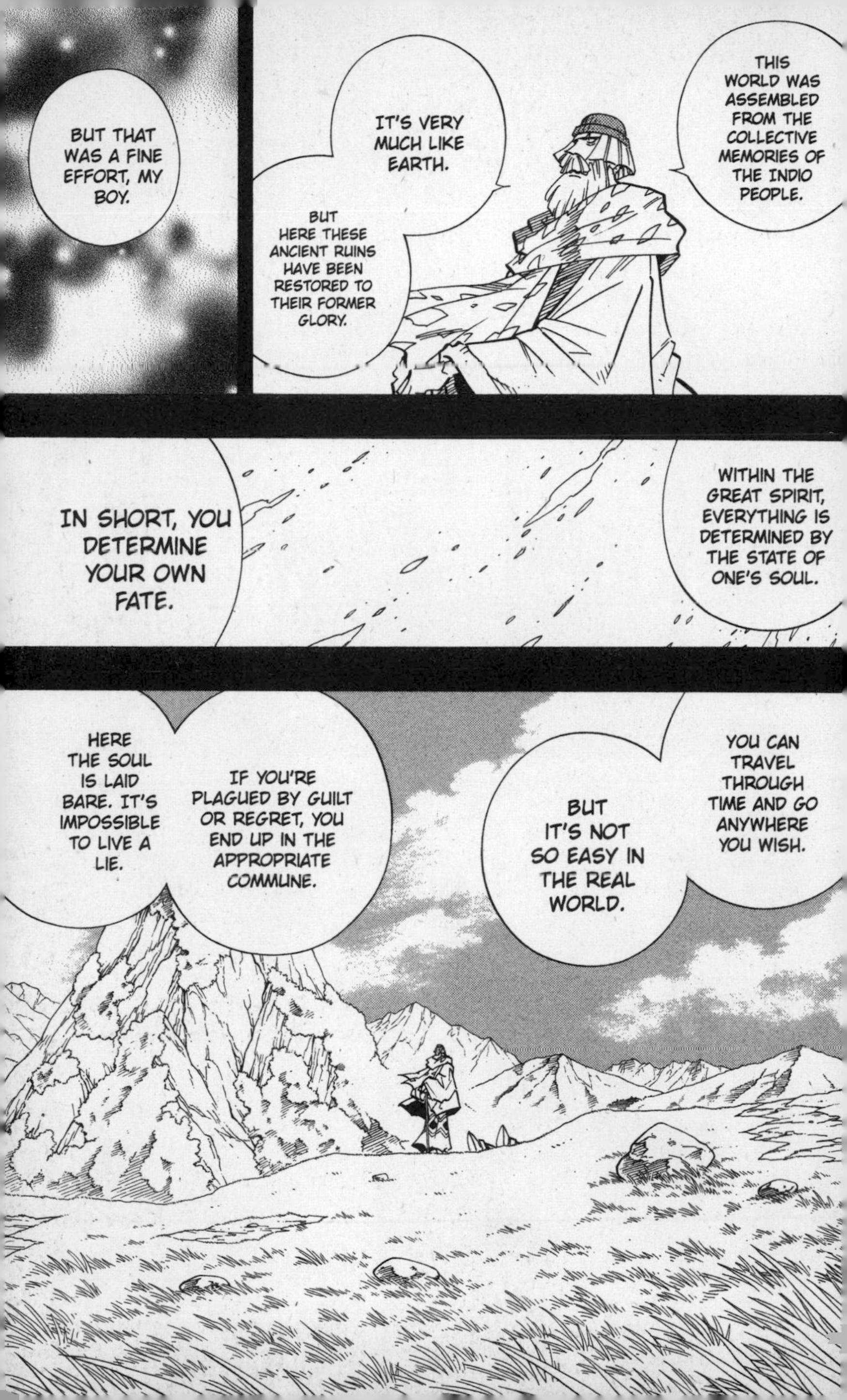
THIS WORLD WAS ASSEMBLED FROM THE COLLECTIVE MEMORIES OF THE INDIO PEOPLE.
IT'S VERY MUCH LIKE EARTH.
BUT HERE THESE ANCIENT RUINS HAVE BEEN RESTORED TO THEIR FORMER GLORY.
BUT THAT WAS A FINE EFFORT, MY BOY.
WITHIN THE GREAT SPIRIT, EVERYTHING IS DETERMINED BY THE STATE OF ONE'S SOUL.
IN SHORT, YOU DETERMINE YOUR OWN FATE.
YOU CAN TRAVEL THROUGH TIME AND GO ANYWHERE YOU WISH.
BUT IT'S NOT SO EASY IN THE REAL WORLD.
HERE THE SOUL IS LAID BARE. IT'S IMPOSSIBLE TO LIVE A LIE.
IF YOU'RE PLAGUED BY GUILT OR REGRET, YOU END UP IN THE APPROPRIATE COMMUNE.

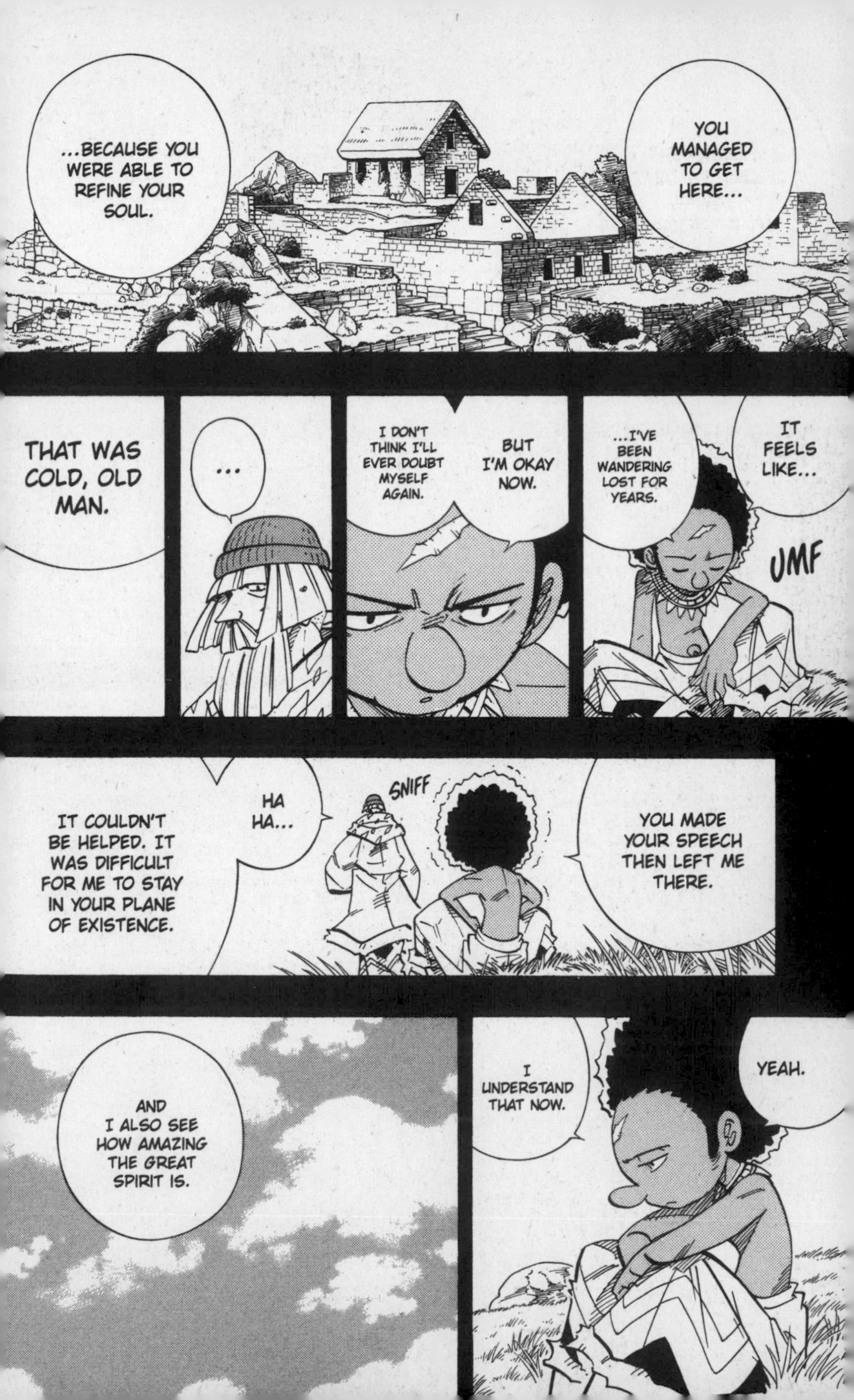
YOU MANAGED TO GET HERE...
...BECAUSE YOU WERE ABLE TO REFINE YOUR SOUL.
IT FEELS LIKE...
...I'VE BEEN WANDERING LOST FOR YEARS.
UMF
BUT I'M OKAY NOW.
I DON'T THINK I'LL EVER DOUBT MYSELF AGAIN.
...
THAT WAS COLD, OLD MAN.
YOU MADE YOUR SPEECH THEN LEFT ME THERE.
SNIFF
HA HA...
IT COULDN'T BE HELPED. IT WAS DIFFICULT FOR ME TO STAY IN YOUR PLANE OF EXISTENCE.
YEAH.
I UNDERSTAND THAT NOW.
AND I ALSO SEE HOW AMAZING THE GREAT SPIRIT IS.

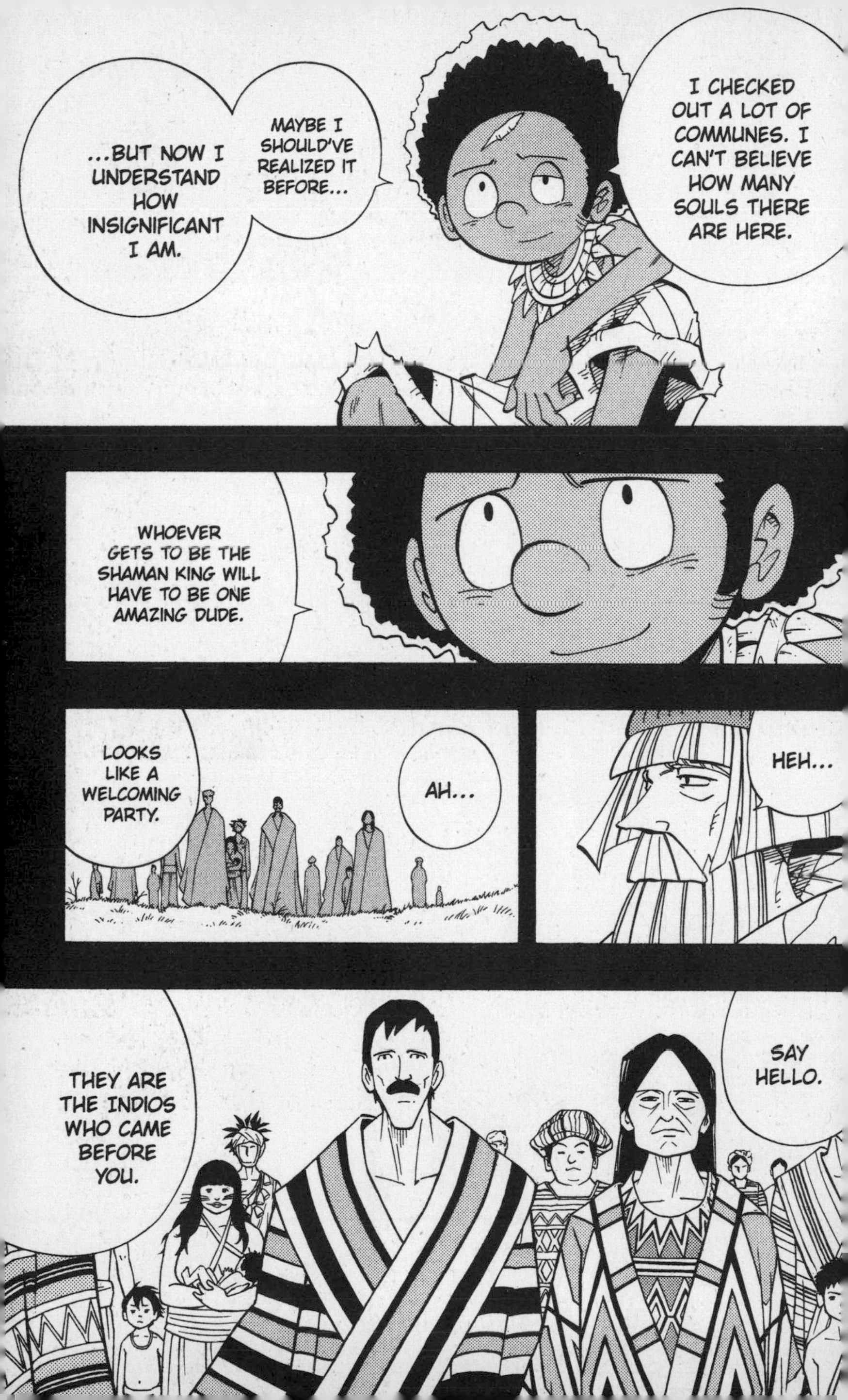
I CHECKED OUT A LOT OF COMMUNES. I CAN'T BELIEVE HOW MANY SOULS THERE ARE HERE.
MAYBE I SHOULD'VE REALIZED IT BEFORE...
...BUT NOW I UNDERSTAND HOW INSIGNIFICANT I AM.
WHOEVER GETS TO BE THE SHAMAN KING WILL HAVE TO BE ONE AMAZING DUDE.
HEH...
AH...
LOOKS LIKE A WELCOMING PARTY.
SAY HELLO.
THEY ARE THE INDIOS WHO CAME BEFORE YOU.

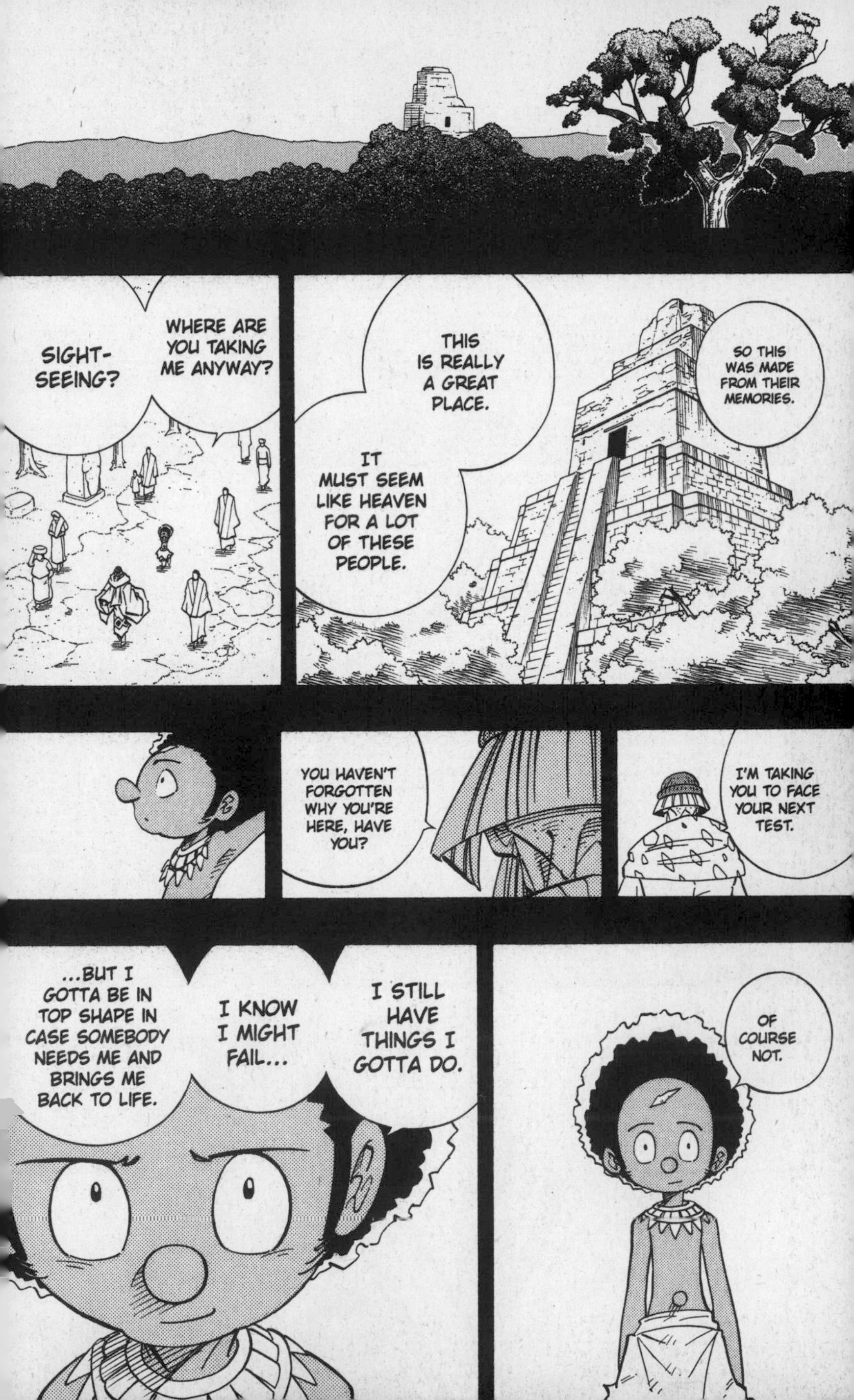
SO THIS WAS MADE FROM THEIR MEMORIES.
THIS IS REALLY A GREAT PLACE.
IT MUST SEEM LIKE HEAVEN FOR A LOT OF THESE PEOPLE.
WHERE ARE YOU TAKING ME ANYWAY?
SIGHT-SEEING?
I'M TAKING YOU TO FACE YOUR NEXT TEST.
YOU HAVEN'T FORGOTTEN WHY YOU'RE HERE, HAVE YOU?
OF COURSE NOT.
I STILL HAVE THINGS I GOTTA DO.
I KNOW I MIGHT FAIL...
...BUT I GOTTA BE IN TOP SHAPE IN CASE SOMEBODY NEEDS ME AND BRINGS ME BACK TO LIFE.

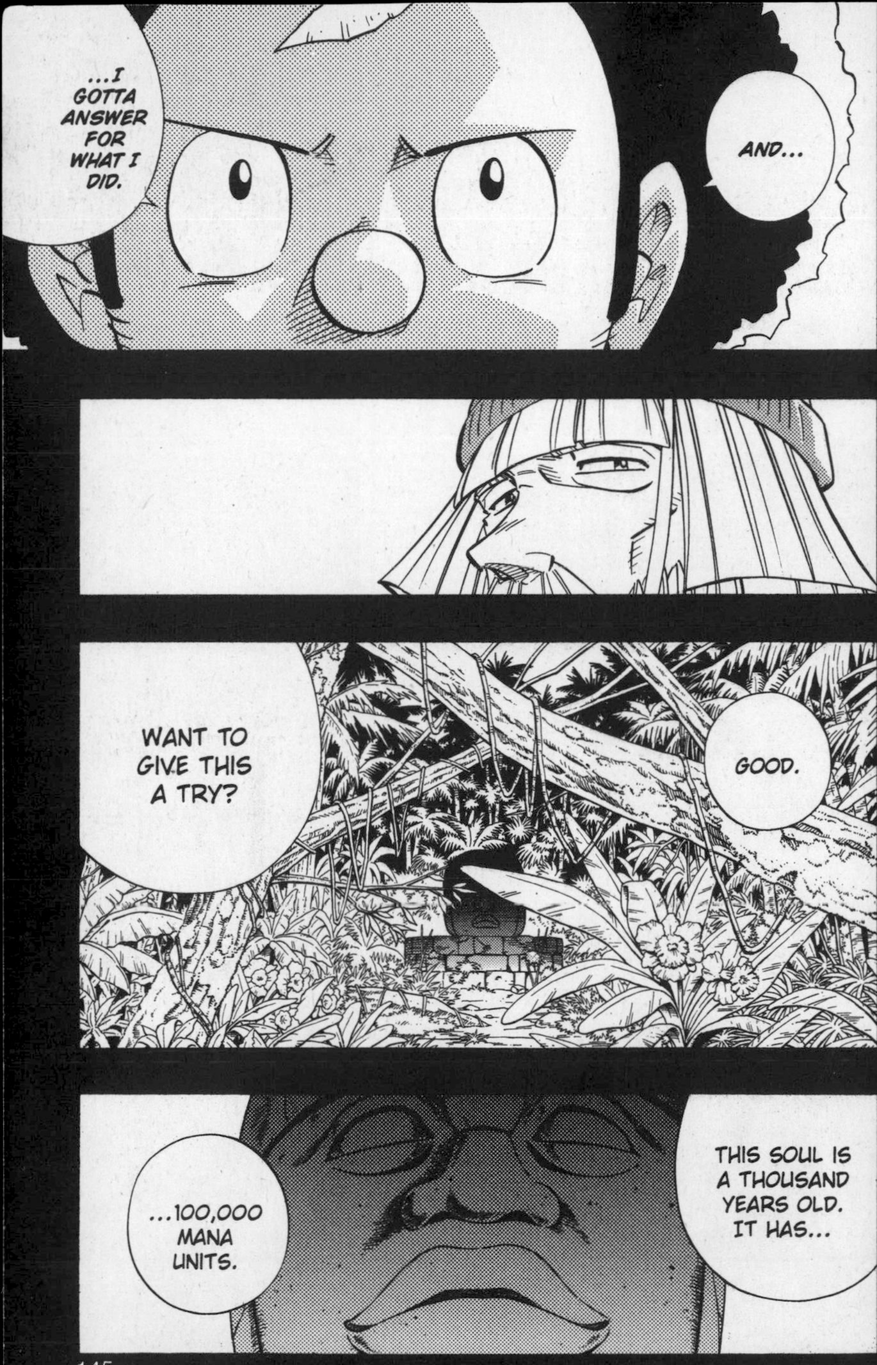
...I GOTTA ANSWER FOR WHAT I DID.
AND...
GOOD.
WANT TO GIVE THIS A TRY?
THIS SOUL IS A THOUSAND YEARS OLD. IT HAS...
...100,000 MANA UNITS.

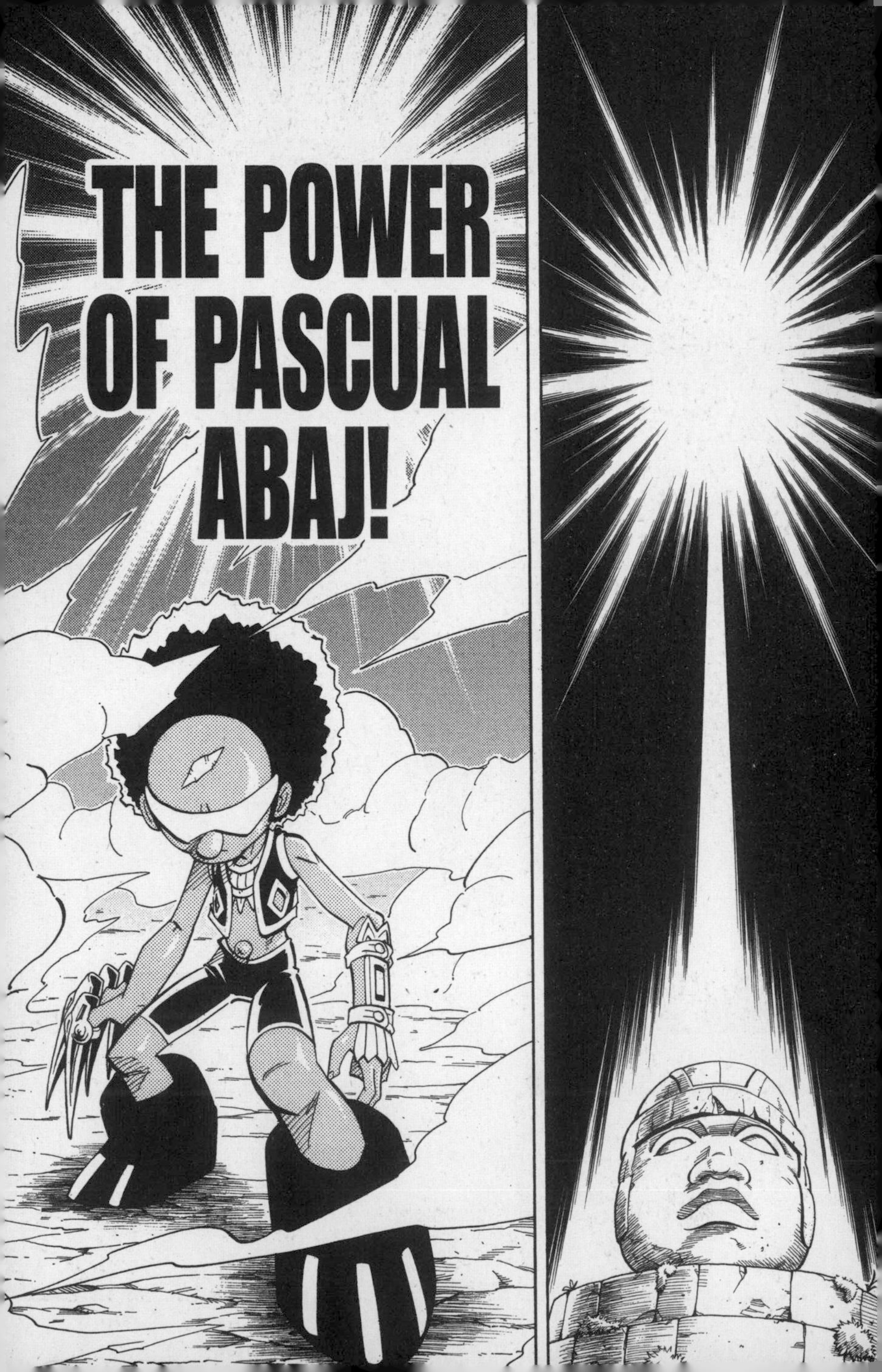
THE POWER OF PASCUAL ABAJ!

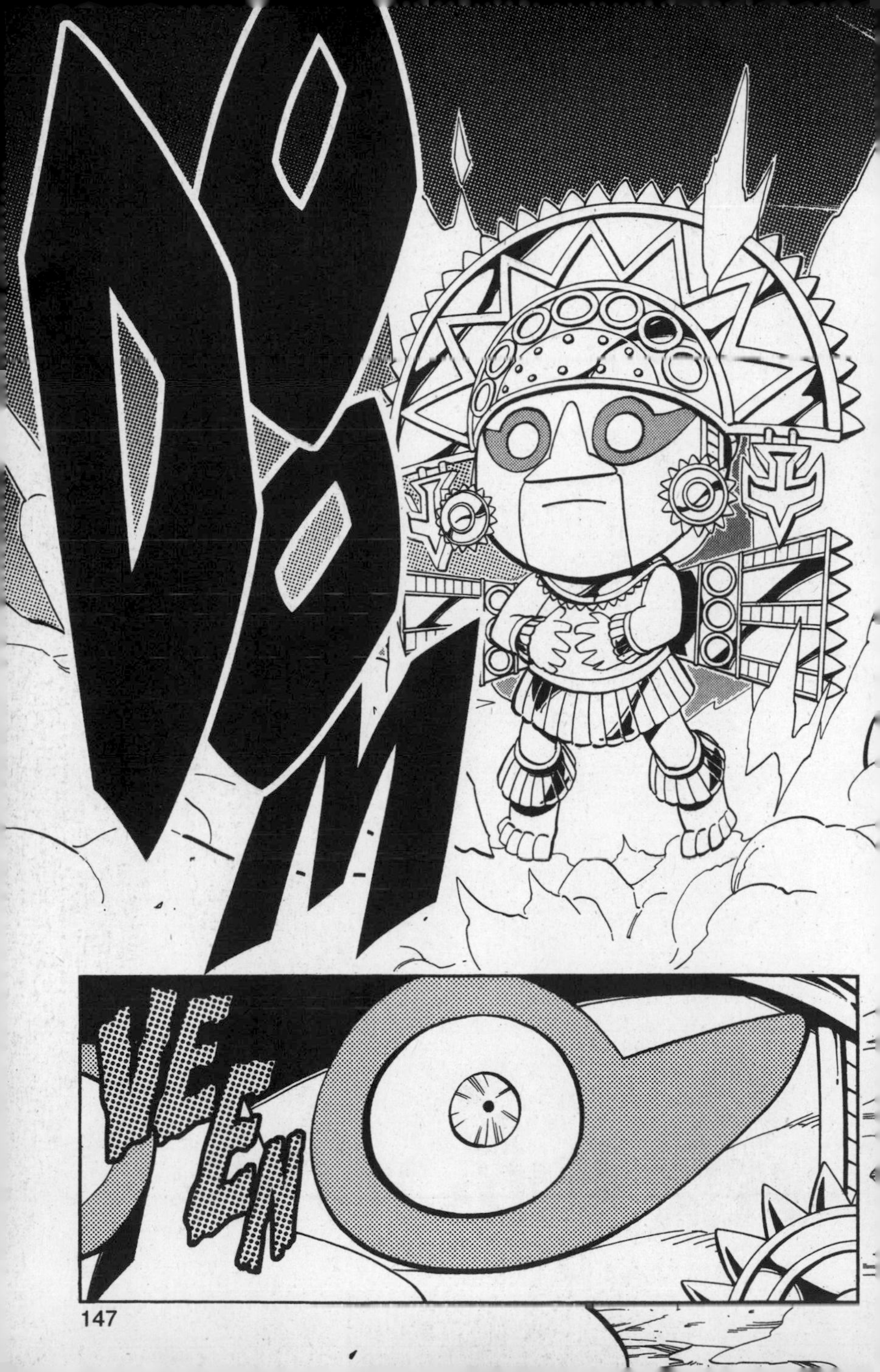
DOM
VEEN

SHAMAN KING CHARACTER FILE No.125

2001
(JAN)

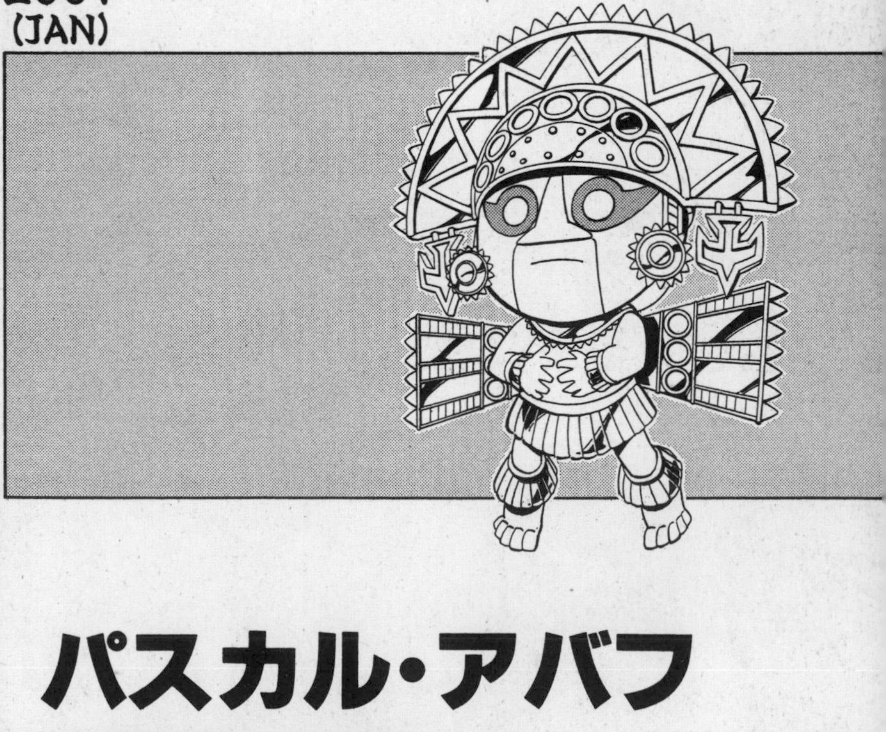

パスカル・アバフ

PASCUAL ABAJ

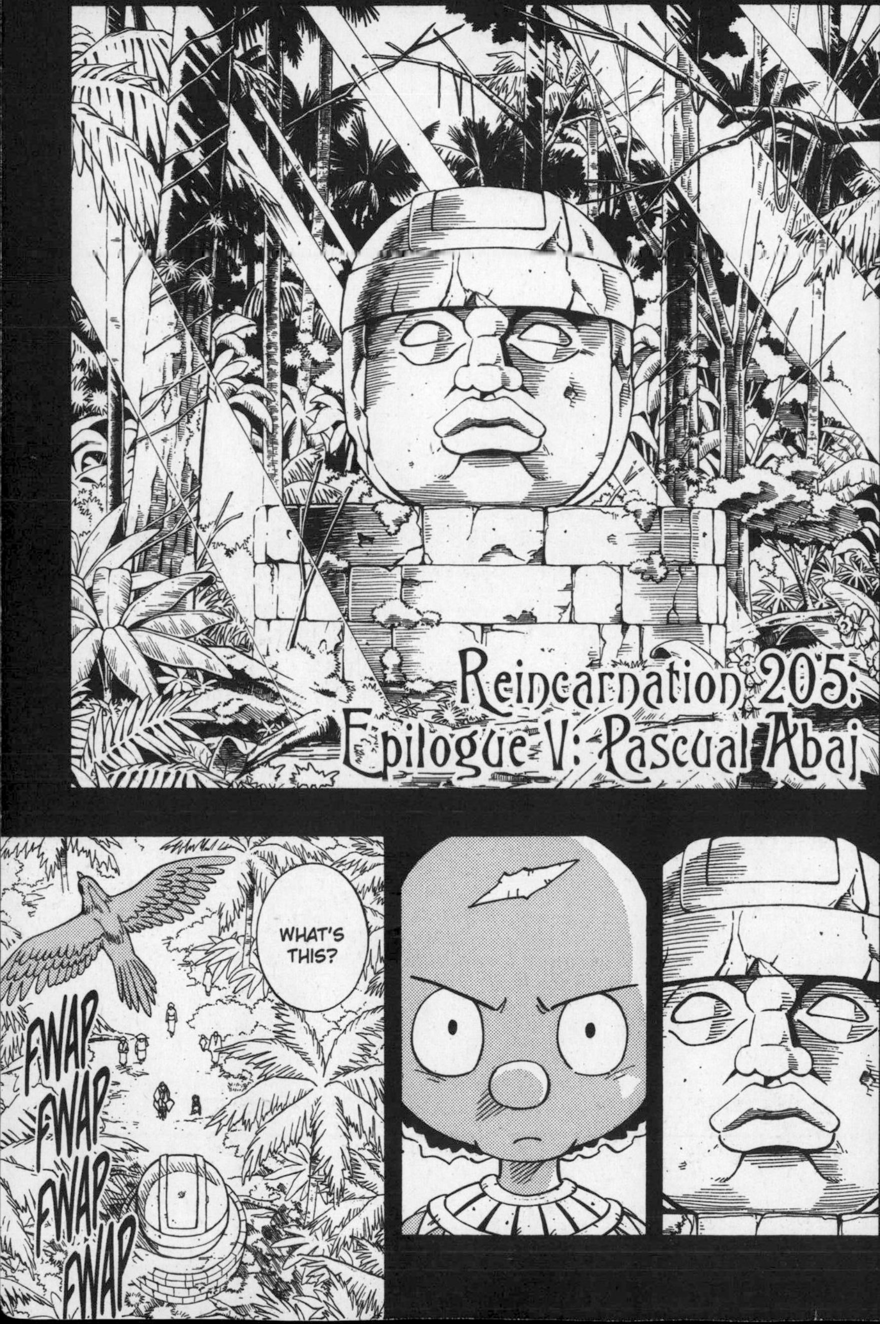
Reincarnation 205:
Epilogue V: Pascual Abaj
WHAT'S THIS?
FWAP
FWAP
FWAP
FWAP

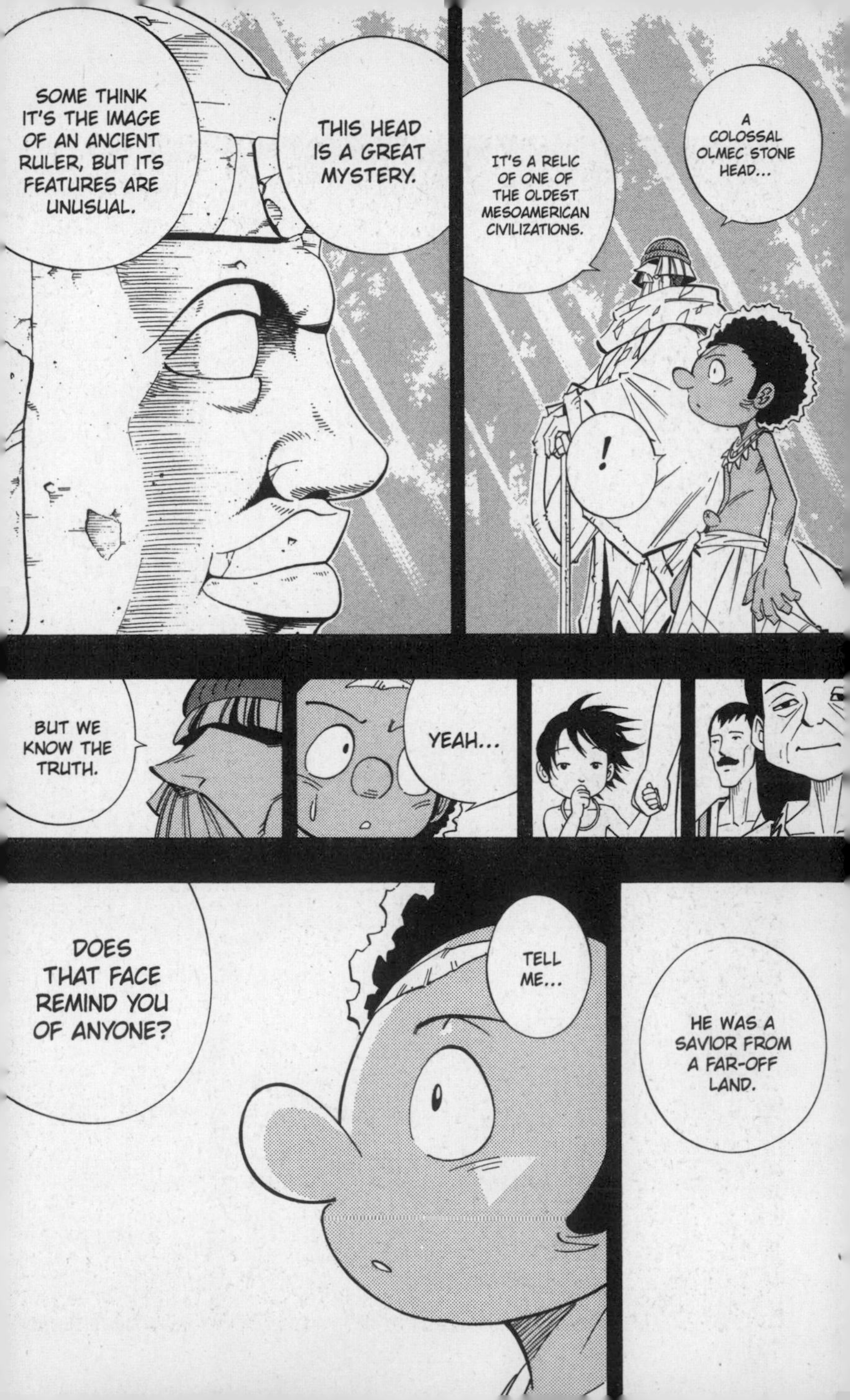
A COLOSSAL OLMEC STONE HEAD...
IT'S A RELIC OF ONE OF THE OLDEST MESOAMERICAN CIVILIZATIONS.
!
THIS HEAD IS A GREAT MYSTERY.
SOME THINK IT'S THE IMAGE OF AN ANCIENT RULER, BUT ITS FEATURES ARE UNUSUAL.
YEAH...
BUT WE KNOW THE TRUTH.
HE WAS A SAVIOR FROM A FAR-OFF LAND.
TELL ME...
DOES THAT FACE REMIND YOU OF ANYONE?

Reincarnation 205:

Epilogue V:
Pascual Abaj

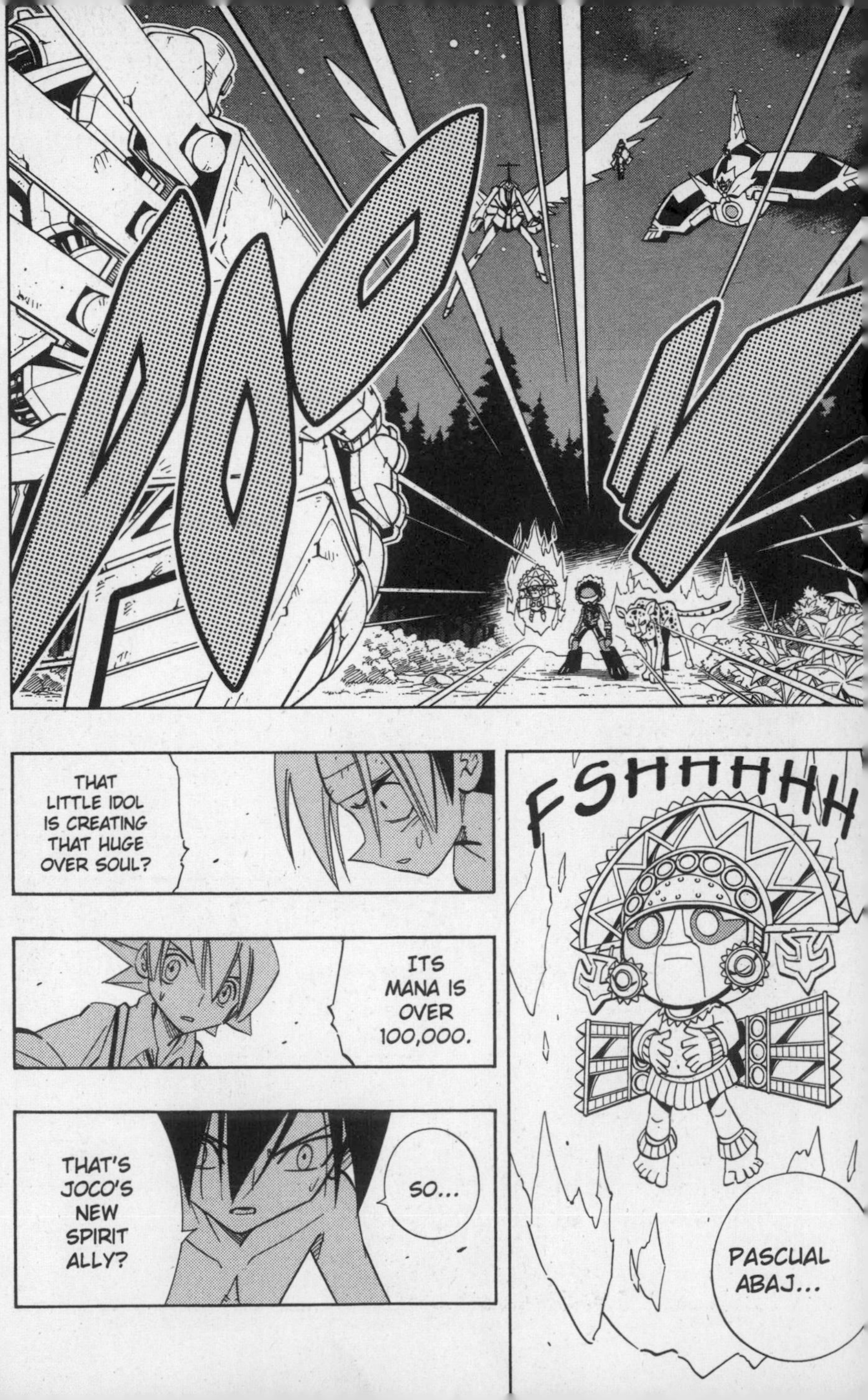
FSHHHHHH
PASCUAL ABAJ...
THAT LITTLE IDOL IS CREATING THAT HUGE OVER SOUL?
ITS MANA IS OVER 100,000.
SO...
THAT'S JOCO'S NEW SPIRIT ALLY?

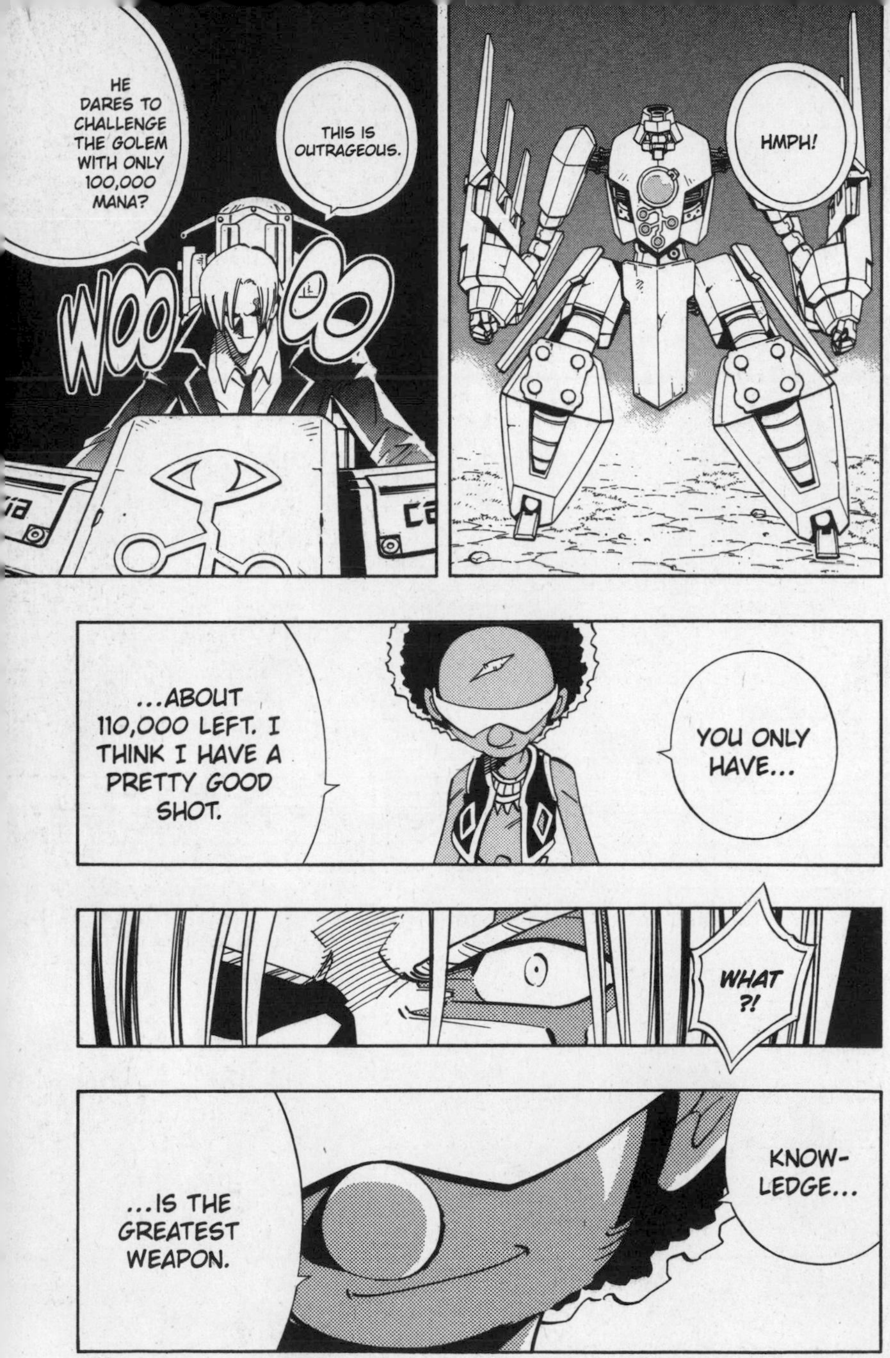
HMPH!
THIS IS OUTRAGEOUS.
HE DARES TO CHALLENGE THE GOLEM WITH ONLY 100,000 MANA?
WOO OO
YOU ONLY HAVE...
...ABOUT 110,000 LEFT. I THINK I HAVE A PRETTY GOOD SHOT.
WHAT?!
KNOW-LEDGE...
...IS THE GREATEST WEAPON.

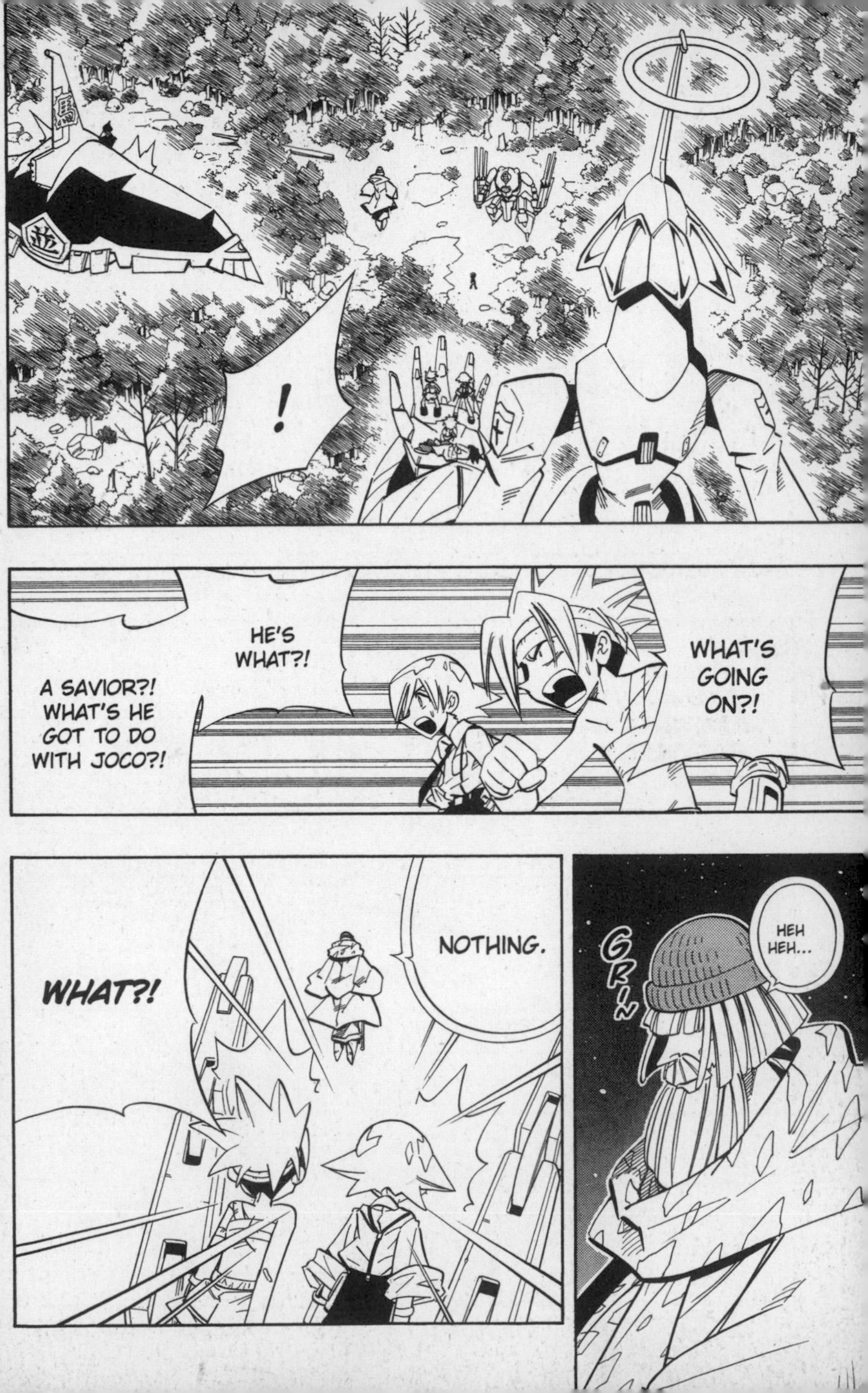
!
WHAT'S GOING ON?!
HE'S WHAT?!
A SAVIOR?! WHAT'S HE GOT TO DO WITH JOCO?!
HEH HEH...
GRIN
NOTHING.
WHAT?!

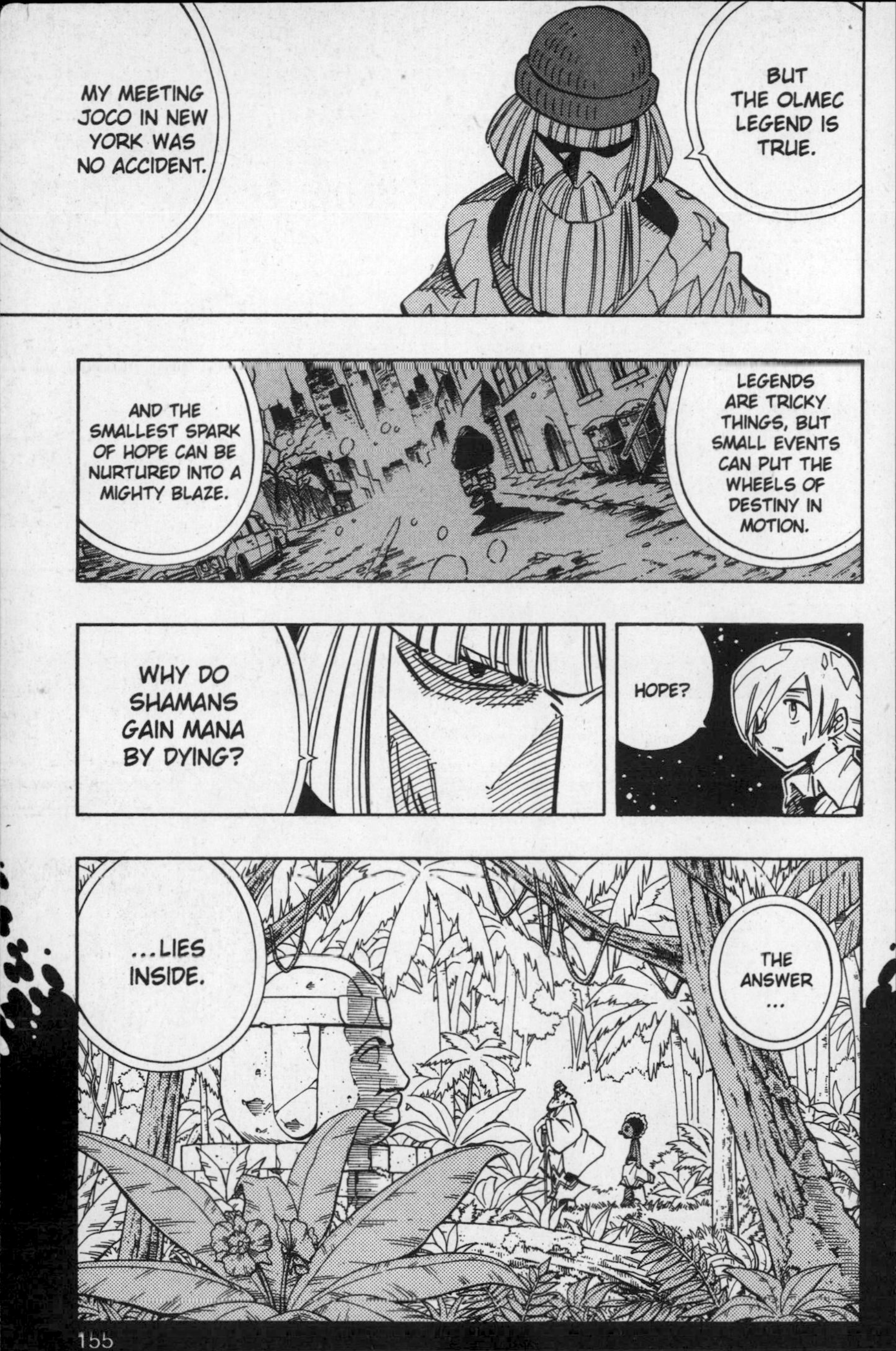

BUT THE OLMEC LEGEND IS TRUE.
MY MEETING JOCO IN NEW YORK WAS NO ACCIDENT.
LEGENDS ARE TRICKY THINGS, BUT SMALL EVENTS CAN PUT THE WHEELS OF DESTINY IN MOTION.
AND THE SMALLEST SPARK OF HOPE CAN BE NURTURED INTO A MIGHTY BLAZE.
HOPE?
WHY DO SHAMANS GAIN MANA BY DYING?
THE ANSWER ...
...LIES INSIDE.

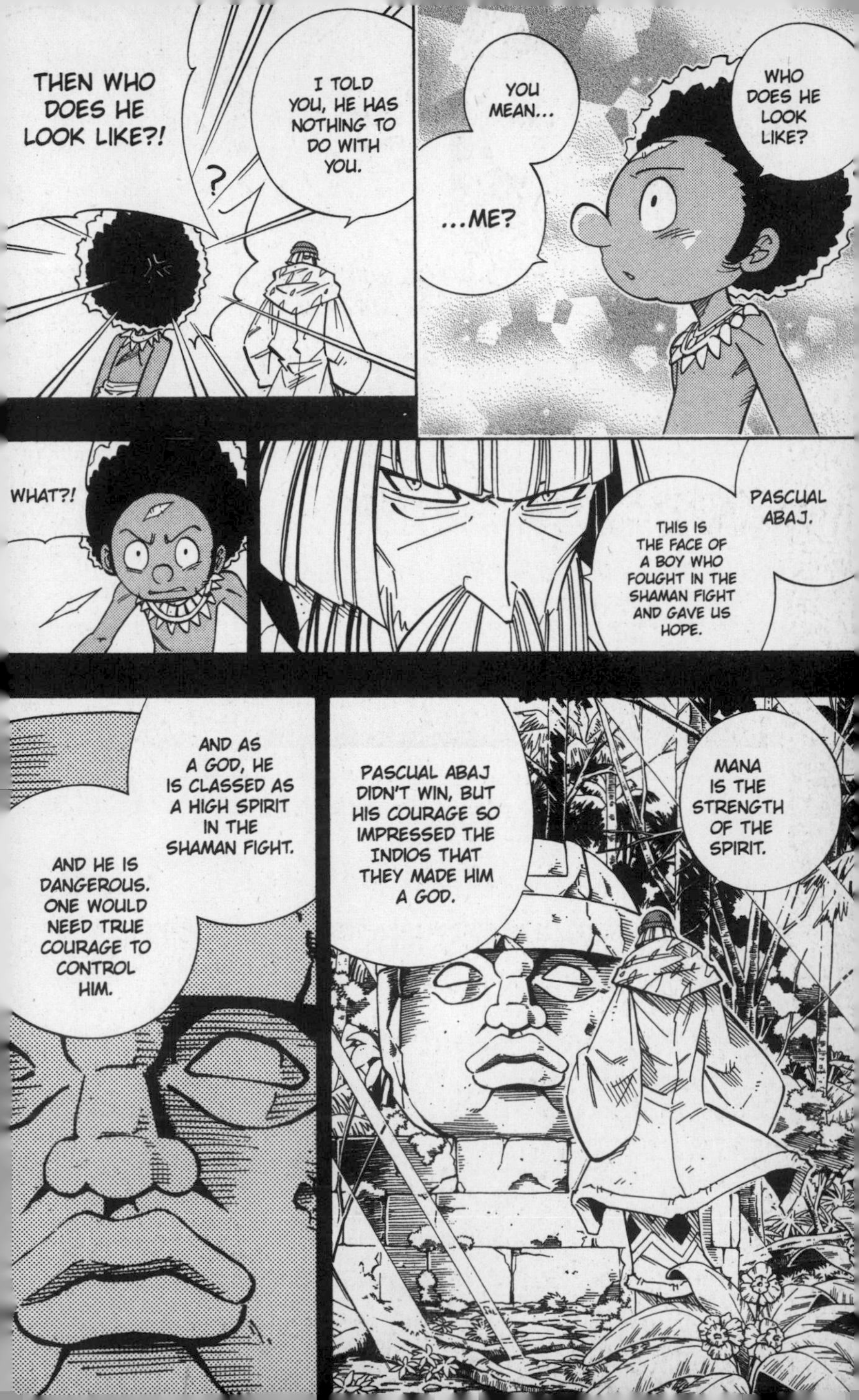
WHO DOES HE LOOK LIKE?
YOU MEAN...
...ME?
I TOLD YOU, HE HAS NOTHING TO DO WITH YOU.
?
THEN WHO DOES HE LOOK LIKE?!
PASCUAL ABAJ.
THIS IS THE FACE OF A BOY WHO FOUGHT IN THE SHAMAN FIGHT AND GAVE US HOPE.
WHAT?!
MANA IS THE STRENGTH OF THE SPIRIT.
PASCUAL ABAJ DIDN'T WIN, BUT HIS COURAGE SO IMPRESSED THE INDIOS THAT THEY MADE HIM A GOD.
AND AS A GOD, HE IS CLASSED AS A HIGH SPIRIT IN THE SHAMAN FIGHT.
AND HE IS DANGEROUS. ONE WOULD NEED TRUE COURAGE TO CONTROL HIM.

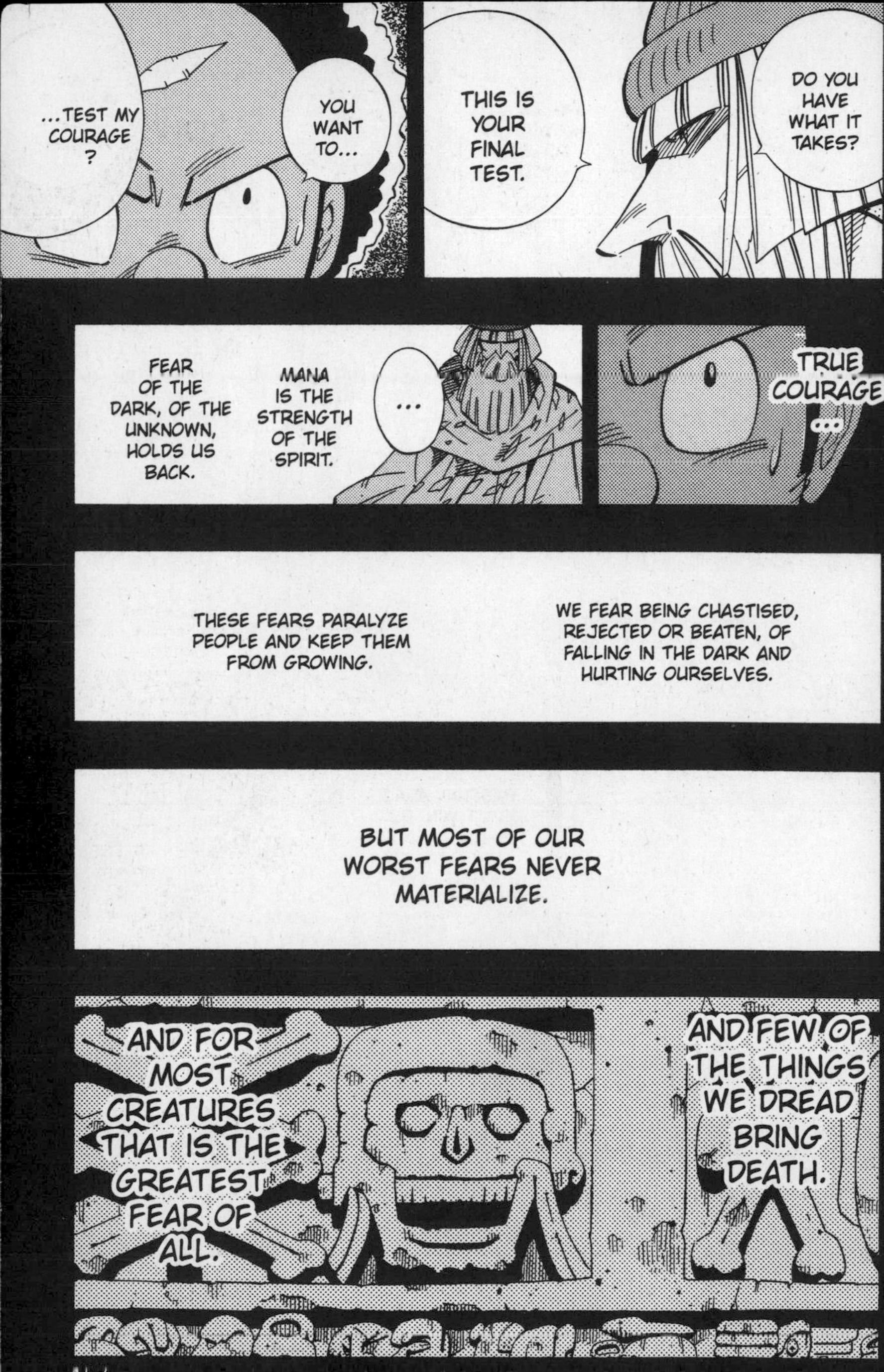
DO YOU HAVE WHAT IT TAKES?
THIS IS YOUR FINAL TEST.
YOU WANT TO...
...TEST MY COURAGE?
TRUE COURAGE...
...
MANA IS THE STRENGTH OF THE SPIRIT.
FEAR OF THE DARK, OF THE UNKNOWN, HOLDS US BACK.
WE FEAR BEING CHASTISED, REJECTED OR BEATEN, OF FALLING IN THE DARK AND HURTING OURSELVES.
THESE FEARS PARALYZE PEOPLE AND KEEP THEM FROM GROWING.
BUT MOST OF OUR WORST FEARS NEVER MATERIALIZE.
AND FEW OF THE THINGS WE DREAD BRING DEATH.
AND FOR MOST CREATURES THAT IS THE GREATEST FEAR OF ALL.

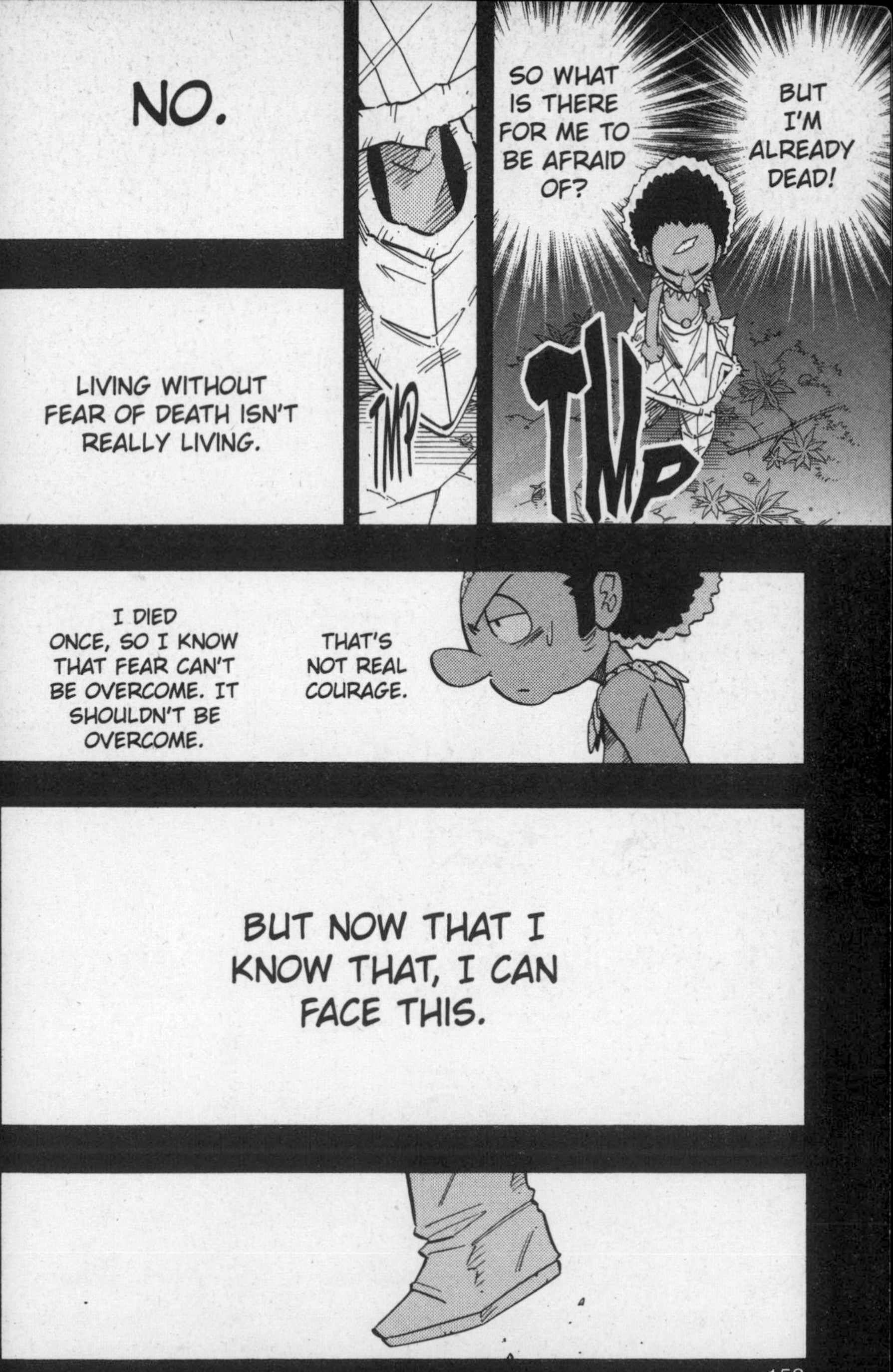
BUT I'M ALREADY DEAD!
SO WHAT IS THERE FOR ME TO BE AFRAID OF?
TMP
TMP
NO.
LIVING WITHOUT FEAR OF DEATH ISN'T REALLY LIVING.
THAT'S NOT REAL COURAGE.
I DIED ONCE, SO I KNOW THAT FEAR CAN'T BE OVERCOME. IT SHOULDN'T BE OVERCOME.
BUT NOW THAT I KNOW THAT, I CAN FACE THIS.

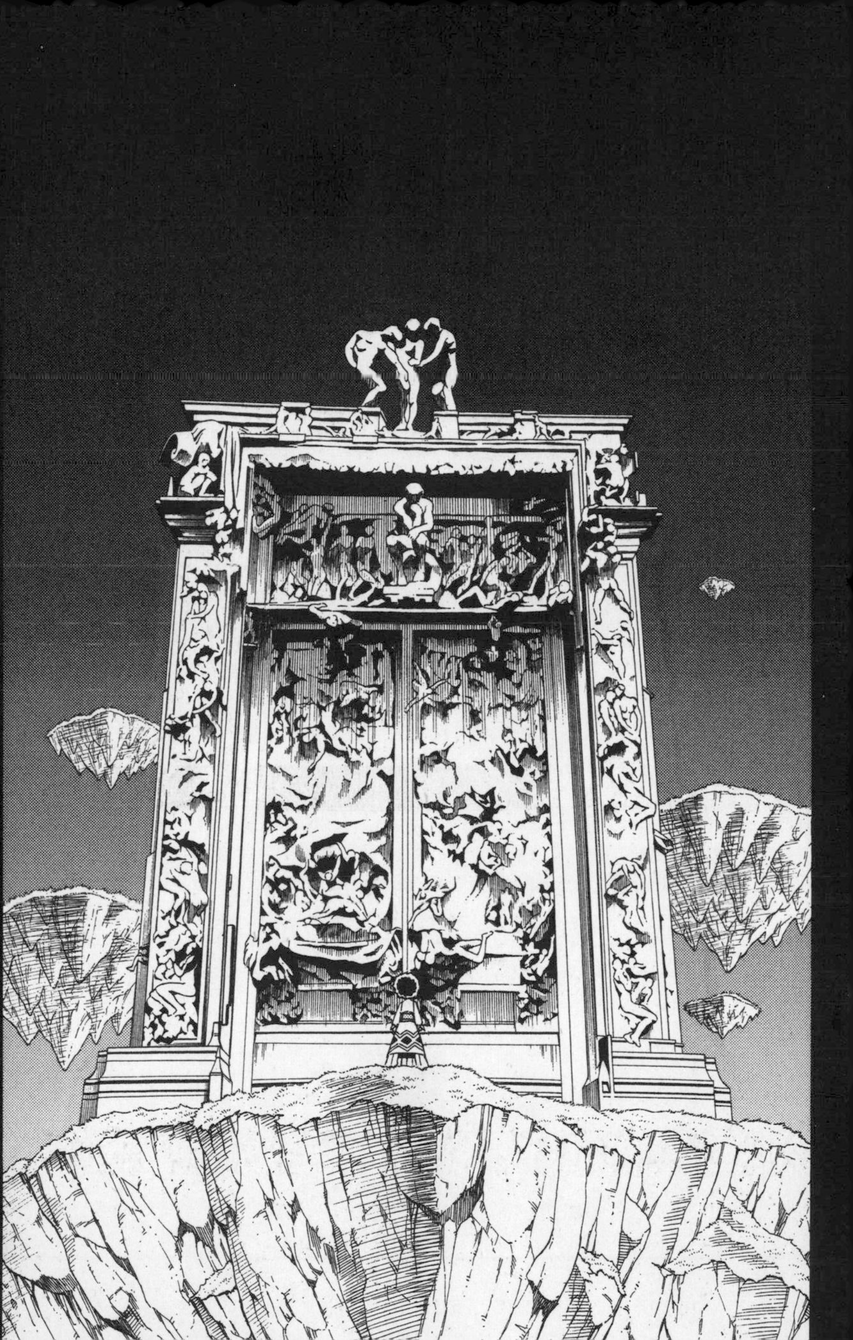

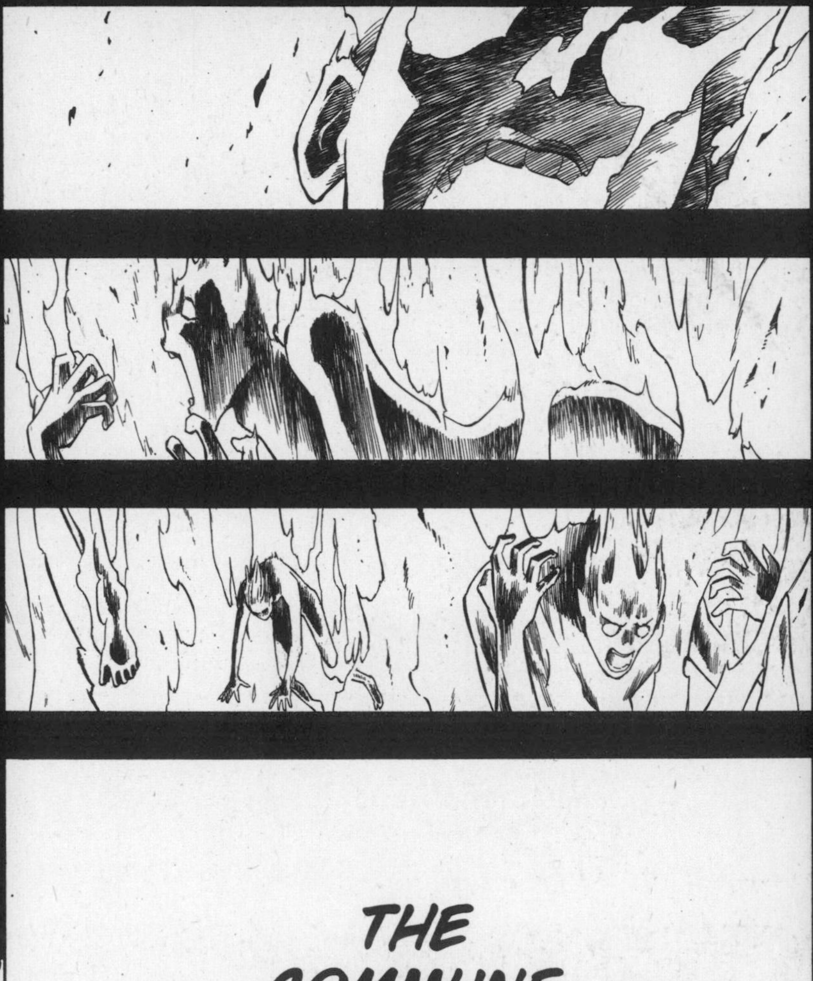
THE COMMUNE OF HELL...

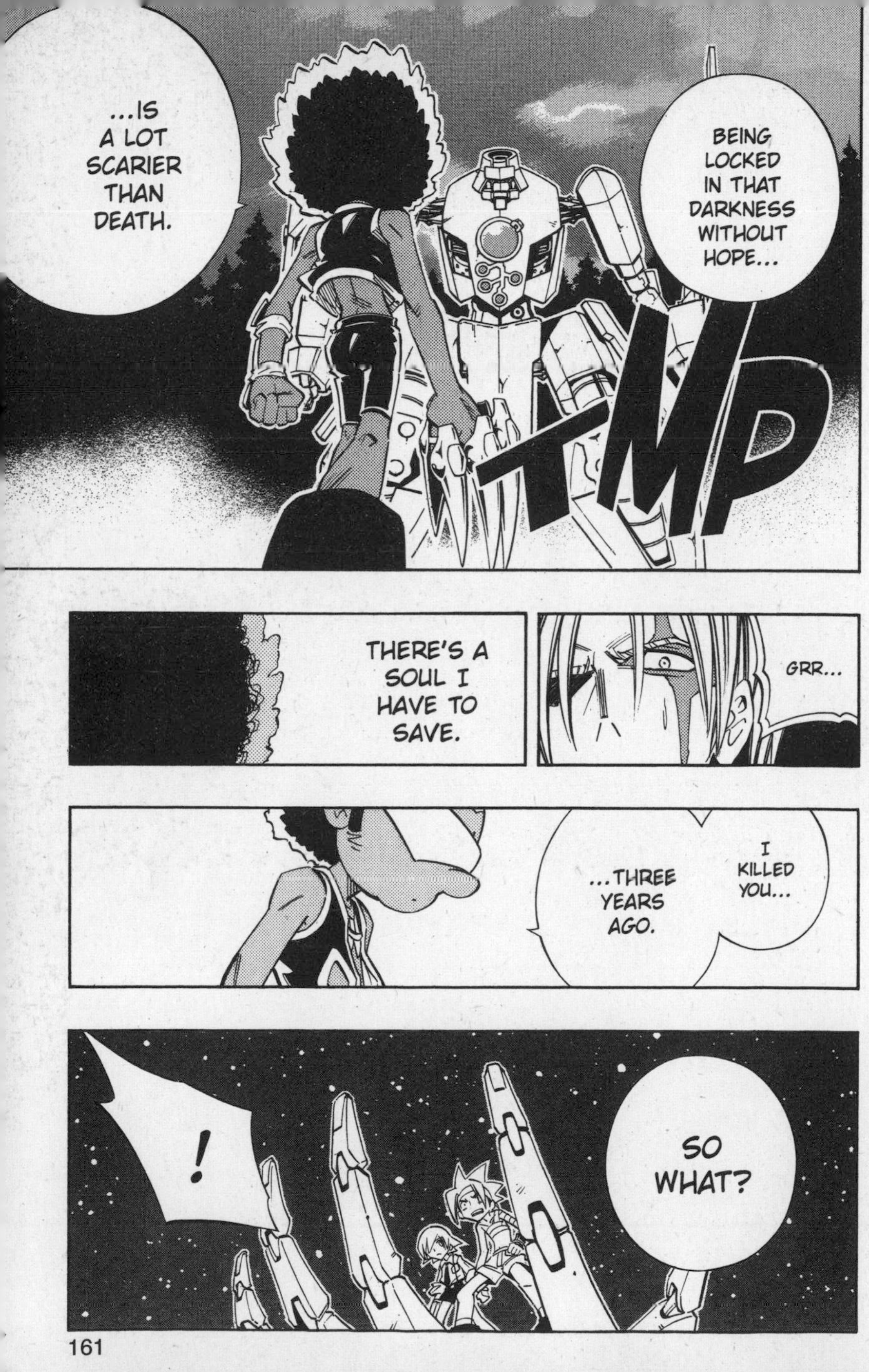
BEING LOCKED IN THAT DARKNESS WITHOUT HOPE...
...IS A LOT SCARIER THAN DEATH.
TMP
GRR...
THERE'S A SOUL I HAVE TO SAVE.
I KILLED YOU...
...THREE YEARS AGO.
SO WHAT?
!

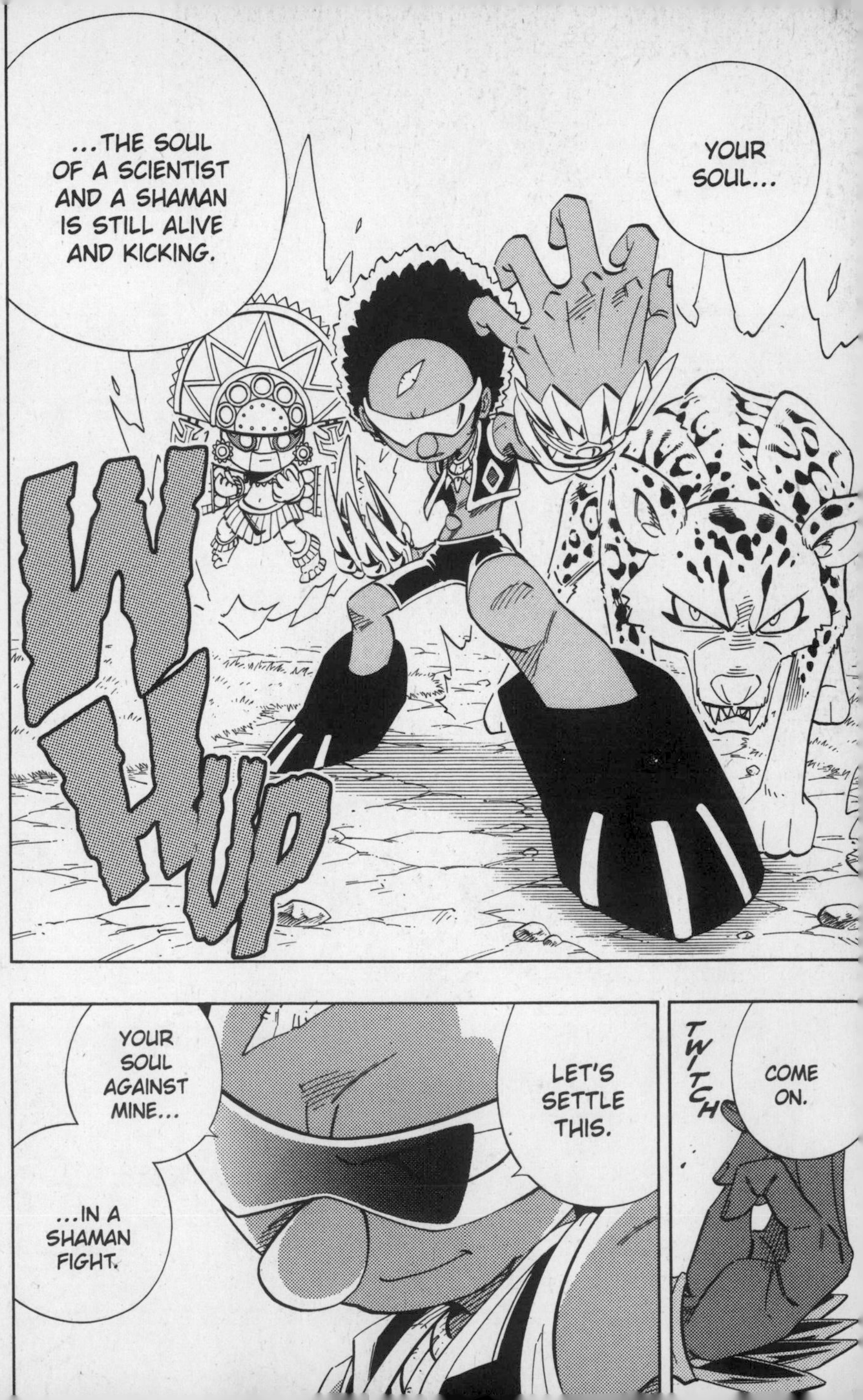
YOUR SOUL...
...THE SOUL OF A SCIENTIST AND A SHAMAN IS STILL ALIVE AND KICKING.
WHUP
TWITCH
COME ON.
LET'S SETTLE THIS.
YOUR SOUL AGAINST MINE...
...IN A SHAMAN FIGHT.

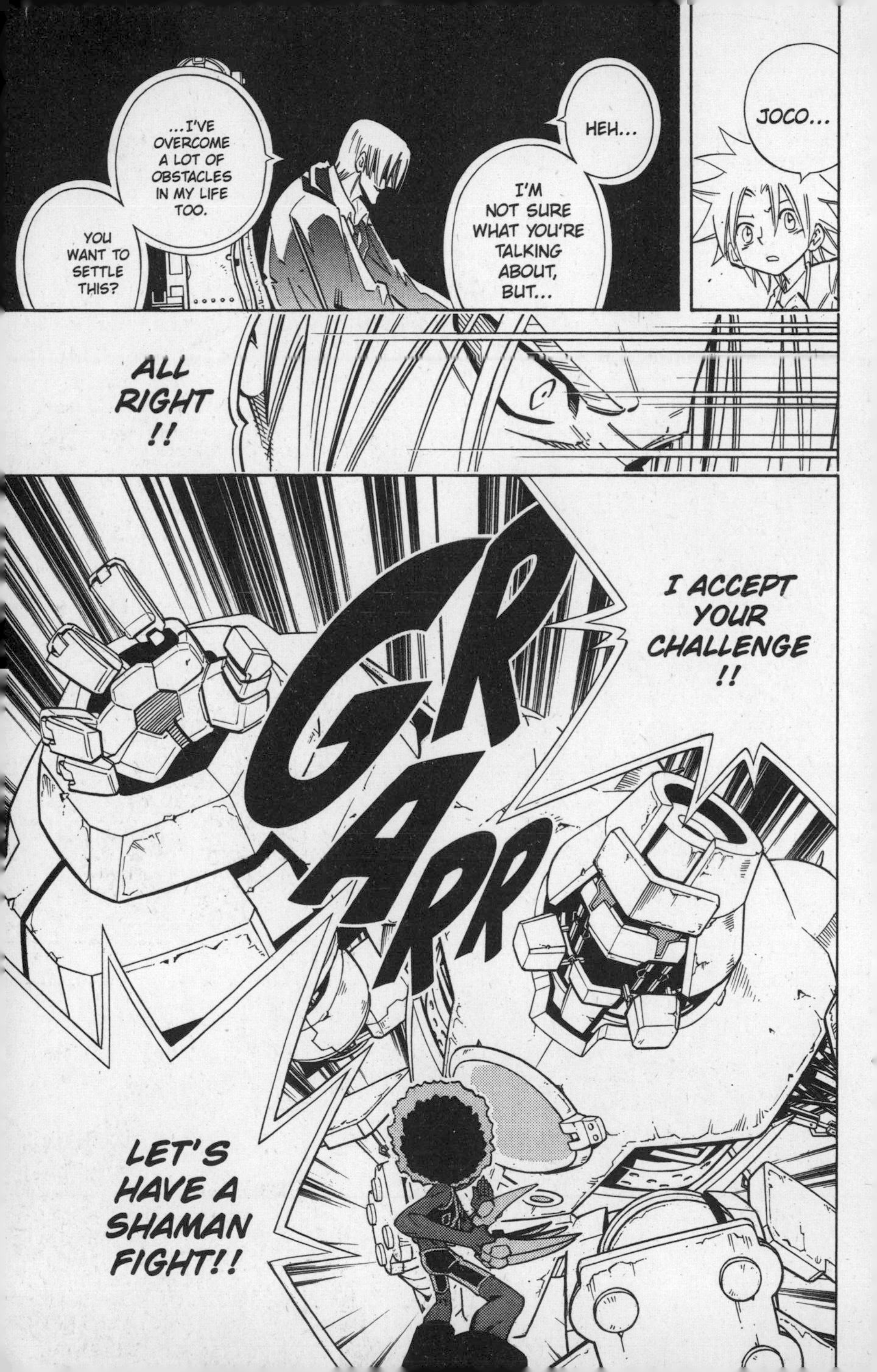
JOCO...
HEH...
I'M NOT SURE WHAT YOU'RE TALKING ABOUT, BUT...
...I'VE OVERCOME A LOT OF OBSTACLES IN MY LIFE TOO.
YOU WANT TO SETTLE THIS?
ALL RIGHT !!
I ACCEPT YOUR CHALLENGE !!
LET'S HAVE A SHAMAN FIGHT!!

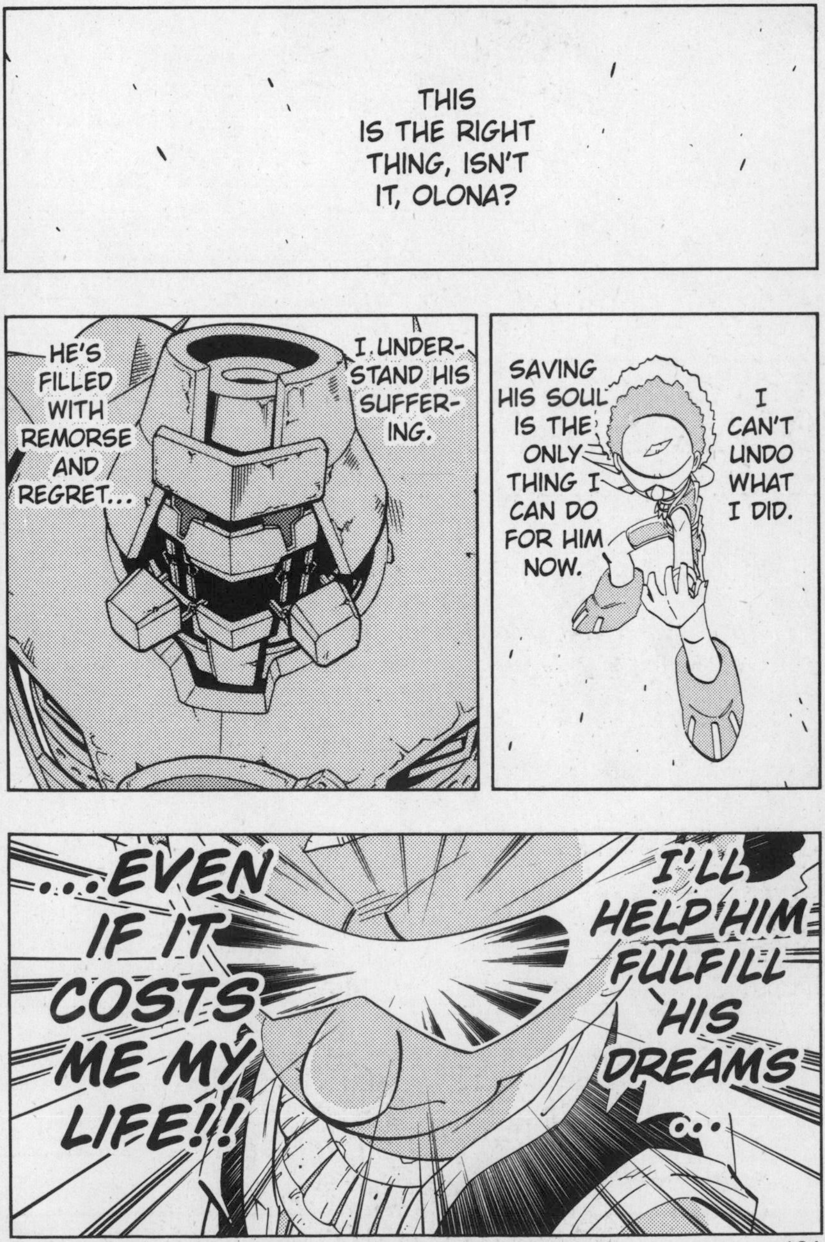
THIS IS THE RIGHT THING, ISN'T IT, OLONA?
I CAN'T UNDO WHAT I DID.
SAVING HIS SOUL IS THE ONLY THING I CAN DO FOR HIM NOW.
I UNDER-STAND HIS SUFFER-ING.
HE'S FILLED WITH REMORSE AND REGRET...
I'LL HELP HIM FULFILL HIS DREAMS...
...EVEN IF IT COSTS ME MY LIFE!!

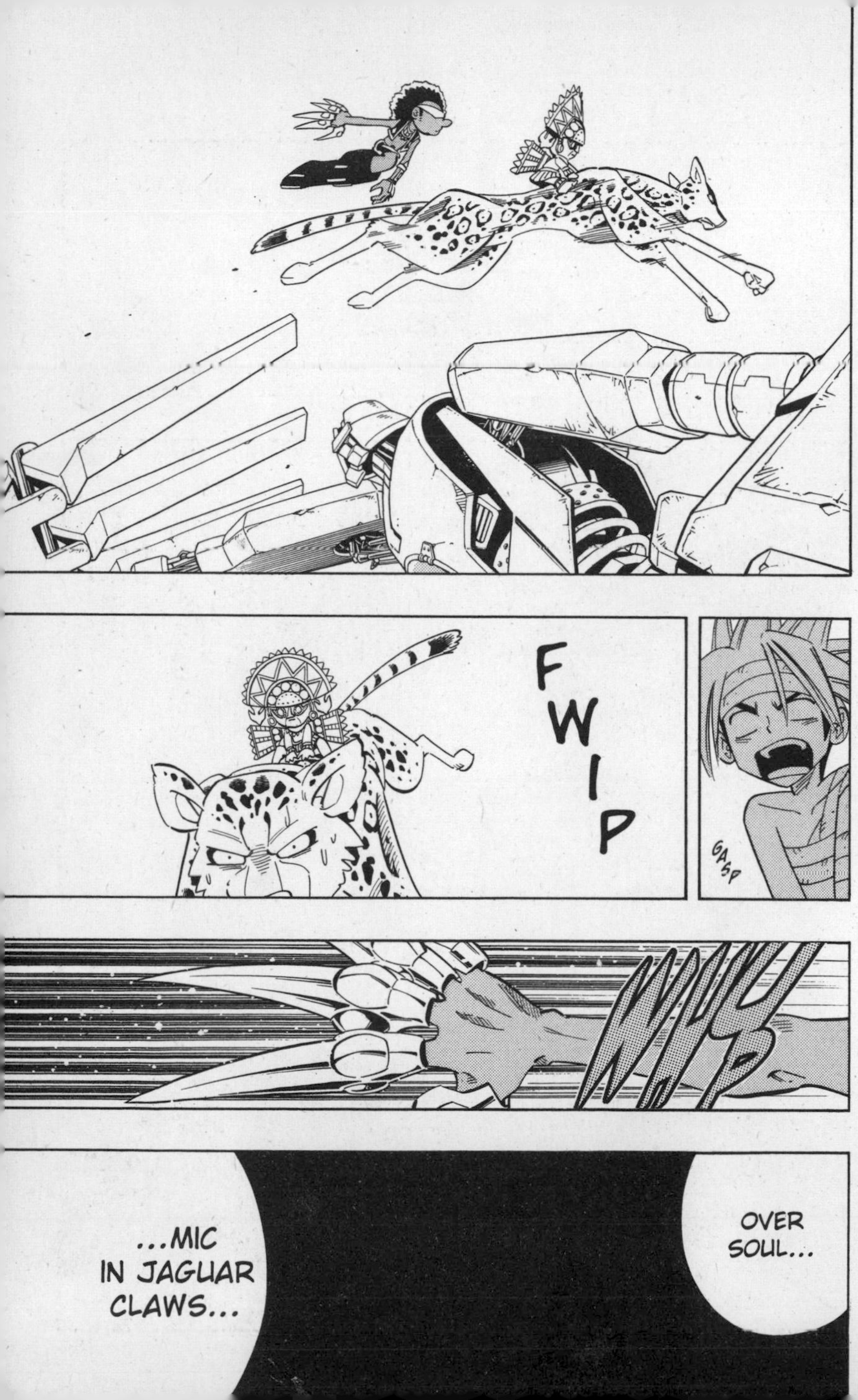
GASP
FWIP
WHAP
OVER SOUL...
...MIC IN JAGUAR CLAWS...

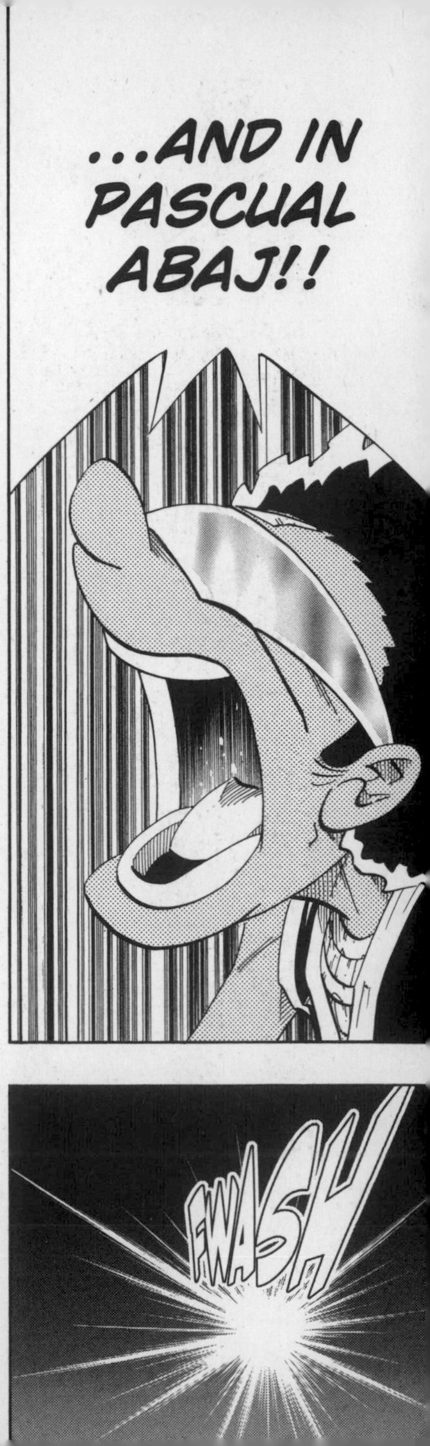
...AND IN PASCUAL ABAJ!!
FWASH
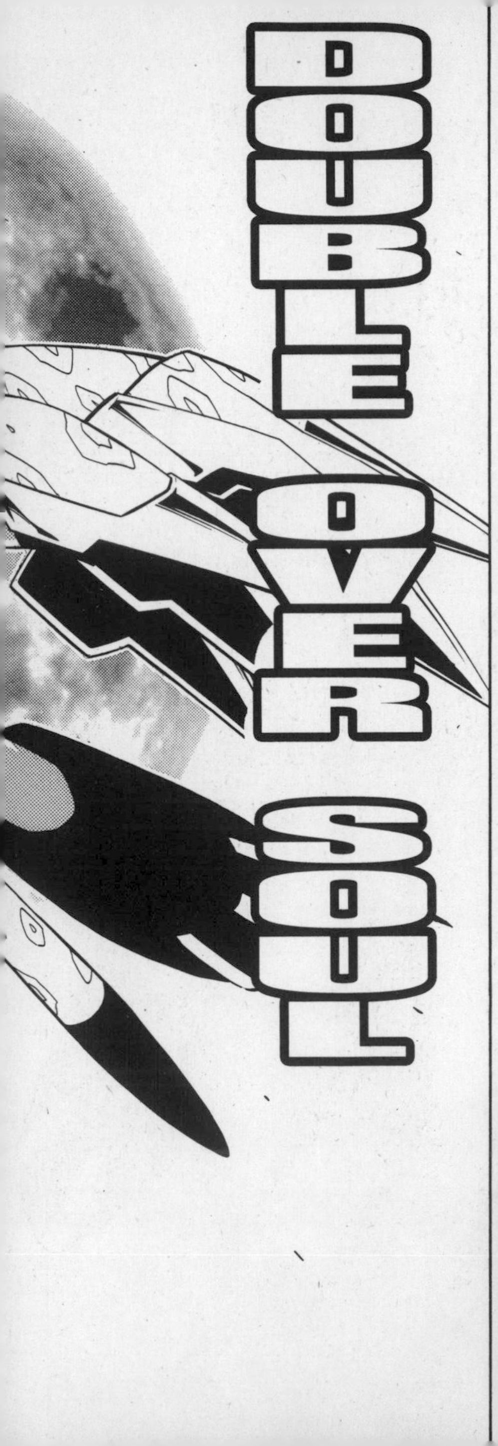
DOUBLE OVER SOUL

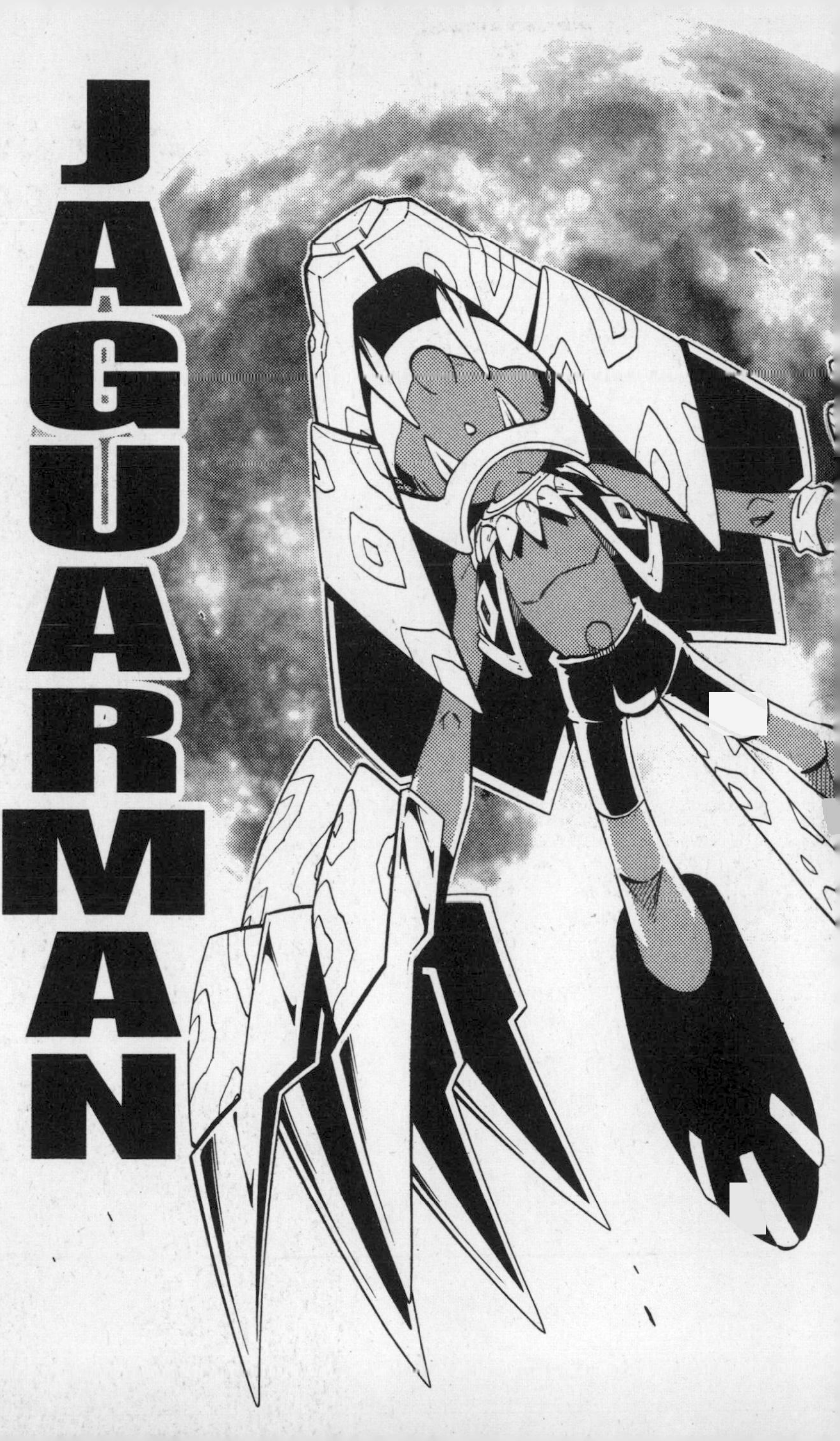
JAGUARMAN

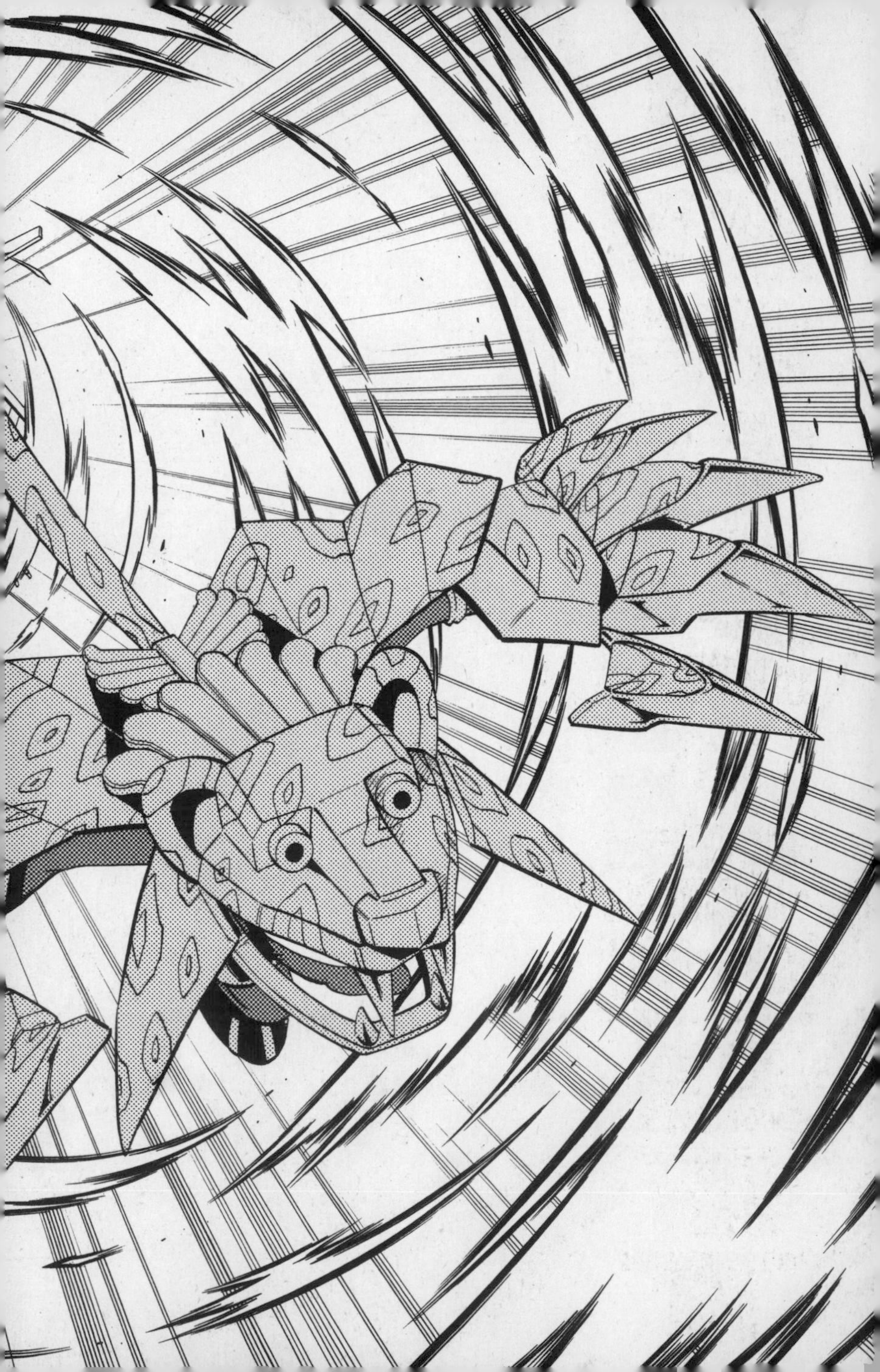

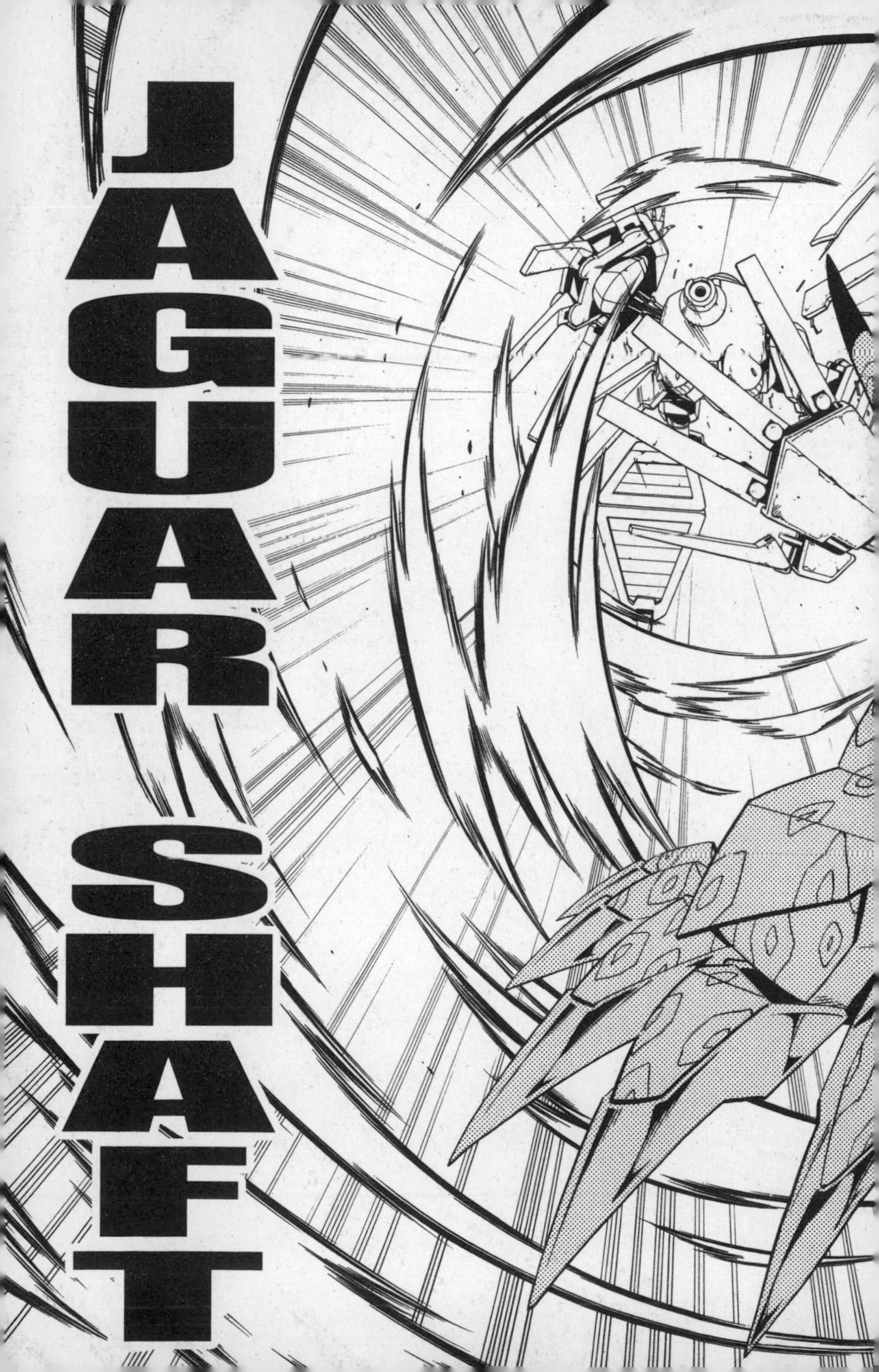
JAGUAR SHAFT

SHAMAN KING ITEM FILE No.61

2001
(JAN)

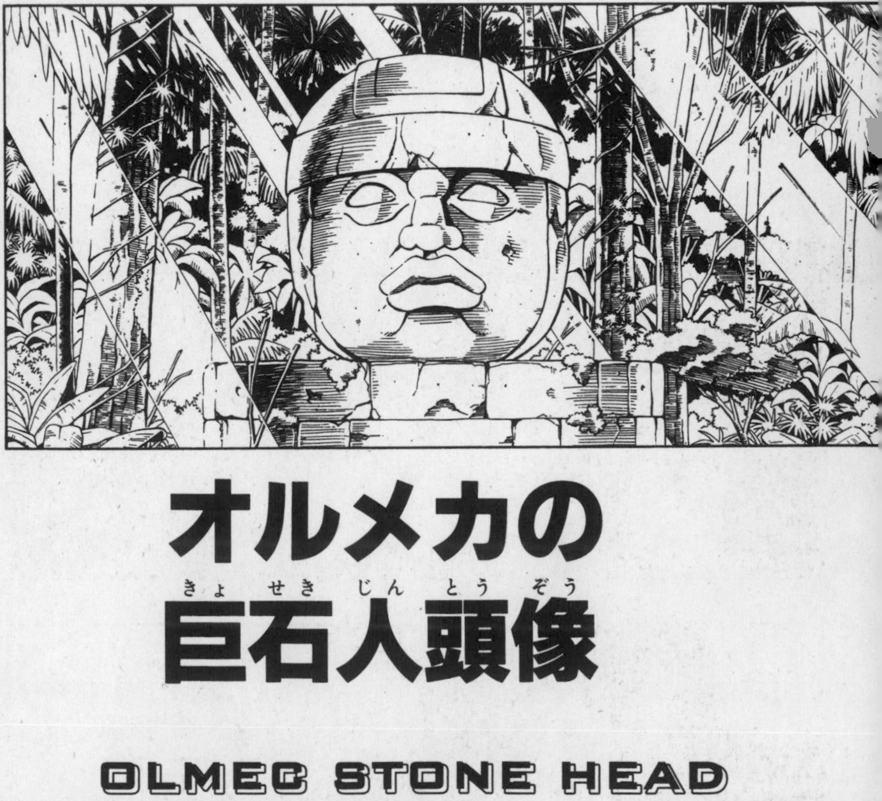

オルメカの巨石人頭像

きょせきじんとうぞう

OLMEC STONE HEAD

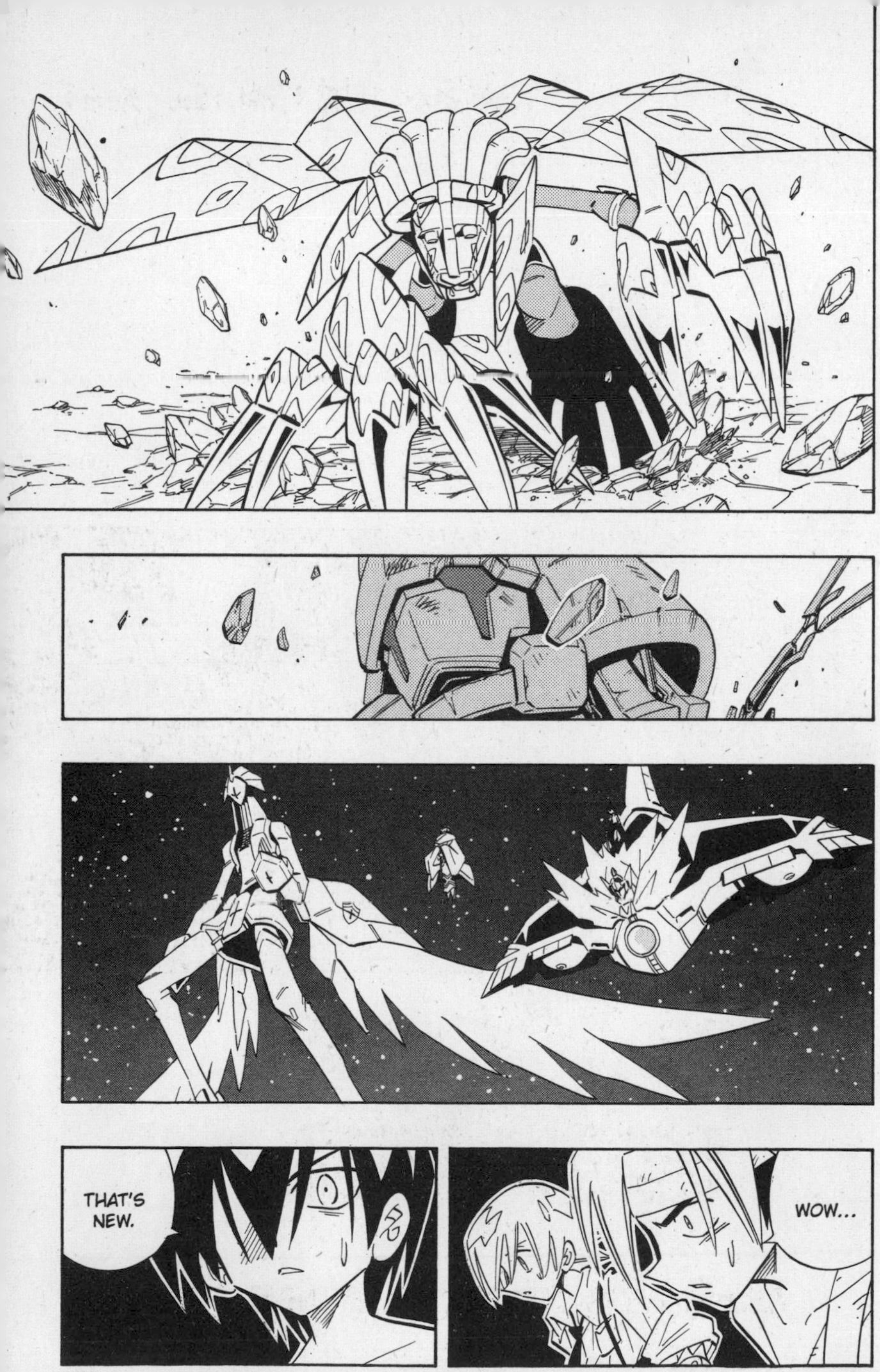
WOW...
THAT'S NEW.

Reincarnation 206: Epilogue V: Settle the Score!

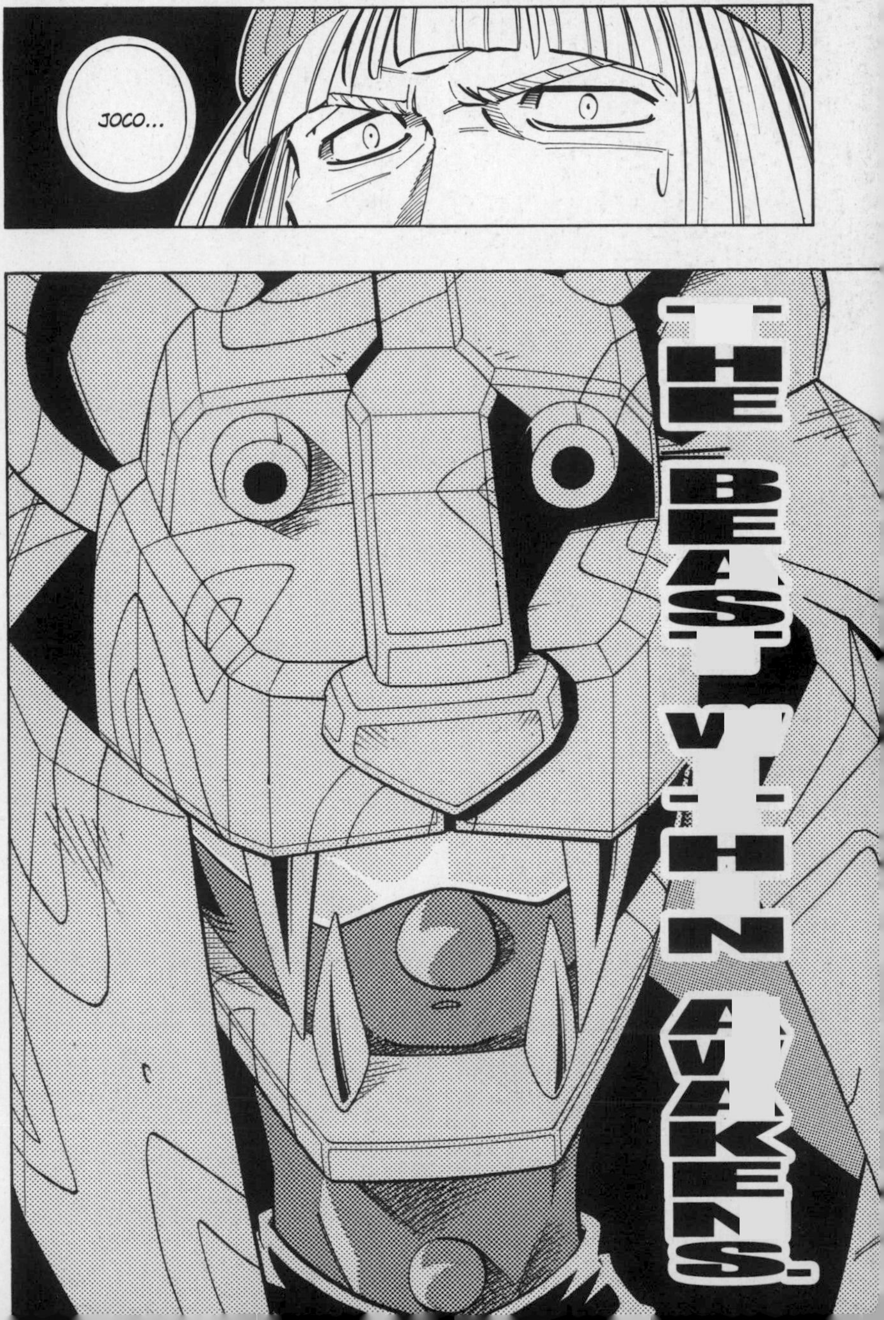
JOCO...
THE BEAST WITHIN AWAKENS.

Reincarnation 206: Epilogue V: Settle the Score!

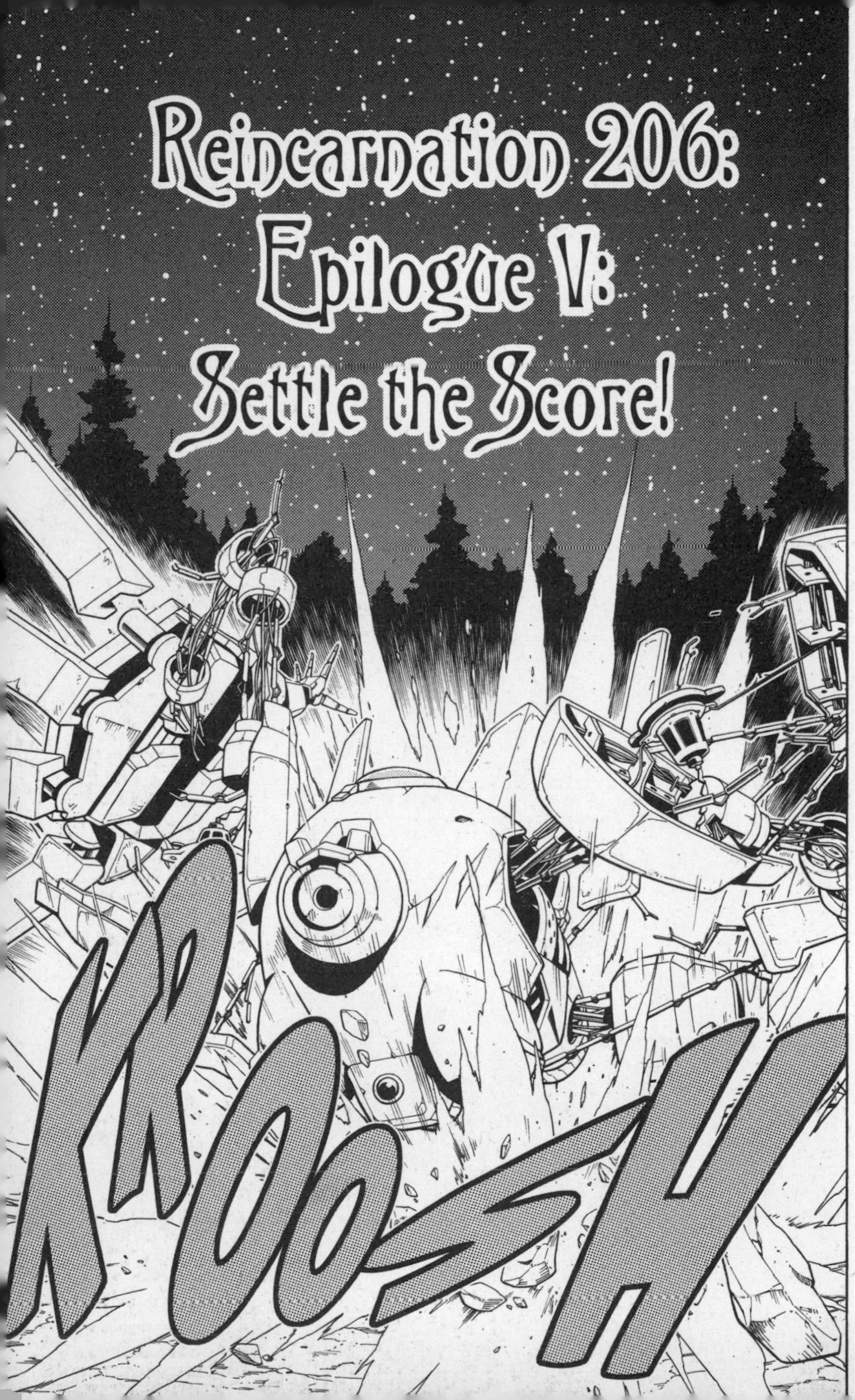
KROOSH

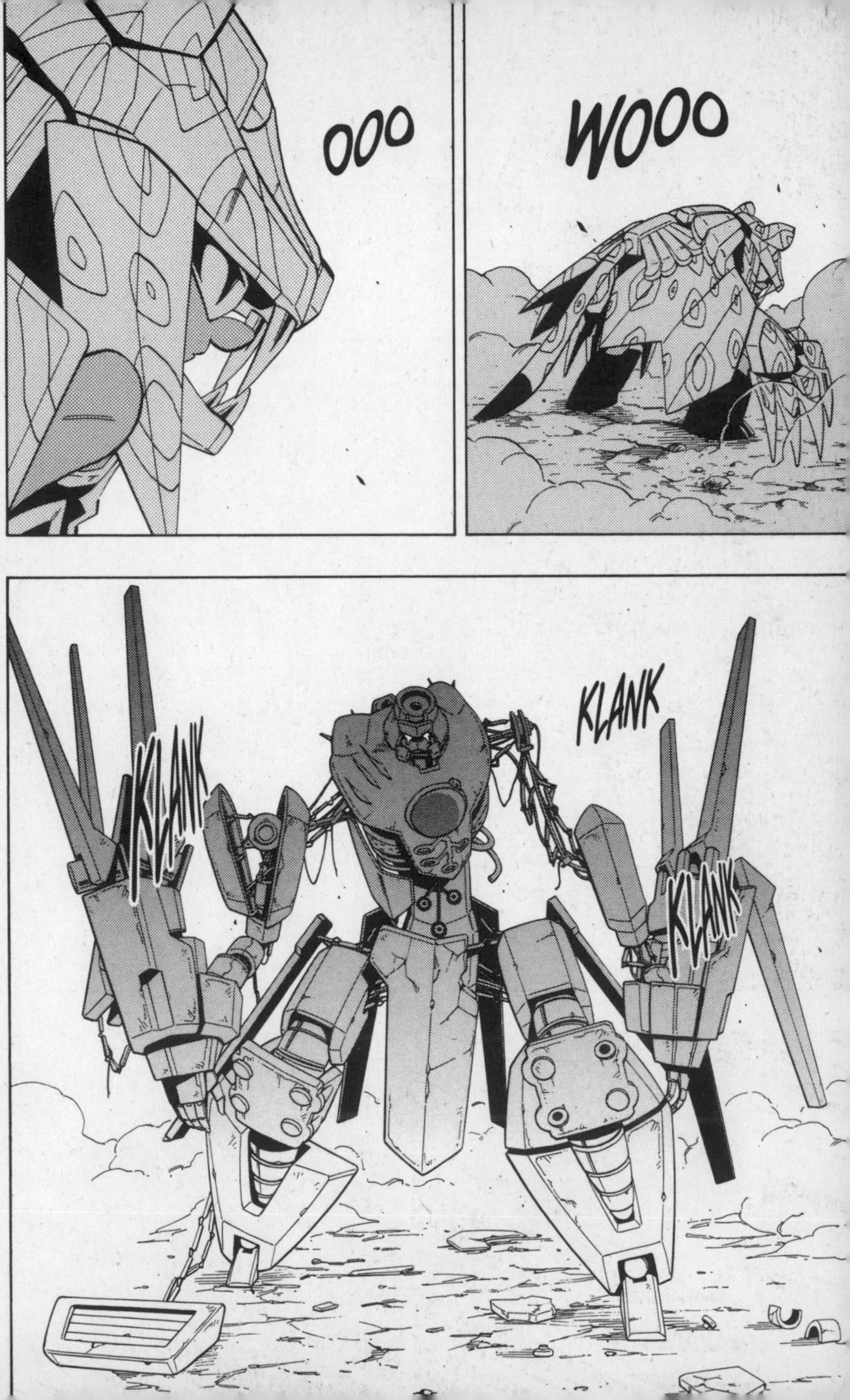
WOOO
OOO
KLANK
KLANK
KLANK

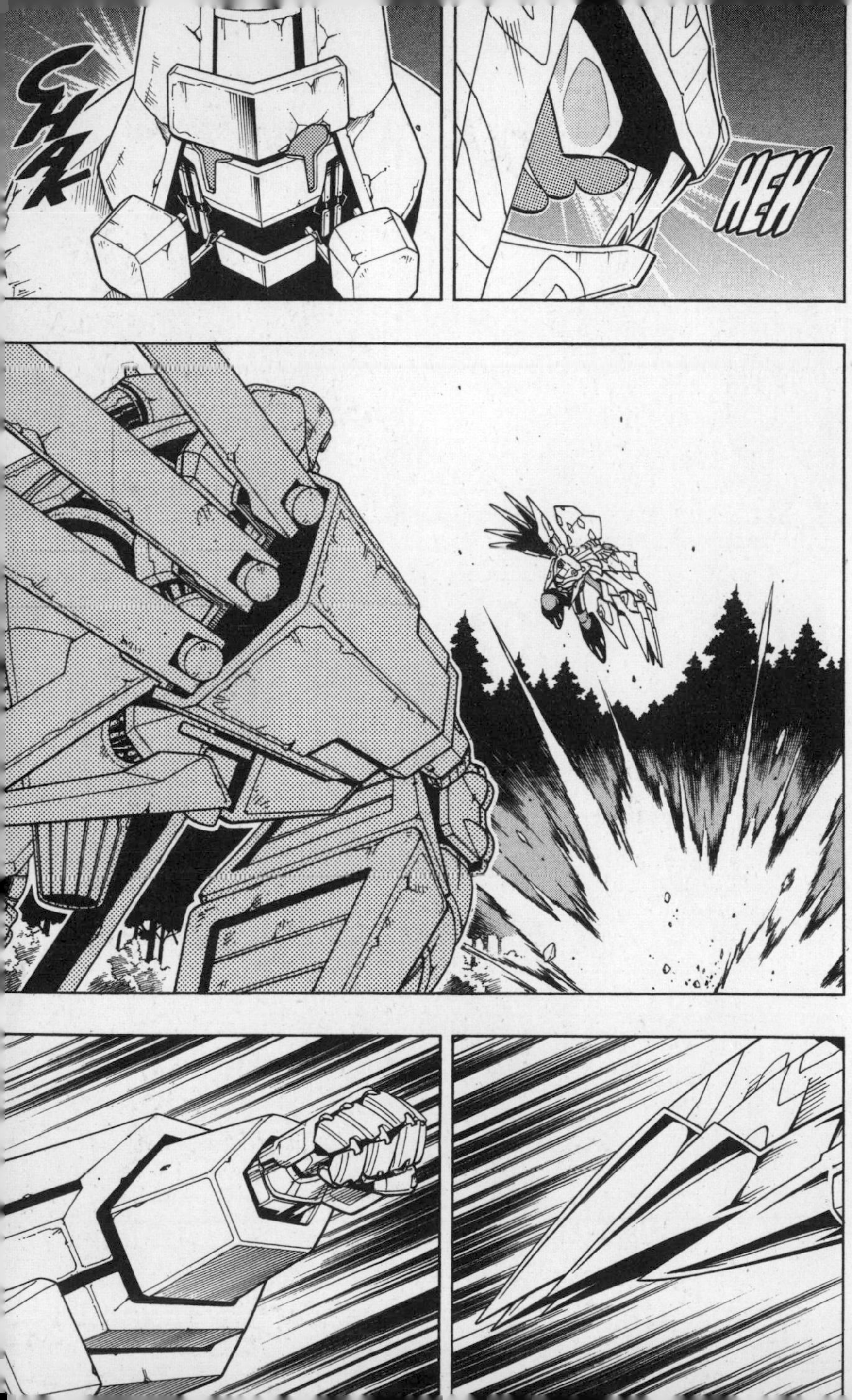
HEH
CHAK

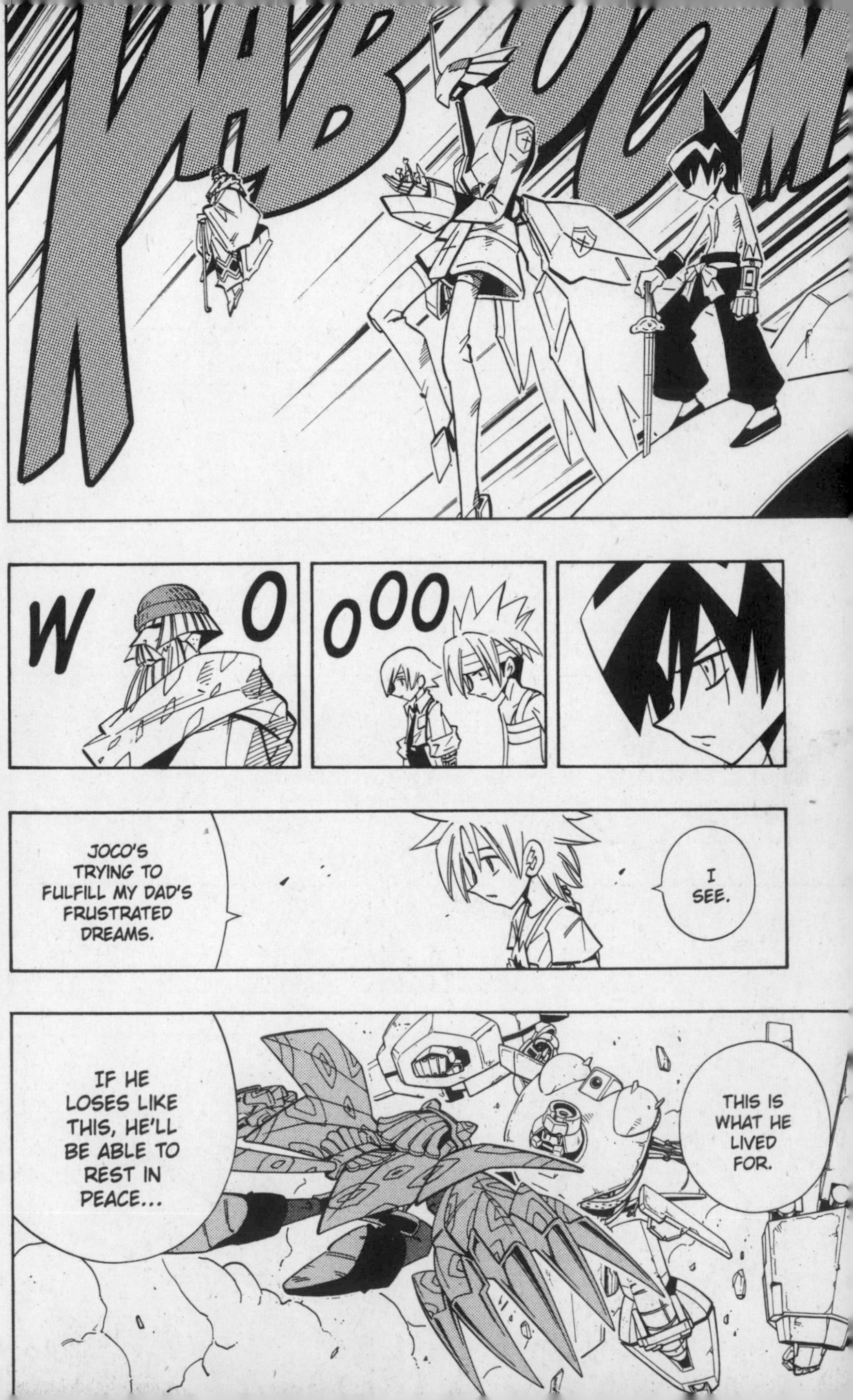
KABOOM
WOOOO
I SEE.
JOCO'S TRYING TO FULFILL MY DAD'S FRUSTRATED DREAMS.
THIS IS WHAT HE LIVED FOR.
IF HE LOSES LIKE THIS, HE'LL BE ABLE TO REST IN PEACE...

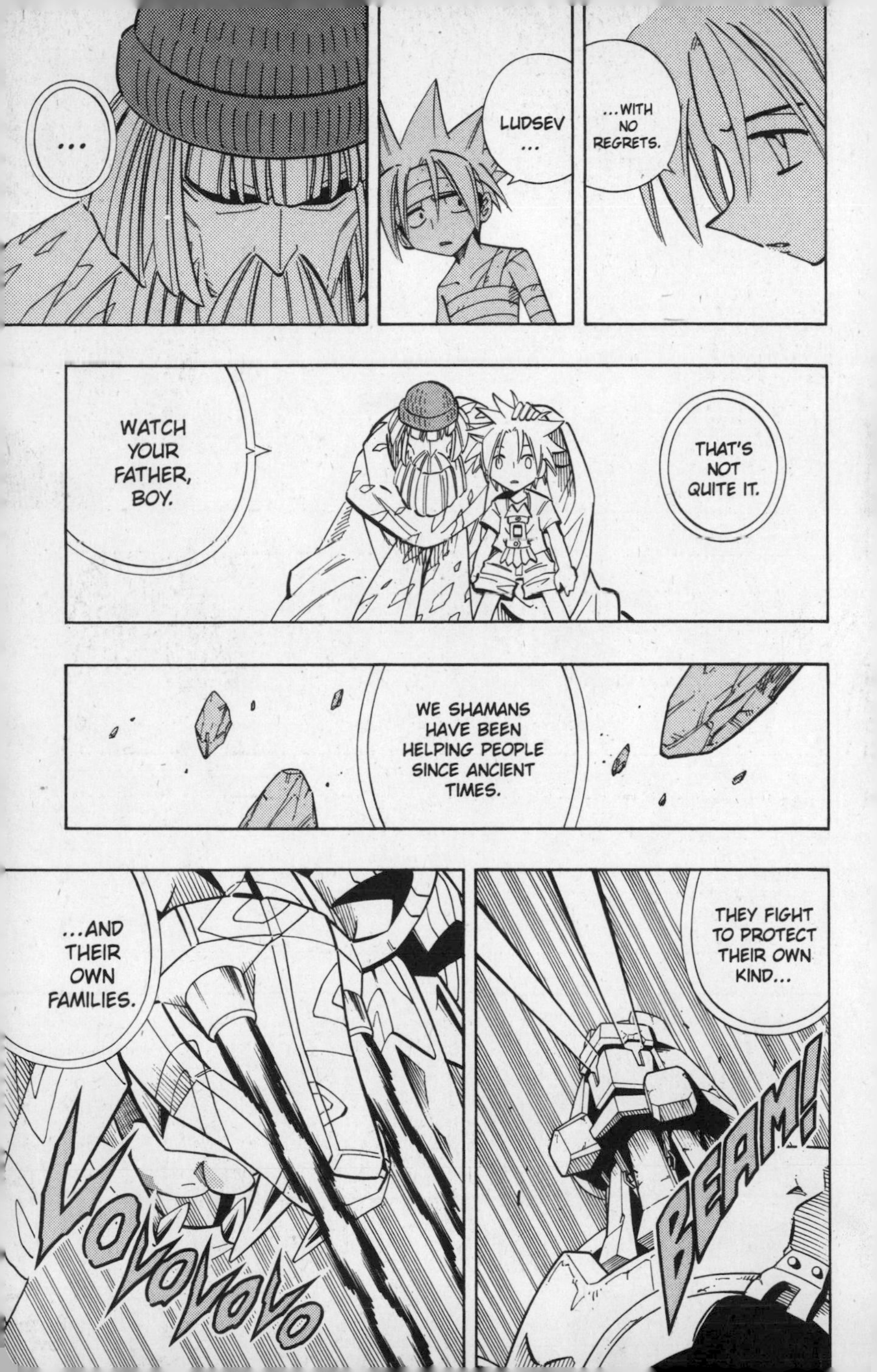
...WITH NO REGRETS.
LUDSEV ...
...
THAT'S NOT QUITE IT.
WATCH YOUR FATHER, BOY.
WE SHAMANS HAVE BEEN HELPING PEOPLE SINCE ANCIENT TIMES.
THEY FIGHT TO PROTECT THEIR OWN KIND...
BEAM!
...AND THEIR OWN FAMILIES.
VOVOVOVO

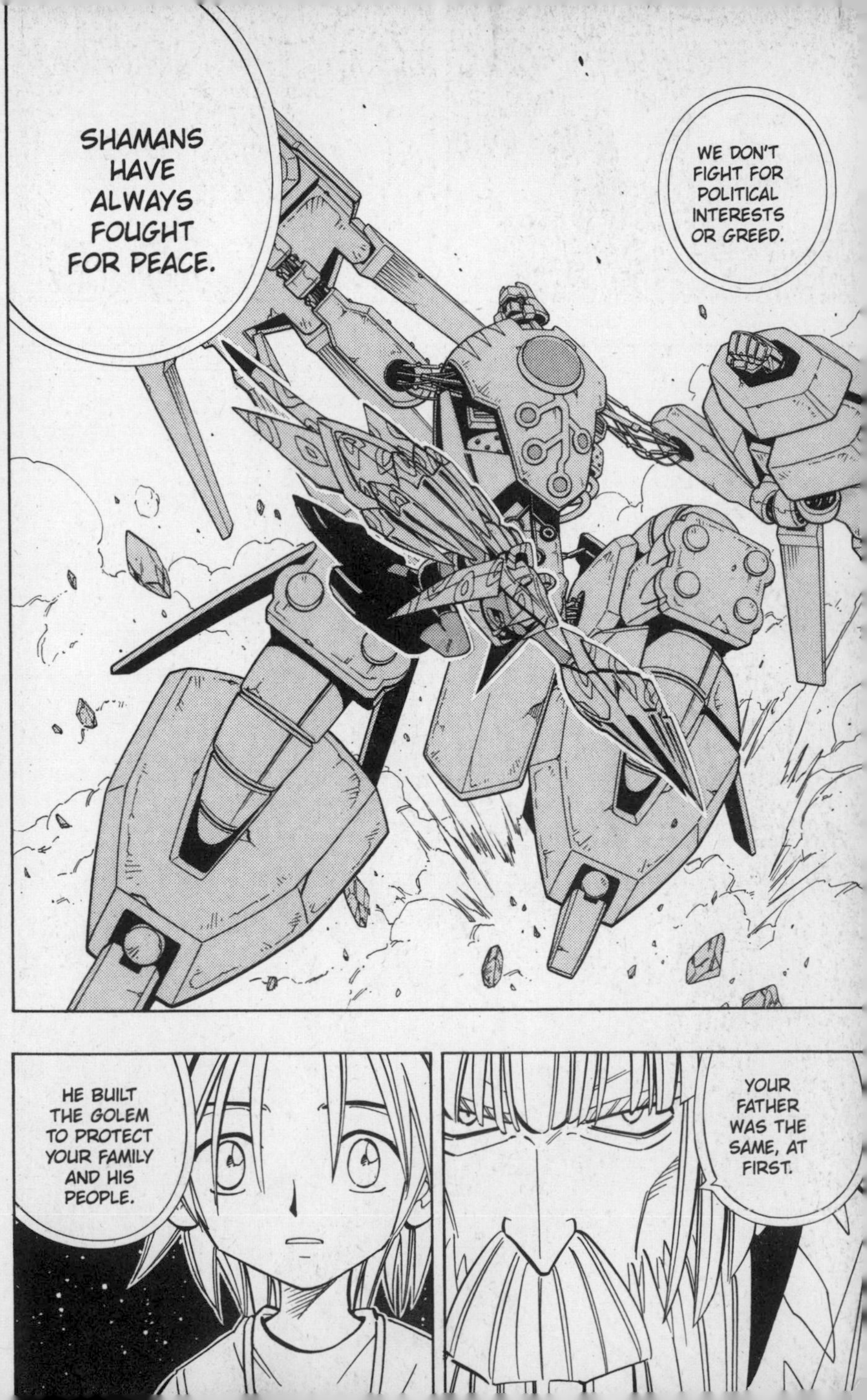
WE DON'T FIGHT FOR POLITICAL INTERESTS OR GREED.
SHAMANS HAVE ALWAYS FOUGHT FOR PEACE.
YOUR FATHER WAS THE SAME, AT FIRST.
HE BUILT THE GOLEM TO PROTECT YOUR FAMILY AND HIS PEOPLE.

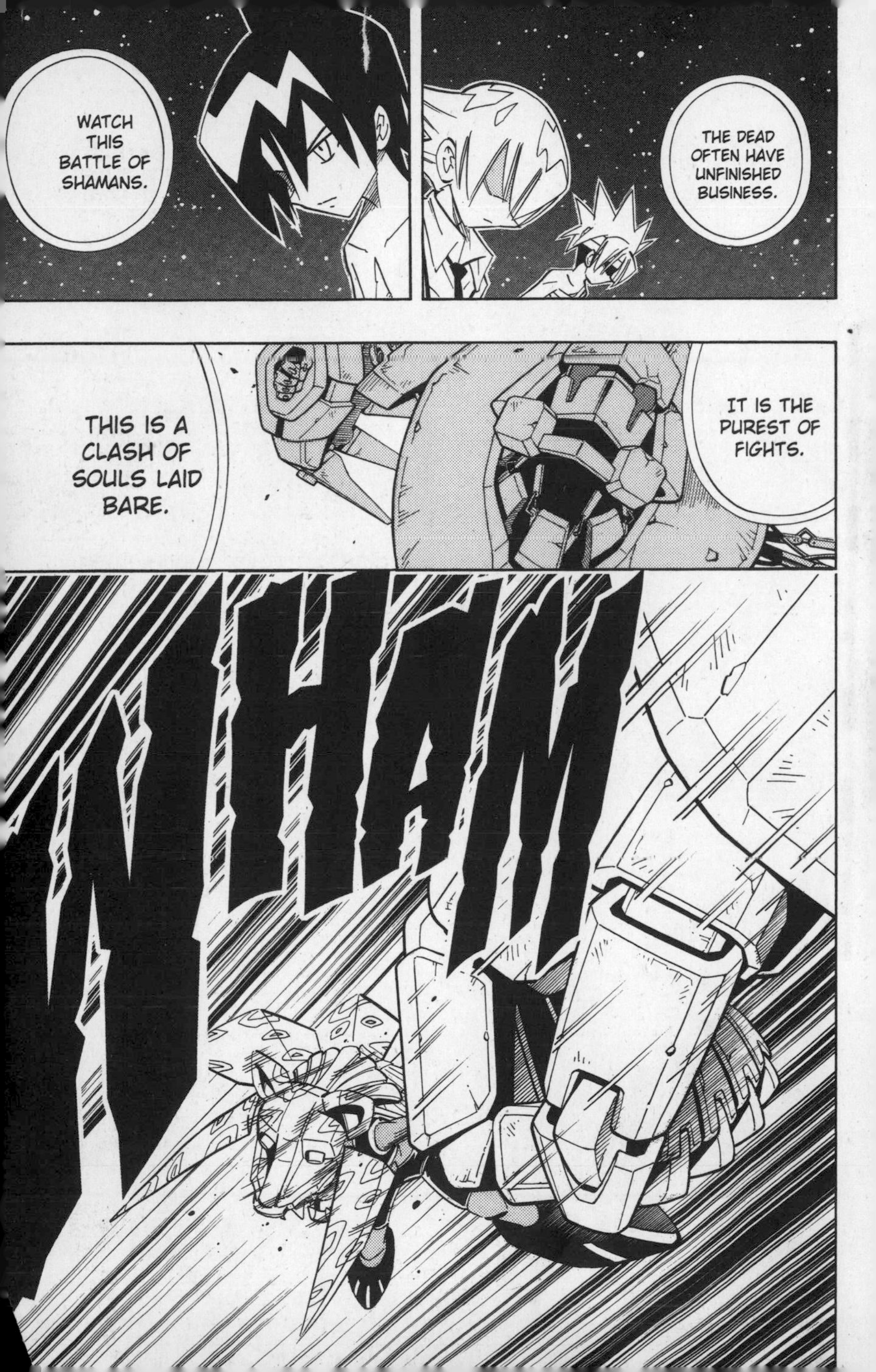
THE DEAD OFTEN HAVE UNFINISHED BUSINESS.
WATCH THIS BATTLE OF SHAMANS.
IT IS THE PUREST OF FIGHTS.
THIS IS A CLASH OF SOULS LAID BARE.
WHAM

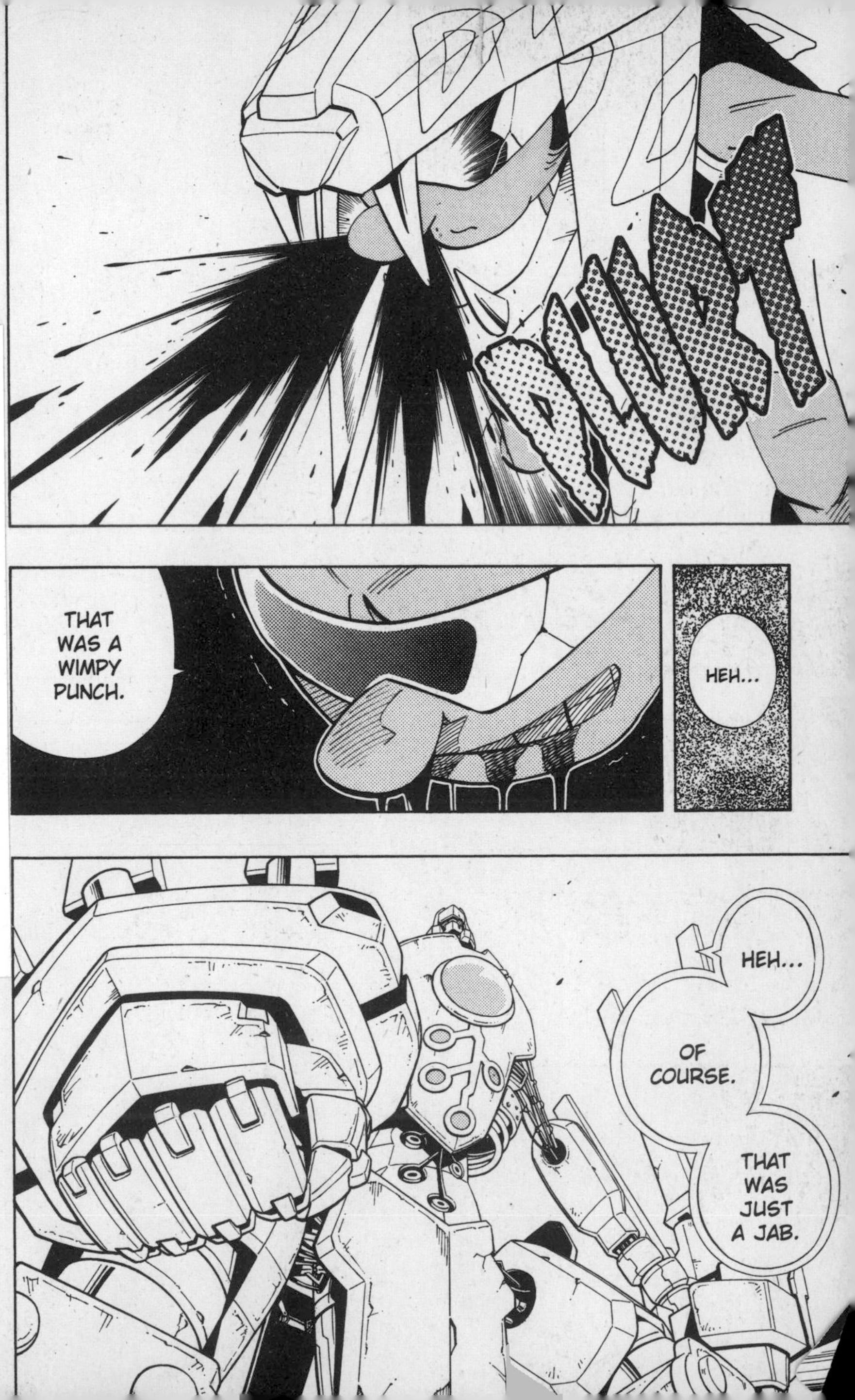
HEH...
THAT WAS A WIMPY PUNCH.
HEH...
OF COURSE.
THAT WAS JUST A JAB.

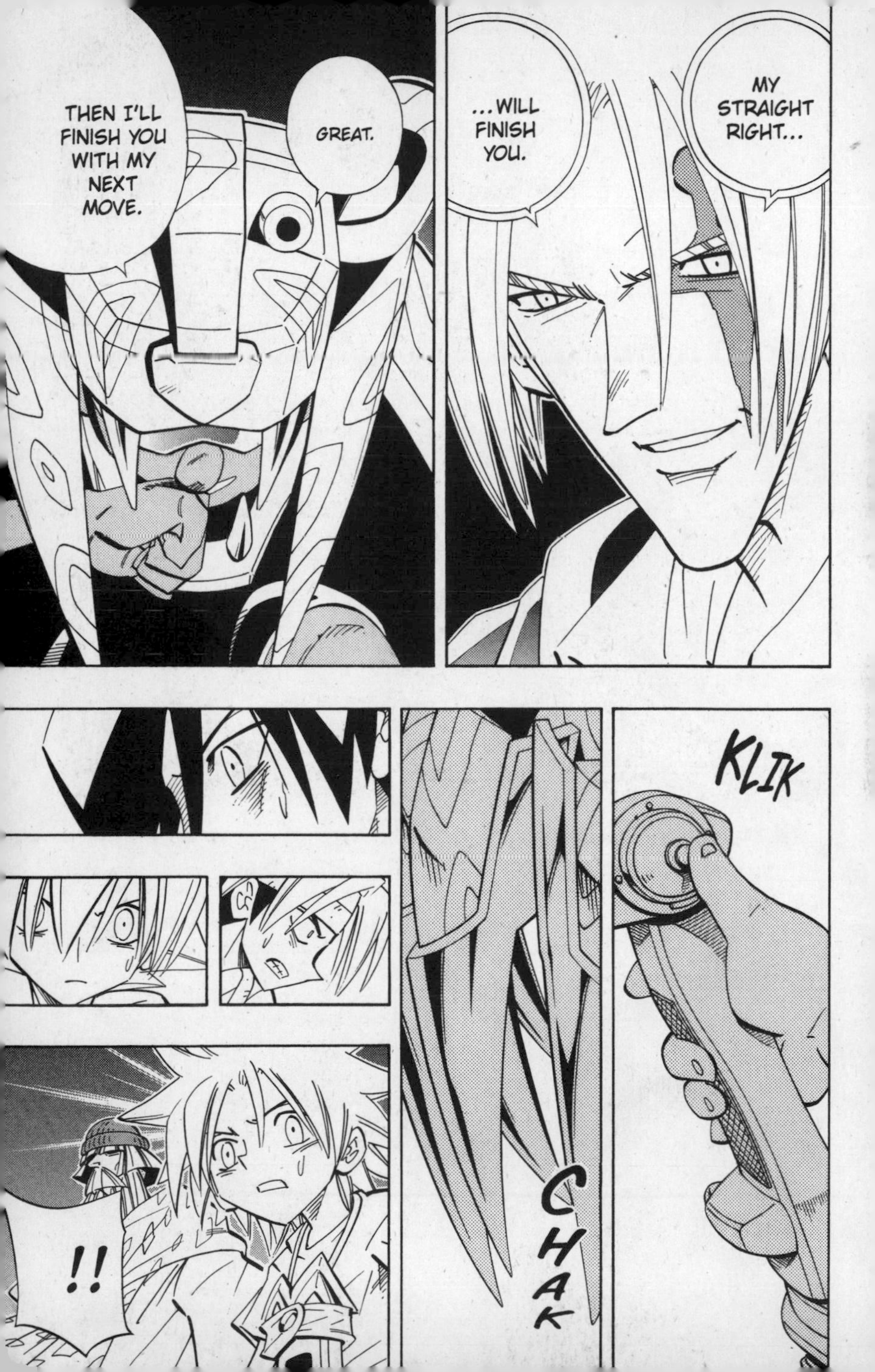
MY STRAIGHT RIGHT...
...WILL FINISH YOU.
GREAT.
THEN I'LL FINISH YOU WITH MY NEXT MOVE.
KLIK
CHAK
!!

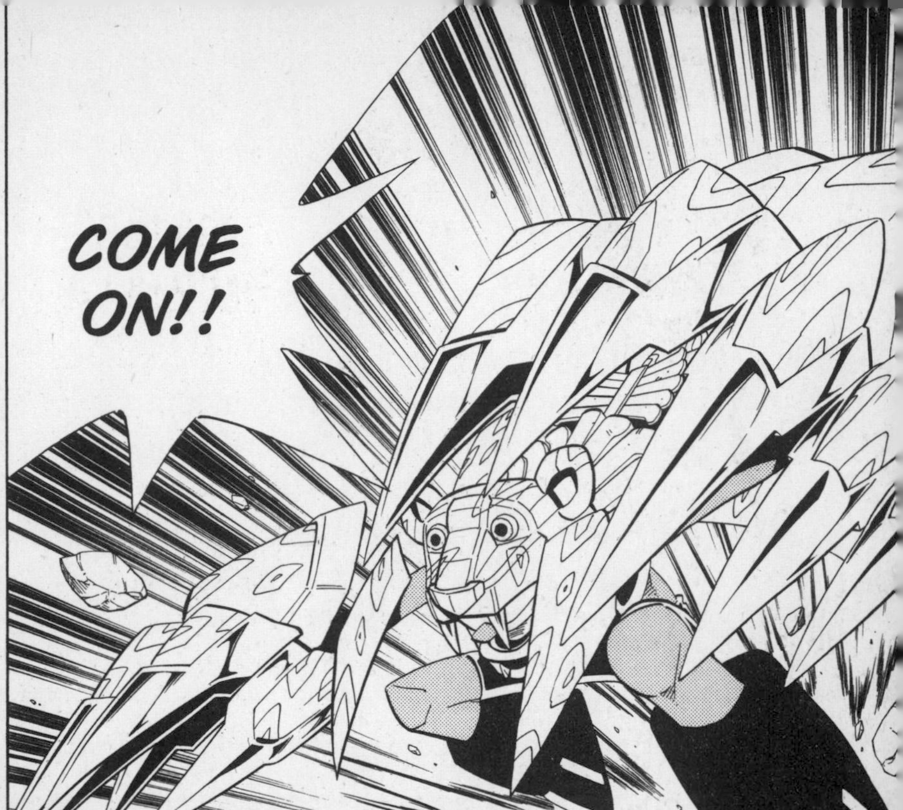
COME ON!!
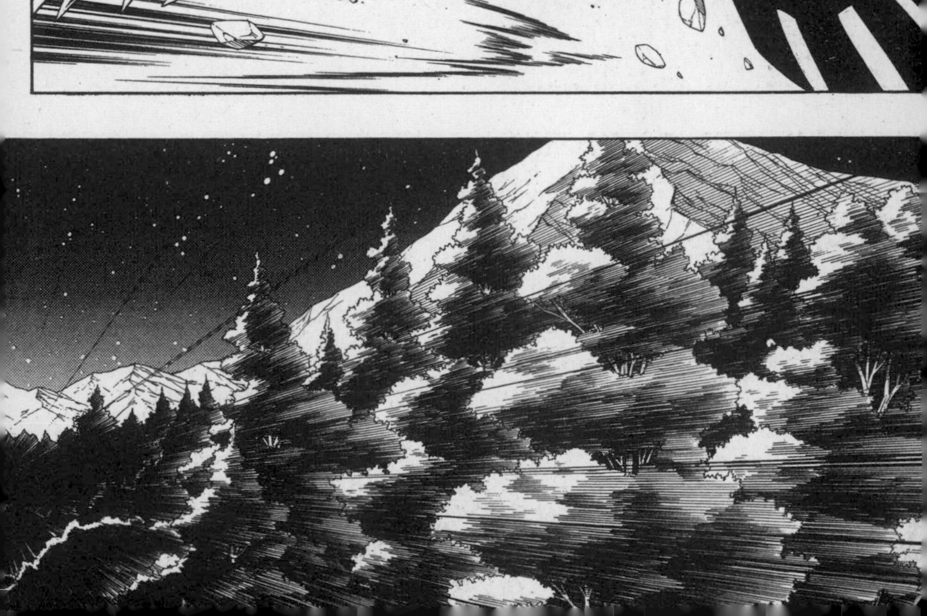

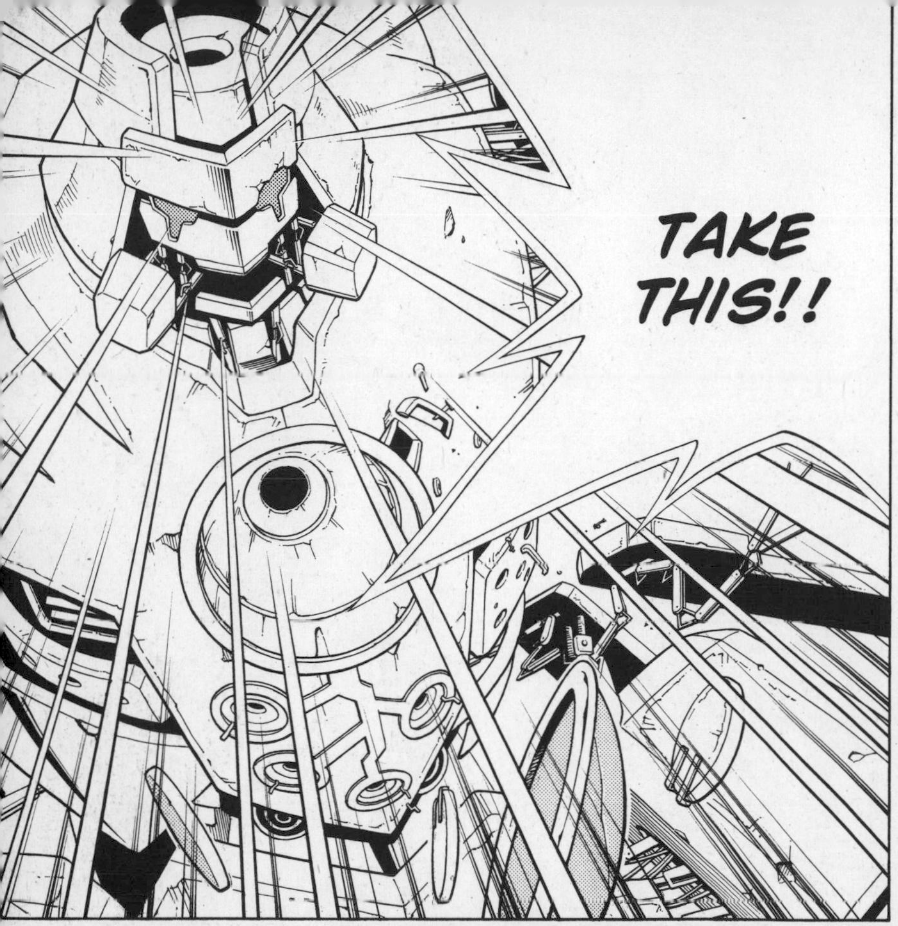
TAKE THIS!!
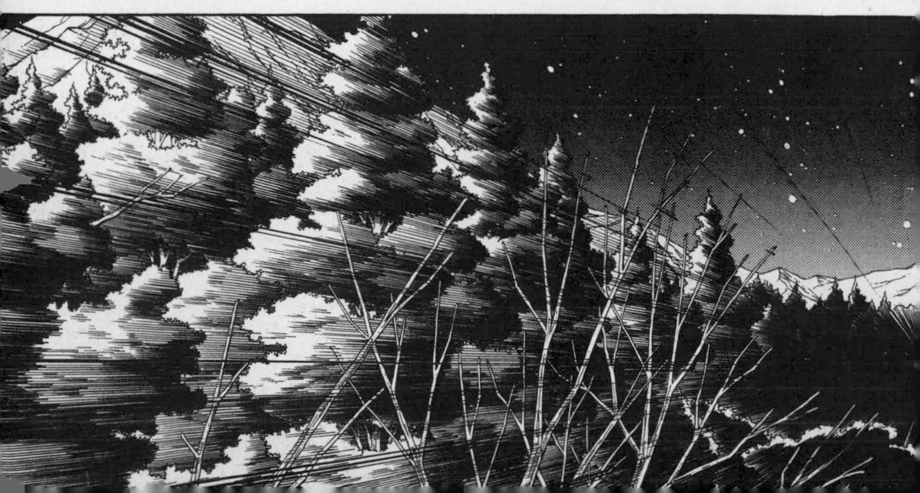

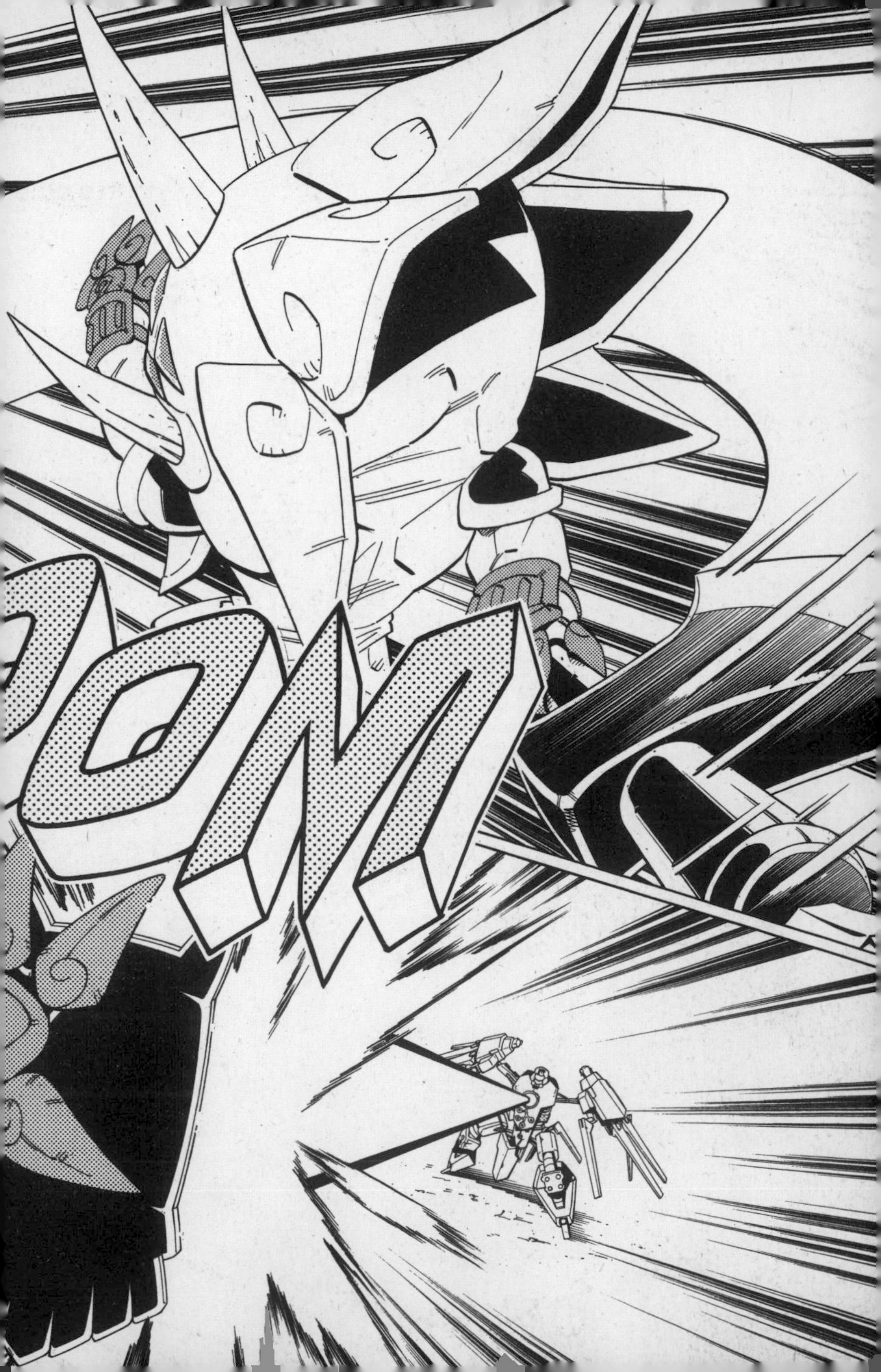

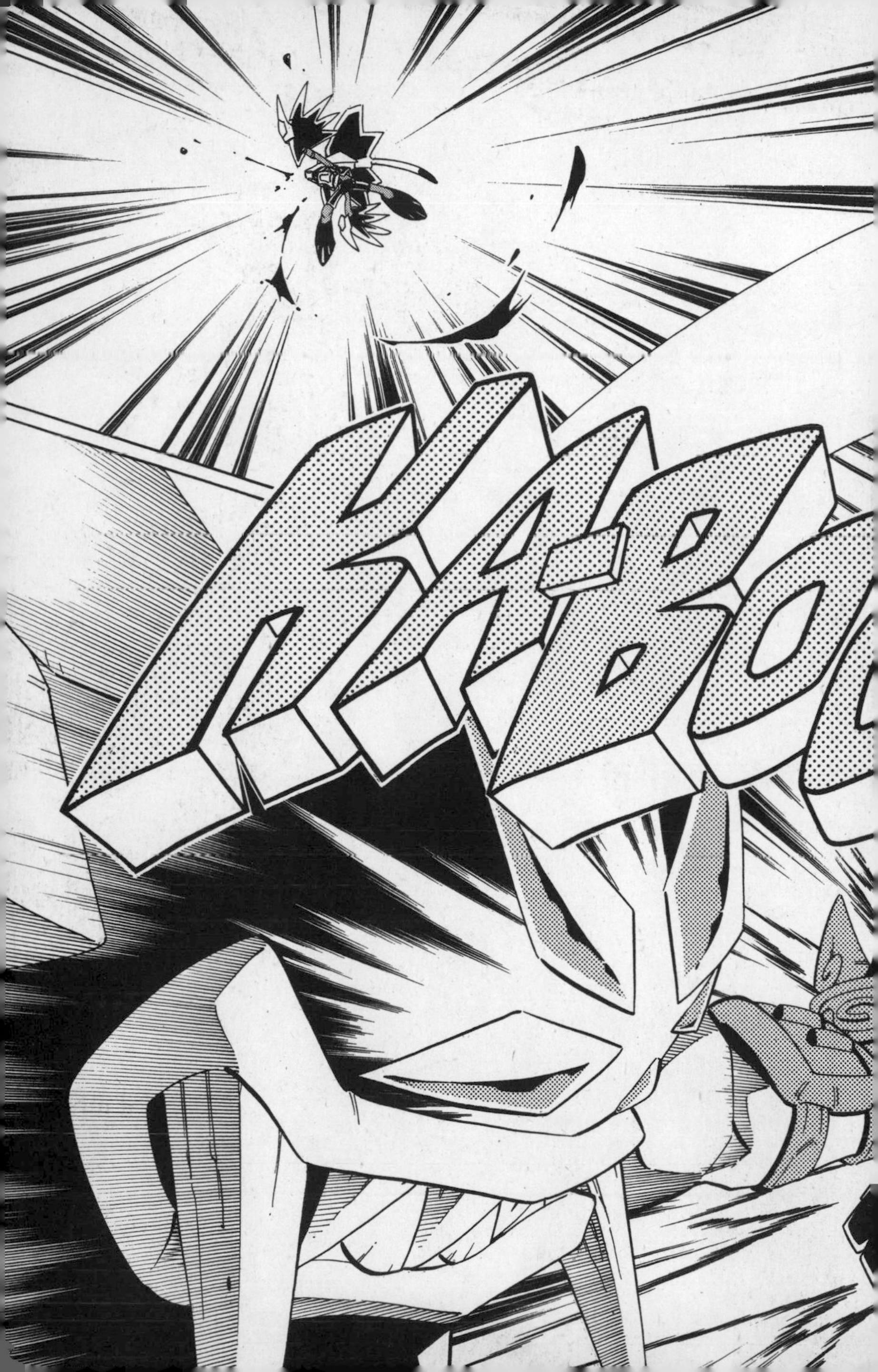
KA-BOO

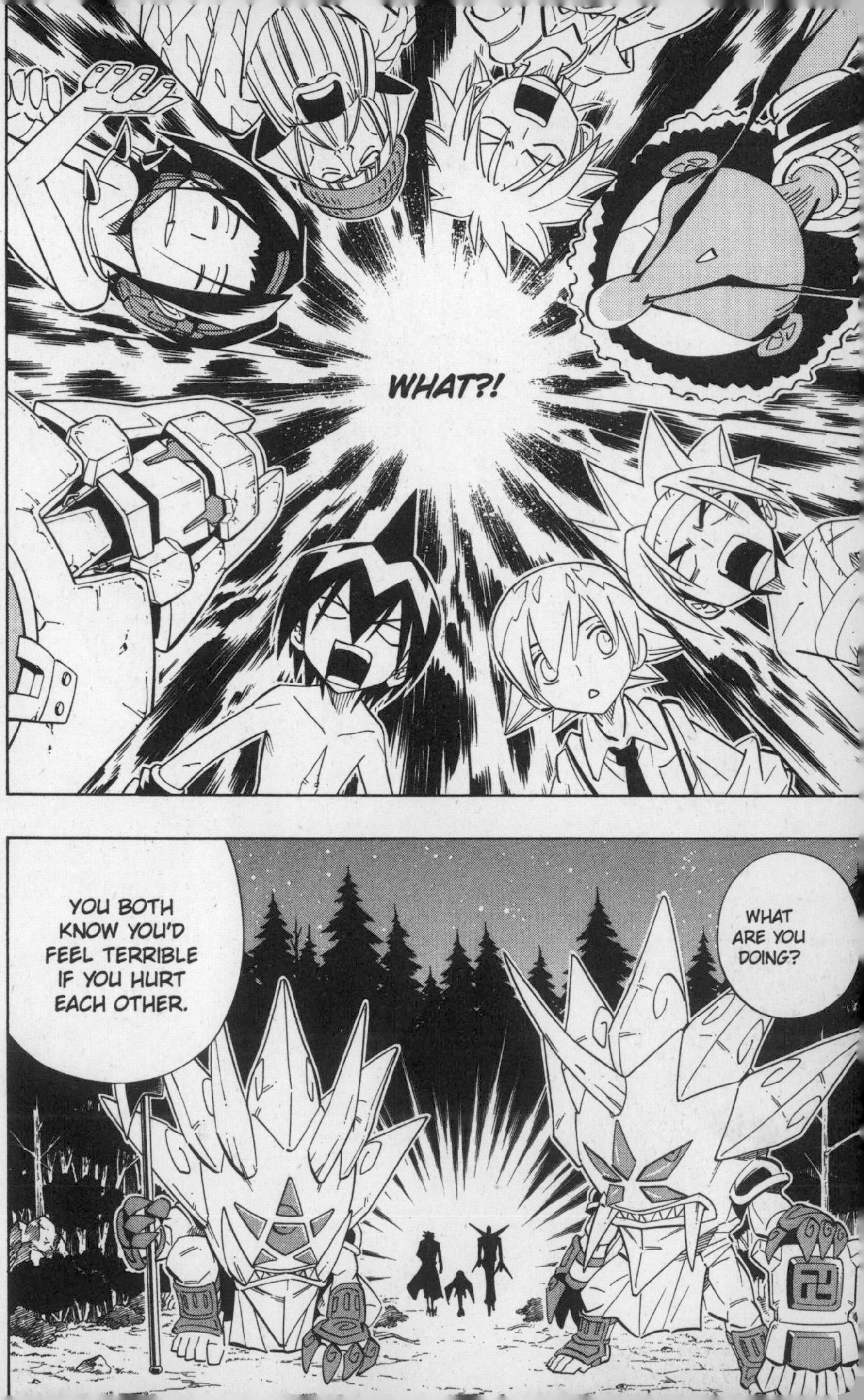
WHAT?!
WHAT ARE YOU DOING?
YOU BOTH KNOW YOU'D FEEL TERRIBLE IF YOU HURT EACH OTHER.

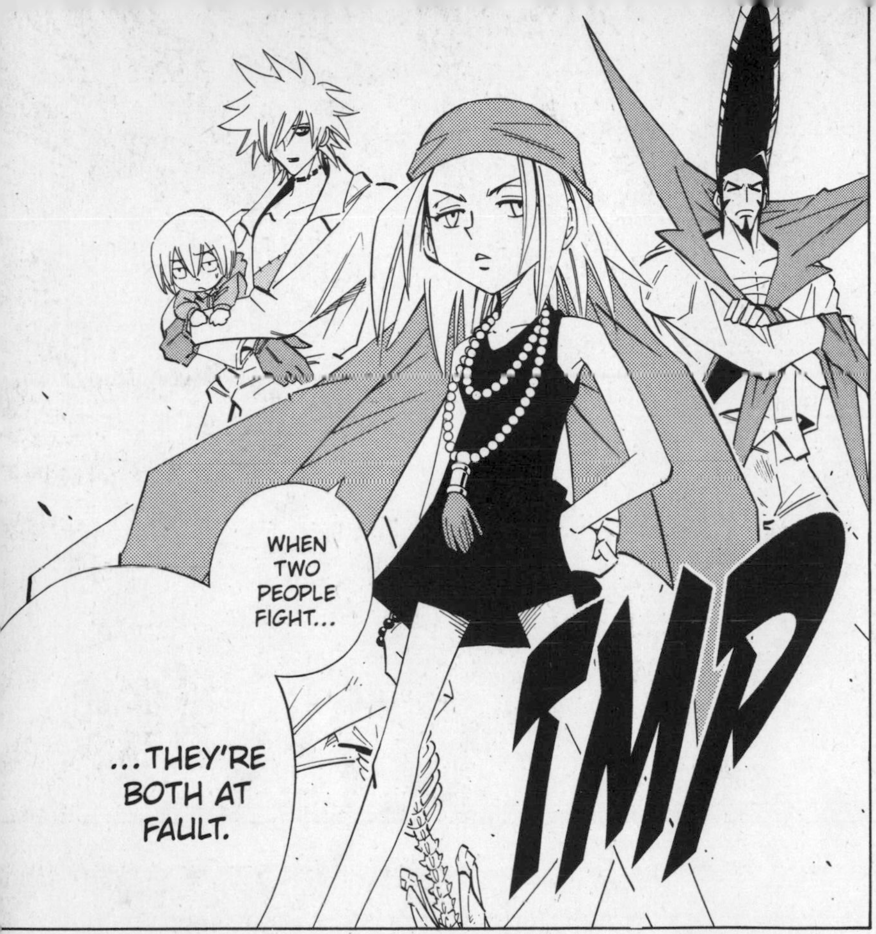
TMP
WHEN TWO PEOPLE FIGHT...
...THEY'RE BOTH AT FAULT.
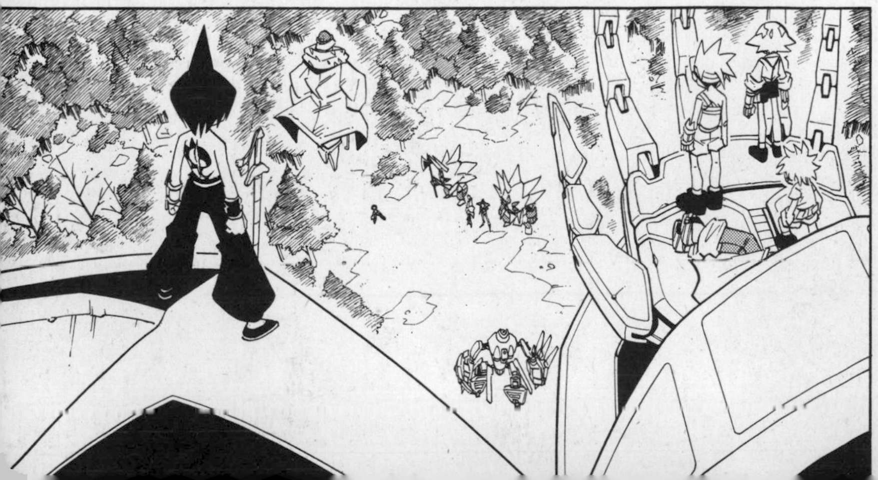

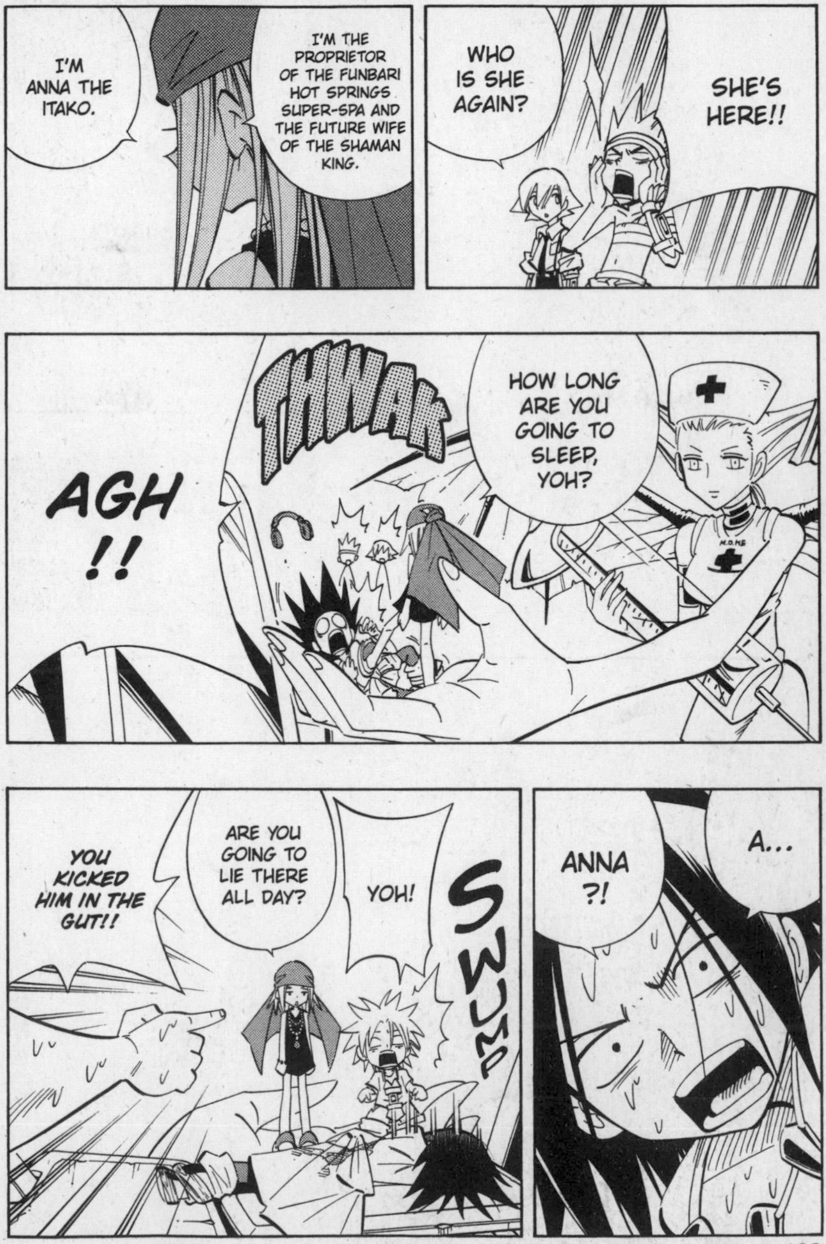

SHE'S HERE!!
WHO IS SHE AGAIN?
I'M THE PROPRIETOR OF THE FUNBARI HOT SPRINGS SUPER-SPA AND THE FUTURE WIFE OF THE SHAMAN KING.
I'M ANNA THE ITAKO.
HOW LONG ARE YOU GOING TO SLEEP, YOH?
THWAK
AGH!!
A...
ANNA?!
SWUMP
YOH!
ARE YOU GOING TO LIE THERE ALL DAY?
YOU KICKED HIM IN THE GUT!!

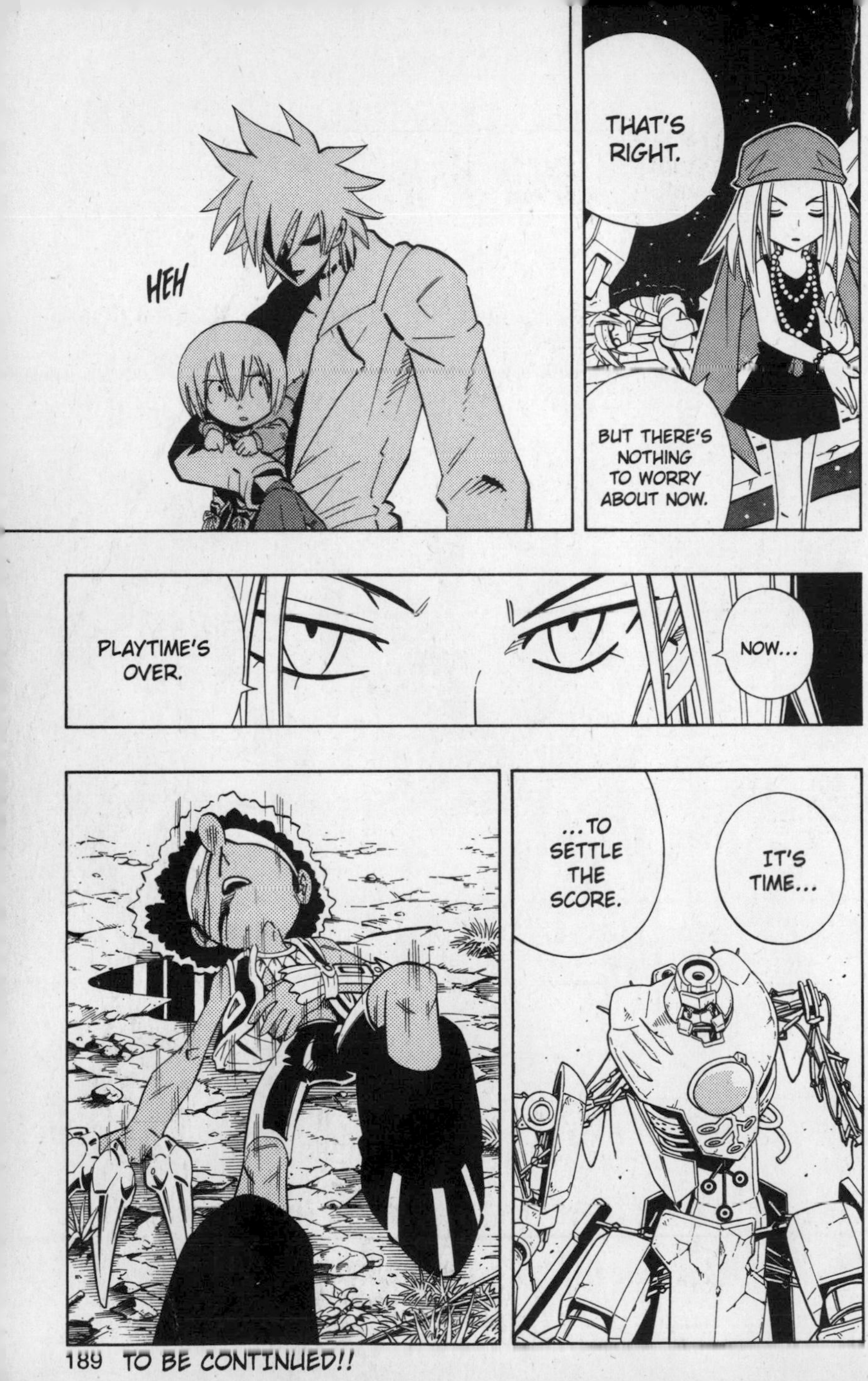
THAT'S RIGHT.
BUT THERE'S NOTHING TO WORRY ABOUT NOW.
HEH
NOW...
PLAYTIME'S OVER.
IT'S TIME...
...TO SETTLE THE SCORE.

 TO BE CONTINUED!!

SHAMAN KING CHARACTER FILE No.126

2001
(JAN)

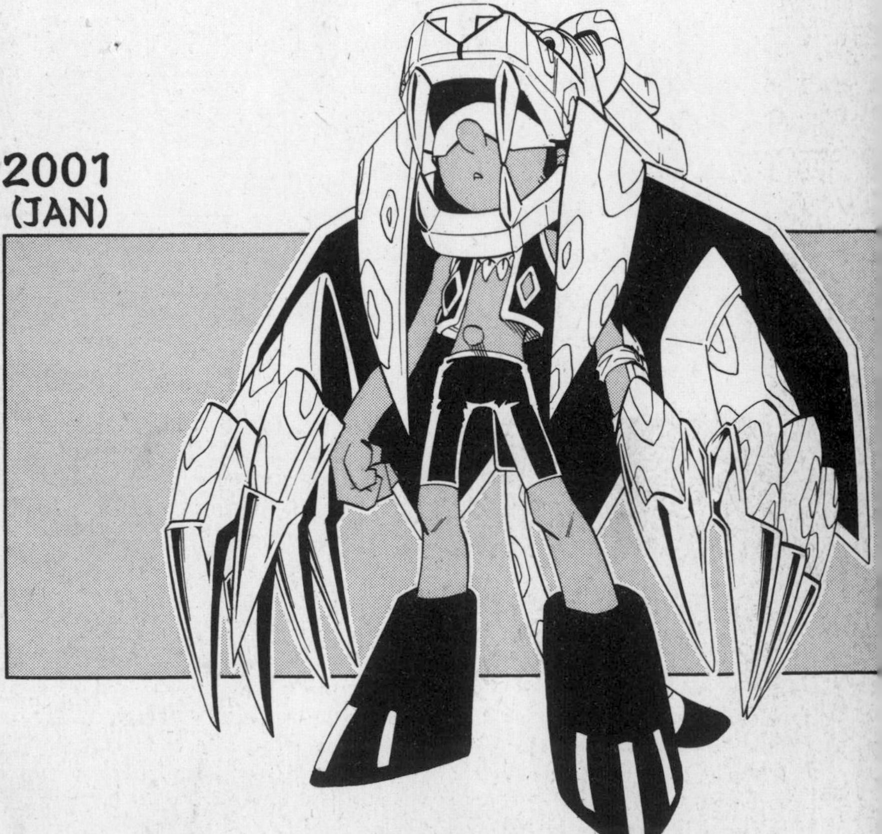

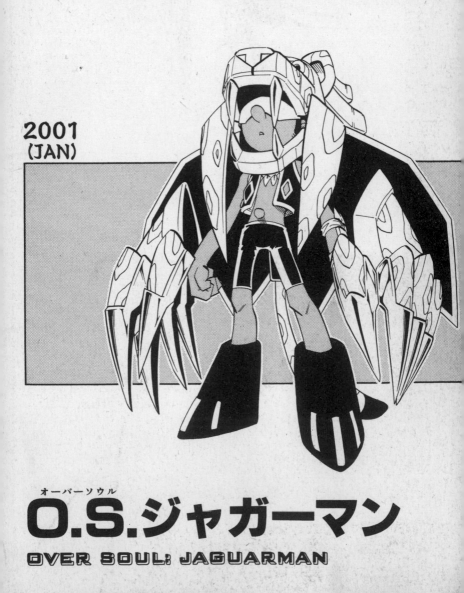

オーバーソウル
O.S.ジャガーマン

OVER SOUL: JAGUARMAN

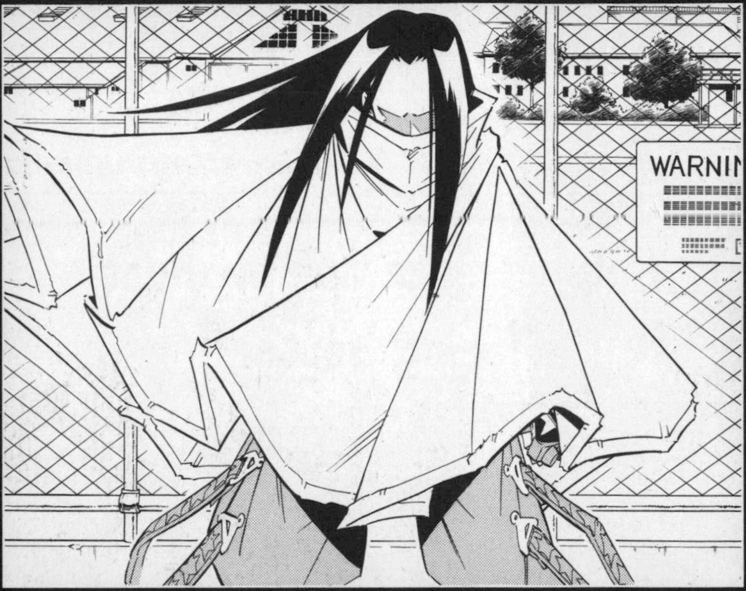
WARNIN

IN THE NEXT VOLUME...

The Golem runs out of energy. Dr. Munzer wants to command it to self-destruct, but Anna wants to keep the Golem as a weapon against Hao. Then Little Opacho shows up bearing a message that Yoh must return to the Shaman Fight...or Hao will destroy both the Golem and the kids!

AVAILABLE SEPTEMBER 2009!